Children everywhere are socialized through language and socialized to use language. Everyday speech activities between young children and members of their families organize and give meaning to social relationships. They are in fact socializing activities, the basis for the transmission and reproduction of culture.

In this study of language socialization among the Kaluli people of Papua New Guinea, Bambi B. Schieffelin analyzes these speech activities and links them to other social practices and symbolic forms such as exchange systems, gender roles, sibling relationships, rituals, and myths. In Kaluli society, as in many others in Papua New Guinea, reciprocity plays a primary role in social life. In families, social relationships are constituted through giving and sharing food, a primary means of conveying sentiment. Although sharing is highly valued, children are also socialized through language to refuse to share, creating a tension in daily interactions. Issues of authority, autonomy, and interdependence are negotiated through these verbal exchanges. Schieffelin demonstrates how language plays a fundamental role in the production, meaning, and interpretation of these activities, as it is the medium of social practice. Through the microanalysis of social interactions, we see how values regarding reciprocity, gender relations, and language itself are indexed and socialized in everyday talk to children, and how children's own ways of speaking express fundamental cultural concerns about their social relationships.

A wide audience of students and specialists in anthropology, sociolinguistics, communication, developmental psychology, and early childhood education will find much of interest in this highly readable and original study.

The give and take
of everyday life

Language socialization of Kaluli children

BAMBI B. SCHIEFFELIN
New York University

The give and take of everyday life:
Language socialization of Kaluli children

Published by Fenestra Books™
610 East Delano Street, Suite 104, Tucson, Arizona 85705 U.S.A.
www.fenestrabooks.com

First edition
Copyright © 1990 published by the Press Syndicate of the
University of Cambridge

Publisher's Cataloging-in-Publication Data

Schieffelin, Bambi B.
The give and take of everyday life : language socialization
of Kaluli children / Bambi B. Schieffelin.
p. cm.

LCCN: 2005920280
ISBN: 1-58736-440-9
Includes bibliographical references (p.) and index.
1. Kaluli (Papua New Guinea people) – Children. 2.
Kaluli language – Social aspects. 3. Kaluli (Papua New Guinea
people) – Social life and customs. 4. Language and culture –

DU740.42.S33 2005
305.23'0899912 – dc20

Contents

Acknowledgments

Ideas, like young children, do not grow by themselves. They must be nurtured if they are to find their expression. They must participate in exchanges with others to become socially meaningful. The ideas in this book have developed over time in varied intellectual, cultural, and personal contexts. At this time I would like to thank the many who have contributed to the construction of those contexts and the completion of this book.

Without the participation and enthusiasm of the people of Sululib, especially Abi, Meli, Wanu, Suela, and their families, who shared conversations and food with me, none of this could have happened. Gigio's humorous commentaries along with his help in the cookhouse and Kulu's own curiosity about language provided invaluable insights into Kaluli ways of thinking about things. Norma and Keith Briggs of the Asia Christian Pacific Mission in Mt. Bosavi helped ease many problems of living in the bush, and Ivor Manton of Mt. Hagen offered much-needed breaks from the bush. Their hospitality and different perspectives on life in a changing Papua New Guinea contributed to the richness of the fieldwork.

Funding for fieldwork was provided through predoctoral grants from the National Science Foundation and the Wenner-Gren Foundation for Anthropological Research. A University of Pennsylvania summer fellowship (1982) helped support the writing. Their assistance is gratefully acknowledged.

Many colleagues and friends encouraged me over the years, offering intellectual guidance and emotional support in conversations and other verbal genres. In particular, Lois Bloom, who got me started, Peggy Miller, and Shirley Brice Heath shared their ideas and feelings about children's language in its many representations and situations. My colleagues in the Department of Anthropology at New York University gave me generous encouragement throughout the writing of this book. Conversations over coffee with Fred Myers and Annette Weiner helped me place the work within broader anthropological issues of reciprocity and social relationships. They always had provocative suggestions when I thought I could go no further. Sandro Duranti offered many important insights that helped clarify my thinking about language in/as context, as well as keeping me sane late at night via e-mail messages. Michael

Silverstein's comments on my 1979 dissertation were still extremely useful in 1989. Faye Ginsburg and Shelah Stein in their own special ways were always there for me during the ups and downs of it all.

As the ethnographer of the Kaluli, E. L. Schieffelin provided missing pieces, from historical material to genealogical backgrounds to subtle semantic distinctions. Without Buck's own interest in the Kaluli, things would have been very different. Ethnomusicologist Steven Feld, my "younger brother" and partner in Kaluli sociolinguistic adventures, generously shared many critical insights along the way as well as providing reality checks on my version of things. Their ideas are woven into the text in a variety of ways.

My son Zachary's presence and participation in the fieldwork was more valuable than he may ever realize. His confidence in me, especially in my completing this work, has always been a source of strength. Esto has supplied a great deal of joy and pleasure. I thank you all.

Finally, two people deserve a very special thank you for their unconditional support and close friendship over many years. The perspective of this work, language socialization, was developed collaboratively with Elinor Ochs, my writing partner since 1974. Always willing to share her thoughts, Elinor has inspired my own. Gillian Sankoff has always made time to give my work her critical attention, and it is much stronger for it. I have learned a great deal from Elinor and Gillian about the give and take of everyday life, and it is to them that I dedicate this book.

1. Introduction

The true locus of culture is in the interaction of specific individuals and, on the subjective side, in the world of meaning which each one of these individuals may unconsciously abstract for himself for his participation in these interactions . . .
                                                                    Edward Sapir (1949:515)

This is a study of language socialization among the Kaluli people of Papua New Guinea. Its starting point is understanding the everyday speech activities that organize and give meaning to the social relationships between young children and the members of their families. These everyday speech activities are in fact socializing activities, the basis for the transmission and reproduction of culture. They are linked to such other social practices and symbolic forms as exchange systems, gender roles, sibling relationships, rituals, and myths. In Kaluli society, as in many other societies in Papua New Guinea, reciprocity is an important principle underlying social life. In families, social relationships are constituted through giving and sharing food: a primary means of conveying sentiment and affection. While sharing is highly valued, children are also socialized through language to refuse to share, creating a tension in daily interactions. Issues of authority, autonomy, and interdependence are negotiated through these verbal exchanges. Language plays a fundamental role in the production, meaning, and interpretation of these activities, as it is the medium of social practice. Competence underlying reciprocity and exchange is indexed and socialized in everyday talk to children, and children's own ways of speaking express fundamental cultural concerns about exchange and social relationships.

Speech enables children to develop social relationships and participate in the give and take of everyday life. Caregivers play an active role in "showing language" to young children. Through language, they create social relationships between their children, themselves, and others. Everyday speech activities in which Kaluli adults tell children what to say, what to do, and how to feel make explicit cultural assumptions and expectations that are usually tacit. By linking these everyday socializing practices to other expressive and symbolic systems, we see how the analysis of discourse is a critical source for understanding how meaning is produced.

1

This book is situated in the context of other ethnographic studies of the Kaluli, principally E. L. Schieffelin's *The Sorrow of the Lonely and the Burning of the Dancers* (1976), a cultural ethnography of the Kaluli, and S. Feld's *Sound and Sentiment* (1982), which focuses on sound as a cultural system. Both are concerned with the ethos and quality of Kaluli life, as is this one. These three works represent three complementary ethnographic perspectives based on field trips by the authors taken separately and collaboratively from 1966 through 1984 and on conversations and ongoing joint projects focusing on the Kaluli. As previous accounts present in detail aspects of Kaluli life not covered here, a short introduction will serve to focus the reader on general aspects of Kaluli cultural life relevant to this study.[1] Additional ethnographic and linguistic information is provided and elaborated on in the course of the book.

The ethnographic setting

The Kaluli are one of four small groups who collectively call themselves *Bosavi kalu* 'people of Bosavi'. In all but a few linguistic details, Kaluli are similar to the three other groups – Ologo, Walulu, and Wisesi – who live in the lush tropical rainforest north of Mount Bosavi on the Great Papuan Plateau in the Southern Highlands Province of Papua New Guinea (see Figure 1). To the north are the Etoro-speaking people (Kelly 1977) and the Onabasulu-speaking people (Ernst 1978, 1984), and to the west are the Sonia-speaking people. Kaluli are speakers of *Bosavi to* 'Bosavi language', which includes Kaluli, Ologo, Walulu, and Wisesi. Many Kaluli are bidialectal, and increasing numbers of men are acquiring other languages. Those who have been employed as contract laborers on tea, coffee, or copra plantations, worked on government stations as cargo carriers, or had extensive contact with missions – for instance, trained as pastors or worked on station maintenance or as household help – often learn Tok Pisin, the national lingua franca. In addition, some Kaluli men know Huli, a local vernacular spoken in the Tari area (Southern Highlands Province), the closest center for government administration.

The Bosavi people, who number approximately 1,200, live in about twenty longhouse communities situated on ridges scattered through densely forested jungle. Each community consists of a single longhouse and several smaller houses around a cleared yard. Kaluli villages are composed of the male members of lineages of two or more named patrilineal clans, plus their wives, children, and other female relatives. Relationships between longhouse communities are maintained principally by ties of marriage and matrilateral affiliation. Marriage is exogamous, and residence is patrilocal.

Villages are separated from each other by at least a half-hour's walk on muddy tracks and over log bridges. Within walking distance of each village

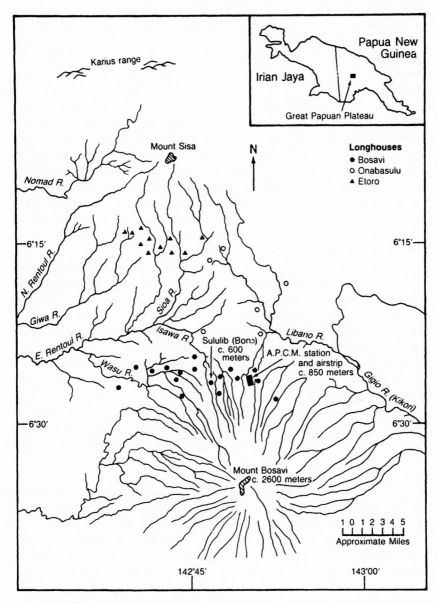

Figure 1. The Great Papuan Plateau (from Feld 1982).

are wild sago palms that grow along the many streams cutting through the forest, from which sago, the staple starch, is extracted. Sago is supplemented by bananas, pandanus, sweet potatoes, breadfruit, and a variety of greens, the produce of extensive swidden gardens. Rivers are the site of fishing activities, and the forest is rich in wild game, including cassowaries and wild pigs. Men hunt and trap these large animals and are always on the lookout for smaller ones. Women process sago, care for the gardens, and bring fresh produce from the gardens to the village on a daily basis. They too are always on the watch for small protein foods such as wild eggs, grubs, crayfish, and lizards.

Gender roles are clearly demarcated, and the daily routines of men and women are separate, but the sexual antagonism between men and women reported in the Highlands is not present in Bosavi; "cooperation" and "complementarity" more aptly describe everday interactions. Men make use of extensive networks of obligation and reciprocity in organizing such work as clearing and planting large gardens and damming streams for fishing as well as in organizing major social transactions like collecting bridewealth. Ties between people in different longhouse communities, however, are particularistic; those individuals who actively sustain relationships are linked, and not the communities as wholes (E. L. Schieffelin 1980:504).

As in many other societies in Papua New Guinea, the theme of reciprocity and exchange underlies the daily organization of both community and family events. In political and economic spheres, Kaluli society is highly egalitarian and does not share the bigman pattern of social organization prevalent in the New Guinea Highlands. Generally, unlike Highland societies where large-scale exchanges result in personal gain, Kaluli society is not primarily organized around formal exchange demarcating political and life-cycle activities. Kaluli exchanges do not involve a competitive bid for status in either formal or everyday exchange.

The major contexts of formal exchange include marriage, which involves exchanging a woman for a negotiated amount of wealth, *su* 'compensation in valuables equivalent in value', usually in the form of shells, axes, and pigs. Because the woman's unmarried brothers usually stand to lose her services once she marries, Kaluli feel a man should provide a wife to the brother, and this type of exchange is called *ga wɛl* 'woman/wife exchange', where *wɛl* is an item exactly equivalent to what was given. After marriage, a number of formal prestations are made between the families (E. L. Schieffelin 1976:58–63). Concepts of *su* and *wɛl* also figure importantly in death, where those who have suffered a loss may be offered compensation (*su*) or (before 1965) someone accused of being the witch responsible for that death was killed as *wɛl* to rebalance the system (E. L. Schieffelin 1980:505). Themes of reciprocity and sentiment about personal relationships are also highlighted in ceremonial contexts, especially in Gisalo performances (E. L. Schieffelin 1976).

Feld (1982a) complements E. L. Schieffelin's work by examining the dynamics of weeping as an expressive means for articulating the same shared feelings about loss and abandonment when someone dies. Formal events, such as ceremonials and funerals, are contexts for the poetic expression of crystallized sentiments about reciprocity and personal relationships. It is in these events, as Feld puts it, that "weeping moves women to song" and "song moves men to tears." These are the domains of adult expression that index powerful feelings through performances of highly conventionalized language and other aesthetic expressive modalities of song and sung–texted weeping.

Deeply connected to these formal events, which are infrequent but nonetheless culturally and symbolically powerful, are the everyday interactions between caregivers and small children that go largely without comment. These routine interactions also express underlying expectations about sharing, reciprocity, and the sentiments of personal relationships. Everyday interactions involve verbal negotiations about giving and taking food and organizing cooperation in domestic activities. In these unremarkable, informal verbal routines between caregivers and children and among siblings, enduring sentiments of affection and trust are created and the discourse structures through which reciprocity is negotiated are established. Social relationships are constituted and validated through exchange, and language plays a critical role in these processes. Myths express the felt sentiments and consequences of breaches in relationships that assume sharing, and ceremony and song mourn the loss of relationships in which people share what they had with each other and contemplate their sense of the future.

From "soft" to "hard"

By the time children are 3 years old, they are expected to participate in the reciprocal sharing that is part of family life, and this is achieved primarily through the use of language. Of course, young children start out exclusively on the receiving end of things. Kaluli characterize infants as "soft" (*taiyo*): Their bodies are floppy, they have virtually no control over what they do, and they have "no understanding" (*asugɔ andoma*). Kaluli talk about children's early development as "firming-up" (*fofandolab*) that involves gaining muscular control, developing strength, and acting purposively. In terms of language, they move from meaningless babbling to well-articulated and socially meaningful speech. The idea is that as both the mental faculties and the physical body mature, things come together in a process called "hardening" (*halaidan*). When I asked for details about development, some Kaluli suggested that the number of teeth children have indicates the extent of this process, since with teeth (especially the back molars) articulation is clearer, but among themselves Kaluli do not spontaneously assess or compare their children's development. The goal of socialization and development is the achievement of "hardening," the production of well-formed individuals in control of themselves as well as able to control and influence others. Active and guided participation in verbal interactions with others constitutes the contexts in which children learn to use language that "makes them hard" (*halaido domɛki*). In this case, the process of becoming "hard" is a literal and metaphoric construct for physical and mental development and for socialization.

Halaido 'hard' and *taiyo* 'soft' are important contrasting concepts in a number of different domains, not just as they pertain to children (Feld & Schieffelin 1982). A man who is strong, assertive, and not a witch (*sei*) is called *kalu halaido* 'a hard man' (E. L. Schieffelin 1976:128), and a major indicator of this "hardness" is the ability to use "hard words" (*to halaido*): to have the fully developed capacity for language.[2] Another domain in which *halaido* figures importantly is dramatic style. In ceremonial performance, songs are intended to be evocative and to move the audience to tears. The climax in aesthetic tension, where the manner of singing and the textual elements coalesce, is what promotes the "hardening" (again, *halaido domɛki*) of a song. A performance that does not "harden" will not be considered successful. The ability to "harden" a song is an important compositional and performative skill (Feld 1983).

The cultural construction of *halaido* in these domains of growth, competence, and presentational style can in part be traced to an origin myth that tells how the world was once muddy and soft. A megapode and a Goura pigeon together stamped on the ground to make it hard. Like the hardening of the land that symbolizes physical and geographical formation, the hardening of the body, language, character, and dramatic style symbolizes the necessity of a person's being socialized in order to become culturally competent.

The term *taiyo* 'soft' is in opposition to *halaido* 'hard'. Within this oppositional frame, *taiyo* is "soft" in the sense of mushy; it is applied to things that decay and rot. Food taboos constrain the association between "soft" substances and young children, who are already soft. For example, certain foods such as eggs (soft consistency) and the meat of certain birds that have "soft" high voices or redundant calls are prohibited lest the process of "hardening" be impaired.[3] Young children are also prohibited from eating all yellow foods, synonymous with decay, debilitation, and weakness – states and associations that must be avoided to insure the desired developmental progression from "soft" to "hard."[4]

The "natural" state of young children is helplessness, and the way in which they get what they want is by appealing to others through begging and whining. These helpless creatures are often hungry, and their endless appeals for food and attention make people "feel sorry for them" (*nofɔlan*); moved by pity, they always give to children. However, this state of dependence, helplessness, and getting what they want by making people feel sorry for them cannot continue forever. Children need to be socialized to be independent and assert themselves, to get what they want by other means than begging and whining. Whereas appeal is the "natural" modality of small children, assertion, the complementary interactional modality, must be socialized through language.

It is through language and through using language that children become participants in all varieties of social exchange as ones who can give as well as ask and take. This is accomplished by teaching children what to say, how to ask, and how to refuse. Once children begin to use words, Kaluli mothers say that they must "show language" (*to widan*) to children if they are to learn to speak. This is part of *halaidan* 'hardening', indicated by the acquisition and use of *to halaido* 'hard language'. Mothers show language through extensive sequences of direct instruction using the imperative ɛlɛma 'say like this', telling 2-year-olds to repeat what they say to other people. This language is always in an assertive modality. It is markedly different in form, function, and content from the language used in appeal, which is not directly socialized because it is considered something children already know. Once a child uses language assertively to ask for food and objects, other members of the household can also ask the child to give and share, and the process of holding the child accountable in exchanges begins.

Linguistic research on Kaluli

The following grammatical and sociolinguistic sketches of Kaluli are based on the materials that inform the entire book: analyses of adults' and children's everday speech.[5] These informal conversational exchanges contain a variety of speech acts and are often highly marked by affect, so providing a rich source of information for analyzing the structure and function of linguistic systems. These naturalistic data also provide socially contextualized material for the analysis of pragmatic and discourse relations, in contrast to elicited data, which are not only difficult to obtain but also frequently unreliable in that they do not capture relationships between the social distribution and the meanings of particular forms.[6] In conversation, participants often make metalinguistic comments about their own and others' speech and these inform the analysis. Misunderstandings, repairs, paraphrases, commentary, and the laughter of adults and older children also provide insights into what is and is not grammatically acceptable and pragmatically appropriate language. Furthermore, children's speech is a surprisingly informative source for the analysis of language structure and function. As a result of children's misanalyses and overgeneralizations of morphological and grammatical rules, underlying forms become apparent; systematic errors in use reveal the distribution and details of pragmatic features. Working monolingually from tape recordings of situated speech, I as a nonnative speaker relied on such essential cues as these.

Linguistic sketch

Kaluli is one of the more than seven hundred languages spoken in Papua New Guinea. It is a non-Austronesian language that is part of the Central and South New Guinea Stock of the Trans–New Guinea Phylum (Voorhoeve 1975). Classified as one of the five languages of the Bosavi family, Kaluli is one of four dialects (Wisesi, Walulu, and Ologo are the others) based on locale and marked predominantly by systematic phonological variation and some lexical and minor syntactic differences.[7] Speakers can be identified by dialect features; children carry their mothers' dialect or, if orphaned, the dialect of the women who raised them.

Kaluli grammar, which I have described in detail elsewhere (1986a), resembles several other non-Austronesian languages that have been described for Papua New Guinea (Foley 1986). It is a verb-final language marking case relations postpositionally on nouns. Subject marking is suffixed on the verb through bound person markers and follows a nominative–accusative pattern. One bound person marker may denote two or several persons. This is common, especially in distinguishing 1st from 2nd and 3rd person, but there is variation in the pattern depending on sentence type. Kaluli has two case-marking systems for nouns, neutral and ergative/absolutive; this pattern follows a semantically motivated split-ergative system. In terms of marking the semantic functions of nouns, Kaluli has a mixed word-order and inflectional system. That is, sometimes word order and at other times case marking is used to indicate semantic function. Kaluli has two allowable word orders for agent and patient, AOV and OAV. Each serves a set of pragmatic purposes. AOV is used in announcements, reports, and narrative accounts, or when the agent is neither in focus nor being negotiated. OAV is used in requests or when the agent is in focus or being negotiated.

Like other languages in this phylum, Kaluli has considerable morphological complexity and irregularity in the verb system. The complex morphological system has elaborate affixation and inflection. There are two sets of independent personal pronouns that operate as nonfocused and focused pronouns. Nonfocused pronouns are multifunctional and are used as subjects and experiencers of intransitive verbs, as agents of transitive verbs in AOV utterances, and as objects and possessives. Focused pronouns are found in (O)AV utterances when the agent is in focus. Some of these pronominal forms are marked for number (singular, dual, plural) and for inclusive, exclusive, and other pragmatic and semantic properties. In addition to expressing agency, some forms are also used as possessives. Subordinate clauses precede the main clause. However, unlike English, which has a variety of lexical conjunctions such as "and," "before," "because," "when," and "if" to join clauses, Kaluli uses a variety of morphosyntactic constructions called medial verb constructions. These, in relation to final-inflected-verb constructions, express the meanings of purposive and temporal conjunctions. These constructions, more than any other, give Papuan languages their characteristic stamp and make them different from those spoken in other parts of the world. They make possible the building of the types of sentence used in "clause-chaining" (Haiman 1979; Longacre 1972; Olson 1978). Through additional morphological markers on the verb, speakers must signal whether the following clause will have the same or a different subject. This system, called switch reference, is found in most Papuan languages. Foley & Van Valin (1984) and J. Heath (1975) have noted the inverse relation between gender systems and switch reference in languages throughout the world. Kaluli, like other languages with elaborate switch-reference systems, lacks gender distinctions throughout the nominal system.

Possession is indicated in several ways: through case-marking suffixes on nouns and demonstratives, through possessive adjectives, and through modified forms of the personal pronouns. The genitive construction typically has the order genitive + head. Unlike the more common pattern of noun-phrase ordering in verb-final languages (as described by Greenberg 1966), modifiers follow the head noun. When an adjective follows the noun, it carries all of the inflectional material of the noun phrase. All adverbial modifiers of the verb precede the verb. Negation is signaled lexically and by both prefixing and suffixing. Nominals are negated with one set of suffixes. Verbal negation varies according to the form of the verb, with imperatives taking only suffixes and other forms taking a variety of prefixes and suffixes, depending on pragmatic as well as structural constraints.

Kaluli employs an elaborate system of emphatic, affect, and evidential particles. These particles are suffixed in word-final and sentence-final position, with evidential particles preceding emphatic particles when they co-occur. These particles encode nonrelational meanings, but are extremely important in conveying information about how speakers feel about what they are saying and how they know about what they are saying.

Kaluli allows a great deal of deletion and ellipsis in all genres of talk. Utterances may consist of a single verb or of a verb with one or more other sentence constituents. When a person opens a discourse, all major noun phrases are usually specified, but if one noun phrase does not change and there is no likelihood of ambiguity, that noun phrase will probably not be repeated.

Modes and codes

While all genres of speaking share many features, several are distinguished by differences in phonology, morphology, syntax, and pragmatic selection as well as by differences in context and content. Within modes shared and participated in by all members of society, such as conversation, ways of speaking follow preferred forms of other appropriate behavior. Consistent with the egalitarian nature of Kaluli society, there are no specially designated speaker roles. If you can speak for yourself, no one speaks for you. What individuals get for themselves is frequently determined by their ability to use language effectively. There are no marked male or female forms or registers; men and women use the same linguistic forms, strategies, and routines when performing the same speech acts and when discussing the same topics. For example, since the organization of domestic affairs and caregiving is predominantly in the domain of women and girls, one frequently hears them talking to babies, arranging for tasks to be accomplished, and arguing about issues pertaining to their social sphere. Men are involved more publicly in political affairs (arranging bridewealth and negotiating breaches in relationships), and the content and organization of their talk are appropriate to those activities. When men do involve themselves in domestic affairs and caregiving, they use many of the same forms of talk as do the women in similar situations. Likewise, when women are negotiating in the political arena or are involved in arguments, they make use of the same linguistic resources as men. This holds for both the phonological and syntactic organization of utterances as well as for the multitude of expressive, emphatic, and affective forms that appear throughout Kaluli speech.[8]

In everyday talk, much is taken for granted, allowing casual or very rapid speech to appear the conversational norm. Vowels are noticeably centralized, and there is a range of speech speeds and volume. Intonation is used both for emphasis and disambiguation, and there is frequent use of quotatives, emphatic and pragmatic particles, and affect expressives.

Outline of the book

In the following chapters I present a view of Kaluli language socialization grounded in the everyday social practices of Kaluli adults and young children. I focus on social relationships and reciprocity as they shape and are shaped through and by speech activities. Chapters in this book are vertical layerings, representing the same events from different stances: some from the caregivers' view, some from the children's, all ultimately from mine. Chapters are linked by cultural themes. I have focused on aspects of socialization that are salient and relevant to Kaluli, but I also acknowledge that they might not see it the way I do.

Chapter 2 sets out the theoretical frameworks, assumptions, and methods that guide this inquiry. Following a description of the fieldwork situation, I make explicit the ways in which I collected, analyzed, and described the interactions and the language used in them. Chapter 3 introduces the children and families, their ideology, and their orientation to cultural change. Since food is important socially and symbolically, food taboos are analyzed in terms of how they convey cultural concerns about children's development. A description of the early contexts of communication for Kaluli children sets the stage for what follows as soon as language appears.

Chapters 4 and 5 present two strategies of Kaluli social interaction, assertion and appeal. Chapter 4 examines the socialization of assertion through direct instruction using *ɛlɛma* 'say it'. It details the multiparty organization of *ɛlɛma* routines and the activities and stances associated with them. As this practice encourages the learning of appropriate language by associating adult and child speech, it is informative to examine the inverse: speech activities created by children that are prohibited by caregivers. Use of assertive language is the way into the system of everyday reciprocity. Chapter 5 focuses on the socialization of appeal through an important relationship between younger brothers and older sisters, who call each other *adɛ*. In this relationship, older sisters are supposed to feel sorry for and give to their younger brothers. Following an analysis of the *adɛ* relationship in myth and a comparative sociolinguistic analysis of sibling kin terms and the *adɛ* term, we shall examine mothers' socialization of the *adɛ* relationship and, through young children's use, what they understand about this relationship term. Assertion and appeal as interactional strategies are examined developmentally and transactionally.

In contrast to Chapters 4 and 5, which present routines having an almost scripted quality with little variation across families, Chapters 6 and 7 focus on face-to-face negotiations between children and caregivers involving giving and taking in which there is both individual and familial stylistic variation. Chapter 6 addresses how reciprocity is socialized and relationships are created through sharing. Sharing is encouraged through caregivers' and older children's talk about social expectations. Another side of reciprocity, however, is to refuse to share, which children are also socialized to do. An important cultural preference throughout is that one ask, not just take. From yet another view, we shall examine the rhetorical strategies of mothers' refusals of children's requests, which happen in some families. Kaluli do not like to refuse directly and have a variety of linguistic resources for accomplishing refusals through inference. The social meaning of food and objects, and how children talk about objects and reciprocity, indicate how food and objects mediate, constitute, and are expressive of personal relationships.

Chapter 7 examines the development of children's requests. Children request food and objects using both conventional linguistic constructions and special forms, varying them according to affect modality (assertion or appeal), object desired (the breast as opposed to other food and objects), and recipient (self/other). Young children sensitively manipulate language to express conceptual and affective categories important to them. Again, variation among children is discussed.

Chapter 8 examines the socialization of gender-appropriate behaviors, looking at how boys and girls are treated differently in the cultural construction of social identity. Mothers constitute siblingship through speech activities, encouraging cooperative acts between same-sex siblings and fostering aggressive acts between cross-sex siblings. Play is an area in which complementary gender roles are established, through hide-and-seek games and role-play activities. Only girls, following their mothers, initiate *ɛlɛma* routines with younger children, demonstrating the salience of this as a gender-specific nurturing activity. Finally, caregivers manage breaches in gender-appropriate activities and through language guide young children into appropriate ways of acting.

Chapter 9 concludes the work by amplifying three structural themes and seeing what they imply about the relationship between language and social life. The first two of these themes, which emerge from the analysis of discourse practices, articulate dilemmas within Kaluli society – autonomy, interdependence and sentiment, and authority. The third theme, gender and reciprocity, is explored through examining discourse practices through which an engendered view of reciprocity and sharing is made possible. This view of reciprocity and sharing considers the roles of all participants, as complementary roles are necessary in the give and take of everyday life.

2. Language as a resource for social theory

The unfolding of childhood is not time elapsing just for the child: it is time elapsing for its parental figures, and for all other members of society; the socialization involved is not simply that of the child, but of the parents and others with whom the child is in contact, and whose conduct is influenced by the child just as the latter's is by theirs in the continuity of interaction. . . . The category ''mother'' is given by the arrival of the child. but the practice or enactment of motherhood involves processes of learning that stretch back before and continue after the birth of the child. Socialization is thus most appropriately regarded not as the ''incorporation of the child into society,'' but as the *succession of the generations.*

Anthony Giddens (1979:130)

This is a particular type of ethnography, one that focuses on the microanalysis of everyday speech and conduct between caregivers and children, linking their practices and patterns to others expressed through myths, rituals, song, exchange, and other symbolic systems. It draws theoretically and methodologically on intellectual traditions within anthropology and sociology concerned with the relationships between language and culture and speech and conduct. It integrates a semiotically based ethnographic perspective with an ethnomethodological interest in examining the details of social interaction and talk for what they reveal about members' methods and preferences. It also draws on psychological traditions that emphasize socially facilitated modes of acquiring knowledge, and places these concerns within a theory of social practice.[1]

My Ph.D. research and dissertation (1975–9) on language acquisition and language socialization, which serve as the basis for this book, can be taken as a measure of some of the changes that have occurred in the study of language and socialization. Until 1975, research on language acquisition drew on psychological paradigms based on work with white middle-class children. While language acquisition was studied in pragmatically sensitive ways, the concept of culture as an important influence on the acquisition process was singularly lacking.[2] Language acquisition was seen as relatively unaffected by such cultural factors as social organization and belief systems. These factors were treated as ''context'' separable from language and its acquisition. The few studies of language acquisition carried out in ''exotic'' cultures failed to document how particular patterns of language use were connected to other aspects of culture, such as local theories of learning, the social organization of caregiving, and the status and role of children. Researchers reported little transcribed speech data, providing neither form nor content for verbal interactions between language-learning children and their caregivers.[3]

Anthropological studies of child socialization and human development, on the other hand, have ignored language used both by children and to children in social interaction as a resource in understanding socialization. For example, the forms, functions, and message content of language have not been examined for the ways in which they organize and are organized by culture in socializing contexts. Starting with Mead's work in Papua New Guinea (1930) and continuing into the present, socialization studies have focused either on psychological issues, both indigenous and nonindigenous, or on formal events such as initiation.[4] Consequently, with the exception of Boggs (1985), Health (1983), Ochs (1988), Ward (1971), Watson-Gegeo & Gegeo (1986a, b), and Wills (1977), anthropologists studying socialization have provided little information concerning the role that language plays in the acquisition and transmission of sociocultural knowledge in particular groups. Language as a source for children to acquire the ways and world views of their culture, and language as a critical resource for the researcher to analyze for what it can tell us about cultural procedures, beliefs, and expectations, has been largely untapped.

My view, influenced by work in the ethnography of speaking (Gumperz & Hymes 1972; Hymes 1962), is that acquisition of language and acquisition of culture are natural contexts for each other and should be studied as such. As cultural values are expressed throughout interactions, an examination of these interactions provides insights into not only what the child is being taught about language and culture but also the relationships that hold between the two. Since 1979 a number of other researchers, linguists, psychologists, and anthropologists have been reporting research on children's language and socialization from a similar integrated perspective known as language socialization. My own work is directed to understanding processes of language use and socialization and also to demonstrating how language is a resource for social theory.

Language socialization

The study of language socialization has as its goal understanding how persons become competent members of their social groups and the role of language in this process. Language socialization, therefore, concerns two major areas of socialization: socialization through the use of language and socialization to use language (Ochs & Schieffelin 1984). Language socialization draws on anthropological, sociological, and psychological approaches to the study of linguistic and social competence within a social group.[5] From the extensive literature in sociolinguistics and the ethnography of communication, we know that vocal and verbal activities are socially organized and embedded in cultural systems of meaning.[6] Everyday verbal activities between caregivers and children are created and constrained by these same cultural and symbolic systems and must be understood in this context.

The notion of language socialization is premised on a set of assumptions about the nature of language, culture, and socialization. Two claims express this perspective:

1. The process of acquiring language is deeply affected by the process of becoming a competent member of a society.
2. The process of becoming a competent member of society is realized to a large extent through language, by acquiring knowledge of its functions, social distribution, and interpretations in and across socially defined situations, i.e., through exchanges of language in particular social situations. (Ochs & Schieffelin 1984:277)

This view of language socialization is tied to an understanding of the nature of culture that I share with most other modern cultural theorists and that can be made explicit in the following principles:

1. Language and culture comprise bodies of knowledge, structures of understanding, conceptions of the world, and collective representations that are extrinsic to any individual.
2. These contain more information than any individual could know or learn.
3. There is variation among individual members in terms of their knowledge. This variation is crucial to the social dynamic between individuals, but it is also socially structured, and as such is extrinsic to individuals.
4. It is important to distinguish between the symbolically constructed contexts in which individuals live and the knowledge, attitudes, interpretations, and understandings they must have to operate appropriately in their place within their culture. These are not the same thing. Thus,
5. One does not "acquire culture"; one acquires a set of practices that enable one to live in a culture.

Social theoreticians, in particular Bourdieu (1977), Giddens (1979, 1984), and Wentworth (1980), emphasize the importance of social practices in everyday life and in socialization. What does a practice-based analysis of language socialization look like? How and where do we directly locate the practices and the processes of social production and reproduction in talk? Giddens's notion of discursive consciousness, "knowledge which actors are able to express on the level of discourse" (1979:5), is a potential bridge to connect speech and conduct. But a specific definition of discourse is not provided in his discussions. The implied notion of discourse is more limited than most linguistic definitions. Giddens seems to associate discourse with explicitness. In this light, discursive consciousness is complementary to practical consciousness, "what actors know (believe) about social conditions, including especially the conditions of their own action, but cannot express discursively" (1984:375). To work with these notions, we need a definition of discourse that underlies the link between talk and conduct. Discourse, like culture, is a form of knowledge, in particular "a set of norms, preferences, and expectations relating linguistic structures to context, which speaker-hearers draw on and modify in producing and interpreting language in context" (Ochs 1988:8). Discourse knowledge is structured by and structures such discourse practices as speech acts, conversational sequences, speech activities, speech events, genres, and registers. This definition allows for both tacit and conscious knowledge of language in context and in this sense differs from Giddens's narrower notion of discourse as a manifestation of conscious knowledge of social conditions. For Giddens, discourse structure is treated as a container of ideas, whereas other definitions add that discourse structure is a form of social action, and discourse is the interpretive underpinning of that action. In this sense, talk *is* practice and displays practical consciousness as well as "discursive" consciousness. Talk is a form of action as well as a symbolic system. Talk needs to be attended to not only for its content but also for its sociolinguistic form.

Discourse practices are a major source of information for children learning the ways and world views of their culture. Speech is always said by someone to someone at a particular moment of some specific socially organized and culturally meaningful activity. As such, it is a medium through which the interactional process of socialization and representation of the world takes place. As Duranti, echoing Vygotsky, points out, speech is better seen "as a mediating activity that organizes experience" than as "a symbol of an already constituted world, whether out there or in the speakers' minds" (1984:36). In the process of socialization, worlds and world views are created through speech. In becoming communicatively competent, one comes to know and experience in culturally specific ways. The ability to participate in speech activities enables children to create additional ways of knowing about the world.

Children acquire linguistic and cultural knowledge through daily interactions with other members of their social group. In these contexts, socializing messages are conveyed by both implicit and explicit means. In socialization, discourse practices are as important a source for the child as they are a resource for the researcher interested in the acquisition of cultural practices and an understanding of world views.

Socialization and social life

Programmatic statements in the ethnographic, ethnomethodological, phenomenological, and hermeneutic literature address the importance of studying socialization (Wentworth 1980), but to date the medium through which the ability to produce and reproduce society is transmitted from member to novice has not been delineated. The role played by language in this process is only beginning to be appreciated. A major goal of the present study is to show how the close analysis of language-socializing contexts can provide that medium. Macro-level social practices must be locatable in micro-level interactions; and the analysis of everyday speech activities is a key to understanding the connections between speech and conduct, language and culture.

The perspective on socialization adopted here draws on symbolic interactionist and phenomenological approaches developed by contemporary social theorists.[7] Socialization is an interactive process between knowledgeable members and novices (children) who are themselves active contributors to the meanings and outcomes of interactions with others.[8] Socialization is a product of interaction. It is constructed by participants; it is not a preexisting process or entity. As an interpersonal process, socialization results in intrapersonal phenomena; for example, the creation and labeling of feeling states. Feeling states play a crucial role in the organization of experience and culture, and so must be part of any account of socialization. H. Geertz, writing about Javanese socialization, states that "a phenomenological approach to the learning of feeling-states or emotions in a particular culture could throw considerable light on the whole process by which a merely human infant becomes transformed into an adult of a specific culture" (1959:225). However, we need to move beyond the hypothetical "could" and see what such an analysis in fact tells us.

Socialization involves social practices appropriate to relationships among interactants. Given that members are knowledgeable and children are active learners, what can we specify about the nature of socialization? Giddens argues that agents know a great deal about the workings of society by virtue of their participation in it, and it is through such participation that learning takes place. Agents tacitly understand what they do through doing it. "The reflexive capacities of the human actor are characteristically involved in a continuous manner with the flow of day-to-day conduct in the contexts of social activity" (Giddens 1984:xxii–xxiii); they monitor settings of actions or behaviors in the context of their happening – that is, linked to particular persons and speech activities.

This notion of what agents do in interaction is a central concern of ethnomethodology and conversation analysis (e.g., Garfinkel 1967; Schegloff 1987). We also see this idea echoed in Bateson's concept of deutero-learning – learning to learn – where "individuals who have complex emotional patterns of relationship with other individuals . . . will be led to acquire or reject apperceptive habits by the very complex phenomena of personal example, tone of voice, hostility, love, etc. . . . The event stream is mediated to them through language, art, technology and other cultural media which are structured at every point by tramlines of apperceptive habit" (1972:170). Given these premises, we should study the actual scenes and occasions that constitute particular circumstances. In these contexts, people encounter, experience, and learn the principles, institutions, and ideals that structure their society and culture. If "mutual knowledge is a necessary medium of access in the mediation of frames of meaning" (Giddens 1979:251), then it is in these actual scenes and occasions that mutual knowledge becomes established.

Much of socialization takes place simply through recurrent participation in interactions with knowledgeable members. In many of these interactions, caregivers make explicit "what everyone knows" (Cicourel 1973:49). In other words, caregivers may place what is tacitly understood into the realm of what Giddens calls "discursive consciousness." Socialization may involve the discursive expression of practical consciousness, on several levels, often simultaneously. Caregivers "show" children what to do and how to feel; make nonliteral statements literal; paraphrase in several ways what they and others have said; correct or model what they want children to say or do. Wentworth states, "Socialization is an actual interactional display of the sociocultural environment, a presentation to the novice of the 'rules' whereby 'respectable' behavior might be construed" (1980:68). In some cases, interactional displays consist of presentations of techniques for accomplishing social routines as these techniques occur in the structure of talk. The extent to which such presentations have been described, however, is still quite limited.

The importance of members' displays and mediation of activities to novices is central to the ideas formulated by Vygotsky (1962, 1978) and others of the sociohistorical school who claim that higher intellectual skills of individuals develop in part through participation in socially and culturally organized activities with more knowledgeable members.[9] These joint activities are socializing contexts in which the more knowledgeable member facilitates and assists the novice in accomplishing what the novice may initially not be able to accomplish alone. In the "zone of proximal development" novices acquire cultural practices with the interactional support of more knowledgeable members. Kaluli socializing practices, in particular direct instruction routines (ɛlɛma), exemplify this particular perspective. The Kaluli theory of "showing language" and the practice of directing children to repeat what caregivers say also illustrate members' facilitating role in the acquisition of sociocultural competence. Such practices lead to a child's independent ability to participate in particular creations of social reality.

A critical part of this interactional dynamic is, of course, the active learner. When we examine children's productions and participation in interaction, we see abundant evidence that they too are agents in many respects. From ethnography of speaking and conversation analysis, we know that speech is always designed minimally according to the relationship between speaker and addressee, which means that addressee identity affects the form and content of all utterances. Interlocutors must be able to assess the relationship between themselves and addressees in addition to recognizing other dimensions of the situation in order to formulate utterances. Work in developmental pragmatics demonstrates that children have this competence as early as the age of 2 (Shatz & Gelman 1973).

Socializing activities are modified by the very structure of interactions; thus, the type of socialization that will be displayed is related to the context of its presentation. The relatively powerless young child actively influences face-to-face socializing activities as members modify the content and form of what they do and say according to the knowledge and stance of the child. This very process points out the importance of face-to-face interaction during which children have the opportunity to discover and be guided through the design of appropriate conduct, to experiment and behave in ways inappropriate for a member. Through these processes children build an initial repertoire of cultural knowledge and practices in relation to specific individuals, which is extended and elaborated throughout the life cycle. Much of everyday social life is constituted through face-to-face interaction. Thus, seemingly trivial conversational procedures have profound effects on social conduct.

Habits are a basic element of day-to-day activity (Bourdieu 1977), and language use is deeply embedded and instrumental in the accomplishment of the concrete routines of social life.[10] Social structures are constantly re-created out of the very resources that constitute them. This is what Giddens called the "recursive nature of social life" or the duality of structure. In and through their activities, actors reproduce the conditions that make these activities possible. For both Giddens and Bourdieu, socialization is not restricted to childhood. All interactions are potential socializing contexts.

The routines of daily social life allow interaction to be accomplished. Socialized in the early years and keyed by predictable metacommunicative devices, routines are extremely important in helping to create a semblance of predictability and providing a framework for contingent responses.[11] Keys define activities of a certain sort and as subject to certain expectations. Thus, participants can identify them and respond in an appropriate manner. Knowledgeable members organize their interactions with children in ways that facilitate children's ability to recognize these keys; recognizing them, children take meaning and acquire knowledge from these interactions. As Briggs (1986) and others have pointed out, caregivers' speech contains contextualization cues that identify what is going on and place affective and propositional aspects of interactions in the foreground. Young children learn to read these cues as part of their own reflexive monitoring processes. The form of the verbal and nonverbal environment makes it possible for children to abstract from the particular instances and form notions of a general nature.[12] Caregivers' utterances are constructed in such a way that their formal features simultaneously key what caregivers take to be the crucial dimensions of the present interaction and its sociocultural background.

Like family life in most places, Kaluli family interactions are highly repetitive, undertaken in like manner day after day. Such interactions constitute "the material grounding" that creates structures of expectations, values, and intuitions. Even predictable routines are dynamic social interactions, however, and we must not forget that their content and boundaries are sometimes ambiguous as participants negotiate and interpret them.

The researcher's analysis of routine speech activities between young children and more knowledgeable members is rooted in what members themselves in concert with children display: their explanations, reasons, and revisions of children's ideas about what they can and cannot do. For understanding cultural practices, language-socializing interactions are natural resources for the ethnographer as members make knowledge explicit through language, often repeatedly, constantly "conforming and informing each other" (McDermott, Gospodinoff & Aron 1978:246). Small children make gaffes and act in ways that do not follow adult preferences. When children offer interpretations of words or about the world that do not match adult expectations, children universally are guided, often through language, into specific ways of talking about (talking or things), as well as specific ways of talking. These breaches, disagreements in interpretation, arguments, and instructions are prime opportunities to observe otherwise tacit cultural expectations and assumptions. The ways in which these cultural practices are negotiated effectively shape the world views of children (Ochs 1988; Ochs & Schieffelin 1984).

Particularly relevant to this study is Bourdieu's formulation of education (socialization) in societies that do not institutionalize it as "a specific autonomous practice which exerts an anonymous pervasive pedagogic action" (1977:87) (formal schools, as I read it). When "it is a whole group and a whole symbolically structured environment, . . . the essential part of the *modus operandi* which defines practical mastery is transmitted in practice, in its practical state, without attaining the level of discourse" (p. 87). While I agree in part with Bourdieu's observation about nonformal education (socialization), I find the suggested role of discourse problematic. It is true that in societies where socialization is not formally labeled "education," attainments of competence and mastery often pass without comment. It is simply assumed that one will become a competent member. Socialization, however, often "attains the level of discourse" because discourse practices provide a medium through which world views and social activities are constituted. "The child imitates not 'models' but other people's actions" (p. 87), drawing on interactional displays of specific people and particular recurring events. That underlying codes have to be inferred from surface manifestations means that novices look to discourse practices. Active learners process social and linguistic information and make sense of it in terms of rationales of their particular society and their own cognitive capacity to create abstract rules from presentations. We must not neglect the fact that discourse carries a great deal of the structure and rationales of society, and while Bourdieu's "structural exercises" (such as riddles, proverbs, games) are important in groups that engage in them, everyday discourse structures convey primary techniques of social problem solving.

Giddens claims that socialization is an active process between children and members that takes place within interaction and involves "mastery of the 'dialogical' contexts of communication" and the accumulation of practical knowledge of conventions drawn upon in the production and reproduction of social interaction. We need to take Giddens both literally and figuratively with regard to dialogic contexts and see discourse practices as media to examine directly. We must relate sets of micro discourse practices not only to each other but to more general or macro cultural patterns, meanings, and paradoxes.

In the close examination of discourse practices, one sees the role of variation. There are several types of variation; for example, across setting and speaker, or in social meaning. Variation in the narrative account restores some of the texture in individuals' lives that gets lost in many ethnographies. A microethnography warrants details and variation; the particular can be situated within and distinguished from the general.

Considerations: time and variation

Although Kaluli society can be characterized as relatively small-scale, homogeneous, and traditional, there is variation in members' speech and conduct. Some variation is directly due to the effects of time. Two kinds of time are relevant to this study.

The first is developmental time. As this is a longitudinal study of children's language socialization, it focuses on children's increasing competence and participation in Kaluli social life. Through developmental time, we see how shifts in the expectations of caregivers and older children affect what constitutes acceptable behavior in younger children and how these shifts are expressed through speech. But the instability of linguistic forms across developmental time is only one aspect of the change and variation that are inherent in children's development. As children grow, they experiment, practice, and creatively manipulate the social and linguistic resources available to them.

The second type of time relevant to variation and change is sociohistorical. Kaluli society continues to undergo important changes, which started in the early 1970s. The introduction of fundamentalist evangelical Christianity by Australian missionaries and increased contact with the provincial government were only two of the sources of change affecting Kaluli society in the mid 1970s. Families responded differently to these changes; some embraced new ideas, and others rejected them. Some families spent more time around the village in their own small houses, and others spent time away in the bush or in the communal longhouse.

In discussing social reproduction, Giddens observes,

All social reproduction is grounded in the knowledgeable application and reapplication of rules and resources by actors in situated social contexts: all interaction thus has, in every circumstance, to be contingently "brought off" by those who are party to it. Change is in principle involved with social production – again in both its basic sense and its "generational" sense – in its very contingency: social systems are chronically produced and reproduced by their constitutent participants. *Change, or its potentiality, is thus inherent in all moments of social reproduction.* It is essential to see that any and every change in a social system logically implicates the totality and thus implies structural modification, however minor or trivial this may be. (1979:114)

This view of social reproduction provides a larger framework for understanding social processes and accommodates change and variation in what we understand as socialization.

In addition to variation due to time, there is variation due to differences in young children's social and linguistic development. Where such individual variation occurs and is culturally significant, I discuss it. Each of the children in the study had certain linguistic preferences and an individual style, as did other family members. I noted shared preferences and styles as well as when and how differences were expressed. Other variability relates to differences in activities between children and adults and between older children and younger ones in terms of what is acceptable, interesting, and appropriate. This variability is important in that it attests to the fact that "shared culture," "stock knowledge," and "mutual understanding" need not be premised on homogeneity of behavior.[13]

The rest of this chapter describes the fieldwork situation, data collection, and interpretation as an ethnographic procedure, and concludes with thoughts about writing this kind of ethnography.

Fieldwork situation

My research in 1975–7 on language socialization was greatly facilitated by an earlier field trip to the Kaluli in 1967–8, when I joined anthropologist E. L. (Buck) Schieffelin for the second half of his ethnographic fieldwork with members of clan Bonɔ in Sululib village. I learned a great deal about the language and culture by participating in village life, and made many Kaluli friends during those fourteen months. When we returned to the Kaluli in 1975 for my doctoral research and Buck's continuing projects on spirit mediums, our son Zachary (4½ yr) was with us. After surveying several villages, we decided to settle again at Sululib, as we knew the people and their histories and considered that fact a resource to build on through fictive kinship and other relationships. Sululib is also centrally located and has the largest population of any village (101 individuals) – an advantage in that there was a good chance that there would always be some families around to work with. Kaluli built us a small house in the village, and once again we become part of the everyday life of the community. We depended on our friends for fresh food and traded salt, soap, fishhooks, and other desired objects for bananas, greens, pumpkins, and papayas. Tinned meat and fish were traded for fresh varieties. As no medical facility was locally available, we took care of the immediate medical needs of village people with antimalarial drugs, penicillin, and bandages.

Fieldwork among Kaluli was an intense experience. Always being right there and able to hear what was going on often made us participants whether we chose to be or not. Crises such as illness and death punctuated routine village activities. Kaluli made their houses open to us, and ours was often full of Kaluli visitors. Men and women curious about what we were doing dropped in at all hours, and we did the same with them for similar reasons. Often people just wanted to sit on our porch, which was a good vantage point, and talk with their friends and visitors from other villages who brought us food for trade. I spent my days either tape recording and observing families or transcribing the taped interactions with paid Kaluli assistants during transcription sessions in the house. On the walking trails, in sago camps, and around the cooking fires, we talked more casually with everyone in the village. Zachary learned to speak Kaluli, played with the children, and was treated affectionately by the adults.

After we had spent a year in the field, Steve Feld, an anthropologist, ethnomusicologist, and close friend, joined us for his dissertation research. Steve came as my "younger brother" (*ao*), and this fictive kin relationship not only made sense in terms of Kaluli social life but helped us understand the *adɛ* relationship, the one between younger brothers and older sisters (discussed in Chapter 5). Steve was Zachary's *babo* 'mother's brother' (one who gives) and Buck's *idas* 'wife's brother' (one who assists and shares). Steve's research complemented my own and Buck's, and we worked with compatible theoretical perspectives. Our research was undertaken in the spirit of cooperation and complementarity as we shared questions, stories, data, and ideas throughout our time in the field.

It will be apparent that this research is not impartial. As Hymes has said, "There is no way to avoid the fact that the ethnographer himself or herself is a factor in the inquiry" (1980:99). As a woman, I was given privileged access to the activities of women and children. No man could have sat in the women's section or gone bathing with small children. As a mother, I was seen as an adult, one who shared some perspectives with other women. Being an impartial observer was neither possible nor desirable. Kaluli incorporated me into their social world and social system, and according to my various relationships I was given kinship or relationship names used by friends. Nevertheless, we were still *kɔle* 'different' and *dogɔf wanalo* 'yellow skinned'. The Kaluli perceived limits to access, just as we did.

Method and interpretation

Selecting families and contexts

During the first three months at Sululib in 1975, I split my time between working on my language ability (for all work was done monolingually in Kaluli) and being with families with small children, watching what they were doing and listening to what they were saying. I hoped to select for longitudinal study four children who were learning to talk. While observing children, I also investigated their daily activities with mothers and siblings. This in itself was an important inquiry: I had to determine the significant and recurring socializing activities for Kaluli children. This meant investigating the social organization of caregiving: who organized activities in which children participated, how children received food, how any arguments were negotiated and by whom, and with whom children interacted. I needed to know the relevant social activities that constituted everyday experience so that unexpected situations could be cast into an appropriate perspective.

I looked for children who were already using single words or just starting to use syntax. In addition, I needed children whose mothers were willing to sit with me, or "school me," as I explained it to them, after each recording session for initial transcription of audiotaped speech. As it turned out, there were only four children in the village who were about the right age, and I began taping the speech of two of them, a girl named Meli and a boy named Abi, after three months of observing and taking notes. I continued following the two younger ones, a boy named Wanu and Abi's younger half-sister Suɛla, taking diary notes on their language and activities until their speech production warranted recording a few months later. The four children are from three families, each of which represents a different orientation to the changes that were taking place in Bosavi in the mid 1970s. These changes included the introduction of religious instruction and a church hierarchy, literacy, instruction in Western health care and hygiene, employment for money as mission personnel (pastors, house help, station maintenance workers), and the increasing awareness of and contact with the Southern Highlands provincial government and developments outside Bosavi. In the three families, adults responded to these new institutions and ideas in different ways, and this affected their cultural ideology and social practices with children. Many of these changes had consequences in the late 1970s and early 1980s for the organization of family life and language use, as I discovered when I returned to Bosavi in 1984.

While establishing relationships with the children and their families, I determined which activities and times of day were best for tape recording. There were three situations in which 2- to 3-year olds regularly participated. The first was early in the morning, when families wake up and mothers stir up the remains of the night fires and begin preparing the first meal. People start talking as soon as they wake up, and usually the first thing on everyone's mind is food. This first period would sometimes extend into mid morning and could involve short excursions from the house to get water at a nearby stream. The second situation was in the late afternoon, when, after collecting fresh greens, pandanus, and bananas from the nearby gardens, mothers return to the village and settle down to cook the main meal of the day. This was an optimal recording time, since children had finished napping and were full of energy. There was enough interaction to keep things going and little chance of an influx of adult visitors (who tend to change the recording situation), because all the people are at home making cooking fires, wrapping packets of sago and greens, or scraping the long cobs of pandanus in preparation for their own afternoon meal. Finally, since trips to nearby streams for bathing, playing, fishing, and drawing water are also times for talking, recordings were made during these excursions whenever possible.

I explored other situations for their recording potential but found that they did not offer the same opportunities for small children to interact with siblings and adults. For example, when mothers went to their gardens for a few hours with their very young children (the older ones often stayed in the village), the young children usually played quietly or slept while their mothers worked at weeding and gathering food. When large family groups went to the bush for several days at a time, their activities were organized around work: cutting trees, clearing brush, building bush shelters, gathering firewood, processing sago. In these situations, small children had excellent opportunities to observe what others were doing and saying, but they did not participate in conversations, as people were oriented toward accomplishing tasks. Since garden sites and sago camps were not optimal situations for 2- to 3-year-olds to talk with other people, I did not record systematically in those situations.

Even though Kaluli mothers are the major caregivers, Kaluli children spend a great deal of time in the company of their siblings and other relatives. The speech samples reflect this; they include extensive conversations among children as well as between children and their mothers, other relatives, and visitors. This is all part of the verbal environment of Kaluli children. At the beginning of the study, the households of the four focus children contained nine other children ranging from 5 months to 10 years of age. The speech of these other children is of course included in the samples. Three of the mothers

Table 1. *Speech samples*

	Sample no.									
	1	2	3	4	5	6	7	8	9	10
Abi										
Age (mo/ wk)	25.1	25.3	27.2	28.2	30	31.2	32.2	33.2	34.2	35.2
Sample length (hr)	0.5	1.5	3.5	4.5	2.75	3.75	3.5	4.25	4.5	4
No. of child utterances	203	566	1,105	982	1,050	1,432	1,250	1,410	1,949	1,693
Wanu										
Age (mo/ wk)	24.1	25.1	26.3	27.3	29	30.3	32.1	—	—	—
Sample length (hr)	2	3	2.5	3.5	4	4	3.5	—	—	—
No. of child utterances	701	1,325	1,584	1,882	2,594	2,289	1,935	—	—	—
Mɛli										
Age (mo/ wk)	24.1	24.3	26	27.3	28.3	30.2	31.2	32.2	—	—
Sample length (hr)	0.5	1.5	3	4	4	3	3.25	4.25	—	—
No. of child utterances	240	603	936	1,513	1,546	1,517	1,260	1,514	—	—

gave birth during the course of the study. The addition of two boys and one girl provided excellent opportunities to observe what happens when a 2- to 3-year-old is no longer the youngest child and the center of the mother's attention. Important social and linguistic consequences in the lives of all of the children followed the arrival of infant siblings. In addition, I had the opportunity to document how infants are introduced into the family and how new relationships are created with them. Unfortunately, Suɛla could not be followed as long as the others, leaving Abi, Wanu, and Mɛli the focus children for the study.

A total of eighty-three hours of naturalistic interaction between children and their mothers, siblings, relatives, and other villagers were transcribed, translated, annotated, and checked in the field; this forms the major data base for analysis (see Table 1). In spite of what must have seemed an endless task that did not make a great deal of sense and in addition was extraordinarily boring, three Kaluli women, Ulahi, Osolowa, and Wadeo, sat with me through transcription sessions lasting seven hours for each hour of recorded tape, nursing infants, holding older children, repeating what they heard on the tape, and answering my endless questions about what was said. I am still amazed that they did it.

Collecting the speech data and preparing the annotated transcripts

Annotated transcripts of the tape-recorded interactions between children and members of their families constitute a major portion of the data. Preparation of such transcripts involved the following procedures.

(1) Since one of my major research goals was to investigate the patterns of verbal interaction between Kaluli and their children and how these patterns changed over time, I collected speech between children and those individuals with whom they usually interacted in everyday family situations. I assumed that this would be the optimal situation for children and would allow me to observe and record them in the recurring social situations in which they learn language. I did not want to act in a way that would elicit the data I would be analyzing, for many reasons. Not being a member of Kaluli society, I could not presume to know the culturally appropriate ways of speaking to and interacting with children, nor would children know how to talk to me. I tape recorded spontaneous speech samples longitudinally in order to document important recurring cultural situations, interactions, and participants in each child's life, children's acquisition of social and linguistic skills, and caregivers' changing responses to their increasingly competent young children.

As a resident of Sululib, I was treated as a participant during recordings and other visits. Adults and children talked to me during the taping sessions, and, depending on their own activities or interests, they would also let me just sit and observe while they cooked food, made net bags, groomed each other, and talked. I was always offered food, some roasted bananas or sago or whatever people were eating, and I usually brought a small item for the child or mother: some soap, salt, tinned fish, or sweet bananas. People were free to leave the situation when they had chores to do or obligations to fulfill; sometimes they just wanted to nap. I began and ended recording sessions when I felt the time was right to do so according to the activities of the participants.

(2) Speech samples for each child were recorded continuously for as long as the situation permitted. This was done in order to analyze how speakers make use of context history and discourse history when talking to each other. Following Bloom's longitudinal speech-sampling procedures (1970), I made detailed written contextual notes along with these recordings (matched to the

counter of the tape recorder) in order to coordinate speech with action.[14] Studying the speech of a few children while taking detailed contextual notes on the setting, scene, and participants (especially the identification of speaker and addressee in multiparty talk) as well as on nonverbal behavior, objects, and displayed affect was fully compatible with the ethnographic perspective I had adopted. For example, in order to understand the use of particular possessive pronouns, one has to know whether an object has been borrowed or if it belongs to the person who has it. To make sense of the pragmatic use of word order or of emphatic subject pronouns, one must know if someone has asked for something earlier in an interaction. Contextual information such as this was essential to the interpretation of the meanings of utterances and interactions.[15] My goal was at least two hours of continuous discourse during each monthly sample, but this was not always possible, as I had to adjust to events in people's lives. The onset of a child's malarial attack, a pig accidentally getting into a garden, the sudden arrival of visitors, and other unforeseeable events sometimes meant that I had to stop recording sooner than I would have liked. Most samples, however, have at least two hours of continuous recording per session.

(3) To reflect the child's maturation, language development, and situational changes, the language samples consisted of three to four hours of speech recorded within a four- to seven-day period at intervals averaging five weeks. Whereas the continuous recording sessions had distinct advantages, spacing

Figure 2. Audiotaping while Suela tickles her brother Sele's foot with a dead crayfish and her mother checks Daibo for head lice.

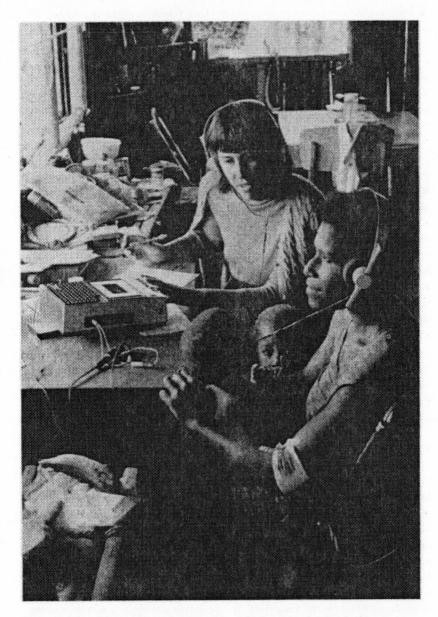

Figure 3. Transcribing session with Osolowa. Mɛli and her brother look on.

the recording over a few days did give continuity between events on a larger scale. I could understand what children were talking about when they referred back to things that had happened in previous visits, as well as to recent happenings in the village. Living in a small village, I heard about or saw what was going on, so even when the tapings were a few days apart, my knowledge of recent events was such that people did not change their speech in order to make sure I would understand. That is, the Kaluli realized what I knew and did not explain things to me as part of the ongoing situation. They knew I would ask if I didn't understand.

As soon as possible after completing the recording of a given sample, I began transcribing the audio tapes, integrating the contextual notes with the transcribed speech. I did this with the assistance of the children's mothers. As it turned out, this "schooling" was one of the first times Kaluli women had had the opportunity to earn any money or trade goods for their labor, and they seemed to be pleased with the exchange. They helped with this initial transcription by repeating both their own and others' speech to me. This was especially helpful in glossing special forms their children used, identifying speakers in multiparty talk, and specifying the history and ownership of objects involved in the interactions. They also freely commented on the interactions. For example, when children played with the sounds of their language or distorted speech, they suggested not transcribing those sections, telling me that it was *ba madali* 'to no purpose' and that we should go on. Their linguistic awareness suggested to me that Kaluli thought that only clearly articulated referential speech was appropriate to write down. In fact, I later found out that these comments were based on metalinguistic notions that included specific ideas about how Kaluli children ought to speak, such as using "hard words" (Feld & Schieffelin 1982). Their responses became part of the annotation and were the basis for generating further questions about interactional patterns, Kaluli classification of speech acts and speech events, and what constituted "good talk" (*to nafa*).

Several months after the initial transcription, I listened to all of the tapes with a young Kaluli man, Kulu Fuale, who did not regularly live in Sululib and who had not been a participant in any recording sessions. He was, however, especially interested in language. I initially saw this as a reliability check, since there were no speakers who could listen to these tapes and check the accuracy of my transcription. But this relistening became more than simply checking transcripts. It was a means of extending and enriching the contextualizing ethnographic and linguistic information provided originally by the mothers. For example, Kulu was able to interpret the significance of many interactions without the contextual information I had recorded. Listening to the tape-recorded message, he could frequently tell how people were feeling from the linguistic forms they used. It was during discussions with him based on these recorded interactions that I came to understand the roles that prosody, voice quality, affect-marked affixes and expressives, and formulaic expressions played in conveying affect, and how the pragmatic use of word order disambiguated utterances and indicated what was at issue. These transcripts of situated speech plus the elicitation sessions based on them, focusing on verb morphology, the case-marking and pronominal systems, syntactic variation, and metalinguistics, provided the data for a linguistic sketch of Kaluli and an analysis of children's psycholinguistic development (B. B. Schieffelin 1986a). For every hour of recorded speech, an additional twenty hours were spent in preparing the annotated translated transcript.

Transcription and annotation were completed in the field. Given the complexities of natural conversation and the ways in which meanings are situated, native speakers are needed to assist in the admittedly time-consuming process of preparing a transcript for grammatical, discourse, and ethnographic analyses. However, it should be emphasized that preparation of the annotated transcript is not merely a mechanical data-collecting task but is itself a deeply ethnographic process. Annotation and translation require an ongoing discussion with native speakers about the cultural significance of the recorded events, culturally recognized types of speech interactions, and named discourse strategies, all of which contribute to the interpretation of conduct and speech.

Even though the speech activities studied involved both children and adults, only adults, mostly mothers, were able to talk with me about the events after the fact. This means that some of the interpretations are admittedly biased in terms of adult meanings and norms. However, knowing this, I took what children said *in situ* as a way of understanding their perspectives and feelings about events. In order to assess what children knew, I examined what they said and did across a range of contexts, how they were responded to, and what the rejoinders were. Older children often talked with each other about events or reported them to others (i.e., complaining, teasing, shaming). These conversations too are part of the tape-recorded samples and contribute to the analyses. Children also made metalinguistic comments, correcting younger children and paraphrasing each other. Thus, my presentation of children's own emergent views is based on their interactional displays to each other and is considered in the context of what adults say about them. Without this type of ethnographic inquiry and resulting annotation, the meaning of these everyday events would have been obscured or at best misinterpreted.

Speech activities, like all other cultural activities, are deeply embedded in belief systems. Local theories concerning the physical, social, and linguistic development of children played an important role in making sense out of what people did and said. The relationship between what people claimed was preferred behavior and what they actually did was taken into account and explored throughout the study. For example, in my interviews with mothers about food taboos I not only asked what they and each of their children could not eat, but when they had last seen particular foods. (Spiny anteaters and echidnas, which are taboo, were extremely rare.) I explored their views about gender-role socialization and language acquisition, taking their spontaneous comments as the basis for further questions. Mothers, and occasionally fathers, were informally interviewed about their ideas on these topics with an eye to how they themselves talked about and conceptualized processes of socialization and development. Given that there was variation in the community regarding certain topics, such as adherence to food taboos, I could explore the reasons for change and the connections with other belief systems. Segments of tape-recorded interactions were used to elicit comments about what children were doing. People also made comments about what I did as a mother; for example, they said I was careless about grooming my son for head lice – he had several cases. They also said that it was a bad idea to let him sleep by himself; it was not safe because of potential witchcraft activities. Instead, he should sleep with me. Zachary's excellent language ability was also commented on and provided an important comparative perspective on Kaluli linguistic ideology. Because of the way the data were collected, with language and context together, the interrelatedness of the various levels of information about speech and conduct could be analyzed in terms of questions not yet formulated at the time of data collection.

A major goal of this study is to describe and account for what Kaluli see as essential for children's language socialization and how this is accomplished. I have taken this perspective seriously, and it is reflected in the selection of topics for each chapter, but there is a tacit comparative perspective that must be acknowledged here. In every society, members believe that certain activities and behaviors are important and others are not. When it comes to what children do, this is particularly relevant, as adults have views about childhood and children's activities. There were numerous children's activities that Kaluli adults claimed were *ba madali* 'to no purpose' and not to be dwelt on. However, some of these activities – for example, sound play – turned out to be rich in terms of displaying children's discourse and metalinguistic skills, in addition to revealing critical cultural ideas about children, language, and the symbolic importance of birds. Previous work on children's discourse practices pointed to the importance of these issues in general, and the comments of Kaluli mothers during spontaneous interactions made them illustrative of culturally specific meanings. Thus, in addition to an ethnographic view that considers what Kaluli say must occur for their children to talk and act like Kaluli, there is a. complementary view from developmental sociolinguistics and psycholinguistics that suggests important developmental processes that should be examined in comparative perspective.

Reading the transcripts and interpreting the examples

As others working on transcribed materials have reminded us, our transcribed data are interpretive records, selected and edited; theoretical descriptions; others' and our memories of events and speech.[16] They are not the events or utterances themselves. One returns to one's transcripts, audiotapes, and field notes repeatedly, checking for additional details that may be more relevant than one previously thought. Every transcript reflects the particular interests and biases of the analyst: What constitutes details for one is less than adequate for another's purposes.[17] I take as a starting point Hymes's position that "the form of the message is fundamental" (1974:54). If the message form is not taken, the rules governing it cannot be captured. "The failure to unite form and content in the scope of a single focus of study has retarded understanding of the human ability to speak and that vitiates many attempts to analyze the significance of behavior" (ibid.). One no longer has to make an argument for the importance of transcription. We know that if we want to understand ordinary, unremarkable, taken-for-granted, everyday events from the perspective of the participants, attention to the detail of talk is especially important. Hymes's observation that "the more a way of speaking has become shared and meaningful within a group, the more likely that crucial cues will be efficient, i.e., slight in scale" (ibid.) is especially applicable to routine and ordinary conversations in families, where speakers are not always aware of exactly what they have said, and even spontaneous requests for repetition do not produce the identical form (Silverstein 1981). Whereas in formal speech genres participants can often repeat what they have said after the fact, in routine conversations that occur simultaneously with other activities (cooking food, trying to hush a crying baby), recapturing what was said by report produces an inadequate account of what was said, and for young children is impossible to do.

Tape recordings and transcripts privilege the said. And as Goffman (1976) observed, the laconicity of talk – what is not said – is always at the heart. This is why we need to work with speakers' interpretations coupled with our own ethnographic and linguistic knowledge. The natives do not rely on the surface only, and neither should we. Moerman claims that working with culturally contexted conversation resolves the problem of interpretation (1988:18). Although interpretation may be less problematic when one examines conversations between adults, the interpretive situation is not always as obvious when one looks at socializing contexts between caregivers and children. It helps to take local theories of interpretation and intentionality seriously (Duranti 1984), along with how adults name speech acts and strategies. But we must not be fooled into thinking that ambiguity and indeterminacy disappear as soon as our data are good enough. Ambiguity and indeterminacy are important social and communicative resources, necessary in conversation; and the best we can do is identify them as such when they occur. Moerman's point is well taken, however, that "culturally contexted conversation permits a description that while never complete is sufficient for showing the nexus between cultural rules and individuals' intentions" (1988:57).

In the chapters that follow, the reader will be presented with sequences of speech taken from annotated transcripts. The conversational details of overlaps and repairs have been preserved, though not with the precision of conversation analysis. Meaning has necessarily been amplified through translation, and linguistic details are given when relevant to the discussion. The explications that follow guide the reader to notice what is relevant to the discussion; Kaluli commentary generated during listening is made explicit whenever possible. The explications are guides to one of many possible discussions; for example, how arguments are initiated, structured, countered, terminated; how keys are shifted; or how relationships are marked. But of course time and space limit the selection and discussion, and what is presented is only a piece of ongoing talk. Topics were often initiated and reinitiated over hours, events, and days; obviously, what is presented is one sequence, but one that represents a pattern. If it does not, that is discussed. My work has been preparing the Kaluli examples so that they are accessible to the reader. They are mostly provided only in close English glosses except for times when language is at issue. One needs to read the examples as representing what particular people say and how they say it in particular instances. As Cicourel and others have pointed out, we must study the actual scenes and occasions that constitute particular circumstances. In interaction, people experience principles, institutions, and ideals that characterize their society and culture. The examples are an integral part of the story and a representation of the voices of the participants.

Readers are invited to consider alternative interpretations; presentation allows that. Examples are multilevel and always display a variety of forms, structures, and messages. Moerman (1988:11) criticizes ethnographers of speaking for not providing or referring to transcripts and for largely concentrating on special sorts of speech events rather than on everyday conversation. This has not been the case for anthropologists or sociolinguists who work on children's language or caregivers' speech.[18] The examination of language use between caregivers and children concentrates on the everyday conversation that constitutes the verbal environment of children. This perspective places the origin of speech production with the participants themselves. Work from this perspective examines how participants arrange what they have to do primarily through talk.

Some thoughts on writing this ethnography

Currently, anthropologists are thinking critically about how to write ethnography; how to represent a version of the experiences, recollections, and interpretations of those experiences at the moment and again in light of recollections of other moments; and where to place themselves in the enterprise.[19] Added to these problems are issues of what we as analysts can expect to know at the moment of observation, then after discussion of the event, and finally during a review of the event in light of information participants themselves only then claim to remember. Clearly there is continual reinterpretation, if not a deepening or broadening of understanding, as we work and rework materials in our sense-making projects.

These processes of interpretation and representation that are troublesome to ethnographers and to participants are also problematic for ethnographers of speaking. First of all, there is the challenge of how to integrate linguistic details within a narrative ethnographic style, a problem noted by Malinowski. His solution was to separate his language analyses from his ethnographic ones.[20] Interactional details such as transcripts of verbal exchanges need to be situated not only in terms of the larger events in which they occur, but also in a broader narrative account. I have aimed for balance between the details and the larger picture. Micro-level interactional and linguistic details are not simply background for macro-level ethnographic descriptions. Just as linguistic and cultural analyses are interwoven, so are particular instances located within patterns of wider cultural import.

Second, for those of us who tape and transcribe events and then annotate them with the assistance of participants, there are always questions about the meaning of what was said. We believe that relistening repeatedly reveals further cues – a tone of voice, a longer-than-expected pause, a particular phrase that had not been quite caught in an earlier gloss. We "reorganize" by slowing down the tape recorder, producing a kind of relistening for details that differs from the on-line hearing and understanding of participants. We pay attention to all verbal contributions, those overlapped or in the background as well as those in the foreground. How different is the experience of the participants at the time and ourselves afterwards, and how does our method affect our interpretation?

These problems are compounded by the fact that research in language socialization focuses on understanding unreportable, everyday activities. These activities are fleeting and routine, and adults assume that they will be accomplished by those who know how. For ethnographer and participants alike, the doing of these activities is largely unexamined and not even talked about except when things do not go smoothly. Only from microethnographies do we see what constitutes the expected and how it is accomplished. But how to write about the routine and unremarkable in an "exotic" culture in an interesting way, where all the background must be filled in so that readers can see both the forest and the trees? If participants think a particular activity is unimportant, what happens when we change its status by giving it our time and attention? Through our transcripts we create objects of study to be mined for ideology. We think about what these situations are for young children in them, and not from the perspective of knowledgeable adults. Where children are participants, routine activities are not always predictable: Almost anything can happen. Everyday activities constitute unknown information. For children, everyday discourse practices contain the cultural keys, tropes, metaphors, norms. They also provide material for learning one of the most important cultural systems and how to use it: language. These everyday routines are for the most part what constitute the child's world.

3. Kaluli children: ideology and everyday life

Sululib village and everyday activities

Sululib, where the members of clan Bonɔ live, is slightly larger than other Kaluli villages. In 1977, the population was 101 individuals, 38 males and 63 females. In the under-10 category, there were 22 boys and 39 girls. While some families still lived in the large communal longhouse, those in this study all had their own smaller houses located around the yard, in which they spent most of their time. The houses of two of the children, Abi and Wanu, were similar to the design of the communal longhouse, with separate sleeping areas for men and women. Meli's family lived in a nontraditionally designed house; her parents shared a sleeping area. All of the houses, however, were made of the traditional materials available from the forest, including sago lath and fronds, black palm, and vines. There were several buildings constructed around the cleared yard to accommodate the government officer and his carriers during their infrequent visits to the area. In the 1970s, a church became part of the village scene (see Figure 4). The Solɔ, a small stream with a spring and pool convenient for drawing water and bathing, was very close to the village, as were some smaller springs. Paths through the forest led away from Sululib to other Kaluli villages, which took half an hour or more to reach by foot on muddy bush tracks and through streams. Walking is the only means of travel in the area.

Kaluli women usually wake up at daylight. Adding firewood to the remaining embers, they stoke up a fire and begin cooking for the morning meal. This meal usually consists of whatever is still around the house from the night before – cooking bananas, sweet potato or taro, sago, pandanus that can be reheated. It is usually cool in the early morning, and as people wake up they turn to the fire to get warm. When it is raining, waking up proceeds very slowly and is accompanied by collective exclamations about the cold and announcements about the rain.

Depending on what needs to be done, men leave the house singly or in groups. Gardens have to be cleared and planted. Fences often need to be repaired so that pigs do not get into the gardens and eat all the root crops. The

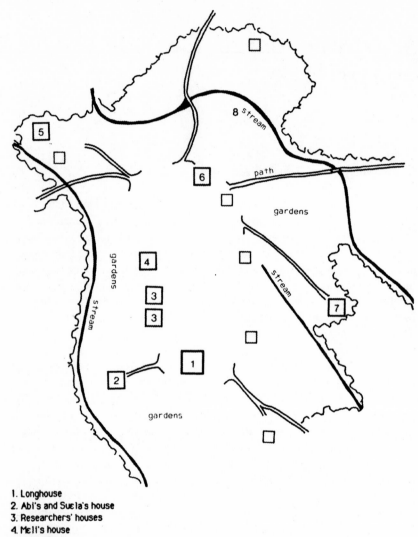

1. Longhouse
2. Abi's and Suela's house
3. Researchers' houses
4. Meli's house
5. Wanu's house
6. Church
7. Pastor's house
8. Solo stream

Figure 4. Sketch map of Bono village.

whereabouts of pigs have to be checked, and someone always has some personal business to transact at another village. Women usually go to their gardens daily to weed and pick various vegetable foods, such as pandanus, breadfruit, and greens, and to collect firewood and cooking leaves for the late-

Figure 5. Children playing in the yard in front of the longhouse.

Figure 6. Meli and her mother visiting with female relatives on the porch of the long-house.

Figure 7. Baseo and others bringing a pig to be cooked.

afternoon meal. Often they leave in mid morning and return in the afternoon. Mothers always take their youngest children on these trips, preferring to leave the older ones in the village unless they need additional help that older children could offer. En route to the gardens, women are on the lookout for birds, eggs, lizards, and landcrabs; they check their traps for small animals to supplement the garden produce. If they are out in the gardens for several hours, they might have prepared a snack, and brought it with them, and they might take a nap.

Upon returning to the village, women organize the late-afternoon meal, the main meal of the day. Older children are sent to draw water from nearby springs in long bamboo water tubes. This is also an opportunity to bathe and collect any firewood that was left on the track earlier. Once these chores are completed, the cooking activities begin. Food preparation and cooking take about two hours and involve different methods, depending on what has been collected. For example, when pandanus is in season, the long red cobs are split and the inner fibers scraped out and eaten raw as a snack. The cobs are put aside. A fire is specially prepared to heat rocks, which are placed inside a leaf cooking packet, which must be assembled. Older daughters assist, cleaning taro and sweet potatoes, which are steamed in the packet with the pandanus cobs. Sago is stuffed into bamboo tubes or crumbled on cooking leaves for baking along with greens or small lizards, fish, or whatever has been

Figure 8. Men laying the pig on the fire to singe off the hair.

brought home. Other vegetables are roasted directly in the hot ashes or cooked over the open flames. Several items may be cooking simultaneously, and this requires organization and coordination among women and their children. As food is ready, it is divided up, passed around, and eaten. These are times when members of the household are either eating or asking for more. During and after eating, family members talk and exchange observations and news; until darkness falls, women also work on net bags, and men sharpen axes. No one goes out after dark: It is considered dangerous because of the possibility of witchcraft. It is a time to talk inside, and children go to sleep as they wish, as do adults. Sometimes, if there are visitors or an issue is up for discussion, those wishing to talk stay up late into the night, stirring the fires to keep warm, not minding that others are sleeping. The next day the same people will take catnaps to catch up on lost sleep.

When a family decides to process sago (when a tree ripens or the supply of processed sago runs out), two families often cooperate. Depending on the number of sago palms to process and how far away they are from the village, groups either go for the day or, more commonly, set up a sago camp and spend several days to a week in the bush. Women build a bush shelter near the sago palms, while the men cut down the trees and split the trunks in preparation for scraping and beating. Infants are in the constant care of their mothers; 2- to 3-year-olds stay close to their mothers, playing while keeping

Figure 9. Ulahi scraping pandanus cobs while Waye stuffs a bamboo tube with sago.

an eye on their activities. Older children play together in the shallow streams that always run through sago camps, hunting for crayfish, throwing pebbles and leaves in the water, and building miniature dams with stones, sticks, and mud. Food is collected from nearby gardens or brought from the village, and a small fire is kept going so that food can be cooked as people become hungry during the day. Once the men have prepared the sago tree and scraped the white pulpy material for the women to beat, the women work steadily at processing the sago, soliciting the help of older girls with the tedious jobs of bringing water to the sago troughs to rinse the starch from the fiber and carrying away the sago garbage to a dumping place.

Children generally seem to enjoy themselves in these sago camps in the bush. There are lots of things to do, and it is a break from the routine of the village. Mothers are present but involved in their work. Fathers are around some of the time and occasionally play with their children when they take a break from processing sago. People seem relaxed and enjoy their time together in the forest.

Whether in sago camps, at the family gardens, bathing in the river, or playing around the house and yard, 2-year-old children are seldom far from their mothers. This is, however, the age when the child's world begins to change; the next child is usually born before the older child's third birthday.

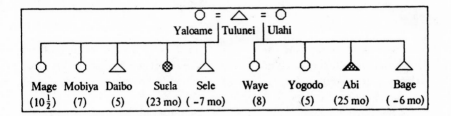

Abi and Suɛla's household

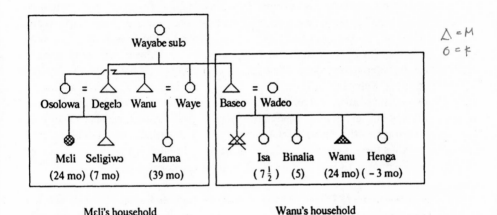

Mɛli's household   Wanu's household

Figure 10

But there were differences among the households in which the children of the study were growing up. The next section examines the differences as well as the common themes in the social worlds of these children.

The children and their families

The four children originally selected for the study were all very close in age. The two boys, Abi and Wanu, were 25 and 24 months respectively at the start of the study; and the two girls, Mɛli and Suɛla, were 24 and 23 months. Abi and Suɛla were children of two co-wives of their father and slept with their mothers in different parts of the same house. Wanu and Mɛli were parallel cousins whose fathers, Baseo and Degelɔ, were brothers. For ease of reference, diagrams showing the kinship relations and household members of the children are provided in Figure 10.

Abi

Abi, who at the start of the study was 25 months old, lived with his mother, Ulahi; father, Tulunei; and older sisters, Waye (8 yr) and Yogodo (5 yr).[1] Six months later a brother, Bage, was born. Tulunei's first wife, Yaloame, and her five children also lived in the same small house.

Of the three families, Abi's most closely followed the cultural practices observed and documented in the 1960s and so could be said to be the most "traditional." Abi's family engaged in the usual subsistence activities, spending time in the bush hunting, fishing, gardening, sago making, and gathering wild edibles. At home, the women wove net bags (*asɔ*) and sago filter bags (*masi*), chopped firewood, cooked food, and looked after their children. Their only store-bought possessions were blankets, axes, and knives, and they went to the mission station only when pressured to seek medical attention for their children. Tulunei, Ulahi, and Yaloame sporadically went to church with some of the older girls, but none of them were involved in church activities or literacy classes, nor were they preparing for baptism. Tulunei's wives did not contribute to the pastor's food supply, and Tulunei only occasionally joined the workforce for church-related projects. Although Tulunei was a village representative to a mission school committee, none of his children ever attended school.

Abi's mother, Ulahi, wore a cloth head cape and made her own and her daughters' skirts out of inner-tree-bark and sago-leaf materials. Abi, when he wore anything, wore a simple cloth pubic cover held on by a string around his waist like his father's. For important events, such as meetings at the mission, Tulunei would sometimes borrow a pair of shorts, but his wives did not own or wear dresses. Both women kept their heads and those of their children shaved in the traditional topknot style. The followed all food taboos, kinship avoidance regulations, and menstrual and postpartum sex taboos. All the children had Kaluli names except the youngest boy, Bage, but he, like other Kaluli children, was named for a namesake (*daiyo*) – in this case, Buck Schieffelin.

The children in this family grew up in a verbal environment where traditional Kaluli topics were spoken about only in Kaluli. Everyone talked about food: who had it, who got it, who gave it. Children first heard about and later talked about catching and eating different kinds of birds, lizards, small animals, and fish. Birds and animals were always of interest; caregivers directed the attention of young children to hearing, seeing, and identifying them and discussed their sounds, movements, and edibility. People talked about the bad things that pigs and dogs did: how pigs got into and ruined gardens and how dogs stole food when people were not watching. Conversations centered on the state of the gardens and the details of work that had to be done in the cycle of food production, distribution, and consumption, as well as on the state of particular marriage negotiations and collections of bridewealth.

Abi and his siblings also heard many discussions about the activities of "witches" (*sei*) during times of illness and death. Sometimes the discussions lasted for weeks on end. At one point, after a senior man had died in the village, Abi's entire family moved into the communal longhouse because they feared that the witch responsible would be coming around after the death and causing more illness, and they feared the isolation of their small house. Ulahi and Yaloame believed in the existence and danger of witches, but also evoked them in order to tease their children, scaring them so that they too would be afraid. Ulahi did a lot of traditional cursing (*weseli salab*), directed especially at the dogs. Abi and his siblings not only became familiar with these topics and activities but talked with each other about them, expressing the same fears and concerns as their parents. These children were acquiring traditional cultural knowledge about the Kaluli world around them, the world of the village as well as the bush, the natural as well as the supernatural.

Furthermore, the family could be said to be traditional in that the members enacted a style that generated a lot of interactional tension through arguments, teasing, and provocation, in both playful and serious moods. Theirs was a comparatively intense emotional environment, with many third-party threats, extended teasing routines, and child tantrums, and a great deal of physical contact, some of it very playful (tickling, cuddling) and some of it aggressive, resulting in hitting and angry crying. With at least ten people in the small house, there were usually several activities taking place simultaneously. Talk accompanied or organized many of them.

Abi's family lived in a smaller, modified version of a traditional longhouse, built on a slight incline off the main yard. The front of the house was on the ground, but about halfway along its length the ground sloped, leaving considerable space between the house floor and the forest floor. The back of the house, which was supported by stilts, extended into uncleared forest. This meant that forest sounds made by insects, birds, and other animals could easily be heard inside the house; the identity of these sounds was often the subject of speculation and excitement. A small path continued along the side of the house leading to one of the nearby springs, and people going to draw water there would stop on their way down or back to chat with whoever was around. A deep trench built alongside the house acted as a barrier to keep the family's pigs, which lived in the surrounding forest, from getting into and destroying the sweet potato and taro gardens, which were very close to the house. The pigs, however, had free access to the area around and under the house, and when called by name they came to be fed. Pigs were often heard under and behind the house, and their noise elicited talk about their identity, health, size, eating habits, and other activities.

The interior of the house was divided into a men's and a women's section

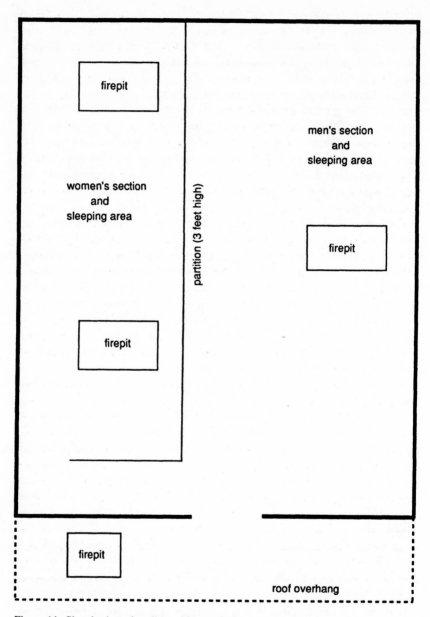

Figure 11. Sketch plan of traditional house design.

(see Figure 11). The two wives, Ulahi and Yaloame, each had her own cooking and sleeping areas at either end of the women's section. These areas were dark, smoky, and private, and restricted for the most part to intimate family interactions. In addition, Yaloame had a second cooking area built as part of a front porch outside the regular house walls but under a roof. Both women enjoyed using this cooking area, which enabled them to see those who came and went on their way to the forest. Tulunei slept in the men's section of the house, often joined by several of his older male and female children around his firepit. Abi slept with his mother in the women's section. During the day, the more brightly lit men's section served as a setting for children's play activities, for Tulunei was almost never in the house then.

Abi, like his father, was solidly built, strong, and sturdy. His quick temper frequently showed itself in situations in which he wanted food, perhaps more than his share, and either didn't get it immediately or didn't get enough. He would scream vigorously when frustrated, and was not easily appeased even when his mother offered generous amounts of food, objects, or attention to buy off his anger (*henulab*). He held on to his anger and was not easily distracted. His mother frequently commented that he was hungry all the time, and he did seem to have an insatiable appetite. Like other boys, he never cooked his own food, but was always monitoring his mother's and sisters' food-preparation activities for what they would have for him. Until the age of 33 months, he usually asked people to do things for him, not only cooking and prechewing his food, but getting him sticks and other things to play with. Around that time his sisters increasingly refused to meet his demands. For example, when his pubic cover fell off, Abi looked at it and then said to Waye, "Put on my pubic cover." Her response was, "What pubic cover?!" and she walked away. He did not do it himself.

Abi was very attached to his mother and demanded that she carry him around the village, although he was capable of walking. He nursed on demand throughout most of the study, taking the breast whenever he wanted it. His mother, even in the late stages of pregnancy, made no attempt to wean him. He continued to nurse even after his brother was born, a practice that was met with disapproval from women in the village. They told Ulahi that there would be no milk for the new baby if Abi continued to nurse. As a result of public pressure and commentary, Ulahi abruptly weaned Abi. Abi was completely miserable for several days and remained moody for more than two months. Sometimes he would display hostile behavior toward his baby brother as well as toward his mother and sisters. He spent hours alone outside his house, smashing small insects, digging in the dirt, and talking to no one in particular. This unusual behavior was commented upon by his mother, but she was not worried about it.

Abi's adjustment to his new brother was difficult and was made additionally so by the sudden change in access to his mother. After his brother was born, he would scream and cry if his mother moved out of his sight. In fact, one of his sister Yogodo's favorite teasing routines was to say that his mother had gone off, when she was really in a corner of their dark, smoky house or just outside cutting weeds. Her words *Nɔwɔ ane* ("Mother has gone") would reduce him to angry tears, and he would begin a frantic search and would call for her, calming down only when he found her. By the age of 3, however, he was no longer upset when his mother was out of his sight.

Yogodo, the younger of Abi's two older sisters, was a thin, scrawny child given to long temper tantrums, which she claimed resulted from being unfairly treated and not getting enough to eat. Yogodo was verbally very facile and quick to deliver sarcastic comments to her mother and siblings. She enjoyed a lot of verbal play with the children of her mother's co-wife, especially with her sister Mobiya and brother Daibo, often teasing and singing with them. She teased Abi extensively when their mother was not attending. Abi in turn refused to share food with her when she begged it from him, even when he didn't want it himself. In addition to teasing Abi about his mother's "disappearance," she also teased him by mocking his speech, repeating what he said but systematically distorting it. She told him to eat foods that were taboo, not good for him, or not properly cooked. Their interactions were often very intense, resulting in someone's getting angry or hit. In the early part of the study, Ulahi teased Yogodo when she was not cooperative, but by the end of the study (age 6) she was frequently told to go away from the house when she was being uncooperative or angry, a common response of mothers to daughters of this age. Yogodo wore a boy's pubic cover until she was over 5 years old, and refused to wear a skirt – she was under only sporadic pressure to do so.

Waye, the elder of the two sisters, was relatively quiet and shy. Some people thought she wasn't very bright or perhaps didn't hear very well. However, once recovered from a long series of ear infections, she was more verbally responsive than she had appeared to be earlier. Like her sister, she was very thin, and did not ask for new skirts or voluntarily bathe very often. While she was usually responsible when taking care of Abi, making sure that he did not hurt himself or others, she did not interact with him very much. Compared with Yogodo, she obeyed her mother with few arguments, choosing to absent herself rather than get involved.

Ulahi came from the eastern Ologo area of Bosavi and had few close ties or relatives in the village. When the two wives, who were close in age, would quarrel, Ulahi, the second wife and the one without connections and allies, was always the one to move out of the small house and take up residence in the communal longhouse until things were patched up. Ulahi was admired for her ability to sing and often sang with Yaloame while they were beating sago together. Ulahi gave instructions and took the lead voice. As a pair, they sang together better than any other two women. Ulahi composed more songs and had more songs memorized than other women (Feld personal communication; recordings: 1982b, A2, A4; 1985, B6, B7).

Ulahi was a very gentle and intelligent woman, articulate and clever, who spent most of her time trying to satisfy her children's and husband's demands. She enjoyed her young son and was devoted to him, always granting his requests for food and attention. She gave in to his angry willfulness as well as to his playful whims. She encouraged his fantasies and always laughed when he did something amusing. Abi liked to climb on her, and they played together physically a great deal, tickling, pinching, and poking. After the birth of her next son, Ulahi found it difficult to carry Abi as well as the baby with her to the gardens every day, especially when she also had to carry heavy loads of firewood and garden produce back to the village.

Increasingly, Ulahi left Abi in his older sister Waye's charge. This was not always successful; Waye would sometimes leave him and he would become distraught. Once Ulahi left Abi in his sisters' care but then came back unexpectedly, only to find him alone, crying by the stream behind the house. After taking him home, where he fell asleep, she located his sisters and told them she did not know where he was. She made them search for several hours in the forest, and when they could not find him there was a lot of angry yelling, and the girls became quite worried. She finally told them that she had found him asleep in my house.

Abi was often unhappy about being left in the village, but he eventually accepted it. He spent time in the main yard, chasing and teasing other children in games of hide-and-seek. Older children, however, would not tolerate his hitting and would leave him alone when he played too aggressively. As Abi got older he spent more time with his brother Daibo and some boys who were two or three years older than himself, but during the major part of the study he kept close to his mother and played with his sisters within sight of her. *GAMES* The games they played were based on domestic and work activities: cooking and eating food, chasing and killing pigs, doing "work" (carrying boxes, building houses), and digging in gardens.

Tulunei, Abi's father, was a well-built man of strong energies and moods. He often expressed his opinions early and loudly in an argument. Some people thought he overreacted and spoke before he had thought things through. In 1968, after he had taken Ulahi as his second wife, he joined the first group of Bosavi men to leave the area and work on a tea plantation in the Highlands. During his time away from the village, he did not learn Tok Pisin, nor did it appear that he was much affected by his experiences outside Bosavi. He returned to a life-style where he participated in traditional subsistence and ceremonial activities. Tulunei spent very little time with his children. In fact, he was never around to be tape recorded with them. Several times after having agreed to watch Abi and Suela (the daughter of Yaloame) while their mothers went off to the gardens with their infants, he also went off into the bush, leaving the two of them crying alone in the yard. Only rarely and reluctantly did he accept responsibility for their care. Others characterized him as lazy in work too. He would begin with a lot of energy and commotion, then leave the bulk of the work for others. Tulunei would occasionally beat Ulahi when he was angry with her for not cooking food or had other domestic complaints.

This was public knowledge; everyone knew what had happened whenever she started crying loudly inside her house. It was not surprising that Abi hit his sisters frequently and that this behavior was not discouraged.

I had a special relationship with Ulahi marked by the reciprocal relationship term *nɛsu* 'my bridewealth'. This stemmed from the fact that in 1967 Buck Schieffelin contributed a kina shell to Tulunei's bridewealth so that Tulunei could marry Ulahi. This meant that Tulunei and Ulahi could call us *nɛsu*, and that is what we called them. Abi's mother encouraged Abi to call me *nɛsu*, drawing on this special relationship marked by support and reciprocity. Abi was outgoing with me and included me in interactions. He called me *nɛsu Babi*, offered me food, and liked me to sit near him and talk to him. Sometimes I was alone with Abi, especially in the last months of the study, when his mother would go off for short periods and leave us together.

I accompanied Ulahi, Yaloame, and their children on several occasions to their sago camps and spent the day with them there, which was very important for observation. Most of the tape recording, however, was of activities in and around the house, at the spring behind the house where water was drawn, and at a nearby stream, the Solɔ, where we all swam. When Ulahi took Abi to the mission for medical attention after he cut his finger badly playing with a sharp bush knife, taping was done there; and when they moved out of the small house during domestic difficulties, taping was done in the communal longhouse. During those times, collecting speech samples from Abi was more difficult because of the large number of people in the longhouse. Multiparty conversations went in many directions, and topics from other people's talk would be included in what Abi would say. This situation, however, resembled the usual experience of children growing up ten years earlier, for then most people lived in the communal longhouse. Children learned how to track many things simultaneously. It was only in the mid 1970s, because of government and mission influence, that smaller houses became the fashion around the village, vastly reducing the number of people who stayed together. This effectively reduced the density and complexity of the verbal environment of the child.

Suɛla

Suɛla was the fourth child to Tulunei and Yaloame, who, like her co-wife, Ulahi, was from the Ologo area. Suɛla, aged 23 months at the beginning of the study, lived with her three older siblings in the same house with Abi and his siblings. Suɛla was a little younger than Abi and quite shy, not as social or verbally outgoing as her brother. She was content to play by herself, and I observed her many times enjoying pretend activities, especially cooking food and sharing it with imaginary people.

Figure 12. Abi and his younger brother carried by their mother.

Her mother was very busy with her baby brother, who was born late in the study, and while she did assist and encourage Suεla to communicate with the other children, she made little effort to understand what Suεla was saying. Suεla's voice was low and soft, and she was often difficult to understand. She tended to imitate her brother Daibo's speech impairment, which caused her mother to complain about how hard it was to understand her.

Suεla had frequent squabbles with Abi, who often tried to take away things she was eating or was interested in playing with. When he teased her while she was playing alone, she had trouble defending herself and would often end up crying. This treatment often elicited annoyed remarks from Yaloame, who denounced Abi's behavior toward his younger sister but, except for verbal charges (''Aren't you a little too big to hit her?!''), did little about it.

Daibo (5 yr) was Suεla's brother, a moody child given to tantrums when he thought he wasn't getting his share of food. He often teased Suεla when she was nursing by pulling the breast out of her mouth or telling her he was going to take it, which prompted angry words from Yaloame but nothing more. As a toddler, Daibo had had an accident in which a stick had pierced his cheek. His difficulty in articulating plosives was thought to be a result of this accident, and at times his mother claimed that he was not easy to understand. Daibo and Yogodo often played together, with Yogodo taking the lead in most verbal games.

Figure 13. Suɛla (held by her mother), Mage, Mobiya, Daibo, and Tulunei.

Mobiya, a sister (7 yr), was a verbally expressive child with a sunny disposition who spent a lot of time with both Suɛla and Abi. She played with them, cooked food for them, and treated them responsibly when they were left in her care. She rarely became angry and often mediated disputes between the other children. She and Yogodo engaged in a wide range of verbal play.

Mage, the eldest sister (10½ yr), spent much of her time away from the younger children. She was involved in domestic chores and organized her activities with girls her own age in the village.

After six months, Suela was discontinued as a focus child in the study for a number of reasons. She was not very communicative verbally, and her mother, who found her speech difficult to understand, had little patience for assisting in systematic transcription. Hence, the social and language data from Suela are not as extensive as for others, but they are informative for comparative purposes and are drawn upon when appropriate.

Wanu

Wanu, 24 months old, lived with his family, which consisted of his mother, Wadeo; father, Baseo; and sisters, Binalia (5 yr) and Isa (7½ yr). Another sister, Henga, was born three months later. Like several other families in the village, Wanu's family followed many of the cultural practices of the 1960s (before government and mission influence), but after the establishment of the mission in the early 1970s they developed an interest in becoming Christian. Baseo and Wadeo gave up smoking and tried not to use profane language. They attended church regularly, joined the workforce that maintained the pastor's gardens, and contributed food to the pastor and his family. Neither Baseo nor Wadeo took any leadership roles in Christian activities, and although they talked about baptism, it seemed like a far-off goal. Neither of them knew Tok Pisin, and though they had bought a literacy book, they never looked at it but kept it stored with their shell and bead valuables in a net bag, and never attended literacy classes. They did not consider sending their children to the mission school.

The members of Wanu's family dressed in traditional clothing. Baseo and Wanu wore simple pubic covers, and Wadeo made skirts out of fine strips of inner bark and string for herself and her daughters. For church and other Christian events such as weddings and baptisms, the parents wore Western clothes that they purchased at the mission store. Wadeo shaved the children's heads as well as her own, leaving the traditional topknot. They gave their children Kaluli names, followed all major food taboos and kinship avoidance regulations, used magic to cure certain maladies, and not only talked about the possibility of witch (*sei*) attacks but genuinely feared them. For example, on one occasion when Baseo became ill, the family moved to his brother Degelɔ's house for several weeks because they feared the *sei* would come around their house and cause more sickness, unprotected and alone as they were. Wadeo, following menstrual taboos, went to a nearby menstrual hut during her periods. The family spent time in the bush processing sago with other families and engaged in gardening, hunting, and fishing activities. They owned few store-bought possessions – some blankets, axes, and bush knives.

Figure 14. Wanu with his sisters Isa and Binalia playing in a stream.

The family lived in a small house, modeled after the traditional longhouse, constructed off the ground on posts and divided into a men's and women's section with a center aisle (see Figure 11). It was off the main yard, away from all other houses except one. The house was surrounded on three sides by forest, so the sounds of birds and other animals were always close by. A notched ladder log went down from the front porch into a small cleared garden area, which was thinly planted with papaya, pineapple, and taro, and not well cared for. In spite of the fact that the family had been living there for several years, the house remained only partially completed. Sections of the house were sloppily constructed, as evidenced by holes in the walls and floor and gaps in the roof thatch, the cause of many leaks. The state of the house was the topic of many heated arguments between Baseo and Wadeo; she wanted the repairs on the house completed, and Baseo acted as if such work could be done at a later time.

Wanu was a small, slender child with a quick smile, an outgoing manner, and a lot of energy. He often pointed things out to me as well as to anyone else who was around, and would seek attention from others, sometimes by acting silly, putting things on his head and saying "Look at me right here!" and sometimes by just running around. His mother called him *debedesen* 'someone who talks nonsense and runs around aimlessly for a short period of time'. His father commented that he was like Newelesu, a character in Kaluli stories who is portrayed as a trickster and an incompetent. While he would cry when he did not get what he wanted, he was easily appeased by offers of food, objects, or attention.

Like his two older sisters, Wanu was a very talkative child, but much of what he said was about what he was doing at the moment, and he often imitated others' speech. During the course of the study, Wanu's language did not reach the syntactic or pragmatic complexity of Abi's and Meli's speech, but he was certainly within the range of normal development.[2] Wanu was weaned at 27 months when his mother was in the later stages of pregnancy. The process was relatively effortless, as Wanu was not very involved in nursing.

Wanu, more than the other children in the study, was much interested in playing with objects. He was able to amuse himself with sticks and knives for long periods of times, and always wanted to play with the contents of my net bag (pencils, extra batteries, tape cassettes). He would stack the cassettes and ask repeatedly to whom each one belonged or roll the batteries around, talking excitedly about how they moved and where they landed. He took advantage of social situations to involve others in what he was interested in – for example, the designs on my rubber sandals, the contents of net bags, the sounds of animals outside. He treated me like an older playmate, asking me questions about the microphone, the batteries, my watch, and my pen.

Because he would happily sustain playing with and talking about objects, the quality of his language and interactions was somewhat different from the other two children. While food was important, it did not play as prominent a role in determining activities or topics of talk in Wanu's life as it did for Abi or Meli. Wanu had an easygoing manner and much of the time was satisfied to be playing games with one or both of his sisters. For example, they would drop sticks through holes in the floor and he would search for them under the house, maintaining verbal contact with the girls the entire time. He would ask questions about the ownership of different foods and objects, but he was not especially interested in having them. His sisters did not cook food when their mother was out, and instead played hide-and-seek games with Wanu in which he would hide or they would hide objects from him. His mother and grandmother commented that his play routines were repetitious (*dedab* 'he repeats'). From my perspective, his routines did not lead to more elaborate solitary or social play, as did the verbal play that Meli and Abi were involved with, but Wanu amused himself easily and seemed to be a happy child.

Wanu's sister Binalia (5 yr) seemed frustrated and unhappy much of the time, especially in the presence of her mother, who made many demands on her. Binalia was the recipient of many sharp and critical comments that were intended to tease or shame her when she asked for food or attention. On many occasions Wanu's mother encouraged him to tease and shame Binalia, telling him what to say to her (using *elema* routines). Like other girls her age, Binalia did not always cooperate with her mother when asked to do such household chores as chopping firewood and drawing water. She had many teary tantrums when denied food or treated, as she saw it, unfairly. But once she was in the bush playing with her sister and friends, she was outgoing and happy.

Another older sister, Isa ($7\frac{1}{2}$ yr), led a more independent life and was out of the house with her same-sex age mates whenever possible. She too had many arguments with her mother, each claiming that the other was making "unfair" demands. Isa was expected to do many chores and would become angry and sarcastic when refusing to cooperate. She did take care of Wanu and enjoyed having him along when she, Binalia, and their girlfriends went swimming or looking for crayfish in the nearby streams. Isa's relationship with Wanu was a trusting one in which there was a great deal of playful teasing.

Wadeo, who came from the western Walulu side, was considered by others in the village to have a sharp tongue and to nag her husband. For example, one time when her husband complained of hunger, she said, "If you are hungry, go cook some food and eat it!" Before the influence of mission and government, in many families this kind of response to a husband's request for food would have been countered with a blow, and local sentiment would have favored the husband. Baseo, however, never laid a hand on his wife, and people snickered and commented that he was afraid of her. Wadeo drove a hard bargain, with her husband as well as with her daughters, refusing them food unless they performed certain chores. There were many angry harangues and exchanges, and she would often go off to the bush with her infant daughter, leaving her husband to look after Wanu, which he did.

Wadeo was a tough and determined woman. Through her verbal abruptness, she played an authoritative role in her family. Her firstborn child (a boy) had died in infancy in 1967. After Wanu was born, she developed a severe breast abscess and nearly died from the infection. She was flown to a mission hospital in Tari where the breast was removed. Against doctor's orders, she left the hospital right after the operation and walked back through the bush to the village (a difficult four-day trip under any circumstances) because she was unwilling to be alone in such a strange and unfamiliar place. When she returned, she resumed nursing Wanu and kept on for several months.

Baseo was different from other Kaluli males of his age cohort in several ways. He had never been away from the area or worked on a labor plantation, as several Kaluli men had done over the years. He was a short man in a society where height was desired, and in social situations he would often take the part of the clown. In 1967, after performing a prescribed act of divination along with other village men to determine who had caused the illness of a woman visiting from another village, Baseo was publicly accused of being the witch (*sei*) responsible. This did not help his growing reputation as someone who might be a witch. Baseo, however, was not a mean or cruel man. Unlike most of the other fathers, he spent time with his children and enjoyed the antics of his son. The time spent with Wanu is reflected in Wanu's tape-recorded samples, which include the largest number of father–child exchanges of any of the families, many of them extended and playful.

Wanu interacted primarily with his family and with the family that lived in the house nearby. The parents often cooperated in gardening activities, and the other family's two daughters, who were the same age as Isa and Binalia, were virtually inseparable from them. Their young son, who was about six months older than Wanu and very shy, was teased constantly by Wanu. After their house burned down, the family moved in with Wanu's family while they were rebuilding, but after a few weeks they moved into the communal longhouse because they said the boys fought all the time.

The only other family that Wanu visited besides mine was Meli's family. He would often visit his paternal grandmother, Wayabe sulɔ, who lived in the same house as Meli (Baseo and Degelɔ were brothers). Sometimes Wayabe sulɔ would keep an eye on Wanu and his sisters when their mother, Wadeo, went to the garden with her infant daughter. However, on these occasions Wanu and Meli did not interact very much with one another, as I had hoped they would; they were shy in each other's presence. In contrast to Abi, Wanu was quite independent and often wanted to go off to the bush with his sisters or father. Sometimes he just wandered off into the main yard by himself, seeking out other children to play with.

As in other families, there were times when energy was at high levels, with great excitement and activity, as well as low times where everyone was falling asleep and mutual attention was minimal. The language samples reflect these shifts in mood and energy. Most of the taping was done in the house with family members and whoever was visiting, though several trips to a nearby stream with Wanu and his sisters were included as part of the data set.

Meli

Meli, aged 24 months, who was the firstborn child of her mother, Osolowa, and her father, Degelɔ, lived with them and her brother Seligiwɔ, who was seventeen months younger.[3] In addition to her nuclear family, several other people lived in her house: Osolowa's brother Wanu and his wife, Waye (Degelɔ's younger sister – a sister-exchange marriage), their daughter Mama (Meli's cross-cousin, fifteen months older than Meli), and Meli's paternal grandmother, Wayabe sulɔ, a widow. Theirs was a small house on the side of the main yard in a part of the village designated in the early 1970s as *kerisɔ hen* 'Christian land', where only Christians were supposed to live. In addition to

Figure 15. Meli with her father, Degelɔ, and her mother, Osolowa, who is holding Seligiwɔ.

the church, infirmary, and pastor's house and gardens, only one other house was in this part of the village, and that belonged to the church deacon and his family.

Both of Meli's parents were recently converted and baptized Christians (1975) and members of the Evangelical Church of Papua. As a result, there were many differences between Meli's family and all others living at Sululib. As baptized Christians, Meli's family professed not to believe in witches (*sei*) and when the topic came up told their children that there were none. They no longer observed most of the food taboos, nor did Osolowa follow the traditional menstrual practices (seclusion in a menstrual hut for the duration of the three-day period) or the postpartum sex taboo (which effectively spaced children at average intervals of thirty-two months) – hence the mere seventeen-month difference in age between Meli and her brother.[4] Osolowa did, however, follow practices of in-law avoidance and did not speak directly to her mother-in-law, Wayabe sulɔ, who also lived in the house (see Example 4.7). Meli, whose name is the Kaluli version of "Mary" (via Tok Pisin "Meri"), was one of the first children to be given a name from the Bible, but she also had a Kaluli name, Hɔidɔ, and a namesake (*daiyo*) relationship in the village. Her younger brother was given only a traditional Kaluli name.

Instead of a bark-fiber and string skirt, head cloth, and shell necklaces and earrings, Osolowa usually wore a dress with a zipper down the front. Christians wore no body decorations at all: Such ornaments were associated with vanity and pride. Degelɔ always wore shorts and had several changes of Western-style clothing that he had collected over the years. Meli usually wore a bark-fiber skirt, but had some shirts and a little dress for Christian events. Her brother, who usually wore nothing, had baby clothes that would also be put on for special occasions. Some of these were bought during the used-clothing sales held at the mission; others were gifts from the Australian missionaries or one of the local pastors. Osolowa did not shave her head or her children's as was still the custom for Kaluli women and children. Instead they let their hair grow out round and full.

Meli's house was different in design from the traditional Kaluli house (see Figure 16). It had no separate men's and women's sections and was divided into three rooms. The first room, through which one entered, was occupied by Waye; her husband, Wanu; their daughter, Mama; and Waye's mother, Wayabe sulɔ. Waye and Wanu were also involved in Christian activities and were preparing for baptism. Waye and her mother shared a cooking area in that room, and though there was no partition, Wanu slept in a separate section of the room from the women. Wayabe sulɔ kept a small pig in the front room of the house.

The second room, which was large and accommodated a dozen people easily, had a large firepit and was where Meli's mother cooked and people sat and visited. The third room was used by Meli's family for sleeping or for

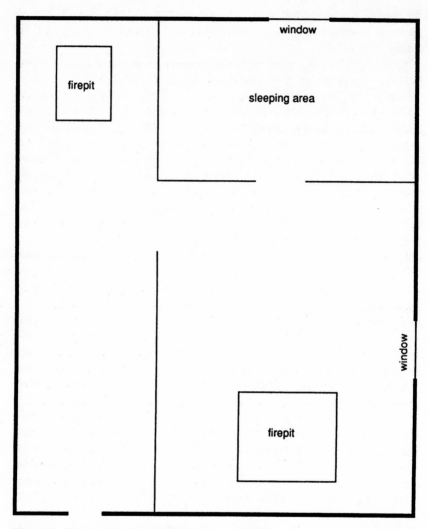

Figure 16. Sketch plan of nontraditional house design.

guests, but sometimes the family slept in the second room around the firepit. Like all other houses at Sululib, this one was constructed from traditional materials (sago and black palm), but in place of the usual open design with low partitions between men's and women's sections, woven bamboo walls extended almost to the ceiling. Several small windows with woven bamboo mats allowed daylight to filter in, making this house the best lit and best ventilated in the village. Store-bought woven bamboo mats were on the floor, identical to others that were put down at night for sleeping. Many dogs of various ages slept in the ashes along the edges of the firepit.

Even though they were in the same house, Meli's family lived quite differently from Mama's more traditional family. For example, Osolowa integrated new cooking techniques with traditional ones. She suspended a large metal cooking pot over her firepit in which she boiled vegetables instead of steaming them in bamboo tubes or baking them in leaf packets as Waye and Wayabe sulɔ did. At night Meli's parents would light a small kerosene lantern they had purchased at the mission store and practice reading their Tok Pisin Bible or literacy booklets in Kaluli, Huli, or Tok Pisin. Instead of net bags hanging from rafters, several small suitcases in which they kept their valuables and clothes were placed along the walls of their room. A few spoons and dishes were scattered around, and a large metal tub in the corner, which would sometimes be filled with warmed water to bathe the children, was stacked with plastic water jugs and bamboo water tubes. Christians from other villages often congregated in their house, and the Papuan pastor and his wife often visited. Osolowa and her husband made frequent visits to the village pastor's house, taking Meli along. They rarely visited non-Christian families in the village, and in the bush only visited the house of Osolowa's father, Kiliyɛ.

As a result of her parents' orientation to the church and mission, Meli was exposed to a variety of objects, practices, and concepts that were foreign to other children. These included literacy books, paper, pencils, and, most important, a set of activities around those objects, such as reading aloud, looking at books, hearing words pronounced syllable-by-syllable, and naming small pictures, all of which fascinated Meli. Meli's father was literate in Kaluli, Huli, and Tok Pisin, and her mother, who was learning to read Kaluli, spent part of every day studying her mission-prepared literacy materials. Meli's parents' participation in church activities also exposed her to new musical forms, such as hymns, and new genres, the Tok Pisin Bible and sermons. Because of her contact with the Australian missionaries and other Tok Pisin- and English-speaking mission staff (teachers, pastors, medical assistants), Meli heard more Tok Pisin and new English-based Kaluli words than other children living at Sululib. She observed the state of concentration and the kind of talk that occurred during religious and literacy events, and her own speech activities (naming, word play, word elicitation) reflected her exposure.[5] Meli's language development during the study showed the most dramatic changes toward complexity, and when I asked, people in the village said that she was *tugusdɔ* 'brainy'.[6]

Soon after Degelɔ's marriage in 1972, he left Sululib to work as a Tok Pisin–Kaluli interpreter for the government in Tari, Southern Highlands Province. After two years, he returned to Bosavi but spent most of his time at the mission station, about two and a half hours' walk from the village. Together

Figure 17. Mɛli's grandfather Kiliyɛ taking care of his grandson Seligiwɔ.

Osolowa and Degelɔ spent several months in a nearby village, where Degelɔ acted as interpreter for a Huli-speaking pastor. As a result of their extensive church involvement, neither of them had the time or interest to engage in traditional subsistence activities. Degelɔ rarely went hunting or fishing, and Osolowa did not process sago at bush camps or do much gardening. Their food was provided by members of their families (mostly Osolowa's sisters and father) and other villagers in exchange for their Christian services (leading sermons, occasionally teaching literacy classes). Unlike other Kaluli children, Mɛli spent very little time at sago camps or gardens. Osolowa, however, often asked for Mɛli's help in watching over Seligiwɔ, preparing the meals, and doing small chores around the house. Since Mama went with her mother to the gardens and Mɛli had no other siblings, she spent more time alone with her mother and brother than other children in the study.

During parts of the study, Mɛli's family spent four days a week at the mission, where both parents attended Bible classes run by the Australian evangelical missionary couple (Asia Pacific Christian Mission). Because marriage is exogamous and residence patrilocal, most other women had no help with child care or subsistence activities from individuals other than their children. However, as a result of clan movements many years ago, most of Osolowa's family were living at Sululib. Two of her unmarried sisters and her father, Kiliyɛ, a skillful hunter, helped with child care and food, leaving Osolowa time to pursue her literacy and Bible studies. She did, however, take responsibility for preparing her family's food.

Mɛli had a strong personality; she knew what she wanted in situations and was persistent about getting it. She wanted to nurse more than her mother was willing, and for much of the study negotiation around nursing was a focus of interaction between her and her mother. She was very much interested in taking care of her brother, repeatedly trying to put him into a net bag and carry him around in spite of the fact that he was too heavy for her to lift. She also paid a lot of attention to his activities and vocalizations. Mɛli was always gentle with her brother and never took her anger out on him when her mother denied her the breast while giving it to him. When he was very small and could not walk, Mɛli was outgoing and personable with people in the village. Once Seligiwɔ could walk and became a personality in his own right, Mɛli became jealous and somewhat withdrawn, and had bouts of temper tantrums. However, she eventually came out of this stage and entered into friendly relationships with her cousin Mama and her other cousins.

Mɛli spent a lot of time with Mama, her cross-cousin (*enesɔk*). There was a lot of teasing, playful and not, in interactions encouraged by their mothers, and little encouragement of the daily cooperation that mothers promoted between sisters. Most of Mɛli's activities were in the company of females, both young cousins and unmarried young women, her mother's sisters. Their more traditional activities also influenced the topics and verbal routines, particularly around reciprocity, that constituted Mɛli's social and verbal environment.

Degelɔ was rarely present, but when he was he would talk to and pay attention to his children for short periods of time. He and Osolowa had a different sort of relationship from other Kaluli couples in that they never argued. This may have come about through their association with both European and Papuan Christians, who espoused an ideology about appropriate Christian conduct between men and women that incorporated the Christian idea that *hɛfɛnolɔ hɛnan* 'one goes softly, easily', the opposite of the exuberant display and assertion valued in this society through the 1960s. As part of their Christian orientation, they talked often about being *sagalɔ alan* 'very happy', and when thanking people for gifts used that phrase as well as *mada ɔm*, which literally means "the very one" but expresses the giving of thanks or "Thank you"; it is also said at the end of a prayer.

Most of the tape recording took place in Mɛli's house with whoever was around at the time. Another favorite taping place was the nearby Solɔ stream, where Mɛli would swim with her mother and brother or, when she was older, go alone with Mama. Mɛli and I had a lot of fun together, as she liked to tease me about dogs stealing my net bag or her brother throwing my sandals in the fire (all elaborate fantasies). Mɛli's mother always encouraged her to cook bananas for me when I visited, and we called each other *ni sɔlu* 'my salt' because of the little packets I would bring her.

In November 1976, after I had been in the village a little over a year, Degelɔ and Osolowa were accepted at an Evangelical Bible school in Lae, on the coast of Papua New Guinea, far from the Papuan Plateau. They left the village for a three-year training course with the plan that Degelɔ would return to become a pastor in Bosavi, which he did. They were the first Kaluli couple to leave the village setting with their children. This departure, unfortunately, terminated Mɛli's participation in the study after nine months of tape-recorded sampling.

Food taboos in childhood

Kaluli greatly desire children, and when they are born they are well taken care of. Kaluli, however, do not have a verbally explicit set of beliefs concerning the nature and development of the child, nor do they elaborate on the metaphor of "hardening" (*halaidan*) when asked about it.[7] There are virtually no rituals in the early years that mark developmental changes, and terms indicating different developmental stages, such as "infant" (*tualun*), "toddler" (*sawalɛsu*), "child" (*sawa*) have vague boundaries. No special practices foster growth, nor are special foods given to children to promote certain abilities.

In fact, no magic is used with small children.[8] Concerns over toilet training or sleep patterns, if they exist, are not voiced.

Kaluli ideas about children's growth and development, however, can be inferred from their caregiving practices. How caregivers interact with children, what they say about them, and what they feel about them are all critical sources for constructing a Kaluli view of children. As food is symbolically and socially instrumental in Kaluli life, it also plays an important part in the development of healthy and competent children. Feeding young children a good diet is important, but more so is preventing them from eating certain foods that are considered harmful at particular developmental points.

Even before a child is born, the mother takes certain precautions to insure that the infant will be healthy. These precautions primarily involve the avoidance of certain foods and are part of a larger system of food taboos important to Kaluli socially and symbolically (E. L. Schieffelin 1976:64–71). Changes in one's social status throughout the life cycle (e.g., puberty, marriage) are marked by adding or giving up dietary restrictions. These restrictions not only index one's particular status but, more important, serve to regulate the sharing of food between people. Whether one eats meat that is fresh (*hɔndɔ* 'wet') or smoked (*suwɔ* 'dry') is a major indicator of one's status. For men, a shift from eating fresh meat to smoked meat comes with marriage and having small children. For women, this shift comes with the onset of menstruation. Other food avoidances are peculiar to individuals and situations; for example, food taboos are adopted during periods of mourning, ill health, and participation in ritual events. Since the mid 1970s, the degree of observance of food taboos is also affected by whether or not one is a baptized Christian; Christianity has served ideologically to undermine Kaluli values.

Women must follow the most extensive food taboos, which begin at the onset of menstruation at approximately age 16. Additional restrictions are added during pregnancy and the child-bearing years. Many food taboos are specific to mothers and young children and can be analyzed as encoding Kaluli concerns regarding children's development. A symbolic analysis of food taboos allows us to infer which aspects of children's social, physical, and cognitive development Kaluli believe are especially vulnerable and can be protected by preventing children from eating certain foods.

I shall be describing some general principles of Kaluli food taboos and the reasons for following them, in addition to the consequences that Kaluli say will befall individuals, particularly mothers and children, who do not follow these taboos. Adhering to food taboos is part of the social responsibility that mothers have in helping their children develop properly. Not only do mothers have to enforce such taboos themselves, but they must also make sure that older children do not give prohibited foods to their younger siblings.

Some general principles

The rationale of taboos is based on the logic of metaphor, the establishment of a connection between things on the basis of a perceived similarity. This logic is basic to the way Kaluli conceptualize identity and distinctness, and operates widely in their thinking. Briefly stated, Kaluli tend to formulate an identification between two people or things if they share the same substance, attribute, or name. Taboos are instituted to interdict this process of identification; that is, to prevent something from being incorporated by a person that would identify him or her with an undesirable quality or condition. When individuals "take on food taboos" (*nɔ mal alilan*), they do not give up whole categories of food, such as all fish or all varieties of bananas. Certain members of each category are either edible or taboo at different points in one's life. These taboos are determined and organized in terms of certain salient and symbolically powerful characteristics that extend across category boundaries. These characteristics may be related to the size, shape, color, and texture of the item or, if an animal or bird, the type of sound or movement it makes. For example, Kaluli associate the color yellow (*wanalo*, from *wan*, tumeric root) with withering and eventual death. The heart of a witch (*sei*) is characterized by its yellow color, which contrasts with the dark color of a normal person's heart. This association is drawn from the plant world, where leaves turn yellow when they are no longer healthy and productive. Thus, all yellow things, whether plants or animals, are prohibited lest by identification the person eating them should become weak, wither, and eventually die.[9]

In addition to food taboos based on physical characteristics, some apply to plants and animals for less obvious reasons. Birds that play prominent parts in myths about the creation of the world are felt to be too dangerous for children to eat and are therefore avoided (Feld 1982a:64). Other tabooed animals, plants, and rivers are believed to have magic in them. For rivers and streams, this means that creatures that dwell in them and plants that grow around them are off-limits to some Kaluli. Therefore, for a complex set of reasons, certain animals and plants must be avoided for all or part of one's life. Kaluli men and women generally agree on the reasons for certain food prohibitions and can elaborate on the consequences of breaking them; some cause both mothers and children to suffer, and others pertain only to children. These negative consequences usually apply to physical, intellectual, social, and linguistic development.

The avoidance of specific foods begins once a woman realizes she is pregnant. During pregnancy, especially the first and second one, a large number of taboos are observed. All varieties of pandanus, fruits, and vegetables that are red are believed to increase the "bloodiness" of women and are avoided in order to prevent heavy bleeding during delivery. Round foods, including melons, pumpkins, papaya, and eggs, are not eaten for fear that during pregnancy the stomach will become large and round like those foods. Also based on metaphor is the idea that pregnant women cannot eat fish that have been poisoned in streams by the sap of particular roots. The fish, suffocated by the poison, float to the surface and are perfectly safe to eat. These fish, however, are likened to the fetus, "a child floating in water," so any association with fish caught in this manner must be avoided.

There are also numerous taboos that lack such clearcut correspondences in images or metaphors; people say that certain foods are simply not eaten out of fear and tradition. For example, certain bananas and sago grubs are prohibited lest labor be long-drawn-out, and sago cooked in bamboo tubes is avoided lest the fetus develop slowly and the pregnancy drag on.[10] Some taboos are held until the child is born, and others are given up several weeks after the birth. For example, during pregnancy women avoid a common cooking banana that is long and thin for fear the newborn will be long and thin like the banana. Once the child is born, mothers may resume eating it.

While the logical reasons and metaphor underlying each taboo are not always available to Kaluli intuition or knowledge or to anthropological analysis, we can nonetheless see what consequences are to be avoided and what, conversely, is the desired state: short pregnancy without a large stomach; little bleeding during a short, easy delivery; and a healthy, well-proportioned child. As Kaluli have no magic to bring about these desired states, whatever might interfere with what is construed as a natural process is avoided, and this is expressed largely through food taboos. Food taboos apply for shorter periods to mothers and also to fathers with each successive child, though Kaluli make no claim that firstborns need to be protected more than later children. Firstborns are thought to attain the greatest height, with each successive child attaining less stature, but this is explained in terms of mothers becoming increasingly less robust with each pregnancy rather than in terms of any effects of what children eat in the early years.

In the first few days of life, infants are offered the breast many times, as well as given it when they cry. In addition, during the first few weeks mothers prechew and feed infants such high-protein foods as insect grubs and crayfish as well as a variety of fruits and vegetables including sweet bananas and leafy greens, which both parents collect. Mothers are careful to avoid prohibited foods, since it is their responsibility to insure the health of their children.

The extensive food taboos that only young children must follow are informative about Kaluli concerns for children's development. Since you can become like what you eat through association and identification, developing children, who are not fully formed physically or intellectually, must adhere to food taboos. I have broadly categorized these taboos, these protective practices to prevent undesirable consequences for the growing child, in terms of the consequences for growth, mobility, and social and language development,

Table 2. *Selected set of food taboos for children*

Object	Problematic characteristic	Consequence
Bush turkeys	Original animal in creation	Heaviness; slowness in
Goura pigeons	myth; stones in stomach	moving; death
Iguanas and large lizards	Slow-moving	Slowness in moving
Ground pigeons	Live on ground	Child will crawl, not walk
Small birds ·	Size	Child won't grow
Snakes	Curved shape	Child won't grow straight
All yellow birds, animals, vegetables	Yellow color	Retardation (*wɛfian*)
Spiny anteaters, echidnas, climbing lizards, pythons	Cling to trees	Child will cling and never become independent
Turtles, crocodiles	Skin texture	Child will have rough skin
Sibɛ bananas	Grow in doubles	Teeth will grow together
Eggs and fish with roe	Roundness; mushiness	Growth goes to stomach; no "hardening"
Mushrooms	—	Convulsion/death
Fruit pigeons, owls, nightjars, frogmouths	Sounds they make	Child will only babble and never learn language
Bats	Bones used in magic; no "voice" (*dagan*)	No language development

and these are presented in Table 2. These aspects of development have uncertain outcomes, and it is in these areas that care must be taken. We can see from the list that Kaluli want to insure that their children become independent, develop language, follow normal growth patterns, and be physically attractive. The assumption underlying food taboos is that children, who cannot take care of themselves, will develop properly provided the individuals responsible for overseeing nurturing and feeding prevent children from eating certain types of food. In addition, caregivers must teach children what they can and cannot eat once they are old enough to be under the supervision of older siblings.

Observing food taboos is a social act as well as a symbolic one, since mothers must either withhold or hide desired but forbidden foods from children who cannot eat them or substitute foods when younger children see older ones eating what they want but cannot have. In situations where children want food that is prohibited, mothers resort to a variety of strategies to avoid giving it to them. These involve distraction and deception, for instance talking about small animals that have been caught as "rocks in a net bag."[11] Outright refusals are rarely heard. Mothers never give children reasons why they cannot eat the food: that it is tabooed (nɔ mal) or that there are serious consequences if they eat it. In fact, mothers do not tell young children that they cannot eat some food, but will instruct them to say to others, "I don't eat *x*." In other words, mothers want their children to take responsibility for not eating prohibited food. One way to do that is to tell them (with ɛlɛma) to tell someone else what they cannot do. Mothers do not make the system explicit or give it authority as the basis of the denial.

In a society with many food taboos, there are situations in which people cannot share food, cannot eat together. Often mothers and children cannot share food with others, and this keeps them socially identified in food-sharing situations. When some children can eat certain foods and younger ones cannot, food taboos can mark status based on age. In Kaluli society, there are few situations formally marking status differences in childhood. No rituals or special activities mark the passing from one stage to another. Subtle differences, however, in what one can eat and share can serve as gentle reminders of a sense of difference in the attainment of developmental markers, such as walking, speech, and social competence. For those involved in nurturing young children, awareness of food restrictions increases awareness of the special status and protective responsibility that go with preventing anything from impeding a child's development.[12]

It should be pointed out, however, that some of the foods prohibited to children are not in fact very commonly eaten, and the issue of taboo in some cases is more ideological and symbolic than pragmatic. For example, spiny anteaters, echidnas, and crocodiles are extremely rare, and bats, large lizards, and snakes are not commonly caught. Tabooed foods do not have any negative nutritional consequences; children have a balanced and varied diet without them.

In the context of social and cultural changes, there are individuals who deny that they hold to certain food taboos. When asked, however, about occasions when they ate tabooed foods, Christians usually say that they have not eaten that food "yet." Christians are encouraged by missionaries to give up all taboos, including those pertaining to food. While Christian families hold the same concerns and beliefs as non-Christians about the effects of certain foods on children's growth and development, they nonetheless feel protected by their new set of Christian beliefs and feed most tabooed foods to their children.[13] Their logical system has not changed, but an alternative construct (Christianity) is evoked as a counterprotective procedure. In other words, as Christians they are protected from the effects of tabooed foods that are still thought to be dangerous.

As a rule, with food taboos as with other practices, women are more conservative in maintaining the traditional ways than men. In addition to having more taboos to adhere to themselves, they are responsible for what actually goes into their children's mouths. As for the families in the study, Meli's family (baptized Christians) maintained very few food taboos; Wanu's family (Christian orientation) maintained all major taboos, giving up only those of lesser consequences; and Abi's family (traditional) maintained all food taboos. Thus, the extent to which food taboos were maintained was consistent with the continuum of social change along which each family could be placed.

The contexts of early communication

In the first two years, children spend almost all of their time with their mothers and siblings. Mothers, who are the primary caregivers, are attentive to their infants and physically responsive to them. When infants cry while being carried in the net bag, mothers gently and rhythmically bounce up and down to soothe them. Their movements are often accompanied by repeated sounds of "Shh," and the whole activity is called *henulab* 'persuade, buy off, distract'. If the crying persists, mothers take their infants out of the net bag, change the soft leaves if necessary, and offer the breast. While nursing their infants, mothers are usually also involved in other activities, such as preparing food or talking to other members of the household.

Infants are always in physical contact with their mothers. When a mother is sitting around with others, her baby will sleep in the net bag next to her body or be held in her arms. Mothers carry their infants in net bags suspended from their heads when they are walking in the bush, carrying heavy loads of firewood and food, and even while working at physically demanding tasks such as beating sago or chopping wood. They never leave their infants alone and only rarely leave them with other caregivers. Kaluli say that mothers must not leave their babies hanging in a net bag from the limb of a tree even if they are working nearby for fear the "ground women" (*hen ga*, a type of spirit) will come and exchange the human baby for one of their own, who would grow up as a dwarf.[14]

Fathers do not spend much time with or associate with their small children. Still, in the 1960s they were prohibited from even seeing the baby for a week or two after its birth, and from touching it until it was 2 or 3 months old. A breach of these prohibitions could result in the death of the infant, and people attributed particular infant deaths to these causes. This attitude changed somewhat in the mid 1970s because of mission influence, and fathers occasionally carry around or amuse their 2–3-month-old infants for short periods of time. The major caregiver, however, is the child's mother, who is with the infant day and night.

Kaluli describe their babies as helpless, "soft" (*taiyo*), and "having no understanding" (*asugɔ andoma*). They take care of them, they say, because they "feel sorry for them" (*nofɔlan*). Kaluli mothers, given their belief that infants "have no understanding," do not treat their infants as partners in dyadic communicative interactions (Ochs & Schieffelin 1984). While they greet their infants by name and use expressive vocalizations for the first few months of life, they rarely address other utterances to them. Furthermore, mothers and infants do not gaze into each other's eyes, an interactional pattern that is consistent with adult patterns of not gazing when talking with others.

Within a week or so after a child is born, Kaluli mothers act in ways that seem intended to involve infants (*tualun*) in dialogues and interactions with others. Rather than facing their babies and engaging in dialogues with them in ways many English-speaking mothers would, Kaluli mothers tend to face their babies outward so that they can be seen by and see others who are part of the social group. Older children greet and address infants, and in response to this mothers hold their infants face outward and, while moving them, speak in a special high-pitched, nasalized register (similar to one that Kaluli use when speaking to dogs). These infants look as if they are talking to someone while their mothers speak for them. Triadic exchanges such as the following sequence illustrate this (see also Example 8.1).

Example 3.1. Abi (35.) is with his mother at home; she is holding Bage (3.), facing him toward Abi. [See appendix for transcription and translation conventions.]
¹Mother → Abi [speaking in high, nasalized voice, moving the baby as she speaks]: My brother! My brother! My *ko*! My *ko*! My brother!
[Smiling at baby]   ²yes! /
³[Speaking in high, nasalized voice] My brother, carry me a little.
[Shifting to sit on his mother's leg]   ⁴I'm on this /
⁵Mother → Abi [regular voice]: Yes, you sit here.
⁶[High, nasalized voice, moving baby] Abi, I'm going to drink the breast. [Mother puts baby to breast; baby waves arm while nursing]
[To BBS]   ⁷wai! / Babi, do you see that? / he startles like that /
⁸Mother → Abi →> BBS [regular voice]: (He) drinks the breast – ɛlɛma.
                                    ⁹(he) startles like that / (I) see the breast /

In this example, the mother is speaking "for" the baby, and thus the baby appears to greet Abi using a kin term (*ni naowɔ* 'my brother') and a term of endearment (*ni ko* 'my *ko*', a tree name that is used affectionately). Abi acknowledges this, saying "Yes," and the mother (speaking as the baby) makes a playful request to Abi. Abi does not respond, and the mother (line 6) initiates talk to Abi, using the special high-pitched, nasalized voice (as the baby), again telling him what the baby is going to do, and then proceeds to put the baby to her breast. Abi, noticing the baby's sudden arm movements, calls my attention to this (line 7), and in her next turn the mother switches from speaking as the baby to telling Abi what to say to me. She uses her usual voice for telling Abi what to say (ɛlɛma 'say it'), but he does not repeat it.

When mothers speak as if their infants are speaking, they use language that sounds more like the speech of 3- or 4-year olds. Utterances are well formed and clearly articulated. They are not modified to sound *taiyɔ* 'soft' like the vocalizations of young children. Only their voice quality (high-pitched, nasalized), the nonverbal movements, and the message content indicate that they are taking the baby's role. When speaking as the infant to older children, mothers speak assertively; that is, they never whine or beg on behalf of infants. Thus, in taking this role mothers do for infants what they cannot do for themselves: act in a controlled and competent manner using language. These kinds of interaction continue until infants are between 4 and 6 months of age.

In these interactions, with mothers taking the baby's part, older siblings are expected to keep up their part of the conversation. Mothers do not tell older children what to say to the baby. Kaluli attempt to establish relationships between siblings at an early age, so that young children will not see infant siblings as amorphous creatures. Through these triadic interactions with the help of mothers, children see infants as individuals with whom they can interact. Infants are presented to older siblings as people with whom they will have enduring relationships and as individuals whose interests must be taken into account. This is repeatedly stressed by "talking," giving infants a voice and making them appear more independent and mature than they actually are. It is during these interactions that mothers socialize both the older and younger child into a sibling relationship, which includes what they are supposed to say and how they are supposed to feel toward each other.

In these interactions, mothers do not look for vocal or nonverbal indications of what infants are interested in and build on those areas of attention as the starting point of the exchange. Instead, mothers structure the interaction according to their own interests and focus on engaging the older child. These triadic exchanges, as well as the dyadic exchanges between mothers and 2- to 3-year-olds, consist of "language that gives thoughts/understanding" (*to samiab*) to the older child, not the infant. Given the claim that infants have no understanding, it is not surprising that Kaluli behave in this way. How would someone without understanding initiate or respond to communicative exchanges?

There is an even more important and enduring cultural construct that helps make sense out of mothers' behaviors in these situations and in many others as well. Kaluli say that "one cannot know what another thinks or feels." Now, while Kaluli obviously interpret and assess one another's observable behaviors and internal states, these interpretations are not culturally acceptable as topics of talk. Individuals talk about their own feelings ("I'm afraid"; "I feel sorry"), but there is a cultural dispreference for talking about or making claims about what another might think, what another might feel, or what another is about to do, especially if there is no obvious behavioral evidence. Kaluli, however, use extensive direct reported speech, and children use this linguistic resource by 24 months of age. As we shall see, these culturally constructed behaviors have several important consequences for the ways in which Kaluli verbally interact with children, and are related to other pervasive patterns of language use and social interaction.

Older infants (6–12 months) interact more directly with people in their environment. They are held in the laps or carried on the shoulders of mothers or older siblings and can easily hear and observe all household activities as well as subsistence activities in the bush. They are greeted by a variety of names and receive a limited set of imperatives and rhetorical questions, largely to control their behavior. Kaluli use no baby-talk lexicon as such, and claim that children must hear *to halaido* 'hard language' if they are to learn to speak correctly.[15] What is important is that the language addressed to these infants consists largely of one-liners that call for no verbal response.

The pattern in which adults do not treat infants as communicative partners continues as infants begin babbling. Kaluli recognize babbling (*dabedan*) but say that this vocal activity is not communicative and has no relationship to the language (*to*) that will eventually emerge. Adults claim that babbling is *ba madali* 'to no purpose', but will occasionally repeat vocalizations back to toddlers (ages 12–16 months), reshaping them into the names of people in the household or into the kin terms of people nearby, but they do not claim that the toddler is saying these names or wait for the child to repeat those vocalizations in an altered form. Vocalizations are not generally treated as communicative and given verbal expression. Siblings aged 2 to 4 will report to their mothers that the toddler has "said" a name or kin term, offering a gloss or interpretation of the vocalization, but caregivers do not support this, and either ignore, deny, or repeat the sounds said by the toddler as the acceptable way to treat such vocalizations.[16] Thus, throughout the preverbal period, very little connected discourse is directed to the child by the caregiver, and what there is is usually done through *ɛlɛma* sequences directed to older children with infants as the intended addressees (see Chapter 4).[17]

Although there is relatively little speech directed to preverbal children, the verbal environment of these children is rich and varied, and from the beginning infants are surrounded by adults and older children who spend a great deal of time talking to each other. Furthermore, as toddlers become increasingly mobile and develop strong interests in people and activities, their actions are referred to, described, and commented upon by members of the household, especially older children, speaking to one another. Thus, the ongoing activities of preverbal children are important topics of talk between members of the household, and this talk about the activities and interests of toddlers is available for the toddlers to hear, though it is not addressed to or formulated for them. For example, in referring to toddlers' actions, siblings or adults will say, "Look at Seligiwɔ! He's walking." Thus, by using the toddler's name, for example, caregivers are socializing young children to pay attention to the verbal contexts that are relevant to them.

Every society has its own ideology about language, including when it begins and how children acquire it. The Kaluli are no exception. Kaluli claim that language has begun once the child uses two critical words, *nɔ* 'my mother' and *bo* 'breast'. The child may be using other single words appropriately, naming siblings, dogs, and food items, and Kaluli recognize these words as such. However, until the child uses the two culturally important words, the child is considered to have not yet begun to use language, and words are said essentially *ba madali* 'to no purpose'.

That *nɔ* and *bo* are culturally selected to mark the beginning of language is evidence of the essentially social view of language taken by the Kaluli. It emphasizes not the learning and using of words per se (such as in the labeling or naming routines important in many cultures) but the use of specific words to express the first social relationship a person has: the mother–child relationship mediated by food from the breast. This is a basic theme in Kaluli social life. The giving and receiving of food is a major means by which relationships are mediated and validated.

Once a child has begun to use the words *nɔ* and *bo*, Kaluli begin to "show language" (*to widan*) to the child "to make language harden" (*to halaido domeki*). This is done principally by the mother, using a language-socialization practice, *ɛlema* 'say like this', which is the subject of the next chapter.

4. *Elema* as a socializing practice

Elema as a speech activity

The Kaluli have a well-articulated notion of how children learn language – it must be taught or shown (*to widan*) to them by competent speakers once children themselves have begun to use language – evidenced by their use of two culturally important words, *nɔ* 'my mother' and *bo* 'breast'. While Kaluli do not specify how in fact they "show language," one can see from interaction the ways in which this is accomplished. Mothers play an active role in their young children's interactions with others, facilitating their participation by enabling the young child to contribute verbally. When a Kaluli mother wants her child to say something to someone, she provides the utterance that she wants the child to say followed by the imperative *elema* 'say like this'. The utterance that the child is to repeat is delivered in the style that the child is expected to repeat, with *elema* usually said in a softer voice and in a clipped manner. The child then repeats what the mother has said (without *elema*), and the mother supplies the next line for the child to repeat. This direct instruction is repeated until mother and child have verbally accomplished what the mother has in mind or until the child loses interest and refuses to cooperate. The use of *elema* is not random in interaction; it is specific to particular speech acts and speech events. Concomitant cues in voice quality, discourse, and situational features signal that response from the child is expected.[1]

Elema is a contraction of two words, *ele* 'like this' and *sama,* the singular present imperative form of the verb "to say." While the contracted form is the most frequent choice, caregivers will occasionally use the full form *ele sama* when telling young children what to say, or the habitual form *ele selan* 'is usually said like this' when emphasizing the habitual or recurrent association of something said in a particular situation.

The presentation of a model followed by an instruction to repeat the same utterance is similar to the ways in which Kaluli teach children to carry out

Some of the material in this chapter appeared in a different form in B. B. Schieffelin 1979, chap. 4.

75

other types of actions. For example, a mother will demonstrate how a simple action is to be done – cupping the hands to drink water from a stream, peeling a hot cooked banana, or pulling weeds from a garden – and will say to the child, *Ɛlɛfoma* ("Do like that"). While the child is carrying out the action correctly, she will say *Ɛlɛ, ɛlɛ* ("Like that, like that") to show encouragement and approval. Caregivers not only provide models themselves but also point to others as examples, instructing children to copy what they see those persons doing.

Ɛlɛfoma demarcates separable actions or single components of a task, much the way *ɛlɛma* is used with a single, usually short, utterance. Neither is used after one demonstrates several sequential steps involved in complex tasks such as lighting a fire or making a net bag; instead they punctuate each separable point. For example, *ɛlɛma* may be placed after single words, phrases, or longer clause units of discourse as the situation and addressee require. There are, however, several important differences between teaching talk and teaching tasks. First, in terms of the linguistic form of the imperative, *ɛlɛfoma* is not a contracted form that can be separated into two lexical items, but is composed of *ɛlɛ* 'like this' plus the adverbial suffix -*foma*, imperative "do." *Ɛlɛfoma* applies to a broad range of actions, whereas *ɛlɛma* is specific to speaking. As for frequency of use, *ɛlɛfoma* is relatively infrequent, in contrast to the highly frequent and variously functioning *ɛlɛma* in speech activities. Finally, Kaluli do not claim that actions or tasks must be "shown" to children for them to learn how to do them, whereas language must be. In fact, there is the sense that children will do things by themselves when they are ready and should not be pushed. This was brought out when Mɛli (31.2) handed her brother Seligiwɔ (14.) my rubber thong and told him to put it on. Her mother turned to her and said, "He'll do it when he thinks of it himself; you shouldn't say anything." This is certainly different from the way in which children are encouraged to speak. Language is also viewed as an interactive and cumulative kind of learning; language gradually "hardens" in the child. No such metaphor exists for learning other activities. Thus, one can infer from Kaluli ideology and practice that they think of language learning as requiring a set of specific social and behavioral assists. As Mɛli's mother said about language, "So that the child will understand, we show it" (*Asulumɛni ɛlɛfɔli ɛna widan*). Kaluli, however, do not make the explicit connection between *ɛlɛma* as that practice and the need to "show language" (*to widan*).

The use of *ɛlɛma* is not restricted to everyday speech directed to small children. There are several situations where adults use *ɛlɛma* among themselves. In daily interactions, when one person does not have a quick answer to a challenge or a clever response to another speaker, a third person will supply lines for the speaker. In these situations, the person who is instructed to speak must quickly decide if he or she is willing to go along with and repeat the suggested utterance. These often become humorous or embarrassing moments, as they reveal the hesitancy of the speaker and can momentarily realign the relationship between participants in the event. Ɛlɛma is also used by members of an audience when participating in traditional storytelling events, in that they supply lines to the teller or echo them themselves after providing them in coproduction of the text (Feld 1988; B. B. Schieffelin 1987 ms.). Yet another important use of ɛlɛma is in ritual contexts, such as in funerary sung–texted weeping (*sa-yɛlab*), where ɛlɛma frames appropriate discourse from a dead person (who has become a bird – *ane kalu ɔbɛ mise*) to the living (Feld 1982a). For example, during a funeral a woman mourner, while weeping, instructs the dead person to tell her where he (as a spirit/bird who has gone to the treetops) can be located. The form this takes is *Nosɔgo, wabɛduno hɔnɔlo ɛlɛliki alolo bedɛlibikɛ ɛlɛmo* 'Cross-cousin, always look up to the top branches of a *wab* tree, I'm going that way – you say like that' (ibid. 111, 118). Thus ɛlɛma in childhood is not only one of the basic socializing practices for teaching sociability and language use but is also an important linguistic and social resource that individuals draw on throughout the life cycle.

[handwritten marginal note: Ɛlɛma present throughout the life-cycle]

The social organization of ɛlɛma

Caregivers use ɛlɛma with young children to perform a variety of functions in discourse and interactions. Depending on the situation and the participants involved, ɛlɛma can occur with high frequency within a given speech event. Ɛlɛma is a verbal form of social assistance that provides children with specific lines tailored to specific addressees. Children are thus able to enter into inter-actions as active participants and accomplish with support what they may not yet be able to do alone. Ɛlɛma routines are important because they provide not only the content of talk but the form and the function as well. They are not staged or done simply for practice, but are embedded in ongoing interac-tion. What young children say in ɛlɛma routines has real consequences for the shape and outcome of an event.

By explicitly telling children what to say, caregivers, especially mothers, are supplying them with both linguistic form and social substance. We shall see later in the chapter how and why it is important to the Kaluli that an adult (read ''hard'') version of the language be learned by children as early as possible. Throughout the description to follow, we shall trace how both lin-guistic form and social propriety are taught to children, often at one and the same time.

Ɛlɛma is used in both dyadically and triadically structured conversational exchanges. In dyadic usage in family settings, an older speaker, usually the mother, tells the young child to say something back to her. In triadic usage, the speaker tells the young child to say something to a third person who may or may not be present. These usage patterns will be referred to as dyadic interactions (involving only two participants) and triadic interactions (involving three or more participants, usually the mother or older siblings, the child, and the intended addressee[s]). Dyadic and triadic ɛlɛma are closely tied together in terms of their socializing functions, however; the goal is that maturing children be assisted to a point where they can generate grammatically correct and socially appropriate lines on their own.

Ɛlɛma provides the context for learning about assertion, one of two major interactional modalities in Kaluli life. Direct instruction with ɛlɛma is only in an assertive modality. Mothers never use ɛlɛma to tell children to beg, whine, or act in the modality of appeal, the opposite of assertion (E. L. Schieffelin 1976:117–34). The two modalities differ both rhetorically and transactionally and are socialized and keyed in particular ways.

Dyadic interactions with ɛlɛma

All young children are involved in dyadic interactions using ɛlɛma, primarily with their mothers. Ɛlɛma is used equally to accomplish three different goals. The first of these is to use ɛlɛma to correct the form (phonological, morphological, lexical, grammatical) or meaning (semantic) of a prior child utterance, as in Example 4.1.

Example 4.1. Wanu (26.3) and his mother are playing with a flashlight battery, rolling it back and forth. I am sitting with them.

[Offering battery to mother]   ¹Mother / over there /
                                       Nɔ /honokɛ /

²You take it – say it.
Ge dima – ɛlɛma.

                                       ³you take it /
                                       ɛno ge dima /

After getting his mother's attention by using a kin term, nɔ 'my mother', as a vocative (line 1), Wanu uses an incorrect lexical item (the distal demonstrative instead of the proximal demonstrative) to refer to the battery he is holding. Rather than correcting the particular demonstrative, his mother tells him to use a different request form, the imperative of the verb "take" (dima), to accompany his offer. Not only is this a more explicit linguistic expression of his action (as evidenced by the mother's response [line 2]), but imperatives are the culturally preferred linguistic form for offering objects or food (see Example 4.5, line 2). Children must learn to use these preferred linguistic expressions in offers and requests, and dyadic sequences with ɛlɛma are one of the ways in which these preferences are displayed, instructed, and corrected. Kaluli distinguish different types of errors metalinguistically, and they are corrected in different ways. Errors categorized as mispronunciations (hala siyɔ) or as grammatically incorrect (togɔde siyɔ) are corrected with ɛlɛma as in the example above. However, errors that are not quite right in terms of their pragmatics (*mahagale siyɔ*) are more usually modeled by adults without the use of *ɛlɛma* (see Examples 5.14, 5.16).

Within dyadic exchanges, *ɛlɛma* is also used to initiate and maintain a fantasy or brief game and to tell children to request something from mothers, usually to switch their attention. Mothers usually initiate these exchanges without any clear indication of interest from the child, and try to involve young children in focused interaction based on their own choice of topic.

Triadic interactions with ɛlɛma

There is some overlap in the ways in which mothers use *ɛlɛma* in dyadic and triadic situations. For example, mothers correct the forms of prior child utterances, directing the corrected responses to a third person (see Example 4.4, lines 21–2), and they encourage children to request food, objects, and assistance from others. However, triadic use of *ɛlɛma* also differs in other important ways from dyadic use. First, triadic use of *ɛlɛma* occurs much more frequently in interaction.[2] Caregivers use *ɛlɛma* more often when directing children to speak to others than when guiding a response back to themselves. It is the most pervasive language-socializing practice used with Kaluli children.

Second, triadic use of *ɛlɛma* pushes children into interacting with a range of individuals in ways the mothers feel are appropriate in a given situation, thus extending the number of social relationships young children have beyond the mother–child relationship. This important socializing practice is a continuation of earlier interaction patterns, where mothers themselves speak for infants while manipulating them. By supplying infants with a voice and with a sequence of appropriate lines before they can spontaneously and appropriately produce them, mothers help children initiate, maintain, and terminate interactions with other family members. For example, mothers use *ɛlɛma* to assist children in requesting objects, information, or actions. What must be emphasized is that in the majority of interactions the starting point is the mother's view of what should be said and what should be happening. Since mothers want children to interact with others in particular ways, to a great extent they must show them what to say and how to say it. Mothers also intervene when they feel an event is not going the way they think it should. This means that *ɛlɛma* sequences are ideal for analyzing what members think they should say and what members think novices should say. Ɛlɛma sequences display how members constitute interactions, and thus they are a rich resource for investigating not only what is said but also how things are said across social activities.

Another important difference between dyadic and triadic *ɛlɛma* lies in the fact that only certain types of speech acts occur within the triadic sequences. These are typically assertive and are used for teasing (*dikidiab*), shaming (*sasindiab*), and confrontation, especially in negotiating claims, refusals, and issues of reciprocity. Mothers tell children to use these assertive forms, in particular requests and confrontational rhetorical questions, with others, but do not tell their own children to use those utterances back to themselves. That is, mothers do not want their young children to tease them or act in a confrontational manner with them. Nor do mothers ever tell children to appeal or beg. What is consistent here is the assertive modality or key in which mothers directly instruct young children to speak to others. This type of support creates confidence in young children, making it clear that they will indeed be able to manage interactions and be taken seriously as interactants. Being able to be rhetorically assertive is critical for getting what you want and entering the system of everyday reciprocity.

Finally, triadic use of *ɛlɛma* assumes an important role in constituting entire conversational sequences. (The sequences of dyadic exchanges are limited.) Triadic exchanges are marked by their continuous (sequential) turns of talk and thus are very effective in teaching such conversational routines as openings and closings of talk and speech-act sequences. While dyadic *ɛlɛma* may be inserted into spontaneous sequences, triadic *ɛlɛma* sequences are themselves used to constitute longer connected discourse.

Whereas dyadic *ɛlɛma* is limited to few turns and a narrow set of functions, triadic *ɛlɛma* generates extensive connected discourse with a wide range of speech acts. These long stretches of talk contain both explicit and implicit *ɛlɛma* instructions. Implicit *ɛlɛma* occurs after the mother has told the child what to say, using *ɛlɛma* to establish the frame, and then continues to provide lines (without repeating *ɛlɛma* each time) for the child to say to a third person (see Example 4.2, lines 4, 6).[3] In longer interactions, after several turns without *ɛlɛma*, *ɛlɛma* is said after the clause-final verb to tie the discourse together (Example 4.9, line 27). It may also be used (after a number of consecutive utterances within the *ɛlɛma* frame) to encourage a child who is beginning to lose interest in repeating the mother's utterances.

Caregivers use *ɛlɛma* to initiate and assist conversations between young children and those just old enough to keep up their end of the conversation. I never observed a caregiver supplying lines to two children simultaneously in order to maintain a dialogue between them. In dialogues with caregiver support using *ɛlɛma*, caregivers assist the youngest language learner. Older children often cooperate in these situations and tolerate some degree of personal infringement in order to give the youngest child opportunities to practice certain discourse routines and to obtain a desired item, even at the expense of the older child. This is especially true of older sisters, who learn early on that their younger siblings, especially their brothers, have priority in goods, foods, and services.

Activities and stance: assertion

In the discussion that follows, three aspects of language use that are specific
to triadic situations are analyzed from cultural and linguistic perspectives. The
first concerns the vocative (addressee name), critical in the opening of conversation and in making requests. The second focuses on calling out, a speech
event that is structured like triadic *ɛlema* except that the intended addressee is
not present and does not answer back. The third set of speech activities concerns confrontational routines such as teasing, shaming, threatening, and
challenging claims of ownership, all part of an assertive modality that is a
major strategy used to get what one wants from others or to refuse the requests
to share that are so common in everyday life.

Vocatives

One of the first things one notices about the use of *ɛlema* in triadic interactions
is the high occurrence of names used in addressing persons. Vocatives with
ɛlema are used as attention-getting devices to indicate that the speaker would
like a particular listener to attend (Keenan & Schieffelin 1976), and as such
they are prerequisites for communication. Using a vocative marks the message that follows it as being intended for someone and also selects the next
speaker in multiparty discourse, which is the usual situation in Kaluli households. In Kaluli, vocatives are also used in maintaining conversational attention and flow. Once into the interaction, speakers may shift to a different
vocative to achieve a particular social end. Vocatives are used to initiate or
maintain talk with individuals who are present, but they are also directed
toward individuals who are not present, as in calling-out sequences. Kaluli
mothers include all of these uses of vocatives with *ɛlema* in triadic interactions as part of the conversational skills children must acquire. Their concern
is additionally registered by the fact that they consistently correct children's
pronunciation of proper names, kin terms, and other naming terms.

Vocatives in all languages are important on both the discourse and interactional level. The selection of a given vocative is based on cultural knowledge and conveys the assumptions and expectations an individual has for that
interaction. Thus, within the framework of *ɛlema*, children are socialized to
select vocatives appropriate to the key and speech act that co-occur.[4] Kaluli-
speakers have many options regarding the vocatives they can select, including
kin terms, proper names, teknonyms, and relationship terms. In the majority
of cases, however, caregivers instruct small children to use kin terms, teknonyms, and proper names (alone and in combination) as vocatives. One
reason for the heavy use of kin terms and proper names is that requests with

ɛlema are in an assertive key, and these terms are unmarked for affect; that is, they can be used in a variety of keys, depending on the prosodic and morphological markings that are added to them. This is in contrast with many of the relationship terms, which are marked for particular affect keys and can only be used in appeal (see Chapter 5). To use these relationship terms in an assertive manner is not appropriate, and children are never instructed to do so.

In my samples, caregivers' use of vocatives co-occurred with a limited number of speech acts, but for all children requests for food and objects were the most frequent accompaniment of a vocative. This is not surprising given that mothers socialize children into culturally preferred means for getting what they want. For Kaluli, this means asking. For Wanu, requests followed more than three-quarters of the vocatives he was instructed to use, with most of the remaining utterances serving to inform the addressee about some topic. For Abi, a little more than half the vocatives (with *ɛlema*) co-occurred with requests; the others were used to threaten, tease, and inform others. For Mɛli, fewer than half were requests; greetings, questions, offers, and informing constituted the remainder. The differences among the children can be understood in terms of gender and family structure. Both boys (Abi and Wanu) were repeatedly instructed to make requests of older sisters, and these requests constituted an important part of their verbal exchanges. Mɛli, a firstborn girl, directed the majority of her requests to her mother's sisters and cousins, who visited but did not live with her. That Mɛli was frequently told to offer to others is indicative of the demand placed on very young girls to give to others.

Calling-out sequences

Kaluli houses are built on the tops of ridges, and many springs and gardens are located within hearing distance of them. When Kaluli need to send a message to someone who they believe is within hearing distance, they call out to that person in a loud, distinctive manner. Calling out with the expectation of response (*holema*) serves a number of different functions. Speakers use it to inform others of important information (for example, that food is ready), to remind someone to pick up firewood, and to relay messages. Calling out is also used to locate people whose whereabouts are uncertain. And a mother tells a child to call out when he or she is doing something annoying and she wants to change the child's focus.[5]

Like other *ɛlema* sequences, calling-out sequences can be analyzed on multiple levels. The following are from two complementary perspectives. The first examines the formal features characteristic of these sequences – prosody, volume, and morphological marking. The second focuses on the cultural information presented to the child, since in these sequences expectations about social relationships are made explicit.

Many calling-out sequences demarcate cultural issues and solutions, and are clearly organized in terms of lexical co-occurrence specifications within particular domains. For example, in the sequence that follows, after the child states, "I am hungry for meat" (Kaluli distinguish between being hungry (*mayab*) and hungry for meat (*telɛnyab*)), the culturally relevant semantic field of hunting is broken down into different highly desirable animals (solutions to being hungry for meat) – bandicoot, fish, crayfish – plus the specific verb that encodes the manner in which they are caught (e.g., trap, snare, shoot). Other calling-out sequences focus on various animals and how they are cooked (e.g., leaf-baked, roasted) and on different vegetables and the verbs for picking them.

To initiate a calling-out sequence, caregivers use a vocative (morphologically marked with the suffix *-o* for calling out) delivered with a distinctively marked prosodic contour (first call) followed by *ɛlɛma*. In the following vocative (line 4), a different prosodic contour is used that indicates second call. These prosodic contours are ordered; that is, one knows from the prosodic contour whether the call is a first or a second. Mɛli correctly adds the calling-out contours and the final *-o* (for distance).

Example 4.2. Mɛli (24.3) is with her mother and father. Her *babo* 'mother's brother' Suwɛlo is nowhere in sight.

¹Mother → Mɛli →> *babo:* Babowo! – ɛlɛma.

²Babowo! /

³Suwɛlowo!

⁴Suwɛlowo! /

⁵Come

⁶come /

⁷pandanus

⁸pandanus /

⁹you too come to eat.

¹⁰you too come to eat /

Father → Mɛli: Mamuwo! – ɛlɛma.

mamuwo! /

No! Loudly! Suwɛlowo!

Suwɛlowo! /

I

I /

now

now /

am hungry for meat.

am hungry for meat /

Bandicoot

bandicoot /

go hunt.

go hunt /

Fishhook	fishhook /
go throw in the water.	fishhook go throw in the water /
Єlin [fish name]	*єlin* /
go catch.	go catch /
At the banks of the Gamo	at the banks of the Gamo /
at the banks of the Yabo	at the banks of the Yabo /
then there	then there /
crayfish	crayfish /
go feel around for (in the water).	go feel around for /

After the framework is established by the initial vocative with *єlema* (the kin term *babo* 'mother's brother'), Mєli repeats his proper name (Suwєlo) and entire sequence without the explicit directive to do so. The first ten lines constitute an invitation to come and eat pandanus. Mєli's father initiates a second message (with *єlema*), initially directed to her grandfather (using the kin term *mamu*), but then switches back to the original addressee, Suwєlo, her mother's brother. When Mєli doesn't speak loud enough, her father tells her explicitly to speak up, and Mєli does so. Children are typically told to make these requests for meat to older male relatives such as mothers' brothers, fathers, and grandfathers.

Sequences consisting of an offer followed by a request outline the prototypical Kaluli paradigm of reciprocity. Mєli offers an invitation to share pandanus, a vegetable food that women prepare, and follows with a request for meat, which men (in this case, mother's brother) typically provide. This request is especially moving from a child who uses the verb *telenyab* 'I am hungry for meat'. A hungry child is a powerful image for the Kaluli. Social information about reciprocity is conveyed in the form and content of the sequence. Children learn to ask particular people and particular categories of people for things they want, and learn what they can offer in exchange.

Through repeated participation in these verbal exchanges, children are socialized to associate particular kinship relationships with a set of speech acts (offers and requests) and to use particular linguistic forms (specific verbs and the nouns that co-occur with them) in conjunction with a set of socially meaningful place names (where family members garden, hunt, and fish together). Small children through these language-socialization sequences come to identify activity, persons, and locality with each other, and later in life, when these connections are evoked in sung–texted weeping (*sa-yєlab*) and song, their significance is deeply meaningful (Feld 1982a, chaps. 3, 5).

Other calling-out sequences, in particular those directed to older children, challenge rights of possession and inform children how to feel about taking what is not theirs to take.

Example 4.3. Mɛli (24.3) is at home with her mother and father. Her cousin Mama (3;3) is outside; she has taken Mɛli's gourd. *Note:* All speech from mother and father to Mɛli is further directed to Mama.

¹Mother → Mɛli: Mamayo! – ɛlɛma.
Mama! – say it.

²// ̄‿Mamayo! /

³Ɛh, Mamayo!! // – ɛlɛma.
Yes, Mama! – say it.

⁴[To Mɛli, softly] Wena siliki holema. Mamayɛ sandabikɛ. Wena siliki holema.
While sitting here, call out. Mama will hit you [if you go out].
While sitting here, call out.

⁵ ̄‿͡Mamayo! /

⁶Sugɔbai diɛmino! – ɛlɛma.
Bring the gourd! – say it.

⁷sugɔbai diɛmina /

⁸Bɔbɔi!
Quickly!

⁹diɛmina /
bring! /

¹⁰Bɔbɔi!

¹¹bɔbɔi /

¹²Diɛmino!

¹³diɛmino /

¹⁴Father → Mɛli: Gɛnɔ kɔlɔ diɛganeyɛ?! – ɛlɛma.
Is it yours to take?! – say it.

¹⁵gɛnɔ kɔlɔ diɛgan?! /

¹⁶Mother → Mɛli: Gɔnɔ mɔsindilowaba?! – ɛlɛma.
Aren't you ashamed of yourself?! – say it.

¹⁷gɔnɔ mɔsindilowaba?! /

¹⁸Sindiloma! – ɛlɛma.
Be ashamed! – say it.

¹⁹Mama! – ɛlɛma.
[Seeing marble on floor and picking it up]

²⁰wekɛ! /
look at this! /

²¹Mabolɔ, ne mabolɔ dike! – ɛlɛma.
Marble, I took the marble! – say it.

At 24.3 months, Mɛli consistently uses the correct prosodic contours for calling out, but she does not always mark her utterances with the word-final suffix -*o*. For example she uses the final suffix -*a* that is used in face-to-face interaction (line 7), but since she is calling out loudly, this error is not corrected. Mothers, who play a backstage role in these sequences, do not speak with high volume themselves when instructing children to call out, but tell children to speak loudly if they are not doing so already. Using the correct prosody, volume, and morphological marking is part of being socialized to call out.

In calling-out sequences, mothers often supply messages for children to repeat (with and without ɛlɛma) before receiving acknowledgment from the intended addressee. These sequences are structurally similar to the usual triadic ɛlɛma routines, but they lack the contribution of the intended addressee. Therefore, the sequence is completely determined by the mother's direction. Mothers usually insist that children repeat the utterances they provide and not spontaneously contribute their own, as in the example above (lines 8–11). Even without a listener's response, children usually cooperate with the directive to call out until either they or the caregivers lose interest.

Mɛli is hearing and repeating the social and affective consequences of taking objects one does not have rights over while she is being socialized into a particular rhetorical strategy for reclaiming something that belongs to her. Mɛli is told to stay inside and call out as a way of avoiding possible physical confrontation with Mama (line 4). Kaluli encourage same-sex children to be verbally assertive but not physically aggressive. The message to "quickly bring back the gourd" is linked to the fact that Mama has taken something that is not hers to take, through a series of rhetorical questions (line 14) meant to shame (*sasindiab*) the person to whom they are directed. This is made explicit (lines 16–18) when Mama is told that she should feel ashamed of what she has done. After Mɛli has lost interest and her mother tries to reinitiate the talk with a vocative (line 19), she draws on Mɛli to tease Mama with her claim to the marble.

Confrontational routines: teasing, shaming, threatening

Speech acts including teasing (*dikidiab*), shaming (*sasindiab*), threatening, and challenging claims of ownership constitute an assertive modality that is socialized through triadic ɛlɛma exchanges, both in face-to-face interactions and in calling out as above. Mothers do not use these speech acts dyadically, but they are extensive in routines directed to others, in particular to older children ranging between the ages of 3 and 10.[6] This assertive modality expressed through these speech acts emerges in the context of 2- to 3-year-olds being socialized to protect what they have and what they want against the demands of older children. The Kaluli consider mastery of this set of rhetorical strategies critical for controlling and influencing others verbally. Face-to-face interactions, which are most frequent, are more complex than those in which there is no third-party input (e.g., calling out or talking to preverbal children). In face-to-face interaction, utterances with ɛlɛma are usually in response to what older children or adults do or say. Young children have to pay attention to the contributions of third parties in addition to what their mothers are saying.

Acts of teasing, challenging, shaming, and claiming constitute extended discourse and are commonly expressed by rhetorical questions. Bolinger defines rhetorical questions as "questions that do not really ask . . . [they] call for no answer" (1975:607). Kaluli direct confrontational rhetorical questions (indicated in examples by ?!) to young children and encourage them to become competent in using them. Kaluli speak about these types of confrontational question as having a *heg* 'underneath', a nonliteral meaning that has to be searched for.[7]

Teasing, shaming, threatening, and challenging claims often occur together in speech events. The following example demonstrates these verbal strategies, their preferred sequencing, and their linguistic expression, and is typical of how mothers socialize small children to be assertive when claims of ownership and distribution are at issue.

Example 4.4. Wanu (26.3), his mother, Binalia (5 yr), and Mama (cross-cousin, 3;6) are at Wanu's house. Earlier that morning, Wanu's grandmother, Wayabe sulɔ, had given his mother a package of cooked pandanus that had been the leftovers from a meal the day before. During that meal, Binalia (according to her mother) had eaten more than her share and had been told that she wouldn't be given any the following day. When she saw the pandanus, however, she began to beg for it.

[1] Mother [examining the pandanus]: It's dried out. I'm going to put it on the fire. Wait a bit.

?! ⇒ rhetorical questions

[She puts it on the fire; Binalia is hanging over her, watching.]
[2] Mother → Binalia: Over there! Go over there!
[3] What are you looking at?!
[4] Did you put yours in there?!
[5] Binalia → Mother [Whining]: Ɛm! (neg)
[Mother angrily picks up old cooking leaf and offers it to Binalia.]
[6] Mother → Wanu →> Binalia: Eat! – ɛlɛma.
[Not paying attention; soft voice]   [7] eat /
[8] Binalia! – ɛlɛma.
                        [9] Binalia /
[10] Pandanus.
                        [11] don't eat! /
[12] Eat pandanus! – ɛlɛma.
[13] Binalia → Mother [Whining]: He says don't eat pandanus.
[14] Ɛm!
[To Binalia]   [15] what are you saying?! /
[Mother takes pandanus out of fire.]
[16] Mother → Wanu [handing him some]: Pandanus.
[Showing me pandanus on his finger]   [17] Bambi /
[18] Eat.
[19] Mother → Wanu →> BBS: Bambi, I'm eating pandanus – ɛlɛma.
[20] Binalia → Mother: Mother, I want to eat pandanus together with Wanu. [Whining] Mother!
                    [21] ɛm! / (neg)
[22] Mother → Wanu →> Binalia: No! – ɛlɛma.
[23] Binalia → Mother: Pandanus.
[24] Mother → Wanu/Mama: Yes, eat, you *two* eat.

²⁵Mother → Wanu →> Binalia: It's mine – ɛlɛma.
                        ²⁶mine /
                        . . .

²⁷Binalia → Mama/Wanu [Watching them eat]: Can you eat that large amount of pandanus by yourselves?!
²⁸Mother → Binalia: What was left of yours from yesterday?!
²⁹Mother → Wanu →> Binalia: Where did you put it?! – ɛlɛma.
[Food in mouth]   ³⁰where /
³¹Is this yours?!
                        . . .

³²Mother → Wanu →> Mama: Mama, you eat some too – ɛlɛma.
                        ³³Mama eat /
³⁴Mother → Mama: "Mama, you eat."
            [15 sec; eating and no talking]
[Binalia tries to get closer to the pandanus.]
³⁵Mother → Binalia: You just try to eat some!
³⁶Mother → Wanu →> Binalia: It's mine – ɛlɛma.
³⁷Is it yours?! – ɛlɛma.
[Wanu is eating; ignores his mother.]
³⁸Mama → Wanu →> Binalia: Did you pick it?! – ɛlɛma.
³⁹Mother → Wanu →> Binalia: My grandmother picked it! – ɛlɛma.
⁴⁰Mama → Wanu →> Binalia: *My* grandmother picked this! – ɛlɛma.
⁴¹Binalia → Mama: Do you usually lick the leaf like that?!
⁴²Mama → Binalia: Why?!
⁴³Binalia → Mama: One usually licks the leaf later.
⁴⁴Mother → Wanu →> Binalia: What do you mean?! – ɛlɛma.
[Offering some pandanus to mother]   ⁴⁵Mother eat / X /
⁴⁶Mother → Wanu: Do I eat too?
                        ⁴⁷yes /
⁴⁸Okay [Takes it] You eat too.
This eating sequence continues. When Wanu has had enough, the mother offers the rest to Binalia. She angrily refuses and whines about it. When the mother finally threatens to throw it away, Binalia takes it outside and eats it.

The mother, becoming more impatient with Binalia's whining and begging for the pandanus, tells her to leave the immediate area (line 2). Binalia's refusal to do so is met with a confrontational rhetorical question (line 3), "What are you looking at?!" meaning there is nothing for her to be looking at. This angry comment also refers to Binalia's staring at the pandanus, a nonverbal form of requesting (*memelab* 'someone begs with the eyes') that is tolerated in very young children but is considered extremely rude in an older child.

Her mother's next remark (line 4) is also a rhetorical question. By asking Binalia, "Did you put yours in there?!" she is implying, "You did not put yours in there" and challenging Binalia's claim to the remaining pandanus. (Her mother knows that Binalia had already eaten her portion.) Her mother does not expect Binalia to answer truthfully, since that would force Binalia to

admit that she is not entitled to have any. The desired effect of this question
is to shame Binalia and stop her begging. Lines 3 and 4 are examples of
sasindiab 'someone shames', a speech act that is a major strategy for controlling (prohibiting) the actions of others. The idea is that the possibility of
confrontation and shame inhibits people from asking for or taking what is not
theirs to take.

In response to Binalia's negative Єm!, her mother angrily holds up an old
leaf (which has the traces of previously cooked pandanus on it) and tells Wanu
to tell her to eat it (line 6). This type of teasing, called *dikidiab* 'one teases',
is used only when someone wants to shame or anger children. Wanu is minimally attending, as evidenced by his soft, low reply. In a second attempt to
draw Wanu into this interaction, his mother uses a vocative (his sister's name
– line 8) with *elema* in a loud voice, and Wanu repeats it. Seeing the old leaf,
and knowing that his mother is heating up pandanus to eat, Wanu confusedly
responds, "Don't eat!," referring (according to his mother) to the real pandanus. His mother's later explanation of this was that he didn't understand
the teasing that was intended by offering the old cooking leaf to his sister.
Binalia reports Wanu's response back to her mother, realizing that he is siding
with his mother and is unwilling to share his food (line 13).

Wanu's response to Binalia (line 15) does not use the appropriate verb
(according to the adult model), but what he says suggests that he understands
some aspects of the delivery and contextual appropriateness of a confrontational rhetorical question.[8] Though the verb is not correct, the prosodic contour of the utterance seems to leave no doubt in the Kaluli listener's mind that
he was responding with a confrontational question to his sister. The mother
reinforces her position (line 22), her unwillingness to give food to Binalia,
and corrects Wanu's negative (line 21) with an explicit "No!" in response to
Binalia's request to share food (line 20). To separate Binalia (who won't get
any) from her cousin and brother (who will), the mother (line 24) uses a dual
emphatic form of the 2nd person pronoun (*gain* 'you two') in her imperative.
To further shame her, the mother urges Wanu to assert his right to the pandanus (line 25), and she succeeds in getting Wanu's collaboration. At this
point Binalia switches from her unsuccessful approach of whining and begging (*geseab* 'make someone feel sorry for/pity') to an assertive style, and
she confrontationally questions her mother and the others. Lines 27–34 show
how these rhetorical questions are responded to. This time Wanu is successfully drawn in.

As Binalia tries to get closer to the food, her mother verbally threatens her
(line 35) and initiates a series of assertions and challenges regarding the ownership of the food in question to prohibit Binalia from taking any and shame
her for trying. Both her mother and cousin Mama turn against Binalia, using
shaming questions as a way of embarrassing and controlling her (lines 36–
44). It is interesting that the reasons given for Binalia's exclusion have to do

with who picked the pandanus (lines 39–40). Kaluli-speakers agreed that these are not valid reasons for denying Binalia pandanus, since Wanu's and Mama's grandmother is also Binalia's, and all three would have equal rights on that basis. The force of these lines lies not in the reason given but in the style of delivery, which is marked as confrontational through increased volume and speed and prosodic contour. Binalia responds not to the content, which is certainly arguable, but to the confrontational style itself. She speaks assertively to Mama, trying to shame her by suggesting (line 41) that Mama doesn't know the proper etiquette for eating pandanus (which involves first finishing the food and then licking the leaf). Wanu does not respond to the *ɛlɛma* utterances (lines 36–40), since he is too busy eating. His mother makes one more attempt to involve Wanu in the conflict (line 44) between herself, Mama, and Binalia, but he does not respond.

involving children in conflicts

These attempts to involve small children in conflicts between others obviously serve a number of complicated ends. In addition to socializing children to assert and challenge rights and to tease and shame others, mothers communicate their feelings and attitudes to older children via younger ones, using them as foils. Kaluli, however, do not think of these strategies in that way. According to them, the goals of these teasing and shaming routines are to socialize small children into saying the right thing back and protecting what is theirs; they make them strong – teach them to be angry when they should be so that they can take care of themselves and be self-confident.

When listening to these tape-recorded interactions, Kaluli consistently respond positively to a child's successful use of confrontational rhetorical questions, both in *ɛlɛma* sequences and spontaneously. In this sequence, Binalia was acknowledged to be skillful in her use of shaming and teasing routines. Wanu was just starting to learn to use them (see line 13). Of the three young children in this study, Meli was said to display the most advanced language and social skills, as judged by her spontaneous and appropriate use of confrontational questions at a relatively early age. These routines are taught with equal enthusiasm to boys and girls, and both become skilled at using them.

Variation in *ɛlɛma*: the importance of the intended addressee

The majority of triadic *ɛlɛma* sequences are directed to older children as intended addressees, but preverbal children, adults, and the anthropologist are also the recipients of directed messages. These messages are embedded in ongoing social interactions, and the utterances vary according to whom they are addressed, inasmuch as language systematically varies according to use. This variation supports the claim that *ɛlɛma* sequences socialize young children to be sensitive to the social identity, knowledge, and capabilities of the addressee.

Infants as intended addressees

Before the introduction of Christianity, Kaluli practiced a postpartum sex taboo that effectively spaced children approximately thirty-two months apart. Children between the ages of 2 and 3 have casual contact with their infant siblings and with other infants, as women visit each other during the day en route to getting water, to borrow embers for making a fire, or just to chat, always bringing their babies with them. Mothers use these opportunities to insure that children learn infants' names and acknowledge social relationships.

Speech with *єlєma* directed to infants and toddlers is gentle compared with the assertive demeanor of *єlєma* routines directed to older children. Mothers use mostly vocatives and expressives with *єlєma* as attention-getting devices to initiate interaction between older children and intended addressees ranging in age from a few days to 6 months (Keenan & Schieffelin 1976). Preferred vocatives include the child's own proper name or the name of traditional story characters, Newelesu for boys and Kobake for girls, and kin terms, such as *nao* 'my brother', *nado* 'my sister', *nɔsɔk* 'my cross-cousin' – all of which can be used with modifiers such as *sulɔ* 'old' or *lєsu* 'little' that mark affection. Mothers tell older children to greet infants with the expressive *Wa!* said exuberantly to get the baby's attention. Several repetitions of a vocative with an expressive are common in a given sequence. In addition to getting the infant's attention, mothers also promote short routines like the one below.

Example 4.5. Wanu (30.) is shaking my pen top at his baby sister (4.), who is being held by his mother.

[1]wa! / wa! / my sister / my
sister! /

[2]Mother → Wanu →> baby: My sister, you take! – єlєma.

[3]my sister / you take /

[Wanu puts the pen top in baby's hand.]

[4]she takes! / X / X /

[Baby drops it.]
[Searching for it]   [5]where is it? / ai! /
[Finding it]   [6]uwo! / X /

In this sequence, Wanu's mother extends his initial greeting by using *єlєma* to tell Wanu to offer the pen top to his sister. In telling him to tell his sister to "take," she is also telling Wanu to "give." In this way, Wanu is encouraged to give something to his sister as part of establishing a social relationship with her.

Messages to older infants are also tied to specific interactions and are related to the actions of either infant or older child. For example, when Seligiwɔ was crying, Mєli's mother would tell her to say to him (using *єlєma*), "Don't cry" or "What are you doing crying?!'"; when Mɛli was offering something to her brother, "Seligiwɔ, take"; when leaving, "Seligiwɔ, I'm going"; when playing a game, "[vocative] + [expressive] + can you touch me?!" Utterances such as these are used as one-liners – they are not part of a sequence of connected discourse. Rhetorical questions with nonliteral meanings ("Can you touch me?!'" = "You can't touch me!'") are addressed to 7-month-old infants. As children become older, rhetorical questions like these become dominant in a variety of playful, teasing, and controlling interactions.

When Seligiwɔ was 9 months old and crawling, he could easily reach things on the floor. When he tried to put them in his mouth, Mɛli was told to say *Nɛsabo!* 'Don't eat!' Mɛli was told to direct his actions using imperatives (i.e., *Mena!* 'Come!') and rhetorical questions (i.e., *Oba hanaya?!* 'Where are you going?!'). As Seligiwɔ began to take things that were not his to take, challenges meant to stop and shame him, such as *Gɛnowo?!* 'Is it yours?!', were issued through Mɛli. Such utterances said loudly did attract his attention. By the time he was 11 months old, Mɛli (28.) was told to say *Dimina!* 'Give!' when she wanted something from him. At this time, connected sequences using *ɛlɛma*, consisting largely of challenges prohibiting Seligiwɔ from taking things that were not his, became part of Mɛli's verbal repertoire.

Example 4.6. Seligiwɔ (11.) has just taken my net bag.
Mother → Mɛli →> Seligiwɔ: Don't take – ɛlɛma.
  huh? /
Don't take! – ɛlɛma.
  don't take! /
This is Bambi's! – ɛlɛma. Is it yours?! – ɛlɛma.
  is it yours?! /
[Mother gently removes the bag from Seligiwɔ.]

People point out interesting sounds and actions for toddlers to notice. Mothers tell the older child to say something to the toddler, using a vocative plus a deictic (*Kokɛ!* 'There!') or (*Wekɛ!* 'Here!') or other attention-getting expressions indicating surprise or interest. Toddlers are encouraged to notice and pay attention to situations with uncertain outcomes, such as dogs fighting, loud talk coming from an unseen source, or someone entering the house. However, at no time are children instructed to say the names of the agents responsible for such interesting actions, nor do adults name the agents (such as "dog" or the name of a person who enters). Instead adults tell children between 2 and 3 to indicate to the baby (using a vocative or expressive plus a deictic) that something is happening. These young children share with the baby the fact that something is to be noticed, and sometimes they pretend fear or surprise, but are not told to tell the baby what is happening – "Dogs are fighting," "Someone is coming," or the like. Nothing is said to the infant that requires a verbal answer; only its attention is elicited and an affective stance is provided.

Mothers encourage sons and daughters to pay attention to infant siblings, involving sons in games and fantasy play, and giving daughters messages about caregiving and social control. Sons gradually lose interest in these routines with infants, and increasingly, when infants are about a year old, single utterances with ɛlɛma are connected sequentially and directed only to young girls to repeat. Mothers tell older sisters or cousins what to tell toddlers – where to go and sit, to eat quickly and then go outside – and tell them to walk around with them. When toddlers take someone's property, they are asked via older girls, "Is it yours?! Aren't you ashamed?!" Mothers tell older daughters to control younger children's actions by gently confronting and shaming them before the younger ones can talk. Thus, the basic controlling strategies are established early, and young girls are given responsibility for monitoring and carrying out orders that originate with their mothers. Toddlers are not expected to answer information-seeking questions, and in fact such questions are not asked. Instead, caregivers issue through their older daughters rhetorical questions meant to control the child's behavior, extending their monitoring to cover an increasing number of contexts. For example, if a toddler starts to put something inedible in his or her mouth, the mother says to the 2- or 3-year-old, "What are you eating?! – ɛlɛma" (meaning "Don't eat that!"), and the child usually repeats it to the toddler with the appropriate force. The older child has the opportunity to gain some control over the actions of the younger sibling even if the mother is directing the entire display.

Mothers' speech to 2- to 3-year-olds with preverbal infants as intended addressees is simple and consists largely of vocatives and expressives. Until the infant is about a year old, there are few sequences of connected discourse, and those that appear are syntactically simple, drawing on a limited number of imperatives, negative imperatives, and rhetorical questions. Much of the material directed to the preverbal child is repetitive, and utterances are topically relevant. Repeating these utterances teaches both older and younger children important communicative skills and a large body of cultural knowledge. When 2- to 3-year-olds are instructed to speak appropriately to a younger child, they are learning the right phrases in addition to the demeanor that goes with each.

Adults as intended addressees

Children's ɛlɛma routines to adults vary in frequency, depending on whom they have contact with, and in form and content, depending on the kinship relationship that mother and child have with the adult participant. As Abi's mother had few relatives in the village, Abi had few interactions (using ɛlɛma) with other adults, and they were limited to greeting passersby. Abi was infrequently told to speak to his father, and when he did he called out requests for food. Wanu did have relatives in the village, but when he visited his paternal grandmother or father's sister, his mother was not there to instruct him in what to say to them. Wanu's experience was similar to Abi's in that most of his time was spent within the nuclear family, and his parents did not encourage him to interact with adults except for greetings and requests.

Meli's experience was different. She had frequent and varied *elema* interactions with many adults. Her paternal grandmother, mother's brother and his wife (her father's sister), and their daughter shared the house. Her mother's unmarried teenage brothers and sisters lived in the village and visited often, bringing food and cooking it there. Her maternal grandfather came by several times a week, bringing small birds and animals for Meli's mother to cook. Meli's house was also a gathering place because of her parents' involvement in Christian activities and because of its central location on the main yard. Christians or relatives going to the longhouse would call out or stop in. Meli participated in many extended calling-out sequences (such as Example 4.2), not only to her mother's brother and maternal grandfather for food, but also to classificatory mothers (her mother's sisters) to fix her skirts and bring her gifts like salt and soap. Mutual teasing between Meli and her mother's sisters was common, focusing especially on food and whether or not to share it. Meli's parents encouraged her to tease other people. These interactions, supported by *elema*, seemed to use Meli as a foil in ongoing teasing routines and often had little to do with Meli's own intentions or interests in a situation.

A complex example of this comes from Meli at age 28.3. In spite of the fact that Meli's mother has given up almost all traditional taboos, she still follows the in-law avoidance taboo and does not speak directly to her mother-in-law. Nor does the older woman speak directly to Meli's mother. While Meli's grandmother is sitting in her section of the house, Meli and her mother in their section are engaged in a calling-out sequence to Meli's cousin Mama ($3\frac{1}{2}$ yr), who is outside with Meli's brother Seligiwɔ and not answering back. The teasing is as follows: Mother → Meli →> Mama: "You have no brother [he died in infancy] – *elema*." Meli repeats her mother's words. "Who will help you cut sago? [when you are older]? – *elema*." The grandmother, hearing the teasing, joins in and says to Meli, "Mama will have your brother."[9] Meli's mother then tells Meli to call her grandmother "an old woman," which is done in a playful way with plenty of laughter to indicate the good humor intended in the teasing. Then she continues:

Example 4.7.

Mother → Meli →> G'mother: Your husband, old Sogobaye, is
coming here – *elema*. [He is long since dead.]
                        [Meli repeats]
[Lots of laughter from all parties]
Your old husband Sogobaye ⁒
G'mother → Meli: ⁒ And what about the ones he fathered?! [Meli's
father, Mama's mother]

And where did *you* come from?!
Did you give birth to yourself?!
You started from one he fathered!
[They all laugh.]
Mother → Mєli →> G'mother: You mean your son Degelɔ? –
єlєma.

[Mєli repeats]
[G'mother names all of her children, and Mєli repeats each one.]

Mєli provides the means of communication between her mother and her paternal grandmother, and receives genealogical instruction: All of her paternal relatives are listed in this exchange. In addition, she participates as a mediator between two people who cannot speak directly to each other, learning about that type of relationship.

In the next example, the issue of the distribution of cooked bananas comes up, and Mєli, guided by her mother, teases her father about not giving him any. His responses are serious and typical of a parent when a child refuses to share.

Example 4.8. Immediately preceding this sequence, Mєli (32.2) and her mother are cooking six bananas. Mєli is supposed to be turning them over, but instead she plays, and the bananas begin to burn. Her mother asks for the tongs back, but Mєli is unwilling to give them back and insists on turning the bananas herself. Her mother takes the tongs, which makes Mєli angry.

[Angrily]   ¹Mother / yours · not · *not will eat /
²Mother → Mєli: Me, why won't I eat?! I'll eat!
                                                ³I'll eat! /
⁴Yes, two *you* (eat).
                                                ⁵won't you eat two? /
⁶Two *I* (eat).
                                                ⁷two – oh – /
⁸Two *Seligiwɔ* (eats).
[They run through the distribution again.]
                                                ⁹will we give two to Degelɔ? /
¹⁰We won't give to Degelɔ.
[Degelɔ walks in.]
                                                ¹¹will we give? /
¹²Mine are spoken for.
                                                ¹³what? /
¹⁴Mine are spoken for. I won't give to Degelɔ.
                                                ¹⁵yes /
¹⁶Degelɔ → Mєli: What! I'll eat!
[High voice]   ¹⁷I'll *not eat /
¹⁸I eat!
[High voice]   ¹⁹this banana I'll not *eat /
²⁰∥Think about it!
²¹Mother → Mєli →> Degelɔ: ∥You don't – I won't give you! –
єlєma.
[To Degelɔ]   ²²I won't give you! /
²³Degelɔ → Mєli: You think about it! I usually give.
²⁴Mother → Mєli →> Degelɔ: Think about it yourself! – єlєma.

²⁵think about it yourself! /
²⁶Degelɔ → Osolowa [changing the topic]: Henga [Osolowa's other
name], when you go to the garden . . .

In the first line of this sequence, Mɛli expresses annoyance at her mother by telling her mother that she will not eat. When one is angry, a first response is often not to share. Her mother then reviews the distribution of the six bananas that they are cooking: two each for Mɛli, her mother, and her brother. Mɛli begins the teasing (line 17) after her father, Degelɔ, overhears the conversation and challenges the distribution plan. Mɛli's use of high pitch frames her utterances to her father as teasing, but she makes an error in the verb she uses (lines 17, 19). Instead of the correct response, *Mɔmienɔ* 'I will not give', she says, *Mɔmɛnɔ:* 'I will not eat', which doesn't make sense. But her father continues. Her mother (line 21) corrects her by providing the right verb ("give") to say back to her father (line 22). Her father explicitly states his expectation that she will share (lines 20, 23), reminding Mɛli to think about and remember what he gives to her. This is frequently said to children who are old enough to know better but still don't want to share.

During transcription, I asked Mɛli's mother why she encouraged Mɛli to tease her father. She said it was so Mɛli would know what to say back to someone when she did not want to share. She called this type of talk *kegab* 'one sounds angry but is not', which she distinguished from *enteab* 'one speaks angrily', which is serious (see Example 4.4, line 21). It is hard to determine how conscious anyone is about the socializing function of these exchanges while they are occurring. On reflection, however, Mɛli's mother did acknowledge that these exchanges help the child learn the right things to say back when she does not want to share.

The anthropologist as intended addressee

Anthropologists do not form a regular participant category in Kaluli life. But since I spent a great deal of time sitting around with families, I too was a recipient of *ɛlɛma* sequences. My social identity as a nonnative resident with extensive fictive kin relationships was unusual. Ways of speaking to me were markedly different from ways mothers told their children to speak to other people, and my special status is reflected in messages directed to me.

Another factor underlying the differences in speech directed to me was that my own ways of using Kaluli, especially in the first few months, were different from those of native speakers. Though I was able to speak the language quite well, I spoke to young children according to middle-class American conventions, and this affected the *ɛlɛma* sequences that their mothers directed to me.

For example, unlike Kaluli adults, I asked children information-seeking questions such as "Where did you go this morning?" or, upon seeing some object, "Where did that come from?" or "Whose is it?" These kinds of question would not have been asked by Kaluli; they would not think it important or they would already know the answer. Mothers, of course, already knew the answers to these kinds of question. My peculiar questions were usually met with no response or, at best, some indication of confusion from the child, such as "Huh?" or "What?" Utterances with *ɛlɛma* helped ease the situation as a mother would repeat my question; if the child still didn't answer, she would provide some answer for the child to repeat to me. Sometimes just enough information to answer the question was provided; at other times a short narrative followed. Narratives sometimes were told to me spontaneously, without my asking a question. However, during the course of the field work, my strange question asking to young children decreased, and so did the prompted narratives.

Example 4.9. Mɛli (27.3), her mother, and I are sitting in her house. The family has just returned from a week's stay at Waiyu, the mission station.

[1]BBS → Mɛli: When you were at Waiyu what did you eat?
[2]what? /
[3]Mother → Mɛli: When you were at Waiyu what did you eat? she says.
[4]when I was at Waiyu ate /
[5]Mother → Mɛli →> BBS: (1) ate sago – ɛlɛma.
[6]ate sago /
[7]Was eating only sago – ɛlɛma.
[8]only sago /
[9]BBS → Mɛli: Did you eat anything else?
[10]Mother → Mɛli →> BBS: (1) ate nothing – ɛlɛma.
[11]ate nothing /
[12]Ate no fish – ɛlɛma.
[13]ate no fish / ate /
[14]BBS: Oh dear. ☺
[15]Mother → Mɛli →> BBS: (1) was really hungry (for meat) – ɛlɛma.
[16]was really hungry (for meat) /
[17]I didn't eat fish – ɛlɛma.
[18]didn't eat fish /
[19]Sago
[20]sago /
[21]only
[22]only sago /
[23]was eating.
[24]was eating /
[25]Plain sago
[26]plain sago /
[27]was eating – ɛlɛma.
[28]was eating /

[29]The sago I will eat
[To Mother]   [30]then enough [of this talk] /
[31]Mother → Mɛli: No, not enough.
[This sequence continued.]

In this narrative Mɛli's mother informs me that Mɛli did not have any meat while at Waiyu – an appeal to me to feel sorry for her and give her some, which I did later that day. The story uses typical narrative conventions, for example, (S)OV word order and subject deletion, since the subject (Mɛli) is known to everyone and remains constant throughout the story. The objects that were or were not eaten are the focus of this story, and the fact that there was no meat is expressed by use of the verb *tɛlɛnyab* rather than the verb *mayab*, which refers to hunger in general. Mothers assisted their children in telling me stories about where they went, specifying ground names and associating them with particular people. Sometimes they would tell me where different people were located, naming garden sites and sago camps, informing me and the child of significant happenings, places, and relationships. Thus the important connections between persons, events, and places (similar to calling-out sequences) that are so meaningful for Kaluli would be woven into these recitations to me. These narratives were rarely told in the here and now (present tense) but were about past events or things that would happen in the future. My role as listener was to acknowledge and express sympathy (when appropriate) but not actually to converse, since the narrative was not dialogic. In later samples there were a few short spontaneous intraconversational narratives from children directed to me and to other adults. However, mothers did not typically direct narratives from young children to others using *ɛlɛma*.

Before their contact with the Christian mission (1971), Kaluli did not use any equivalent of a politeness formula such as "Please" or "Thank you" in asking for or receiving objects. The missionaries introduced politeness conventions such as "Thank you," and many Kaluli saw this "Christian behavior" as appropriate for all nonnatives. Consequently, when I gave Mɛli some salt or food, her parents would often say the equivalent of "Say thank you," using the Kaluli expression *Ɔmo!* or *Mada ɔm!* 'The very one!' followed by *ɛlɛma*. However, with traditionally oriented families such as Abi's, children were told to say *Ni Babi* 'My Bambi' or *Nɛsu Babi*, thus expressing the relationship established by the giving. When siblings or adults gave something to the child, the child was not told to say "Thank you," since that giving helped constitute the kinship relationship. Instead, after the receipt of, for example, a food item, the child would be instructed to tell someone else who it was who gave it. Children never used the expression "Thank you" spontaneously with me.

Mothers told children to make offers to and requests of me, but children were learning that I was to be spoken to differently from other adults. Notably absent in speech directed to me were teases, challenges, and playful threats.

Mothers were consistent in formulating language appropriate to the intended addressee, with situation, interests, competence, and relationship always taken into account.

Problematic speech activities

Utterances with *ɛlɛma* support young children's involvement in a variety of everyday activities, and mothers assume that children will spontaneously speak in the ways they have been shown. Through *ɛlɛma* and repetition, caregivers promote a positive and desirable association between "hard language" (from the caregiver) and young children's developing linguistic skills. Children, however, initiate speech activities that are unlike any their parents have shown them, for example sound play, word play, imitating and distorting speech, and monologue. Kaluli say that these verbal activities can impede young children's language or promote an undesirable symbolic association. Like certain foods which are taboo for children, these verbal activities must also be avoided. They are unacceptable for young children and are terminated by mothers when they hear them, a fact that shows the importance of linguistic ideology in shaping everyday practice. In particular, Kaluli concepts of "soft" and "hard" language explain why, in addition to the symbolic associations between children and birds, these speech activities are problematic.

Monologue

Unlike many white middle-class children, who when playing alone or before going to sleep often talk to themselves, Kaluli children rarely engage in monologues. Recordings of children alone or lying quietly by themselves before sleep (itself unusual) do not have the stream of monologic talk that one can easily record in similar contexts in middle-class American homes. This includes singing and rhymes, sound and word play, and often two-part conversations created by a single speaker. I never asked Kaluli directly about what they thought of children speaking to themselves – there being no Kaluli word for "monologue" and having no adult examples of the phenomenon – but I did have the opportunity to find out. My own son, who was 4½ at the beginning of the study, engaged in extensive monologues, initially in English and later in Kaluli, while playing alone in his room. Upon hearing him, Kaluli would ask, "Whom is he playing with?" and when I answered that he was alone, playing by himself, some commented that it was "different" (*kɔle*). Others said I was teasing and just didn't want to say whom he was with. After seeing that he was indeed alone, people would shake their heads in mild astonishment, saying *Kɔle sele* 'Really different'. Clearly they found his behavior uncommon and a little odd. With this attitude so clearly expressed, I looked for situations of Kaluli children's monologue and could find only occasional instances when a child was alone and talking to himself or herself.

When Abi was 31 months old, his brother was born, and as a result of village pressure Abi was weaned abruptly. This had a negative effect on his disposition; he was angry and more fretful than ever. One of the things he did during the two or three months following this traumatic experience was talk to himself. Fortunately, I recorded several of these short monologues, as Abi did not mind my sitting nearby as he played and talked. When I played the tape back to his mother as part of the transcription process, she claimed that she did not understand what Abi was saying when he talked to himself. She called it *ba madali to* 'talk to no purpose', and since it was *ba madali* 'to no purpose' she claimed not to understand the words. Needless to say, I found her reluctance intriguing, since she was always so helpful and tried to understand passages containing noise or overlapped speech. This seemed to be something else. I knew Abi was not babbling or doing sound play, for I could understand some of the words. When my assistant Kulu listened to the tape with me, he was able to help me transcribe it, but agreed that it was *ba madali to*.

Example 4.10. Abi (34.2) is playing by himself outside, picking up pieces of wood and breaking splinters off.

	nɛwɛlɛsu died / just died / nɛwɛlɛsu · I'm going to throw in a hole / there //
[To me, showing me splinter]	uh · died /
BBS: Huh?	
	died / mother's brother died /
Mother's brother died?	
	yes /

Nɛwɛlɛsu is the name of a character in Kaluli stories after whom people call boy babies before they are given their own proper names. It is also the name of a phasmid, a long thin stick insect. It is impossible to know which Abi is referring to (baby brother or insect) as he plays with the wood. Perhaps it is a fantasy related to the splinters, which resemble the insect, but there is no way to know. In speaking without an intended addressee, Abi's voice is soft (*hɛsa*). It was this type of speech that his mother could not understand.

The few times I recorded children on the verge of sleep, they spoke in a soft voice, not intended as conversation. Mothers assisting in transcription had no difficulty understanding what children were talking about in these situations.

Example 4.11. Abi (35.2) and his mother are around the firepit. Abi is lying on his back, very sleepy, playing with a piece of string. His mother is cooking bananas.

[In a soft voice using a descending major third]   ¹nɛ gimi andoma / nɛ gimiyɔ / X /

I have no fishhook / my fishhook / X /

²Mother → BBS [in speaking voice]: Nɛ gimi.

My fishhook.

³nɛ gimiyɛ /

⁴Mother → Abi [following his melodic contour]: Gimiyɛ nɛ gimiyɛ

[Continuing in a songlike voice]   ⁵nɛ gimiyɔ / nɛ gimi andoma / X / X / X / ɔɔ / andoma / nɛ gimi andoma / X / X / Way-eyɛ diɛgane /
Waye took it away /
nɛ gimi andoma / X / X / X /

⁶[Songlike] Nɛ gimi
⁷[To Yogodo]: Siɛfinɔ!   andoma / X /
none / X

[Abi continues.]
Siɛfinɔ sɛlɛ!!
Fire tongs! Fire tongs, I'm saying!!!
Siɛfinɔ. Siɛfinɔ halo dimino! Yogodo!
Fire tongs. Give me the fire tongs from up there! Yogodo!
[Yogodo is asleep; no response.]
Abi! Siɛfinɔ! Siɛfinɔ dimino!
Abi! Fire tongs! Give the fire tongs!

⁸huh? /
what? /

[Getting up]   ɛm! / nisa diɛno /
no! / I'll take /

Ɛm, o deliyɔkɛ!
Okay, over there!

In this sequence, Abi draws on two different genres, *sa-yɛlab* and *heyalo*, in lines 1, 3, and 5 and then switches into conversation in line 8. In his first turn, the phrase *nɛ gimi andoma* 'I have no fishhook' is similar to the formulaic phrase "I have no *x*" found in *sa-yɛlab* 'sung–texted weeping'. This poetic form of lamenting the loss of a loved one is performed by women at funerals (Feld 1982a:92). Here Abi delivers this poetic form in a songlike voice, singing the interval of a descending major third, a melodic contour that he has often heard his mother sing. This interval, however, is not found in *sa-yɛlab*, but in *heyalo*, one of five Bosavi ceremonies with a distinct song style. Thus, while there is a disjunction between the source of the poetics and the melody, the poetics express his sadness about the loss of a fishhook, and while the loss of this item is not nearly so significant as the loss that adults mourn, Abi nonetheless expresses his own feelings of sadness through the poetics of the genre associated with this expressive form. Learning song is also learning the appropriate evocative mode of lament. Song is associated with moving another to do something about one's loss. As Feld points out, song is an outgrowth of sung weeping.[10]

Abi's mother turns to me and repeats his words in her usual speaking voice, but then she shadows his vocalization, following the melody in a songlike voice with a clear enunciation of the full descending major third. Even though Yogodo is asleep, which for Kaluli is not the privileged state it is for middle-class Americans, her mother does not hesitate to ask her to get the fire tongs. She is taking hot bananas out of the fire and cannot manage without them. Getting no response from Yogodo, she asks Abi to get the fire tongs even as he is falling asleep. Children frequently did the same to their mothers, asking them for things as they were falling asleep or were already asleep, and jumping on them if they did not respond.

There are several reasons for the infrequent occurrence of monologues among Kaluli children. One is that people are rarely alone. Nor is it desirable for children (or anyone) to be alone, since when alone one is more vulnerable to negative forces such as witches. In addition, anyone who is alone or who likes to spend time alone is suspected of being up to no good, since no sane person would want to take chances and leave himself or herself open to witches' attacks. There is security in company and in relationships. Finally, language is considered to be essentially social. Talking to oneself, especially if one can talk to others, is considered "different" and incomprehensible.[11]

Sound play

Sound play has been discussed in terms of the vocal/verbal activity of a single speaker and as dialogic exchanges between young children.[12] In these exchanges, children pay attention to the phonological shape of one another's utterances and repeat or modify slightly a sequence of sounds just produced. These sequences, which may be referentially meaningless, are nonetheless textually cohesive in that utterances relate to each other by similarity of phonological shape. Furthermore, as a single speech event, sound play is coherent on a social level.

The occurrence of sound play has been reported in a number of different cultures. Most middle-class Americans think of sound play as one of many verbal or vocal activities young children engage in. They are not disturbed by sound play as such, provided the language does not disturb others. Kaluli children also engage in and enjoy sound play, but the response of Kaluli adults to this activity is different from that of middle-class Americans. For important cultural reasons, young children's sound play is discouraged and terminated when it is heard. All young children were involved in sound-play interactions with older children; Mɛli and Abi participated in especially varied and elaborate routines. These routines can be analyzed in terms of form, content, and the turn-taking procedures established and agreed upon by participants. They can also be examined for the formal features of language that can be played with (pitch, prosody, timing) and for evidence of metalinguistic awareness of conversational conventions and conversational cooperation.

Mɛli enjoyed sound and word play, and such activity took place with her mother and her cousin Mama, fifteen months older than Mɛli. In the following sequence, the two girls are in the house with Mɛli's mother and grandfather. Her mother is cooking and talking to him.

Example 4.12. Mɛli (30.2) and Mama (3; 9) have been playing together all morning and were earlier engaged in a repetition game. They are waiting for Mɛli's mother to finish cooking. Mama is banging rhythmically on a plastic water jug. [Transcription conventions in this example: Lines above utterance show general pitch contour of the vocalization. A colon after lexical item indicates vowel lengthening. Double vowels indicaie vowel gemination. Position of word in each turn pair roughly indicates amount of time between termination of first turn and onset of second turn of the pair.]

¹Mama:	Mɛli Mɛli Mɛli Mɛli Mɛli Mɛli
²Mɛli:	oh yes?
³Mama:	oh yes?
⁴Mɛli:	obɛ what?
⁵Mama:	obɛ what?
⁶Mɛli:	oh okay
⁷Mama:	oh okay
⁸Mɛli:	oh yes?
⁹Mama:	oh yes?
¹⁰Mɛli:	obɛ: whaaat?
¹¹Mama:	obɛ what?
¹²Mɛli:	oo:
¹³Mama:	oo:
¹⁴Mɛli:	obɛ:
¹⁵Mama:	obɛ:
¹⁶Mɛli:	o:h
¹⁷Mama:	oh
¹⁸Mɛli:	uu
¹⁹Mama:	uu

²⁰Meli: u͡wu:

²¹Mama: u͡wu:

²²Meli: u͡u:

²³Mama: u͡u:

²⁴Meli: u͡bu:

²⁵Mama: u͡bu:

²⁶Mother: Wai! To nafa se sɛlɛiba! Ɔbɛ towɔ we.
Hey! Try to speak good talk! This is bird talk.

This sequence demonstrates the transition from language to rhythmic sound play, and is one of many instances where two children collaborate and maintain this type of verbal activity. Mama's use of Meli's name in initiating talk to Meli (line 1) is different from the usual ways in which speakers use vocatives to secure the attention of the listener in conversation. Her calls to Meli are accompanied by rhythmic banging on a water jug and are rapidly repeated six times, without an interval to allow Meli to respond. In addition, they are high-pitched and staccato, and do not follow the usual prosodic contours used in conversation.

Whereas Mama is playing in her opening line, Meli responds in her next turns in conversational style. After her name is called, Meli acknowledges Mama (line 2) with *Oh* 'Yes?' When Mama imitates Meli's opening acknowledgment (line 3) instead of providing a line of conversation, Meli requests clarification with *Obɛ* 'What?' Mama again repeats Meli's utterance. Next, Meli responds to Mama's turn with a closing acknowledgment *Oh* 'Okay' (line 6), which Mama again imitates. While Mama's imitations of Meli's utterances are playful, Meli is still in a conversational frame and is using conversational features. However, when Mama repeats Meli's utterance in an even higher-pitched voice with a shorter than usual interval between turns, Meli's following response (line 8) is also higher-pitched, and the play is on. Thus, the mood or key initiated by Mama is finally recognized by Meli, and play is agreed upon as indicated by her rise in pitch.

By the tenth turn, there is overlap between the two speakers, with Mama imitating Meli's utterances. The overlap is within turn pairs, never across turn pairs; that is, there is no overlap between turns 13 and 14, only between 14 and 15. As in other play sequences based on words, Meli always waits for Mama to complete her turn before starting the next pair part.

Up to this point, turns 10–11, the girls are playing with the conventions of opening and closing up talk (Schegloff 1968). That is, there is a vocative as a summons (Meli's name), a response ("Yes?"), a clarification request when a message is not forthcoming ("What?"), and the closing confirmation ("Okay"). In this sequence, however, there is no content, topic, or message between the opening and the closing. Thus, lines 1–11 consist of playing with some formal devices of conversation, the opening and closing.

Then there is a shift: From turn pairs 12–13, the intervals between the turn pairs become shorter, the pitch becomes higher, and the vowels are lengthened and then shifted. What has been a sequence of words dissolves into a sequence of sounds as the girls play with the phonological shape of the words. Here, the younger child, Mɛli, takes the lead. From turn pairs 12 to 17, the prosodic contours remain similar to those of closing contours, following a descent in melody. From pairs 18 to 25, they shift into a more playful modality. Other changes occur during these turns. The vowels rise, and the turn-taking pattern becomes less conversational and more like the pattern of lift-up-over-sounding (*dulugu*) characteristic of women's songs or more generally of collaborative voicing in women's and men's informal work and leisure activities (Feld 1988). The two little girls started out playing with the words used to signal the opening and closing of talk, correctly sequenced, and then jointly renegotiated the sequence into one of playing with sounds. They cooperated for twenty-five turns, signaling their ongoing agreement to maintain this play-speech activity, using pitch (high voice), prosody (exaggerated intonation and descent in melody), and timing (shortened within-pair turn intervals). Mɛli acknowledges the imitation on the part of Mama as playful, evidenced by her collaboration. In other sequences Mama mocks Mɛli's speech by imitating it and changing the phonological shape, and Mɛli refuses to respond in those cases except by getting angry.

[margin handwriting: what they uled in the dialogue]

After turn 25, Mɛli's mother, who has been busy scraping taro and having a conversation with her father, turns abruptly to the girls and in a loud, authoritative voice says, "Hey! Try to speak good talk! This is bird talk." The girls immediately stop and become quiet. Both girls were enjoying this activity, so why did Mɛli's mother respond as she did?

Mɛli's mother's termination of the sound play was not due to mild irritation caused by the noise the girls were making. Similar noise levels caused by other verbal activity would never have prompted this reaction. Her particular response, which was consistent with that of other Kaluli, has a cultural and symbolic basis related to Kaluli ideas about language development and the broader notion of taboo. Recall that Kaluli see the process of language acquisition as a "hardening" process. They do not use special baby-talk words and have clear ideas of how children's language should sound. They have no word for sound play. It is grouped with babbling as *ba madali* 'to no purpose'. Mothers encourage their children to speak "hard talk," "good talk," by both telling them what to say and correcting errors of grammar and pronunciation. The goal of language development is to produce speech that is both well formed and socially appropriate, enabling individuals to establish and maintain sociable relationships.

Kaluli also believe that birds and children are connected in complex symbolic ways. One manifestation of this relationship was discussed earlier with regard to food taboos, which prevent the association between children and certain birds. Kaluli say that if small children were to eat certain pigeons, they too would only coo and never learn "hard language." The prohibition is necessary to protect the child's developing language and, by implication, social ability. Birds and children are closely associated in other contexts. The calls of some fruit doves are felt to be similar to the whining voices of small hungry children. Both have high-pitched vocalizations with melodic descent, trailing off. It is the descent that makes their vocalizations birdlike, songlike, less "hard" and more ɔbɛ gɔnɔ to 'bird sound words'. Yet another association turns on the fact that upon death a person's soul becomes a bird.

Given these powerful and problematic symbolic associations between birds and young children, the two must be kept separate. This means not only that children must avoid eating certain birds, but that they must not sound like them either, even in play. Mothers discourage their children from emulating or imitating qualities associated with certain birds. In order to insure that "hard language" develops, mothers prevent a dangerous association: They terminate sound play. They make it explicit to children that they are to speak "good talk, not bird talk."

Imitation and distortion: what older children do to the speech of younger ones

It is important that older children not engage in speech activities with younger children that contradict the efforts made by adults to ensure "good talk" and "hard talk." When older children imitate and distort the speech of a younger child within the mother's hearing, she does not tolerate this behavior.

Example 4.13. Abi (27.2) and his sister Yogodo (5;6) are alone; their mother has left the house to get firewood. Abi wants Yogodo to cook bananas for him, and she begins to do it.

[To Yogodo]	[1]give bananas /
[2]Yogodo → Abi: Give bananas.	
	[3](I) will eat / give bananas /
[4](I) will eat.	
	[5]Yogodo /
[6]Dogodo.	
	[7]huh? /
[8]Huh?	
	[9]Yogodo! /
[10]Dogodo.	
	[11]ɛm? /
[12]ɛm?	

[Lines 11 and 12 are repeated six times.]
[As the mother returns, the bananas fall in the fire because of Yogodo's distraction; both children cry. Mother cooks another vegetable (*jun*) and hands it to Yogodo to peel for Abi.]
[13]Mother → Yogodo: Peel it.

[14]peel it /

¹⁵Yogodo → Abi: What *jun*?!

¹⁶*jun* peel it / my *jun* peel it /

¹⁷[Slurring words] My *jun* peel it.

¹⁸huh? /

[Lines 17 and 18 are repeated three times.]
¹⁹Mother → Yogodo: Speak language!
　　　　　To sama!

In imitating Abi's request for bananas, Yogodo follows his utterances with virtually no interval between her turn and his. When he addresses her, she distorts her pronunciation to tease and annoy him. This continues after their mother returns. When Abi repeats his mother's request to Yogodo (line 13), he is challenged with a rhetorical question, "What *jun*?!," implying that there is none. Abi clarifies his utterance, adding the words *jun* and "it," producing an incorrect double referent, which Yogodo repeats and distorts, including his error. He seeks clarification several times from Yogodo, who confuses him with her distorted imitation, and finally his mother, who has been busy cooking, turns to Yogodo and says, "Speak words/language."

Mothers see this type of activity as not only mocking or teasing the young child's not yet well-formed language, but as also confusing the younger child about language, its correct form and appropriate use. Thus an undesirable language interaction is terminated with the explicit directive *To sama!* 'Speak language!'. By focusing on the form of talk rather than on its specific content or on a way of speaking, the children are not discouraged from speaking to one another, but are encouraged to do it properly, on the model of "hard words."

Playing with words

Once children's language is sufficiently "hard" (at about age 3½ to 4), they are free to play with words. This activity, which is unnamed by Kaluli, usually occurs in situations involving minor disputes over food or when teasing is involved. What often starts out as something serious can turn into something playful. This depends on who is involved and the use of closely timed rhythmic and repetitive formulaic utterances. While this speech activity is appropriate for older children, mothers do not want their older children negatively influencing the younger ones whose speech is not yet well developed. The following sequence started as a dispute and evolved into speech play.

Example 4.14. Abi (27.2), Yogodo (5;6), sister Mobiya (7;6), and brother Daibo (5;6) are with Abi's mother, all sitting around cooking and eating bits of food. Yogodo has been begging for food from Abi.

¹Mobiya → Abi: Abi brother, don't give!
²Yogodo → Mobiya (distorted): Abi brother, don't give!
³Mobiya → Yogodo: You eat already!
⁴Yogodo → Mobiya: You eat already!
[Lines 3 and 4 are repeated twice.]

⁵Daibo → Girls: I eat!
⁶Yogodo → Daibo: I eat!
⁷Mobiya → Yogodo: You don't eat!
⁸Yogodo → Mobiya: You don't eat!
⁹Daibo → Girls: I eat!
Niyɔ nan!
¹⁰Yogodo to both: I eat!
Niyɔ nɛn!
¹¹Mobiya → Yogodo: You don't eat.
Giyɔ mɔnan.
¹²Yogodo → Mobiya: You don't eat.
Giyɔ mɔnan.
[Loudly]   ¹³nɛ babɛ / nɛ nɛ / nɛnɛ / hɛhɛ /
[The others laugh.]
¹⁴Mother → Children: Speak hard!
Halaido sama!
¹⁵Yogodo → Mother: What?
¹⁶Mother → Yogodo: Speak hard!
Halaido samɛ!

After Mobiya tells Abi not to share food with Yogodo, Yogodo mocks her by repeating what Mobiya has said, phonologically distorting her speech. Mobiya responds to this with a formulaic tease *Gi na* 'You don't eat'. Yogodo continues, imitating Mobiya's speech, and Daibo joins in. From line 5 to line 14, the three older children engage in a closely timed teasing routine about who will and will not eat. Food, however, is no longer the issue in this interaction; there is increasing overlap in word boundaries, and a rapid speechplay rhythm develops.

Abi has been sitting and watching it all, but at line 13 he loudly interjects a contribution of his own. He imitates the speech of the older children, making them laugh. His vocalization is nonsensical, but he does retain one phonological element from the speech that has gone before, *nɛ* from *niyɔ* 'I'. His vocalization breaks the rhythm of the ongoing interaction, and the laughter of the older children calls the mother's attention to it. She terminates the play by telling the older children to "speak hard," implying that the speech before that point was something other. Such a reference is always to speech in an ongoing context. In situations like this, mothers are careful to see to it that their young children do not sound less mature than they actually are. Later on, the older children resumed their speech play, and as long as Abi did not participate, his mother did not interfere. When she listened to this tape, Abi's mother said that Abi's contribution was *ba madali to* 'talk to no purpose'.

Word play with mothers

In contrast to this sequence with children, we shall examine a sequence in which Mɛli's mother takes her through one of the teasing routines in the correct sequence with the right rhetorical force. (See also Example 8.8.)

Example 4.15. Mɛli (30.2) has just been given a sweet potato by her mother.

	¹my mother! /
	nɔwo! /
²Yea.	
Oh.	
	³you don't eat sweet potato /
	siabulu ɛnɔ gi nakɛ /
⁴Wa?	
Huh?	
	⁵sweet potato /
	siabulu ɛnɔ /
⁶Is it yours?!	
Ɛnɔ ginɔwɔ?!	
	⁷it /
	ɛnɔ /
⁸I eat sweet potato!	
Siabulu ni nan!	
	⁹no /
	ɛm /
¹⁰You don't eat!	
Ge mɔnan!	
	¹¹you don't eat! /
	ge mɔnan! /
¹²You don't eat!	
	¹³you don't eat! /
¹⁴I'm saying the truth!	
Hindi sɔlɔl!	
	¹⁵I'm saying the truth! /
	hindi sɔlɔl! /
¹⁶You didn't dig up any!	
Ge andoma wali!	
	¹⁷you didn't dig up any! /
	ge andoma wali! /
	¹⁸I sweet potato /
	niyɔ siabuluwɔ /
¹⁹You didn't cook sweet potato!	
Ge siabuluwɔ mɔsɔfɛ!	
	²⁰you didn't cook sweet potato! /
	ge siabuluwɔ mɔsɔfɛ! /
²¹Don't eat!	
Mɔnan!	

Mɛli initiates this sequence using a formulaic expression *Gi na* (see Examples 6.4 and 6.15) meaning "You don't eat." Her voice is pitched higher than usual, and her prosodic contours are exaggerated to produce a singsong effect. Mɛli is smiling, and her mother commented to me that this was play. Her mother poses a rhetorical question (line 6) as a challenge, to which Mɛli has no response. Then the mother starts the formulaic "I eat, you don't eat." Mɛli's initiation of a new line, "I sweet potato" (line 18), is not correct, and her mother supplies a line (19) that Mɛli can follow. All of these utterances are well formed and clearly articulated. The high pitch is maintained throughout by both Meli and her mother. Intervals between utterances are shorter than the usual conversational turn. This bit of play followed a conventionalized sequence, and improvisation was corrected. The formulaic expressions are critical in that they index the type of speech event, teasing.

Language socialization, assertion, and reciprocity

When ɛlɛma is used in triadic situations, the modality of assertion prevails. In socializing language in the modality of assertion, mothers are socializing assertion itself. For Kaluli, this means being strong and independent and is related to the notion that ''a man is expected to look out for his interests himself'' (E. L. Schieffelin 1976:117). In interactional terms, this means to request with imperatives, to challenge, and to confront with rhetorical questions – to say something powerful to get what you want but to say it without destroying social relationships. Through their participation in socializing routines with ɛlɛma, young children learn to use language to ask for what they want and to hold on to what they do not wish to share. The modality of assertion is an integral affective component of triadic utterances with ɛlɛma, but assertion itself is never made verbally explicit except through prompts such as ''Speak loudly!'' or ''Say it again!'' That is, parents do not say ''Be assertive!'' but socialize children into ways of speaking that express assertiveness, which for Kaluli is a major modality in which to act.

Caregivers' socialization of assertion through ɛlɛma routines is carried out through activities in which both sharing and speaking are mediated at the same time. In these socializing contexts, a triadic relationship eventually develops into a dyadic one. Participation in talk starts out as a three-way relationship as caregivers speak for infants and supply lines to young children. Eventually the primarily triadic organization of talk shifts so that even when talk is multiparty, it is no longer heavily mediated by one person on behalf of another. Through these exchanges, one is initially given a voice, and then one eventually develops his or her own. This is what happens in terms of sharing as well: Caregivers guide children through routines of giving and taking. This type of mediation is also critical in socializing appeal. The organization, however, is different, because children are socialized to respond to the appeals of others. Again, as we see in the next chapter, a triadic relationship between mother, infant, and older child is necessary for the initiation and development of the dyadic relationship of adɛ.

Talk, like other forms of social action, requires giving attention to the other and taking into account what the other wants or needs. Turns of talk, like other forms of social exchange, are given and taken, negotiated and refused. Talk is not only instrumental but is also a metaphor for what happens in exchange: Meaning is offered and taken, asked for and given. Children through these exchanges of mediated or assisted talk are learning about reciprocity as well. They are learning about the form and functions of giving and taking, *reciprocity* that reciprocity and social relationships are bound to one another, and that language and sentiment are instrumental in effecting the bond. Reciprocity, then, is also mediated in several ways, socially by the fact that caregivers play such an active role in determining the sequencing and outcomes of sharing encounters, and by language, which itself can be given in place of food, objects, and attention. Eventually, the active role of caregivers in these exchanges diminishes as children are able to negotiate their own way through interaction. The role of language, however, in this process of mediation and negotiation becomes even more important as children become increasingly autonomous, confident, and interdependent.

5. Socialization of appeal and the *adɛ* relationship

A major modality of Kaluli children's language socialization is assertion, one of two major interactional strategies of Kaluli everyday life. The contrasting modality, which is also essential, is appeal – a strategy in which one person attempts to get something by making others "feel sorry for" (*nofɔlab*) him or her. A person making a request based on appeal is seen as being helpless; this state in turn is responded to by compassion and assistance. Persons responding to such an appeal, however, must feel that they are giving of their own free will (*inɛli asulɛsɛgɛ* 'having thought of it himself/herself'). Reasons for giving or helping are not phrased in terms of meeting a demand as in assertion, or in terms of obligation or duty, but rather in terms of sympathy: "Because I felt sorry for, I gave" (*Nofɔlabiki, mi*). These terms, assertion and appeal, apply to modalities of action (E. L. Schieffelin 1976:117–34), and though Kaluli have no metalinguistic terms for these modalities, they are nonetheless central.

Children do not have to be socialized to learn how to appeal. Because very young children are thought to be helpless and vulnerable, people feel sorry for them and thus give to them. Until children begin to use language, they have no other stance, and the only social role they play is recipient, one who receives. Instead of teaching children how to appeal, the concern is with socializing children to respond sympathetically and empathetically to the appeals of others, to feel sorry for and give to others who appeal, and thus to take the role of one who is moved and gives. To participate in Kaluli society, one must draw on a range of interactional strategies acquired in childhood: One must be able to ask assertively as well as respond appropriately to assertive requests and statements; one must be able to move others to give or help as well as be moved by others and respond by giving or helping.[1]

The essence of appeal is embodied in the *adɛ* relationship that develops between siblings, particularly between older sisters and younger brothers. *Adɛ* is one of the profound social and sentimental relationships; outside of mar-

Portions of this chapter appeared in my "A sociolinguistic analysis of a relationship," *Discourse Processes* 4(2) (1981): 189–96, and are reprinted with permission of Ablex Publishing Corporation.

riage, it is the most important bond between men and women. The *adɛ* relationship is important in everyday interaction, is evoked in song poetics, and is presented in myth. Feld (1982a:20–43) analyzes the use of *adɛ* in poetic song texts. On ceremonial and funerary occasions, people sing about "having no *adɛ*," which is extremely powerful in evoking sadness and weeping. In myth, where the relationship is idealized, its violation elucidates its significance.

The *adɛ* relationship in myth

The boy who became a muni *bird*

Once there was a boy and his older sister; they called each other *adɛ*. One day they went off together to a small stream to catch crayfish. After a short while the girl caught one; the brother as yet had none. Looking at the catch, he turned to her, lowered his head, and whined, "*adɛ, ni galin andoma*" – "*adɛ*, I have no crayfish." She replied, "I won't give to you; it is for mother."

Later, on another bank of the stream she again caught one; her brother was still without. Again he begged, "*adɛ, ni galin andoma.*" Again she refused. "I won't give to you; it is for father." Sadly he continued to hope for a catch of his own. Finally, at another bank, she again caught a crayfish. He immediately begged for it, whining, "*adɛ*, I really have nothing." She was still unwilling: "I won't give to you; it is for older brother."

He felt very sad. Just then he caught a tiny shrimp. He grasped it tightly; when he opened his palm, it was all red. He pulled the meat out of the shell and placed the shell over his nose. His nose turned a bright purple red. Then he looked at his hands; they were wings.

When she turned and saw her brother to be a bird, the older sister was very upset. "Oh *adɛ*," she said, "don't fly away." He opened his mouth to reply, but no words came out, just the high falsetto cooing cry of the *muni* bird, the Beautiful Fruitdove (*Ptilinopus pulchellus*).

He began to fly off, repeating the *muni* cry, a descending *eeeeeeee*. His sister was in tears at the sight of him; she called out, "Oh *adɛ*, come back, take the crayfish, you eat them all, come back and take the crayfish." Her calling was in vain. The boy was now a *muni* bird and continued to cry and cry. After a while the cry became slower and more steady, "Your crayfish, you didn't give it to me. I have no *adɛ*, I'm hungry." (Ibid. 20–1)

In order to understand the socialization of the *adɛ* relationship in a broader cultural frame, I draw on the myth of the boy who became a *muni* bird. Feld analyzes this myth in terms of seven major cultural themes. These include male, female, and the *adɛ* relationship; food, hunger, and reciprocity; sorrow, loss, and abandonment; birds; weeping; poetics; and song. As we have seen, in socializing the *adɛ* relationship, food sharing is frequently from older sister to younger brother. Younger brothers feel "owed" and appeal to their older sisters to give them what they want. Older sisters are socialized to respond to this type of appeal and to give. Thus, for an older sister to deny her younger brother's request based on appeal is a violation of the expectations he has about the *ade* relationship.

Comparing mothers' socialization of the *ade* relationship with the way *ade* is depicted in myth, we see the consequences of a breach of expectations. The young boy in the myth, who Kaluli said was like Abi or Wanu, appeals to his older sister, who is likened to Abi's or Wanu's older sisters, for food. Both the little boy's utterance "*Ade*, I have no crayfish" and his voice quality (*geseab*) are aimed at making his sister feel sorry for him and give. However, each request is refused as the sister places other family members before her younger brother. This entire sequence, in fact, runs contrary to all norms of Kaluli social practice, especially in light of the expectations created by mothers socializing their children into the *ade* relationship. In denying food to her younger brother who has appealed to her, she is denying a basic role obligation.

Building on analyses by E. L. Schieffelin (1976), Feld discusses sorrow, loss, and abandonment, emphasizing how Kaluli deeply fear loneliness. No companionship, no assistance, no one to share food with is perhaps the most frightening human state. Loneliness is seen as nonassistance, the condition of being without relationships. It is clear that sharing with others is extremely important to Kaluli. "As human relationships are actualized and mediated through gifts of food and material wealth, so these things come to stand for what is deeply felt in human relationships" (E. L. Schieffelin 1976:150). And, as Feld points out, "It thus makes sense that Kaluli equate breakdowns in reciprocity, assistance, sharing, hospitality, and camaraderie with vulnerability, loss, abandonment, isolation, loneliness, and ultimately, death" (1982:29). The fact that the older sister consistently denies her younger brother food signals the fact that he has no *ade*, no one in the relationship of giving in response to his request based on appeal. No one feels sorry for him; no one is moved by his situation. As Feld further suggests, "For the boy hunger becomes isolation; denial of the expected role becomes abandonment. The anxiety that results is both frightening and sad; instantly the boy is diminished to a nonhuman state" (ibid. 29).

Feld takes up a number of other important themes in his analysis of this myth, but one particularly relevant to this discussion is the symbolic importance of birds to the Kaluli. Reference was made earlier to the significance of birds in Kaluli beliefs: Children must not eat certain birds, lest they never speak. Kaluli perceive children, with their high-pitched voices and their repetitive vocalizations, to be like birds. Children are told not to speak "bird talk" (*ɔbe to*) but "good talk" (*to nafa*), "hard words" (*to halaido*). In addition, Kaluli believe that birds are *ane mama*, spirit reflections of their dead. In actual or symbolic death, one becomes a bird. Thus, the consequence of the breach of the *ade* relationship is that the boy turns into a bird; his crying is the origin of weeping.

The significance of the *adɛ* relationship is not limited to children; it is not just a strategy that mothers use to get older daughters to assist with the younger children. By socializing the *adɛ* relationship in childhood, where events and associations are largely out of the control of young individuals, mothers provide their children with a very meaningful bond between siblings, one in which appeals will rarely be refused and one that is important throughout their lives.

While the kin relationships of brother (*ao*) and sister (*ado*) are "given" by virtue of the Kaluli notion of shared substance (E. L. Schieffelin 1976:55), *adɛ* is a unique relationship between older sisters and younger brothers encouraged by mothers in early childhood. *Adɛ* behavior is rooted in gender-role socialization in which younger brothers are socialized to appeal to an older sister for goods, services, and attention. The older sister is moved and "feels sorry for" her younger brother and acts toward him in an unselfish and nurturing way. While the brother and sister interactions involve both assertion and appeal, *adɛ* relationships are realized exclusively by the demeanors appropriate to appeal.

Adɛ is not a term that Kaluli talk about. In family interactions with small children, however, it appears in transcripts of the earliest interactions recorded.

Example 5.1. Mɛli (24.3) is with her mother and baby brother Seligiwɔ (7.). There is a large bush knife near the little boy.

[As the mother leaves the room, in a soft voice to Mɛli]: He will accidentally cut himself. Stay here and watch over *adɛ*.

inexplicability or explaining adɛ

When I asked adults about this term, they could not explicate its meaning, but would point to Abi or Wanu and their older sisters, or to Mɛli and her younger brother, saying *Adɛyɔm* 'That's really *adɛ*'. When I asked what two siblings called each other or how they referred to each other, Kaluli gave me proper names or kin terms, but never the term *adɛ*. This term was used in family interactions, but I could not get Kaluli to explain it to me as they could explain kin terms and other reciprocal relationship terms (e.g., *daiyo* 'namesake'; *nɛsu* 'one who gives/receives bridewealth').

Linguistic marking of kin and *adɛ* terms

From the time they are small, siblings spend a great deal of time together, eating, bathing, playing, and sleeping in the same house. Only when they are 4 or 5 years old do they form more independent relationships with same-sex peers and begin to spend less time with younger siblings and more time with older ones. Throughout their time together in the house, at the streams, and walking around in the bush, brothers and sisters develop a sense of shared experience in relationship to everyday routines, associating actions and events with particular places and with each other. Mothers are quick to point out and comment on ground names, significant events that happened at a particular place, who has planted gardens. A whole world of associations develops for children in the context of time spent together with siblings.

In these situations, brothers and sisters use a variety of different names for each other. The selection of one or another of these names depends on a particular aspect of the relationship that the speaker wants the addressee to attend to at that moment. Siblings use proper names, kin terms, and relationship terms, affectionate names and teasing names.

Kaluli kinship terms for brother and sister are relatively uncomplicated linguistically. They do not indicate sex of speaker, age in relationship to speaker, or whether the relationship is full or half. The kin terms for brother and sister are:

nao 'my brother'	*nado* 'my sister'
gao 'your brother'	*gado* 'your sister'
ene ao 'his/her/their brother'	*ene ado* 'his/her/their sister'

The 1st and 2nd person possessive prefix (*n-*, *g-*) and the 3rd person possessive pronoun *ene* are part of the kin term. In address, the terms are used (1st/2nd person) with or without the unbound possessive pronoun; e.g., *Ni nado!* 'My sister' or *Nado!* In reference, the possessive pronoun is used with the kin term; e.g., *gi gao* 'your brother'.

Contextual constraints on kin and adɛ terms

Sociolinguistic evidence points out important differences between kinship and other relationships and the special *adɛ* relationship. These sociolinguistic differences (i.e., at the morphological and pragmatic level) index critical social differences between the sets of terms and the relationships they mark.[2] Morphologically, *adɛ* functions differently from kin and other relationship terms. All kin and other relationship terms take a possessive prefix or pronoun (e.g., *enesɔk* 'his/her cross-cousin'; *ni daiyo* 'my namesake'; *gɛsu* 'your bridewealth giver/recipient'). *Adɛ* does not conform to the rules of marking possessive or referential relationships, and unlike those other terms, *adɛ* cannot be expressed with a possessive form.[3] In address, one says *adɛ;* **nadɛ* and **ni adɛ* are not said. Nor can one refer to someone else as **gadɛ* or **ene adɛ*.

Kin terms are used often and in a wide variety of social situations. In address they are used:[4]

· in greetings, exuberantly and reciprocally; proper names can be used with them (e.g., *Nao!* 'My brother!'; *Nao Wanu!* 'My brother Wanu!')
· as attention-getting devices in conversations, as openers, or for calling out

- in requests as vocatives when the speaker is either demanding something or asking in a neutral way (e.g., *Nao, helebe dimina* 'Brother, give me the knife')
- after hearing a report of a sad event, used following an expressive word to show compassion (e.g. *Heyo, nao* 'Alas, my brother')
- in any situation in the assertive modality (e.g., in sequences with *ɛlɛma*)

In reference, kin terms are used:

- when reporting an event, or in reported speech (e.g., *Gi gadowɛ, "Mɛn mɛni meno" ɛlabe* 'Your sister said, "Come and eat!" ')
- in making inquiries after an individual (e.g., *Ni nao hɛh?* 'Where is my brother?')

Sibling terms may be extended to a variety of individuals beyond the immediate family. Classificatory brothers and sisters, regardless of whether they reside within or outside the village, are called by these terms, and the range of usage for address and reference described above applies to them as well. Contextually, *adɛ* is more restricted than kin terms. In fact, *adɛ* cannot be used in any of the situations listed as appropriate for the sibling kin terms.

There is only one speech act in which it is appropriate to use *adɛ* as a vocative, namely, when one is begging for something or wants someone to feel sorry for one and fulfill a request. Consistent with the appeal modality, *adɛ* must be uttered in a soft, plaintive voice, which the Kaluli call *geseab* 'makes someone feel sorry'. Older children and adults use *adɛ* as a vocative in such requests, sisters use it reciprocally, and brothers use it with older sisters. Brothers, however, never use it with each other, and instead use *nao* 'my brother' when appealing for something, letting voice quality and demeanor convey the affective stance. Mothers use the term *adɛ* in reference, addressing one child and referring to the other as *adɛ*. They use it only with their own children (or grandchildren), referring to sons up to the age of 6 and to daughters up to the age of 15 or such time as they no longer have control over their activities. In contrast to the wide range of people one calls brother or sister (classificatory siblings both in and out of the village), only a limited number of individuals get referred to and addressed with *adɛ*: only those siblings with whom one has grown up and shared everyday familial experiences.

The referential use of *adɛ* can (with few exceptions) be illustrated in this way:

	Referent	
Addressee	Older sister	Younger sibling
Older sibling	—	*adɛ*
Younger sibling	*adɛ*	—

Thus, there must be two persons who are in the appropriate relationship to each other in order for the term to be used. In addition, the *adɛ* term is reciprocal in reference – that is, mothers, who primarily use *adɛ* with children in this manner, can address an older sibling and refer to a younger sibling as *adɛ*, or address a younger sibling and refer to an older sister as *adɛ*.

Adɛ is a context-specific, linguistically marked relationship term. It evokes the *adɛ* relationship. The *adɛ* relationship differs from the sibling relationship in that the latter is *independent of situation* – a child is a brother or sister whether walking in the forest, playing, or sleeping. The *adɛ* relationship is evoked only under particular circumstances and is specific to situations in which a person needs something and appeals to someone to feel sorry for him or her. These situations in which *adɛ* is used become part of the meaning of the relationship created. While it would not be pragmatically inappropriate to use kin terms ("brother" or "sister") in any of the contexts in which *adɛ* is used, the rhetorical force of the utterance would not be the same. A speaker's use of *adɛ* makes the proposition in which it is embedded far more compelling. Since a sister (*ado*) or brother (*ao*) is someone you can sometimes hit (see Examples 8.3, 8.4) and not share with (see Example 4.4), the use of the kin terms is not specific to the affective compassionate response mothers (and others) wish to elicit in certain types of interaction.

In conversation, the kin terms "brother" and "sister" do not have the specific affective components that *adɛ* has. Kin terms are general and too diffuse to have the strategic and rhetorical force of a relationship term like *adɛ*. This particular relationship term is affect-marked in that it is never used as a neutral term. The meaning of *adɛ* is situationally specific: It conveys expectations of nurturing, sharing, and giving out feelings of compassion. *Adɛ* indexes the complex of affect and expectations that the mother is both creating and drawing on every time she uses the term with her children. The choice of a lexical item is "constrained by what the speaker intends to achieve in a particular interaction as well as by expectations about the other's reactions and assumptions" (Gumperz 1977:196).

Socializing the *adɛ* relationship

Adɛ is socialized through linguistic and social referencing. The recurrent use of paralinguistic phenomena such as intonation, voice quality, volume, and pitch in addition to the term *adɛ* create the *adɛ* relationship. These phenomena, which Gumperz (1977) has called contextualization cues, are used to signal how contexts are to be interpreted. The appropriate use of and response to contextualization cues presuppose certain linguistic and sociocultural knowledge. Children acquire the knowledge necessary to interpret, respond to, and produce socially appropriate interactional sequences through participation in them. The *ade* relationship is socialized as it is displayed through predictable verbal exchanges organized by mothers and in which children play an active role.

In families with two young children, many opportunities arise in which mothers create the *ade* relationship. In ongoing interactions, a mother stops what she is doing, focuses her attention on the two children, and secures the attention of the older child. Speaking with a soft, plaintive quality (*geseab* 'make someone feel sorry'), using an expressive word, *wɔ* 'have pity' or *heyo* 'feel sorry (for someone else)', she addresses the older child softly and slowly, marking a switch in tone (key) from whatever was previously occurring. She tells the older child either to terminate or to initiate a specific activity with a younger sibling, referring to that sibling as *ade*. What mothers say (message content) tells the child how to act. How mothers say it (message form) communicates to the child how he or she is to feel. The way in which the mothers speak, voice quality, and use of expressive words and the relationship term *ade* (contextualization cues) create an ambiance of intimacy, appeal, and compassion. Message form and message content socialize children to feel compassion, feel sorry for a helpless infant, and comply with their mothers' requests.

In these interactions, mothers, using the *ade* term (in reference) and its co-occurring contextualization cues, socialize children into a set of motivations, expectations, and assumptions, informing them how they should act as well as how they should feel. In addition, since two children are involved, mothers create "structures of expectations" (Tannen 1979) for the younger one, showing how acting in an appealing or begging way will elicit compassion and assistance. Given that mothers repeatedly use this formulaic set of contextualization cues in recurring situations, the appropriate mood and behaviors are presented in and as a unified scenario. Both children are socialized into their *ade* relationship roles, and as additional children come into the family, the roles of younger and older sibling are played out between different members. Children who know how to appeal are socialized to feel sorry for and give to others.

In addition to telling children what they must not do to *ade*, mothers express three salient positive concerns in creating the *ade* relationship: Children must share with and give food and objects to *ade*, take care of *ade*, and be with *ade*.

[margin note: positive concerns in the ade relationship]

How not to act

Given their energy, curiosity, and lack of social knowledge, 2- to 4-year-olds will sometimes treat younger siblings in ways the mother views as inappropriate. They may play too roughly, tease them with objects, bother them while they are nursing. Reprimands (negative directives) to the older child take the following form:

Example 5.2. Mɛli (26.) is playfully offering my rubber sandal to her brother Seligiwɔ (9.).

Mother → Mɛli → Seligiwɔ: You take! – ɛlɛma.
[Waving sandal at baby]   gu! / gu! / there! /
[As baby reaches, Mɛli pulls the sandal away.]
Mother → Mɛli: No, what's this?
[Softly] *Heyo*, don't do that to **adɛ**.

Example 5.3. Abi (35.2) is with his mother and baby brother (3.). Abi tries to pull off the baby's string belt.

Mother → Abi: Heyo, don't do that to **adɛ**.

In sequences like these, mothers verbally tie the two children together by speaking to the older child and referring to the younger one. Her appeal to the older child to "feel sorry for" is conveyed by her voice quality (*geseab*) and sympathy-eliciting expressive *heyo*, and that is the affective stance being socialized as a response to a younger, helpless sibling. Children between the ages of 2 and 4 receive many negative directives, such as "Don't disturb *adɛ*" (who is asleep), "Don't take *adɛ* outside" (it's cold), "Don't startle *adɛ*," and "Don't tease *adɛ*" (*dikidiɛsabɔ*). Reasons and consequences are sometimes given (Examples 5.1, 5.6) but at other times are not (Examples 5.2–5.5).

It is important not to hit or hurt *adɛ*, and this message is repeatedly brought to the child's attention. In fact, if a mother thinks that her child is about to hit a sibling (younger or older) for no apparent reason, she will use the term *adɛ* in reproaching the child.

Example 5.4. Wanu (27.3) is with his mother and baby sister (1.), who is crying.

[Pretending to hit baby]   ¹don't cry! /
²Mother → Wanu [softly]: One doesn't hit **adɛ**.
                                              ³**adɛ** · **adɛ** · don't cry! /
⁴Mother → Wanu →> Baby [softly]: Don't cry.
[Softly]   ⁵don't cry /

Example 5.5. Wanu (27.3) hits his sister Binalia (5 yr) for no apparent reason.

Binalia → Wanu [yelling]: Wanuwɛ!
Mother → Wanu: You don't do like that to **adɛ**. Stop, don't hit.

Example 5.6. Mage (10 yr) begs salt from Suɛla (23.), and Suɛla threatens to hit her with fire tongs.

Mother → Suɛla: One doesn't hit. One doesn't hit.
                                    no! /
What do you mean, "no!"? Did you come by yourself?! Did you go by yourself?! Having been carried, you came. **Adɛ** comes and carries you. One doesn't hit.

In Example 5.4, the mother appeals to Wanu not to hit his baby sister, referring to her as *adɛ*. When he says, "*Adɛ*, don't cry!" in an inappropriately

Figure 18. Isa sharing food with her younger brother, Wanu, and her friend Ea.

loud voice, his mother repeats "Don't cry," omitting the term *adϵ* but using a comforting tone of voice. *Adϵ* is not used as a vocative with a negative imperative.

While the *adϵ* term usually refers to a younger sibling, it is also used to elicit compassionate feelings toward an older sister who takes care of the younger child. In Example 5.5, the mother uses the *adϵ* term as part of the reason why Wanu should not hit his sister in that situation. Hitting for no reason is treated differently from specific events organized by mothers where they encourage their sons to chase and hit their older sisters (see Examples 8.2–8.4). After Suϵla (Example 5.6) is told not to hit her older sister and says, "No!" her mother confronts her. Using rhetorical questions, she emphasizes that *adϵ* (her older sister) takes care of her and carries her in the bush; that is reason not to hit her. Sisters are not supposed to hit each other in any situation (see Chapter 8).

Giving and sharing

Mothers are explicit about what children ought to do in responding to *adϵ*. One of the most important things is sharing and giving. Mothers display the model behavior that they want their children to emulate.

Example 5.7. Wanu (29.), his infant sister Henga (2.), older sister Binalia (5;6), and mother are sitting around the cooking fire. Wanu is holding a crayfish that his mother wants to cook.

Figure 19. Mobiya carrying Suela, her younger sister.

Figure 20. Yogodo digging sweet potatoes with her younger brother Abi.

[1]Mother → Wanu [plaintively]: *Wɔ*, after cooking let's give it to
adɛ, to Henga.
                                        [2]huh? /
[3]After cooking, let's give it to Henga.
                                        [4]huh? /
[5]To Henga.
[6]Binalia → Wanu →> Mother: Yes – ɛlɛma.
                                        [7]no! /
[Other talk for 1 min 20 sec]
[8]Mother → Wanu: To **adɛ**, after it's cooked I'll give it to **adɛ**.
[Holding out crayfish]   [9]this? /
[10]Yes, for **adɛ**, I'll cook it for **adɛ**.
[Re crayfish]   [11]this? /
[12]Yes.
[Wanu gives crayfish to mother and she cooks it.]
[Other talk for 2 min 10 sec]
[Mother has cooked crayfish; Wanu sees
it.]   [13]to me! /
[14]Mother → Wanu: *Wɔ*, I'm giving to **adɛ**, I'm giving it to **adɛ**.
[15][Offering Wanu a piece]: You eat this.
[16]Binalia → Mother [whining]: *Wɔ*, to me.
[17]Mother → Binalia: You eat something else!
[18]Binalia → Mother: *Wɔ*, to me.
[19]Mother → Binalia: *Wɔ*, I'm giving it to **adɛ**. You'll eat greens,
I'm giving it to **adɛ**.
[Wanu tries to grab a piece of crayfish.]

[20]Mother → Wanu: You've had enough. The head is mine. It (the meat) I'm giving to **adɛ**.
[Loudly to mother]   [21]*don't give adɛ! /
[22]Mother → Wanu [plaintively]: Wɔ, I'm giving **adɛ**, to Kobake, she's hungry.

The mother introduces the idea of giving the crayfish to the baby (line 1), framing her suggestion with the expressive *wɔ* 'feel sorry for' and the term *adɛ* followed by the baby's name, Henga, thus associating the two. Binalia (line 6) tells Wanu to agree, but he refuses. The mother brings up the idea again (line 8), referring to the baby only as *adɛ*, saying, "I'll give to *adɛ*." In using the 1st person present tense of the verb "give," instead of the imperative form, she tells Wanu what she will do, rather than telling him to give. She tries to get him to agree to her proposal, which depends on his voluntarily giving up the crayfish, which he is holding. After the crayfish is cooked, Wanu asks for it, and rather than refuse Wanu directly, his mother responds plaintively (line 14) "Feel sorry, I'm giving it to *adɛ*." However, she offers Wanu a piece. Binalia, who was not offered any, appeals to her mother, and this elicits a sharp refusal (line 17). After Binalia's second appeal (line 18), the mother reframes her response, soliciting compassion from Binalia, claiming that her own action is on behalf of the baby and that Binalia's self-denial should be as well. After claiming the head for herself, the mother tells the others she is giving the best part, the meat, to *adɛ*.

Wanu protests, using a pragmatically inappropriate utterance "*Don't give *adɛ*!" (line 21). His mother uses several linguistic resources in response to emphasize that the recipient is the baby: plaintive voice, an expressive, the *adɛ* term, the name Kobake (what Kaluli call a newborn girl before she receives her own proper name), and a reason, "She's hungry." (The 2-month-old infant has shown no interest throughout.) The linguistic resources she uses are the reasons for giving. The idea here is that sharing with the younger child constitutes the relationship between siblings; one should anticipate desires as well as fulfill explicit requests.

While mothers (for socialization purposes) propose the desires of infants too young to pay attention, they are sensitive to indications of interest from toddlers and young children and frequently ask older children to be responsive to the initiating moves of younger children.

Example 5.8. Mɛli (28.3) is eating a banana, and her brother (11.) is looking at her.
Mother → Mɛli [softly]: Wɔ, give half to **adɛ**.
[Mɛli doesn't; the baby crawls away.]

Example 5.9. Abi (31.2), his sister Yogodo (5;6), and their mother are eating ginger. Abi drops his.
Mother → Abi: *I'll* look for it, you wait.
Mother → Yogodo: Yogodo!

Yogodo → Mother: Yea?
Mother → Yogodo: Give your ginger to **adɛ**.
Yogodo: I'll break mine in half and give.
Mother → Abi →> Yogodo: Yogodo, I want ginger – ɛlɛma.

Example 5.9 illustrates how mothers switch between the term *adɛ* and the proper name when asking for food. Once the mother asks Yogodo to give ginger to *adɛ* and Yogodo agrees, the mother no longer evokes the *adɛ* relationship. She tells Abi to ask for ginger, using Yogodo's proper name. The *adɛ* term is not used, because Yogodo has already agreed to give the ginger; in addition, it would not be appropriate in this type of request with ɛlɛma.

Sometimes mothers initially refer to the younger child by name instead of by *adɛ*, and if the older child does not comply, they recast the request substituting *adɛ* for the proper name, appealing to the older child on behalf of the younger one in a plaintive voice using expressives. The use of *adɛ* adds rhetorical force to requests and implicitly adds the reasons why the child should do as the mother says. However, when children do not comply, there is little else mothers can do, and the issue is dropped for the time being. In contrast, when *adɛ* is used in address, speakers use it as an initial vocative; it is not used to escalate or add force to a request that is not met.

In many cases, older children comply when asked to give something to a younger one. However, there are times when the younger child has begged and the mother has intervened on behalf of the younger child, using *adɛ* in her request, and still the older child does not want to give. On rare occasions, mothers physically intervene and take the desired object from the older child, which results in angry tantrums from the older child. It is important not to frustrate a young child who has begged for something, but it is not good to force someone to give up what he or she has.

[handwritten margin note: when adɛ is not successful]

In most cases when *adɛ* is used in reference, older children are asked to act with regard to the younger one. However, the reverse also happens (see Examples 5.5, 5.6). Mothers encourage sharing between siblings, using the *adɛ* relationship when possible, especially when the older one is a girl and there is nothing to be gained by not giving. Thus there is some reciprocity expected in the *adɛ* relationship, but not a lot.

Example 5.10. Abi (35.2) is eating sugar cane. Yogodo (6 yr) begs for some.

Yogodo → Abi: Abi, I want (some) sugar cane.
[Abi gives a piece to his mother.]
Mother → Abi: *Heyo,* give it to Yogodo, if you are unwilling (to eat it yourself), give to Yogodo, half to **adɛ**.
                                  no! /
[Abi gives the rest of the sugar cane to his mother.]
Mother: I'll break it in the middle.
[She does and gives half to Yogodo.]

Nurturing and caregiving

Another important component of the *ade* relationship is nurturing and care-giving, and this aspect of the relationship is gender-specific – mothers are socializing girls to be mothers. While boys are asked to give food and objects to younger siblings, they are rarely asked to assist with caregiving. This con-trasts with the many requests mothers make to older girls to help with child-minding activities: to "watch over *ade*," "check on the location of *ade*," "bring food to *ade*," "draw water to bathe *ade*." When speaking to older children who have "understanding" (*asugɔ*), mothers often provide addi-tional reasons as a way of adding force to their requests, making the conse-quences of noncompliance more explicit, as in Example 5.1. When daughters are acting on these requests, mothers want them to feel compassion and be moved, to act of their own free will, as all mothers are supposed to. This is what responding to appeal is about and how it differs from responding to an assertive demand. The ability to respond to someone who needs help, to re-spond out of compassion, is instilled from the earliest age, as soon as there are two children. Mothers use *ade* as a way of putting children in this partic-ular role relationship with one another, which makes it harder for one child (in the presence of the mother) to refuse to fulfill the wishes of another, es-pecially the wishes of a younger child.

Recall that the *ade* term is reciprocal in reference and that mothers may also speak to a younger sibling and refer to the older sister as *ade* (see table following Example 5.1 and Examples 5.6, 5.10). For example, when mothers want a young child to seek help from an older sister, they use the term *ade* to encourage the younger child.

Example 5.11. Abi (34.2), Waye (8;9), and their mother, who is carrying an infant and a heavy load of firewood, are returning from bathing. The mother asks Waye to carry Abi up the hill, and she agrees.

Waye → Abi: I'm going!
Mother → Abi: She's going! Go be carried by **ade**.
[Abi refuses.]
You go up there! You go get carried by **ade**.
                                                            no! /
No!
[Abi starts to cry, refusing Waye, and the mother finally carries Abi and everything else.]

As in this example, mothers sometimes have to urge a 3-year-old to submit to the care of older sisters when the younger child is insisting that the mother take care of both him and the infant. Mothers hope to draw on the good feelings that have developed in the context of giving and sharing between younger and older children. When asking younger children to go to the older ones for help, mothers do not use expressives (*heyo* or *wɔ*), nor do they use a plaintive voice (*geseab*). They use *adɛ* with a neutral voice in this context, because they are not eliciting pity but evoking the relationship of trust and caregiving.

Togetherness

The third cultural component of the *adɛ* relationship is togetherness. In reference, this involves the use of the 2nd person dual emphatic pronoun *gain* 'only you two together'. In the example below, Mɛli emphasizes this togetherness by using the 1st person dual emphatic pronoun in encouraging her brother.

Example 5.12. Their mother is settling Mɛli (30.2) and Seligiwɔ (13.) down together.

Mother → Mɛli: Sit on here, then **adɛ** and you two together sit on this.
[To Seligiwɔ]   sit on this / only we two sit /

Using adɛ in reference with same-sex siblings

While *adɛ* is usually used between cross-sex siblings (older sister and younger brother), mothers occasionally use the term to refer to a relationship between young sons under 6 years of age (e.g., Example 5.3). After that age, the *adɛ* term is not used. Mothers more commonly use the kin term *ao* 'brother' when speaking to one boy and referring to another, establishing the general pattern of adult usage, where brothers never use the *adɛ* term to address one other. Because of the closeness that brothers share, they effectively appeal to each other for objects and assistance without invoking the *adɛ* relationship, using kin terms and such other relationship terms as shared names (*wi ɛlɛdɔ*).

The situation between sisters is different. Mothers use the *adɛ* term to speak to one and refer to the other until they are teenagers or no longer under the mother's direction. Sisters continue to use this term with each other as adults, evoking the *adɛ* relationship when asking for help or requesting special objects. Mothers use the *adɛ* relationship as a way to encourage cooperation between sisters as well as to serve their own ends. They will ask one sister to help the other with a chore, using expressives, the *adɛ* term, and a plaintive voice in making the appeal.

Example 5.13. Their mother is speaking to Waye (8 yr) about Yogodo (5 yr), trying to persuade Waye to help her younger sister.

Heyo, **adɛ** is all alone, by herself.

The appeal is based on the fact that if the older one did not help the younger one, the younger one would have to be alone and do the task herself. This is particularly undesirable when the chore requires going any distance into the bush. Using this form of request presupposes that the younger sister has already agreed to do the chore; when mothers get one to agree, they can turn around and use that fact on the other one. Older girls resist this manipulation when it is obvious what mothers are doing.

Mothers actively socialize siblings into a set of shared expectations and behaviors that constitute the *adɛ* relationship. There is predictability across the contexts in which these socializing messages occur, the form and content that these utterances take, and the affective feelings that they display and are supposed to elicit. These verbal interactions constitute how one is to act in the *adɛ* relationship.

Children's understanding of the *adɛ* term

Young children (2–3 yr) make many requests on their own behalf based on appeal. They use only one of the two major expressives, the egocentric, sympathy-eliciting expressive *wɔ* 'have pity for me', but not the sociocentric, sympathy-offering expressive *heyo* 'I feel sorry for you'. Using the expressive *wɔ* with proper names or kin terms (as a vocative), they follow it with the affect-marked 1st person pronoun *nelɔ* 'I want'. In these requests they speak plaintively (or whimper and cry), and because they are still small and people feel sorry for them, this is effective. While many requests are directed to mothers, children with older sisters seek their help and goods as well. Young children, however, use the term *adɛ* infrequently and, according to adult norms, most of the time incorrectly. In one sense, they have no need to use this particular address term; their requests are still effective without it, especially as mothers intervene and use it in reference. During this time, they are being socialized into the *adɛ* relationship; their use of the *adɛ* term is important evidence of what they know, both linguistically and socially, and what they do not.

In spite of the fact that children repeatedly hear their mothers use the term *adɛ* in reference, none of the children use it to refer to other people – which is correct: Only caregivers can use it in reference. In address, all children applied *adɛ* to individuals who could be *adɛ* in the appropriate social situation, showing their sensitivity to addressee selection. The main difficulty children had was use of *adɛ* with an inappropriate verbal demeanor (loud voice) or speech act.

Abi used the *adɛ* term only twice in the recorded samples. In the first, Abi addresses his sister.

Example 5.14. Abi (31.2) is playing with a large tree nut, a wild almond.

[Calling to his sister Yogodo (5;6)]   **adɛ**, look at my wild almond! /
Mother → Yogodo: "Sister, look at my wild
almond, sister!"

Abi is correct in his choice of addressee – in some situations his older sister is called *adε;* however, this is not one of them. Abi was using *adε* in an exuberant way as a vocative to call out and direct someone to look at something. This violates the co-occurrence rules governing *adε* and other linguistic behavior (Ervin-Tripp 1972; Gumperz 1967). Neither this modality (assertive) nor this speech act (directive to look at) can co-occur with *adε*. While his utterance is syntactically correct, it is pragmatically inappropriate.

Mothers are sensitive to children's use of *adε*. In this and other examples (see 5.14, 5.16), they recast children's language and re-present culturally preferred usage in order to inform children both what is to be said and what is to be heard. In repeating Abi's utterance with *adε* as reported speech, substituting the kin term *nado* 'sister' for *adε*, his mother models the appropriate vocative for that particular speech act.

In another use of *adε*, Abi addresses a possibly appropriate addressee and uses one of the contextualization cues, the expressive *wɔ*, but again the situation and speech act are not appropriate.

Example 5.15. Abi (32.2) is playing alone with his sister Suεla (26.). He has tucked some leaves into her string belt, and she, being unwilling to have them there, has pulled them out.

[As Suεla runs from Abi, he calls out]   wɔ **adε!** / wɔ **adε!** /

As in the previous example, Abi uses *adε* assertively in calling out. In both cases, the kin term *nado* 'my sister' is correct. Kaluli described Abi's use of *adε* as "not quite right" (*mahagale siyɔ*). The situation is not one in which the speaker can reasonably elicit sympathy. That might have been what Abi was doing, but his use did not match adult norms.

With a brother only seventeen months younger than herself, Mεli heard the *adε* term in reference from the time she was quite small. However, she had no older siblings she could have called *adε* in making requests, and she did not use it in address to other members of her household, such as her older cousin Mama, which was correct.

In one situation, however, Mεli used *adε* three times, twice in reporting the vocalizations of her brother.

Example 5.16. Mεli (28.3) is playing a peeking game with her brother Seligiwɔ (12.), who is sitting on his mother's lap.

Seligiwɔ [babbling]: adεadεadεadεadε etc.
[To Seligiwɔ]   *say "**adε!**" /
[Baby continues babbling.]
[To mother]   that one is saying / Mother! / that one is
                                         saying / that one is saying / Mother!! / (he)
                                         says "**adε**" /

Mother → Mεli: Yes, he says, "My sister
Mεli."
                              (he) said, "**adε**" /

Based on the similarity of her brother's vocalizations and the word *adε*, Mεli interprets those babblings as his saying *"adε"* and tells him to continue to do so (using the future imperative form of εlεma 'say it'), which is pragmatically incorrect from the adult perspective. Her mother, who is not attending to what the children are doing, initially makes no comment. While Seligiwɔ continues to babble, Mεli excitedly reports his vocalizations to her mother. In her response, her mother provides the adult interpretation of what Mεli is supposed to hear: *nado* 'my sister', not *adε*. Mothers recast an infant's babbling into what is pragmatically appropriate and culturally possible in that situation. In this situation, Mεli is being socialized into a culturally preferred interpretation of the vocalization. Mεli disagrees, and the topic is dropped. Like Abi, Mεli used *adε* inappropriately (*mahagale siyɔ*) in both utterances. *Adε* is not used playfully, assertively, with εlεma, or aside from requests.

These examples illustrate how caregivers actively guide interpretive processes, in particular when children's interpretations violate co-occurrence expectations (Cook-Gumperz & Gumperz 1978). Speech act and mood of the interaction determine mothers' interpretations. Therefore, when children use the term *adε* without the appropriate co-occurrence of message form, content, and contextualization cues, it is uninterpretable as such. Mothers consequently reinterpret children's utterances, reshaping them to conform to co-occurrence expectations. Adults do not support children's nonconventional use of the *adε* term or relationship. By insisting upon and maintaining the restricted context of usage, mothers define, and when necessary recast, children's own emerging interpretations of utterances and events. They display the rules of use and interpretation to children (and researcher) through these exchanges.

Mothers treat children's incorrect use of *adε* differently from errors that are purely linguistic or referential. For example, when children address someone with the wrong proper name, mothers say the correct name or kin term, followed by εlεma, and expect the child to repeat. However, when children use *adε* inappropriately, mothers repeat the correct form of what to say (as in Examples 5.14, 5.16) but do not ask children to repeat it. They do not call attention to the nonconventional usage or make it as explicit as they do with other types of incorrect or inappropriate language.

Mεli did not use *adε* again in the recorded samples, and her response to being told to call her brother suggests that she knows not to call out *Adε!*

Example 5.17. Mεli (27.3) is at home with her mother. Seligiwɔ (11.) is crawling toward another part of the house.

Mother → Mεli: Call out for Seligiwɔ!
[No response from Mεli]
[Soft voice]: Call out (for) **adε**, Mεli.
[Loudly]   Seligiwɔ! /

Here one might have expected Mεli to call out *Adε!*, since her mother used *adε* in the second of her utterances, followed by the imperative "call out" (*holema*), and Mεli could simply have repeated the last utterance. Mεli may have been cued by her mother's shift in voice quality – lowered volume and pitch – when she urged Mɛli to call out and used *adɛ* to add rhetorical force and provide the reason for Mɛli's compliance. By calling out "Seligiwɔ!" Mɛli is calling out appropriately.

After his sister Henga was born, Wanu's mother often told him how to act toward her, using *adɛ* in those interactions. Wanu used the *adɛ* term with the highest frequency of the three children, and like the others he always addressed someone who, in the right context, could be *adɛ*. He also used the term in the wrong modality and with the wrong interactional force in all but one instance.

In Example 5.4 Wanu's inappropriate vocative choice of *adɛ* directed to his infant sister (line 3) (*Adɛ, adɛ,* don't cry!) is similar to Example 5.7, line 20, when after his mother says, "I'm giving to *adɛ,*" Wanu says, "Don't give *adɛ*!" In both instances he uses part of his mother's prior utterance in constructing his own, and in both cases combines the *adɛ* term with his own assertive utterances, producing a pragmatically incorrect utterance.

At 29 months Wanu uses *adɛ* as a vocative plus *wɔ* when begging for food from his older sister Binalia. The form of his utterance is correct. However, since he already has the bigger piece of food, his sister does not (and can't be expected to) give hers to him. She ignores him, as does the mother.

At 30.3 months Wanu used *adɛ* in address once again to his older sister, again an appropriate addressee.

Example 5.18. Wanu (30.3) is watching his sister (8;6) prepare food.

[Neutral voice]   "**adɛ**, I want," later I will say /
                    "adɛ, nelɔ," tifa ɛlɛmɛno /

This example is informative about the development of Wanu's metalinguistic knowledge as he displays what one is supposed to say when appealing for food. He uses the affect-marked 1st person pronoun *nelɔ*. Telling his sister he will ask for food, however, is an inappropriate use of *adɛ*. His sister does not respond to this utterance, and later, when the food is ready, Wanu does not say, "*Adɛ,* I want" to his sister.

By the time girls are 5 years old, they use *adɛ* as a vocative in requests based on appeal, primarily directed to their younger brothers and older sisters. They always use it with the correct demeanor, modality, addressee, and speech act. Unlike adult usage, which is more restricted (only younger siblings may address older sisters as *adɛ*), older girls (but not boys) use it on occasion to beg from their younger brothers. Yogodo and Binalia use the dual exclusive form of the 1st person pronoun (*nani* 'we two') in their requests to siblings, emphasizing that both of them eat – a framing device that is very persuasive. While older children use the *adɛ* term with the appropriate interactional force, it does not always bring the desired effect. Sometimes mothers intervene and undermine the request, but even without the mother's interference, siblings sometimes refuse appeals evoking the *adε* relationship. For children, the occasional refusal has consequences only for immediate events. For adults, it is a different matter. To refuse someone who has evoked the *adε* relationship can cause a serious breach and create tension between the siblings involved.

Assertion and appeal

A developmental perspective

One way to understand young children's socialization into the complementary modalities of assertion and appeal is to assume a developmental perspective, starting with infants who are "without understanding," "soft," helpless, and socially unresponsive.

Mothers with older children repeatedly present infants to them, animating the infants and giving them a voice as they "speak for them," eliciting social responses and creating social relationships between siblings within a triadic (Mo $\rightarrow$ Ch $\rightarrow$> Ch) arrangement. Mothers in this role speak as the infant in an assertive manner, presenting the infant as responsive and articulate. Their presentations of the infant complement what infants already do. Mothers never beg, whine, or appeal to others in the voice of the infant. Older children are socialized to feel sorry for the infant through mothers' speech about infants, but mothers do not elicit those feelings when they speak as the infant. Throughout their first eighteen months, people continue to "feel sorry for" small children and give them what they want. No one likes to see such small children frustrated, angry, or hungry, and people go to great lengths to avoid such situations.

Once children begin to use language, a transition takes place. While people still feel sorry for young children, they say that it is not good for them to go around begging and whining all the time. No longer speaking for children directly, mothers now assist them in speaking to others, using *εlεma* and telling them what to say in triadically organized interactions. Children are socialized through specific linguistic routines into an assertive style of speaking in order to ask for food and objects from others, to get what they want, and to participate generally in social relationships. In these exchanges, as in those with prelinguistic children, mothers provide the verbal skills and the assertive affective modality that is understood as being complementary to the children's "natural" ability to appeal.

As children become more socially and linguistically competent, caregivers increasingly expect them to respond to requests and to share with others. When the child is around the age of 30 months, a new sibling usually arrives, and other important changes in the socialization process occur. The new baby is the center of the mother's attention, the one for whom the mother now provides a voice that constitutes an identity for the infant and a relationship with the older child. At the same time, in the context of the *adɛ* relationship, caregivers socialize older children to de-center themselves and to feel sorry for and give to the infant. When speaking to older children and referring to the younger one as *adɛ*, mothers socialize feelings of compassion, using the very stylistic devices that children will later use themselves when making verbal requests based on appeal. This is different from the direct instruction of ɛlɛma sequences, where as part of an assertive demeanor children are learning communicative skills to obtain things, to protect what is already in hand, and to report information, along with other rhetorical and social skills.

During this time, 2- to 3-year-olds are increasingly cared for by older siblings while mothers go to the gardens with their infants. Older siblings also socialize younger ones to feel sorry for and give to them, and to participate within a framework of social reciprocity. The assertive language strategies that small children acquire help them protect what they do not wish to give up. This is what "hardening" (*halaidan*) and "gaining understanding" (*asugɔ*) are about. Through language, children are socialized into the culturally preferred verbal expressions for, interpretations of, and responses to assertion and appeal. First they must be able to ask in an assertive Kaluli manner, and then through the *adɛ* relationship they are socialized to feel sorry for and give to others.

Transactional consequences

The modalities of assertion and appeal have different rhetorical strategies and interactional outcomes. Speakers' assessment of situations and the demeanor of other participants influence their choice of strategy and type of request. Once a move has been made, speakers must evaluate how the interaction is going and switch strategy if they find that their initial approach is not accomplishing the ends desired. Small children usually adopt one strategy in a given interaction and repeat it in their attempt to get what they want. This is in contrast to older children, who recognize that what they are doing is not effective and try other rhetorical strategies or interactional approaches. One indicator of increasing verbal competence in children is this ability to shift to change strategies during ongoing interaction.

Assertion and appeal have different transactional consequences, too. Young children need to learn both in order to participate in everyday social reciprocity. In this egalitarian society, the emphasis in socialization is on making one's own way, through the establishment and maintenance of social relationships. Individuals are both very independent and dependent on one another. Everyone lives within a complex social network that must be continually rebalanced through sharing and cooperation.

When people appeal to others for food or assistance, they put themselves in a "helpless" position. Their self-presentation is one of vulnerability, which in turn elicits compassion. When someone responds to that appeal, she or he does so having thought of it herself or himself. Kaluli see transactions resulting from such interactions as originating with the one who gives, not with the one who asks. There is no obligation carried over from this interaction to return what is given, since the one who gives "thought of it herself or himself." The one who asks is in this sense not responsible for the giving act. Beginning in infancy, the transactional consequences of appeal are similar throughout the life cycle.

On the other hand, the transactional consequences are different for requests in an assertive modality. When individuals ask in an assertive manner, the giving originates with these demands. In making assertive requests, speakers take responsibility for the subsequent transaction. This is evidenced by individuals who, upon receiving a refusal, remind the other of previous transactions in which the one who is now asking complied with the addressee's demands. This can be done in a joking or a serious manner, adding force to the request. If an individual continues to refuse, he risks the other's anger and a possible breach in the relationship.

This is not to suggest that Kaluli keep close score on all interactions, but rather that sharing is the ideal, the expected, in everyday social interaction – though of course things do not always turn out that way. If someone only begs and appeals to others to give, that person will be viewed as a child to be pitied and considered less than a full participant in social life. On the other hand, if someone is overly demanding, that person will have to be prepared to meet the return requests that are forthcoming, or end up owing returns to the individuals with whom an exchange was not completed. Both modalities provide Kaluli with options and interactional procedures to realize their social relationships.

In family interactions, language plays an important role in enabling children to enter the system of everyday sharing and reciprocity. Before children can use language, very few demands are made on them to share or cooperate. People rarely try to persuade small children to give up anything or demand anything lest the child become angry. Furthermore, since preverbal children get what they want because people feel sorry for them, children who have not yet begun to use language are not seen as initiating any transactions. They are not yet in the system of daily reciprocity.

The situation changes when children begin using assertive language supported by *ɛlɛma*. When children are able to ask without the verbal support of older siblings or adults, they become potential givers. Caregivers ask them to reciprocate, to share food that others have given to them. They also appeal to their children for food, addressing them with a variety of kin and affect-marked relationship terms. When children do not comply, caregivers switch from a strategy of appeal and challenge them, reminding them, often in a sarcastic manner, that they always give and that reciprocity is expected. Thus, in being socialized to ask assertively for what they want from others, children also become accountable and responsible for their demands. When children can initiate exchanges, they are expected to reciprocate and become participants in reciprocal relationships. As children's rhetorical abilities develop, parents, siblings, and other close relatives increasingly demand that the children be responsive and comply with the requests that are made of them, particularly with regard to sharing food.

6. Socializing reciprocity and creating relationships

The story of the boy who became a *muni* bird articulates a central tension in Kaluli social life: the importance of giving and sharing in the face of the desire to keep what one has for oneself. Among intimates, giving and sharing food is an affirmation of relationship, an expression of sentiment and positive feeling. These meanings are expressed in a variety of verbal genres from the formal to the mundane. Song poetics remind us that death, the loss of a relationship, means that particular acts of giving or sharing will no longer occur. Myths recount the expectations of sharing and the consequences of violations, usually loss or abandonment. Everyday interactions are punctuated not only by requests, but also by questions and answers about who has given what to whom.

And yet, not surprisingly, Kaluli refuse to share with one another. At times "uncertainty" and "conflict" best describe situations involving requests to share and give. Daily exchanges between caregivers and children are dominated by negotiations over who will get or give what portion of food. Adults get annoyed, even angry, and children sulk and cry as they are disappointed. Given the enormous amount of verbal energy participants put out to get a small piece of banana or sago from one another, one might think that Kaluli do not have enough to eat; but to the contrary, Kaluli live in an environment with a rich and varied supply of plant and animal foods. There is always enough to eat. The real issues are when to give and how to refuse.

Sharing is not encoded by a specific verb, but is expressed through the verbs *dimina* 'give' and *dima* 'take'. These verbs encode the directionality of action in transferring objects and nothing more. The verb that comes closest to encoding the notion of sharing is the concatenated verb *gulumina* 'having broken (off part), give'. This verb is rarely used in requests, but instead is used when talking about how to share something (breaking it and giving part). It does not encode anything about the socially significant aspects of sharing, nor does it occur in negated forms, as in protests or complaints (*mɔgulumiab* 'he is not breaking off and giving'). The negated form of *dimina* 'give' is used occasionally to complain about someone's not sharing, generally in the

136

habitual tense (*mɔmian* 'one doesn't give') or in the past tense (*mɔmi* 'did not give'); it is seldom used to comment on present or ongoing activities.

The most common way to talk about not sharing is to use one of the very few negative verbs in the Kaluli lexicon, *kidiab* 'one does not share; one refuses to give'. It is used in contexts where the speaker assumes that the other should share, with the implication that a breach in the social relationship could result from this negative behavior. The negated form of the imperative *kidiesabo* 'don't not share' is used to persuade one who is not sharing to do so.

Sharing must be negotiated through talk. In interactions involving food, participants often differ in their goals; reciprocated sharing is not always the desired end for everyone. This creates a tension between autonomy and interdependence, expressed through daily demands and appeals to share food, to cooperate in tasks, to participate in conversation, and even to pay attention. In this egalitarian society, individuals cannot easily compel one another to act. They depend on sociable relationships in which they can expect or negotiate daily cooperation and reciprocity, and through which they can define their personal autonomy. Caregivers use language to constitute these sociable relationships between their children and themselves, mediating both the sharing and the talking about it.

Tension between autonomy and interdependence is evident in children's arguments and complaints and in domestic situations where husbands and wives have similar verbal exchanges. Between intimates, there is never an easy resolution of the problems of interdependence and autonomy of desires. Caregivers rarely hit children, but husbands do have the option of expressing their anger or frustration at their wives through physical as well as verbal means. In public contexts, adults seek ways to keep their feelings less obvious through subtle use of language and the avoidance of direct confrontations, though they are not always successful.

Through language, young children are socialized into culturally specific ways of managing such tension. Young children are socialized both to give and share and to refuse to give and share through elaborate verbal routines. Children learn when and how to share and when and how not to, entailing a sensitivity to considerations of face, relationship, gender, and key. Children's own desires also significantly influence the ways in which a particular sequence is played out. Their responses to given situations affect caregivers' choice of rhetorical strategy and linguistic form. Children, by virtue of their daily participation in such events, acquire a range of interactional options. They experiment with alternative solutions to interactional problems and experience the consequences of their choices. They participate directly as addressees and indirectly as observers of others involved in the negotiation of giving and taking, sharing and refusing. Young children observe or overhear almost everything that goes on; few events are managed privately. In family interactions, requests for sharing and cooperation are repeated daily. Older siblings and parents take predictable roles and stances, drawing on the outcomes of previous events to support their behavior in current ones. Within these repeated events, children develop a set of social expectations and cultural intuitions in addition to the linguistic and rhetorical resources for understanding and participating in them.

In this small community of a hundred individuals, most interactional strategies are common across families. Certain strategies and affective stances, however, figure prominently in some families but not others. In terms of affective stance, Meli's, Abi's, and Suela's mothers all favor persuasive strategies based on appeal to encourage their children to share and cooperate. They evoke kin role reversals, appealing to their children as *nɔ* 'my mother' in requests for food and assistance. They also create non-kin-based relationships marked for positive affect between themselves and their children. These include shared-name relationships (*wi ɛlɛdɔ*) based on sharing special foods (usually meat) evoked with those names. These relationships carry expectations of continued sharing and giving.

Strategies of appeal used by these parents contrast with the strategy predominant in Wanu's family. His parents use a more assertive and demanding style. Threats, statements about the consequences of refusal, and sarcastic comments are often exchanged between Wanu's parents and his older sisters in attempts to control and change each other's behavior. Whereas this style of social control is part of the verbal repertoire in other households, it is limited to last-ditch attempts or to situations where participants are exhausted by frustration.

The caregivers in these families also differ in their responses to children's refusals to share and cooperate. Wanu's mother displays a significant amount of anger and often threatens her older daughters when they flatly refuse or just do not do what is asked of them. Abi's mother expresses her frustration verbally with affective expressives and words like "Why is it like this?!" and usually ends it there. Meli's mother relies on playful teasing and joking to persuade Meli. Parents are not always able to exercise authority or compel their children to do what they want when they want. Everyone has a stake in maintaining some degree of personal autonomy, but all are connected by strong ties of interdependence. In the following sections, we shall examine strategies used by older children and caregivers to socialize the cultural sentiments that underlie reciprocal behaviors and the postures used to avoid compliance.

Sharing: creating expectations

Wanu's mother rarely asks him to share food with her, but his sisters and father ask him often.[1] Requests to Wanu are simple and straightforward, and when he refuses, there are few attempts to persuade him using alternative or affect-intensified request forms, affectively marked proper names (such as *ni Wanu* 'my Wanu'), or other relationship terms. Instead, his father and older sister Isa talk about Wanu's refusals and relate them to immediate or future consequences in other food exchanges.

Example 6.1. On a visit to tape record Wanu (24.1), I brought three sweet bananas for the children and gave one each to Wanu and Binalia. Their sister Isa was not home; their mother, Wadeo, was sleeping. Wanu's father, Baseo, came in and asked Wanu to share some of his banana.

[1]Baseo → Wanu: Feel sorry, some to me.
Wɔ, nuɔ ne.
[Wanu does not give. Baseo sits by the firepit; I give the remaining banana to Baseo.]
[2]Baseo → BBS: My Bambi!
Ni Babiyɔ!
[Wanu, holding his banana, begs for
more from his father, reaching up.]   ε / ε / ε /
[3]Baseo → Wanu: It's finished!
Kɔm!
[Baseo really has another piece, and
Wanu, seeing it, begs.]   ε / ε / ε /
[4]Baseo [eating the remaining piece] → Wanu: No! You didn't give (any of) yours. You don't usually give to me, but I gave to you!
A! Giyɔ mɔmi. Giyɔ nelɔ mɔmiɛsen, kɔsega niyɔ gemɔ miyɔkɛ!
[5]Baseo → Others: My child does a good job of eating sweet bananas.
Nawa magu gen kobale nab.

Baseo's comment (line 4) to Wanu, "You didn't give (any of) yours" states explicitly his reason for refusing as well as expressing his expectation of reciprocal sharing. He makes it clear what sharing entails between himself and Wanu. His second comment (line 5) is directed to other family members about Wanu, and its sarcasm is meant to shame Wanu. Comments stating explicit reasons for refusing were frequently made in conjunction with comments meant to shame.

Kaluli say that these comments made directly to children and made in their presence, talking about them in the 3rd person ("my child") to others, accomplish two important things. First, they are "said to make children think about what they are doing" (*asulumɛki siyɔ*). They remind children of what is expected of them in social relationships. These comments are always said in front of children, never behind their backs. Not only is this consistent with the Kaluli notion of avoiding gossip, but – the second point – it is important for children to hear sarcastic or negative comments made to others about them, because the comments are "said to make them feel ashamed" (*sindi-lomɛki siyɔ*). Sometimes they are told to feel ashamed and asked rhetorically if they are not ashamed. Young children do not answer either of these types of comment. Comments addressed to others are especially not to be challenged. These remarks, always said when situationally relevant rather than at some later time, are made by older children and parents. They are not necessarily aimed at changing immediate behavior, but to affect what they do the next time. Caregivers constitute relationships through sharing and also use sharing to express relationships.

Older siblings join in and make comments when younger children are not sharing. Abi's older sisters often made comments about how infrequently Abi shared what he had, in spite of the fact that he was always getting things from others. They also gave support to their mother when she complained.

Example 6.2. Abi (32.2), his mother, and sisters Yogodo (5;6) and Waye (8 yr) are outside the house. His mother hands him a packet of biscuits, telling him to give some to his sisters. Abi refuses his mother's requests, even those based on appeal using the term *nɛsu*. She has now asked him just to break off a little piece and give it to her.

[Abi is breaking off a small piece of biscuit.]
[1]Mother → Abi: I'll eat (that) [holding out her hand].
Ɔ ne mɛno.
[He gives her a very tiny piece.]
[2]What's that?!
Hɛh ko?!
[3]Yogodo → Waye: He gives only a little to Mother.
Nɔwɔ ba hɛlu lɛsu miab.
[4]Mother → Yogodo: It was really none!
Andomale!
[Abi continues eating.]

Evaluative comments such as lines 3–4 about not sharing or giving enough criticize children indirectly. However, when children are directly challenged, comments usually take the form of sarcastic assertions or rhetorical questions. Neither of these types of utterance, either direct or indirect, is meant to be answered. Indirect comments are not addressed to the person about whom they are made, and direct remarks, rhetorical questions, and sarcastic comments call for no answer. The purpose, however, is similar for both: They are said to shame children and make them think about what they have said or done.

Caregivers are sensitive to children's positive behavior (from the caregivers' perspective), but they never praise children for sharing or giving. They do, however, verbally confirm and support children's comments about sharing. Casual reinforcing comments (line 4) are interwoven with those that are more direct, as in the example that follows.

Example 6.3. Baseo and Wanu (29.) are eating pandanus together, and Wanu has given some to his father.

[1]Father / I just gave / X /
Do / ɔ ne miyabe / X /

²Baseo → Wanu: You just gave?
ɔ ge miyabeyɔ?

> ³I just gave /
> ɔ ne miyabe /

⁴You *too* should give!
Giyɔlo miyalu!

In informal interactions such as these, reciprocity has no finite boundaries; it is continuous and expected. Kaluli follow through on particular exchanges and do not forget a breach, as insignificant as it may seem. And they socialize their children to do the same. Later the same afternoon, Isa cooked a banana for her father and gave it to Wanu to hand over to him. Instead of giving it, Wanu ate it himself. Family members were annoyed and spoke to Wanu directly and indirectly. Among other things, his mother said to Wanu, "Maybe you'll give some of yours" (to your father, since you ate his), and to his sister Isa, "He'll do the same to yours!" (eat your food). A little later, Wanu, who was eating a banana, begged the sweet potato his father was eating. His father responded with two rhetorical questions and no sweet potato.

Baseo → Wanu: What about the sweet potato?! Who ate that (other) banana?!
Siabulu hɛh?! Magu ko abe naba?!

Wanu, however, continued to watch and whine, and kept begging from his father until he was given half the potato. A little later, Wanu begged again, this time for food already in Baseo's mouth, which Baseo took out and gave him. Wanu then begged from his mother, who also gave him food. All of these positive responses were because his parents, feeling sorry for him, gave (*nofɔlabiki, mi*). But when Wanu then grabbed the salt bag and put his food into it, he was met with a very negative outburst from his father: *Seilɔwɔ!* 'You are obviously a witch!', and the bag was quickly removed. When Wanu took without asking, their anger flared. If small children ask, they are usually given food, but one must not take without asking. Calling a child a witch is not a light remark; witches are greatly feared in Kaluli society. They are evil, prey on and kill others, and never participate in reciprocal relations.

Wadeo's requests to Wanu are stylistically consistent. They are generally assertive and straightforward, and when there is an appeal, it is without persuasive elaboration. The majority of Wadeo's requests are framed as demands either to share food or cooperate in tasks. When making requests, Wadeo uses her children's proper names rather than kin or relationship terms (*nɛsu*, 'my bridewealth'; *nɔ* 'my mother'; *wi ɛlɛdɔ* 'shared name') or positive affect markings in conjunction with the names. When the older girls do not share, their parents also make disapproving comments, followed by threatening not to give food or telling the child to go outside when cooperation is not forthcoming. These comments are similar to those made to and about Wanu except that, rather than statements, they are usually rhetorical questions meant to shame. Negatively marked names (*kegayɔ* 'skinny thing'; *kuf aba* 'big belly'; *wɛfi* 'retard') are also used only to older children.

An exception to this demeanor in Wanu's household is in requests on behalf of others, in particular the infant daughter. Wanu's mother begins to draw heavily on the *adɛ* relationship with Wanu and his sisters when little Henga is born. She uses elaborated requests, with expressives and intensified forms, to encourage Wanu and the girls to share food with the baby (see Example 5.7). She also uses the *adɛ* term to encourage Wanu to treat his sisters well and share with them, but there is no great amount of elaboration in these contexts.

Baseo also appeals to his children for food, and like Wadeo, he does not use relationships terms, preferring proper names and simple request forms. His appeals to his son are similar in form to those made to his daughters.

Example 6.4. Baseo repeatedly begs banana from Binalia (using a single form, *Nuɔ diemina* 'Bring some to me'), telling her that he has salt to give and she should give banana; but she refuses. Then Wanu asks Binalia for some banana.
[1] Baseo → Wanu: Did she say, "I'll give to you also!?," that lizard over there!
Gelo miɛnɛnɔ!?, wɔgɔlɔ honomɛyɔ!
[Binalia gives nothing. Several minutes later, Baseo is still annoyed.]
[2] Baseo → Binalia: You don't eat. You often give to me like that.
Gi na! Giyɔ nelɔ mianɔ aun.
[Binalia whines and begs her father for salt. After ignoring her for a while, he finally gives some to her.]

In a great number of exchanges in Wanu's family, such as the one above, there is little elaboration after the initial request is made, but once a request is refused, expectations are made explicit, and elaborate sarcasm, insult, and teasing ensue. When someone continues to refuse, there is little to do but register one's feelings through words, hoping that shaming might effect a change. Notice that Baseo finally gave in to his daughter's request, but not until after he had registered his feelings. Endless playful and not-so-playful arguments centered on issues of not giving and not sharing between parents and children of all ages.

The situation in Mɛli's family differs in several ways. As Christians, her parents describe themselves as following an interactive style called *hɛfɛnolɔ henan* 'one goes softly', a counter to the argumentative and exuberant traditional style. As there are older siblings, it is not clear whether the lack of more assertive "hard" talk around sharing is an artifact of family size or the conscious adoption of this "soft" presentational style. Mɛli's family also has many visitors, including her maternal grandfather and her mother's brothers and sisters of varying ages. These various family members make many requests of Mɛli to share food and also provide contexts for *ɛlema*-supported routines for her to refuse their requests. At the beginning of the study, Mɛli was only 24 months old and was hardly expected to share food. As she got older, however, requests to Mɛli changed in tone, and she was expected to comply.

While relatively few requests for assistance or for food sharing were made of Mɛli in the early samples, the requests that were made were in a well-marked playful key.

Example 6.5. Osolowa is leaving the house and tells Mɛli (26.) to eat with her father, Degelɔ. Both already have food.

Degelɔ [laughing] → Mɛli: You give yours to me! Quickly give it!
Giyɔlɔ nelɔ mina! Boboi mina!

Mɛli does not respond to this request. Degelɔ's rapid delivery and laughter signal that he is playfully teasing her and does not expect her to give him her food when he has plenty. Degelɔ may have been trying to draw Mɛli's mother into a teasing routine, but she was leaving and did not follow up. By the time Mɛli is 26 months old, close relatives playfully ask her for soap, fish, and money, using appropriate kin or, more frequently, relationship terms. Other relatives, overhearing such requests, would turn these dyadic exchanges into triadic ones, telling Mɛli to challenge back, using ɛlɛma plus rhetorical questions like "Who are you?!" or "Is it yours?!" These claims have a playful tone. Through ɛlɛma routines, Mɛli is socialized to respond to a variety of requests made of her, refusing with clever rhetorical questions and challenges. These routines are marked by adults' laughter and enjoyment of Mɛli's ability to hang on to what is hers. Contradictory messages are conveyed – the importance of sharing and the importance of refusing – but both are necessary to the development of social and verbal skills.

In addition to making playful requests Osolowa and others appeal to Mɛli using verbal markers that key serious interaction. These markers include tone of voice and expressive words as well as nonkin reciprocal relationship terms that evoke the sentiment of sharing. Nonkin reciprocal relationships are based on the pervasive Kaluli notion of shared substance. For example, when two individuals share something special, for instance, food, that becomes the basis for sharing a name, usually the name of the food. This reciprocal name, *wi ɛlɛdɔ* 'named alike', indexes a special relationship of expected continued sharing and affection between those two people. It makes public an act of giving; puts it on record and makes it an interactional resource. A particular shared name has currency as long as it is used. These terms provide options to individuals to create additional social relationships based on sharing and affection both within and outside of formal kinship relations. Individuals in any kin relationship except those that involve avoidance can designate and active these relationships, regardless of generation or gender.

Most *wi ɛlɛdɔ* are based on highly desirable protein foods, including *ni mahi* 'my bandicoot', *ni handa* 'my landcrab', and *ni ɔbɛ inso* 'my baby bird'. Names between individuals may change if another shared item replaces an earlier one in importance; for example, two people may call each other *ni oga* 'my pandanus' but later on share bandicoot and call each other *ni mahi*. Mεli's mother encourages her to use *wi εlεdɔ* not only with her but with cousins, her father, and me. Abi's mother seldom uses *wi εlεdɔ* with her children, but she encourages them to use the names with their father. Wanu's family does not use *wi εlεdɔ* terms.

There are other named reciprocal relationships in Kaluli society used among adults but extended to children that encode strong positive affect and sentiments of sharing. One of the most important of these is *nεsu* 'giver/receiver of bridewealth', a reciprocal address term used between a married couple and the individuals who contributed bridewealth to assist the husband's family. *Nεsu* is a combination of the words *nε* 'my own' and *su* 'compensation' (what is given to the wife's family in return for the loss of their daughter). It is used exuberantly in greetings among adults as well as in appeals. The primary adult usage indexes the personal connection between individuals through specific bridewealth contributions (axes, shells, pigs), with the expectation of return when a daughter from that union marries. In the *nεsu* relationship there is the expectation of general sharing and cooperation, and adults may use this relationship with each other as much or as little as they please.

Within families, the affective range of *nεsu* is restricted in that it is used only in appeal or when expressing empathy; its range of application is extended to use between caregivers and children and between older siblings. Caregivers use *nεsu* only as a vocative to evoke this relationship and appeal for food or assistance from children or to soothe a child during a temper tantrum. Food is offered, and the child is appealed to as *nεsu*; the child is urged to eat as a way of *henulab* 'buying off his anger'. When Mεli took my rubber thong away from Seligiwɔ, Osolowa appealed to her thus: "*Nεsu*, feel sorry and give the shoe back to your brother." And when Mεli hurt her foot, her mother, offering her sympathy, said *Nεsumalε* 'My poor *nεsu*'. Older children also use this relationship term when appealing to younger ones, but young children are not socialized to use it with others. *Nεsu* thus gets mobilized to accomplish everyday sharing and cooperation. The term is intensified with affect-intensifying suffixes, is used with expressives such as *wɔ* and *heyo*, and co-occurs with the same contextualization cues as one finds with *adε* (e.g., soft voice).

Another nonkin reciprocal term, similar to *wi εlεdɔ*, indexes the first sharing relationship between mothers and children and is used only between nursing children and their mothers. Mothers call their nurslings *ne bo* 'my breast' only in appeal when trying to encourage cooperation. In the sequence that follows, Mεli's mother, after making an initial appeal and being refused, adds a relationship term, *nεsu*, speaking in a soft voice to elicit empathy. When she is refused, she uses a more affectively intense vocative, *ne bo*, but that too fails to persuade Mεli to give up the piece of paper she is playing with.

when repeated refusal occurs

Mothers infrequently just take objects when they are refused, and Mɛli's angry outburst is rewarded by the return of her paper.

Example 6.6. Mɛli (28.3), sitting with her mother, is playing with a piece of paper.

[1]Mother → Mɛli [soft voice]: Hɛbɔ nelɔ.
Half to me.

[2]ɛm /
no

[3]Hɛh **nɛsu.**
Come on, nɛsu.

[4]ɛm /
no

[5]Mɔ, **ne bo.**
No, my breast.

[6]ge oba! /
who are you! /

[Mother takes paper.]
[Angry]

Nɛ diɛnowɛ! /
I (true owner) will take it! /

[Mother returns paper.]

Mothers also try to persuade small children to share food by addressing them with the kin term *nɔ* 'my mother'. Evoking that relationship, they appeal to children (of either sex) to feel sorry for them and give, as mothers give to children. Abi's, Suɛla's, and Mɛli's mothers all used *nɔ* in appeal on numerous occasions, but Wanu's mother did not use this term or *nɛsu*. Some fathers appealed to children using *dowɔ* 'my father' in the same manner. The reversed use of the kin terms *nɔ* 'my mother' and *dowɔ* 'my father' to children is available to anyone whom the child calls *nɔ* (e.g., mother's sisters). For example, on separate occasions of appealing to Mɛli to share food, Osolowa's unmarried sister Auwe first addresses Mɛli as *adɛ*, then corrects herself and uses the more conventionally appropriate term *nɔ*.

Adults' appeals to children are heavily marked to elicit feelings of compassion. They use expressives such as *wɔ* 'feel sorry for me'. And if the vocative is the child's name, it is marked for intimacy either with the possessive pronoun *ni* 'my' preceding it ("my Suɛla" – see Example 8.7, line 27) or with a word-final morpheme (-*a* or -*o*: Mɛli*ya;* Abi*yo*). Alternatively, a relationship term is selected; except for *adɛ* and *nɔ*, these take the intimacy markers -*a* and -*o* (*nɛsuwa; ni mahiyo*) for added emphasis. Other kin terms, such as *nelɛ* 'my daughter', that are affect-neutral are almost never used as vocatives in requests based on appeal. Adults use request forms identical to those used by children with soft voice quality (*geseab*) when begging: *nelɔ* 'I want'; *hɛbɔ ne* 'half to me'. Repetition plus the use of affect intensifiers increases the rhetorical force of these requests. Mɛli's, Suɛla's, and Abi's mothers all use these strategies of appeal with their young children, and Suɛla's and Abi's mothers use them with older daughters as well. Requests using these terms

ranged from requests for assistance in domestic activities (get nearby firewood; turn bananas in the fire) to asking children to give food, salt, or some
other item.

Meli is often reluctant to help her mother with household chores and share
food with her. When she does not comply, her mother repeats her requests,
but little else is done. Her mother's response in Example 6.6 – physically
taking the object – is rare. One makes requests, repeats and intensifies them,
and uses appeals and special relationship terms, but compliance cannot be
forced without provoking anger, which is to be avoided. Meli enthusiastically
helps, however, when her mother asks her to help with the care and feeding
of her brother Seligiwɔ. In almost every request on his behalf in connection
with caregiving, Meli complies. Requests by her mother on behalf of her
helpless younger brother are marked for positive affect. Perhaps Meli is com-
pelled through her feelings toward him that have been socialized into the *adɛ*
relationship.

The patterns, however, change rather dramatically when Meli is 32.2 months
old. First, demands escalate, especially to share food with family members.
Meli can provide responses of refusal without prompting; however, she still
has to learn when and to whom to give and when to tease and refuse. This is
socialized explicitly and directly. Previously, an adult would say, "If you
don't do *x* now, you won't have *y* later," but then would give in to the child's
whining and repeated requests. Now, however, adults follow through on threats
and the consequences of refusal.

For example, Osolowa is cooking mushrooms and asks Meli to go and get
the sago needed for cooking, which is in the corner of the room. Meli refuses,
and Osolowa repeats persuasively, *Mɔ, nɛsu* 'no, *nɛsu*'. Meli starts talking
about another topic, but her mother responds, annoyed, *Mo mobiɛsabo!* 'But
don't be unwilling!'. Meli still refuses, and her mother in a sarcastic manner
asks, *Ge kɔlɔwɔ mɔmɛnɔwɔ?* 'You won't eat mushrooms?' Meli refuses to
get the sago, and her mother goes to get it herself. Meli is not given any
mushrooms and sago in spite of her repeated requests. After one of her many
requests for mushrooms and sago, her mother reminds her, "You said, 'I am
unwilling.' " Her own words are used to hold her accountable.

Around this time Meli is socialized into the idea that though a request from
a close family member can be challenged initially, if that person continues in
a serious manner, using appeal markers, the request should be honored. For
example, Auwe, one of Osolowa's unmarried sisters who spends a lot of time
with Meli and often gives her food, begs for salt, saying she has none, using
both *adɛ* and the kin term *nɔ* in her requests. Initially, others sitting around
encourage Meli to tease her back and refuse, which Meli does. But Auwe is
serious and continues her request, saying, "Feel sorry for me, my mother,
my bandicoot!" – an appeal using *nɔ* plus their *wi ɛlɛdɔ ni mahi* 'my bandicoot' (highly valued meat that Auwe shares with Meli). Meli responds with a

challenge and refusal. Auwe turns to Mɛli and says angrily, "Okay, you won't eat animals [meat = special food] in my house again!" Osolowa tells her sister just to take the salt; Mɛli protests, and Auwe refuses to take it. Osolowa shows her anger toward Mɛli, telling her to tell Auwe, *Dima!* 'Take it!' Mɛli however, walks out as the adults call her *wɛfi lɛsu* 'little retard'. She does not yet understand; she misjudges the seriousness of the relationship and the request.

There are many ways Kaluli remind their children that they are to share. Around the time that Mɛli is 32 months old, when she refuses her mother's appeals to share food her mother comments, "And what do we call each other?" to remind Mɛli (*asulumɛki siyɔ*) of their shared name (*ni yɛsi*, a small animal that they shared) and the continued expectation of reciprocity in that relationship. Mɛli's father, seeing her with several ripe bananas, asks for one, and Mɛli teases him and does not share. He then says to her, "Feel sorry for me, your father, your bandicoot!" Her father not only reminds her of their kin relationship but marks the seriousness of his request by using their *wi ɛlɛdɔ*. Mɛli's response is "What bandicoot?!" Osolowa then tells Degelɔ not to carry Mɛli anymore, and he replies that he will not. This response is treated as *wɛl* 'payback' for Mɛli's refusal to share and as a way to shame her.

When Mɛli does not comply, her father says in a serious manner, "Think about it, I give (to you)" (*Asuluma, ne miɛni*). She is told to reconsider her action in terms of the consequences it might have for their social relationship, consequences that are rarely made explicit to young children. By 30 to 32 months, children are expected to move from "having no understanding" (*asugɔ andoma*) and only being capable of taking, to being able to think and participate responsibly in giving. Once children have understanding, they have the ability to establish and maintain different social relationships. Adults' responses to young children socialize them to assess situations so that they can react appropriately to requests to share and cooperate. They are reminded of the consequences that follow from their responses. Through participation in these activities, children develop cultural intuitions concerning the key of the activity and the relationships between themselves and others that are invoked, and these intuitions in turn allow them to assess when and how to give.

Older siblings socialize sharing

Older siblings take an active role in socializing 2- to 3-year-olds into sharing. Away from their mothers, they tease and challenge younger children about not sharing through verbal play routines. Older children also use many of the same strategies adults do when younger children are not sharing, including shared names (*wi ɛlɛdɔ*) to evoke special sharing relationships.

For example, Mɛli (32.2) and her cross-cousin (*enesɔk*) Solia (age 10) are playing in Mɛli's house. Solia lies on top of Mɛli's father's suitcase, and Mɛli wants her to get off so she can get on instead. After telling her to get off, Mɛli pushes her, saying, "That's not yours!" (*Ko ginɔma!*). Solia's response, "Are you not my baby bird?!" (*ɔ ge ni ɔbɛ insoma?!*), evoking their *wi ɛlɛdɔ*, reminds Mɛli of their special relationship, which includes cooperation in play. Mɛli backs off, letting Solia stay on the suitcase. The meanings of these terms do not draw on any given expectations of kinship relationships, but rather develop and are sustained through occasions of use marked by sharing and cooperation between individuals.

Abi's refusals to share and cooperate give his older siblings many opportunities to express directly and indirectly their expectations about each other in addition to sharing. These exchanges show particular ways siblings feel about and socialize each other. Yogodo (5 yr), Mobiya (7 yr), Abi (31.2), and Suɛla (29.) are sitting around the fire together, eating and talking, when suddenly Abi tries to take his younger sister Suɛla's cooked sweet potato. Yogodo intervenes, telling Abi that Suɛla is still scraping off the burned part; in other words, he should wait for his share, for she has not even finished preparing it for eating. After Yogodo walks away, Mobiya asks Abi, "Abi brother" (*Abi ao*), not to take Suɛla's food, telling him that Suɛla will cry if he takes it from her, emphasizing that one does not want to make younger siblings cry. Abi grabs the potato anyway, and Mobiya tells him to say, "You take it" (*Ge dima*) and give it back to Suɛla, but he refuses. As Suɛla is whining unhappily, Mobiya leaves with her, saying to Abi:

Example 6.7

¹Ge asulɔ! Ali ni bigiyɔ ɛna olɔsɔfɛ.
You understand! Yesterday we shared bigi.
                              huh? /
²Ai! gɔnɔ ɔli dowaba?!
What! Aren't you ashamed?!
[Abi is left by himself.]

Mobiya, taking her lines from a verbal teasing routine that children frequently use, challenges Abi's behavior by reminding him that the day before they had all shared *bigi* (a wild fruit). Now, by taking Suɛla's food away from her, he is not acting in the spirit of cooperation, and Mobiya shows her annoyance and shames him directly. She also leaves him alone, which is a common tactic among older children when they disapprove of younger children's behavior. This is typical of older children socializing younger siblings to act appropriately. While older siblings often appear to be after what is good for them, they also intervene on behalf of younger siblings when they think they are being treated unfairly.

Reciprocity is a serious topic of verbal play among children. The few verbal play routines that Kaluli children regularly repeat reflect their concerns with the serious business of sharing. These routines maintain and balance social relations. Children often pull one or two lines out of these routines (see Example 6.7); the following sequence contains the complete formulaic teasing routine (lines 18–21). It makes explicit the importance of sharing food as a way of being together, something that is highly valued in Kaluli life.

One afternoon in the house while their mother is asleep, Yogodo (5 yr) and Waye (8 yr) prepare a cooking fire, cut up and put sweet potatoes into bamboo tubes, and finally cook them. During the very lengthy preparation, there are arguments, teasing routines, and word play among the children. Abi (30.) makes the whole task more difficult by breaking up the fire, jumping around, and kicking ashes and dirt on his sisters. Finally he offers Waye a raw sweet potato to add to the tube; when she does not take it immediately, he withdraws it.

Example 6.8

[To Waye]   ¹ge kadɛfoma! /
                                             you forget it! /

[Abi gets up.]
²Yogodo → Abi: Gelɔ gasa mɛnɔwele?!
I wonder if you are going to eat together with us?!
³Waye → Abi: Gelɔ gasa mɛnɔwo?!
Will you eat together with us?!

                                             ⁴gelɔ gasa mɛnɔwo?! /
                                             will you eat together with us?! /

⁵Yogodo → Abi: Gi olɔsɔfɛyɔ?!
Did you put yours in the tube?!

                                             ⁶gelɔ gasa mɛnɔwo?! /
                                             will you eat together with us?! /

⁷Waye → Abi: No gelɔ gasa mɛnɔwo?!
And will you eat together with us?!

                                             ⁸gelo mayɛ / X /
                                             you eat it too! /

⁹Yogodo → Abi: Gelo mayɛ!
You eat it too!
¹⁰Waye → Abi: Gelo mayɛ!
You eat it too!
¹¹Waye → Yogodo: We henɔliyɛ, sofɛdo!
This is cooked with dirt, you boob!
¹²Yogodo → Waye: Ɛh, wɛlifɛnɔlɔbi ɔngo!
Yes, it might fill (the tube) like that!

.
.

[Talk continues about cutting potatoes; Abi is told to sit still.]
¹³Waye → Yogodo [looking at the dirt on the sweet potatoes]:
Ama henɛ!
Oh, this dirt!
¹⁴Yogodo → Waye: Hɛh! Ibu wemɛ
What about it! With this stick (to scrape it off).

¹⁵Waye → Yogodo: ɔ "Gi ibu wemɛ diɛnɔwɔ?!" ɛlabeyɔ?!
And did I say, "You take and do it with this stick?!"?!
¹⁶Yogodo → Waye: Bigiyɔ – olɔsɔfɛyɔ!
Bigi – cooked in a tube!
[All start laughing.]
¹⁷Waye → Yogodo: Oba bigiyɔ?!
What *bigi*?!
¹⁸Yogodo → Abi: ɔ gelɔ gasa mɛnɔwɔ?!
Will you eat together with us?!
¹⁹ɔ gi olɔsɔfɛyɔ?!
Did you cook yours in a tube?!
²⁰Ge mɔ olɔsɔdɛlale.
You didn't cook it in a tube.
²¹Gɛli mɔsaleyɔ.
You won't be very happy.
[Abi loudly babbles nonsense sounds.]
²²Yogodo → Abi: ɔli dowaba?!
Aren't you ashamed?!
²³Waye → Abi: ɔli dowaba?!
Aren't you ashamed?!
[Sweet potato falls on the ground, all eyes on it.]

Bigi (a small wild fruit that children collect and eat when they are in the bush together) are put into thin bamboo tubes about twelve inches long. When the tubes are filled, a stick is inserted. Pushing it up and down crushes the *bigi*, releasing juice and seeds. Everyone then passes the tube around and shares the mixture. Bamboo tubes (*olɔ*) are commonly used for cooking sago and many other foods; this cooking method is called *olɔsɔfɛ* 'bamboo tube-cooked'. Though *bigi* are not cooked, the activity of putting them into tubes and sharing them is called *bigi olɔsofɛyɔ*. The important components of this activity, then, are collecting *bigi* together, putting them into tubes, and sharing them around. This is typical of the way people prepare and distribute cooked food in families.

Cooking sweet potatoes shares many features with this favorite children's collective activity. Waye and Yogodo pool their resources, putting potatoes into tubes (not the usual cooking method) with a plan of sharing them. When Abi refuses to contribute his, Yogodo takes a line from the formulaic routine, repeated by Waye (lines 2–3). They challenge Abi's right to eat together with them (share), as he has contributed nothing. Abi, in keeping with his usual boisterous mood, loudly repeats what they have said. Yogodo, emphasizing her point, adds the second line of the routine (line 5), another rhetorical question meaning that he didn't contribute his share. Waye repeats the first line. Abi yells out (line 8), "You eat it too!," which is not part of the routine. Abi had not been on many *bigi* trips, so he may not have been familiar with the lines that his sisters are using, but he certainly understands that he is expected to share.

The girls continue examining the potatoes and the dirt that are in the tube, talking about who will eat the yellow ones, the dirty ones, and so on. In line 16, Yogodo reintroduces the idea of sharing, referring to collecting *bigi*, to which her sister responds with a rhetorical question, "What *bigi*?!," meaning that there is none to share. Yogodo then recites the entire piece, said to shame Abi (*sasindiab*). The first two lines (18–19) pose the rhetorical questions of whether the person is going to be eating together with the others and whether that person has the right to do so (from contribution). The third line (20) asserts that the person did not contribute and therefore (line 21) won't be very happy; that is, will not get anything to eat. But Abi only babbles loudly, eliciting the last comments from the girls that make explicit that what he is doing is not all right: He is not acting appropriately and should be ashamed. Later on when Abi begs for potato, Yogodo simply responds, "You really didn't 'cook in a tube' [share]" and refuses him, repeating this several times. Abi, though, persists, and finally Waye gives him a small piece of hers, telling Yogodo that he has none. Later, as Yogodo is enjoying hers, she taunts Waye, who has none left, with a popular teasing routine: "Some still there [I still have some and you don't]." Waye's response is a challenge: "Say it again! [I dare you]" (*esama*), and the two of them go through that sequence till they tire of it.

In contrast to Abi's mother, who displays an almost idealized type of sharing, giving what she has to others, it is his siblings who put verbal pressure on Abi to share. Older children repeatedly use lines from this four-line formulaic piece (see Example 6.7), using them to remind each other and younger children that one won't be happy if one doesn't participate and share. When Abi refuses to share, they remind him of what they have given. When they refuse his requests, they recount his previous refusals when they have requested something. Thus they hold him responsible for their refusals, making the consequences of previous refusals explicit and immediate. Young children from about 30 months spend increasing amounts of time with older siblings and are encouraged to participate in the give, as well as the take, of everyday interactions. Verbal reminders from other children, especially older sisters, play an important role in socializing younger children into sharing.

[margin note: child-on-child strategies on sharing]

The importance of asking

One way in which small children indicate their desire for food is by staring at it. Kaluli call this nonverbal begging *memelab*, and it is considered rude, something done by small children and dogs, and particularly annoying when people are eating and enjoying their food. People curse dogs, hit them, and chase them away when they sit and watch and whine. Young children are verbally discouraged by indirect means from doing the same. They are not directly told to stop, but adults and older siblings talk to each other about the

[margin note: rude to stare]

child's inappropriate behavior as a way of discouraging it. Abi's siblings' comments about Abi's behavior were made to make him feel ashamed (*sindilɔmɛki siyɔ*) and stop staring. Another term, *meselab* 'coveting', is also used, but this term includes both watching someone intently while he or she eats and making negative comments about the manner of eating. Older children are verbally reprimanded directly when they exhibit any of these behaviors.

This dispreferred behavior, "asking with the eyes," points to a cultural preference in Kaluli interaction for asking explicitly and verbally. Asking is important in establishing one's social relationships and assuring their continuity. Through *ɛlɛma* sequences, children are instructed to ask as a way of building relationships involving sharing. During my early visits to the families, mothers instructed children to ask me to give them things to play with, such as my net bag, batteries, and rubber thongs. In encouraging these requests, mothers were building relationships between their children and me based on giving and eventually on expectations of reciprocated sharing. Mɛli's mother encourages her to call me by a *wi ɛlɛdɔ* (*ni sɔlu* 'my salt') because I give her small packets of salt when I visit. Abi's mother also uses relationship terms in defining my relationship with Abi, frequently referring to me as *gɛsu Babi* 'your *nɛsu* Bambi' and reminding Abi in conversation that because I always give him things, like small pieces of soap or food, he should ask for what he wants and address me as *nɛsu*. These transactions provide the basis for further interaction and relationship, and are referred to in reminders to children when they do not give when asked.

Asking is a preferred initiating move in casual sharing and everyday distribution of food. This preference could be interpreted as meaning that the one who wants something has to ask permission to take, but Kaluli view it as providing the one who has something with the opportunity to give. Remember that the two major interactional strategies, assertion and appeal, have different transactional consequences. If someone begs, then the giving that results is seen as originating with the giver, who feels sorry and is moved to give. If someone asks assertively, then the one who asks is seen as initiating the exchange and can be asked for something in return at a later time. When someone takes something without asking, an opportunity to give is removed.[2]

Young children are encouraged to persist in asking, but they also have to figure out when to stop. For example, Ulahi instructs Abi (28.2) in asking his sister Waye for food, saying to him, "Sit here and keep asking" (*Wɛna siliki, hɛyamelea*). Abi keeps asking, and after each request Waye gives until Ulahi again intervenes to stop Abi, saying sarcastically to him, "Doesn't Waye give to you?!" (*Wayeyɔ gelɔ mɔmiaba?!*). The use of rhetorical questions calls attention to, challenges, and attempts to modify children's unacceptable behavior. Yogodo, who had not quite caught the sarcastic tone of her mother's comment, responds, "No! She gave enough already!" (*A! Eyɔ miyabega!*).

This comment makes explicit what Ulahi had intended to convey using less direct means.

Another component of requests is that once an individual asks and another agrees to give, the one who asks is expected to see the transaction through to the end and take whatever has been requested. Thus, children learn that their asking is a commitment and not a play activity. Their request holds them accountable to complete the transaction and can be the basis of a challenge if they change their minds. Among adults, a refusal to take after a request has been granted can be an insult and grounds for a serious breach. It denies an opportunity to give after one has been established through the request.

For children, taking without asking is almost always a transactionally inappropriate move and must be reformulated to fit Kaluli preferences for giving and taking. Kaluli prefer children to ask (*henima*), not just take or whine. The importance of asking is socialized through direct instruction (using *ɛlɛma*) to repeat requests using the imperative form of the verb "give" (*dimina*) or the pronominal form *nelɔ* 'to me/I want'. This is further supported by comments to and about children who take without asking.

Mɛli and Wanu usually ask for what they want. In fact, Mɛli (26.) seems to understand this preference at a metalinguistic level. One day Mɛli was holding an empty adhesive-tape dispenser while her brother Seligiwɔ (8 mo) was vocalizing. Mɛli gave him the tape dispenser, and when her mother turned to see what she was doing, Mɛli said, " 'Give me that "picture," ' he said" (*Pikisa ko dimina ɛlabe*). (Mɛli called the tape dispenser *pikisa* 'picture' because the hole reminded her of looking through a camera, which she saw the missionary and anthropologists do.)

In contrast, Abi often grabs objects and food or confidently announces that he is taking something. His mother and siblings frequently express their disapproval of his behavior to him. In spite of frequent instructions (with *ɛlɛma*) telling him what to say, reminders to ask (*henima*) for what he wants, and his participation in verbal routines to socialize children into the preferred procedures for giving and taking, Abi persists in his ways. Abi's mother had encouraged him to take the breast without asking whenever he wanted it, unlike the other mothers, who expected their children to ask. Perhaps because of expectations that developed out of this feeding experience, Abi does not usually ask before taking food (and objects) from his mother and other family members. Instead, Abi often asserts that he will take them, using declarative forms such as *Ne diɔlo!* ("I'm taking it!"), *Nisa dienɔ!* ("I (not you) will take it!"), or *Nɛno!* ("Mine!") as requests. He was often corrected by his mother, using *ɛlɛma*, and told to ask, to say the preferred forms, usually *dimina* 'give' or *nelɔ* 'I want/to me'.

Asserting "I will take!" does not pass for acceptable child behavior in any of the families. Wanu occasionally asks for food with *Ne diɔl!* 'I take!', and both of his parents correct him with *Dimina ɛlan* 'One says give'. However, directives of this type are relatively infrequent in both Mɛli's and Wanu's families, as these children generally use appropriate request forms. In contrast, imperatives and other directives to ask are frequently directed to Abi, especially between the ages of 27.2 and 30 months. Abi's mother repeatedly says, *Ge miɛni, mo gi dia!* 'I'll give it to you, but don't take it!' Unlike literal phrases commonly used when Abi was younger, this phrase incorporates an idiomatic expression with no surface negative (*gi dia* 'you [don't] take'), which is part of a set of formulaic teasing routines. These idiomatic expressions are pragmatically more complex than straightforward directives (see Example 6.15). While Abi is frequently reminded of the appropriate ways to ask and corrected on the pragmatic level, his phonology and syntax go largely without comment. In interactions with his older sisters, the focus is on immediate outcomes rather than details of pronunciation and grammar.

In other families, mothers and other members of the household corrected phonology, morphology, and syntax as well as pragmatic use of requests:

Example 6.9. Mɛli (26.) is at home with her mother's brother, Wanu.

[To Wanu]	*diɛmiya / *diɛmiyɛ /
	*bring / X! /
Huh? Ɛh, dimina, dimina! – ɛlɛma.	
What? Yes, give, give! – say it.	

Example 6.10. Mɛli (27.3) is cooking bananas with her mother.

[Looking for the fire tongs]	siɛfin abamiyo? / siɛfin hɛh?! / X / X /
	where's the fire tongs? / what about the fire
	tongs?! / X / X /
"Hɛh?!" ɛlɛdomogɛluan!	
One shouldn't just say, "What about?!"!	
	Nɔ ge ni siɛfin kelima /
	Mother, you look for my fire tongs /

Kaluli are sensitive to ambiguous or partially formulated requests; they put an interpretive responsibility on the addressee, especially when food is the issue. In Example 6.9 Mɛli's uncle corrects her pronunciation; in Example 6.10 her mother challenges her pragmatic choice. Though asking in the appropriate manner helps, it is no guarantee of getting what one wants, especially for older children. For example, when Waye asks her mother for a particular food item, she is told, "It is yours to ask for?!" (*Ginɔ kɔlɔ henaya?!*), denied the food, and also shamed.

Taking without asking obviously has rhetorical consequences that vary according to whether the owner is present or absent. For older children and adults, the consequences of taking without asking are more serious than for young children. Strategies of verbal control will therefore vary according to the ages of the participants and the extent to which the event is framed as serious.

When young children do not ask and take something that is not theirs to take, they are shamed (*sasindiab*) through rhetorical questions, sarcastic comments, formulaic expressions, and third-party threats. At an early age, small children are told that something belongs to someone else, followed by a rhetorical question like "Is it yours?!" As children become older, increasingly less literal tactics are used.[3]

Caregivers and older children rarely make direct statements of authority where they claim they will punish someone who takes something without asking. When older children argue amongst themselves and turn to their mothers to intervene, their mothers usually avoid getting involved, preferring to let children resolve their own problems. They issue rhetorical questions like "Is it my concern?!" and "What do you want me to do about it?!" When adults intervene with small children, they make extensive use of third-party threats to create authority where none actually exists: "Someone will say something to you!"; "Your father (not present) will say something!" The threat is that one will be publicly and verbally confronted with the challenge "Is it yours?!" Mothers never threaten small children with what they themselves might do; rather, they refer to a third party who is not present as the agent who will act.

Young children also use third-party threats in their interactions with others when someone is taking something without asking. Initially, these third-party threats are delivered in a playful manner, but still with the appropriate sequencing and discourse constraints. For example, Meli (24.1) is alone with her grandfather, who has a few small things belonging to her cousin Ofea in his bag. Each time she tries to take one of them without asking, he playfully says, "Don't take! Don't touch!" (*Diyɛsabo! Golɛsabo!*). Meli's next turn, following his utterance of prohibition, is what he might also say: "Ofea will say something. It's really Ofea's" (*Ofea sɛmeib. Ofea ɛnɔlɔbɛ*). He then follows her turn, confirming her assertion. They repeat this sequence – (1) Meli touching objects → (2) grandfather's prohibition → (3) Meli's reasons → (4) grandfather confirming reasons – as a verbal play exchange for different items Meli reached for in the bag. Meli knows and can state the reason for not taking something: The object belongs to someone who has not agreed to give it to her.

Before the age of 3 years, children find themselves in situations where they want something and the owner, or the one who can give, is absent. These situations are problematic in that authority is often ambiguous, not located in any specific person, and must be created by other participants for any given situation. In these situations, reasons are given why one should not take, and some of these are phrased as third-party threats. Young children learn that their relationship to the owner is critical to their access to the object. Depending on who the owner is, they do not always need ask, especially if they want to borrow something. Claims of ownership and relationship become part of the rhetoric of sharing and reciprocity.

Figure 21. A mock threat. This photo was taken in 1968, when body decoration for weddings was common.

Example 6.11. Abi (31.2) takes an ax that is lying on his father's sleeping platform.

¹Mother → Abi: A! Kabiyɔ diyɛsabo!
No! Don't take the ax!

²ɛm / (neg)

³Golɔ sɛmɛibkeyologa!
Your father will say something. I said!

⁴a! Daiboweno /
no! it's Daibo's /

⁵Daiboweno, sɛmɛib.
It's Daibo's; he'll say something.

.

.

[Daibo (5;6) enters, having heard them talking.]
[To Daibo, showing ax]   ⁶dowɛnowele? /
                                           is it really Father's? /
⁷Daibo → Abi: Ɛh. Ninoma ninomale, doweno.
Yes. It's not mine, not really mine, it's Father's.
[Abi puts down the ax.]

In this segment, Abi counters his mother's third-party threat (line 3) by claiming that his older brother, not his father, is the owner of the ax. This is his justification for taking it without asking. His mother then agrees with his claim of ownership, using that to support her assertion that it is *not his* in any case, so he cannot take it without asking. Abi puts down the ax when Daibo confirms what Abi suspects, that the ax is his father's. Young boys do not own axes.

Abi knows the appropriate response to threats, but he does not issue such threats to others until he is aged 32.2 months. From this point on, he regularly uses third-party threats to control actions of his siblings, though he is usually unsuccessful. Other important strategies develop in dyadic interaction, where children negotiate with others directly. As early as the age of 27.2 months, Abi talks about reciprocity to get what he wants after trying to take something without asking.

Example 6.12. Abi (27.2) had been begging salt from his sister Mobiya (7 yr), who was giving it to him. Then, he tried to take it himself, and she put it under her skirt out of his reach.

¹Mobiya → Abi: Sɔluwɔ ge miɛni.
I will give you salt.

²ɛm? /
huh? /

³Mo gi dia!
But you don't take (it)!

⁴Nelɔwɔ / nelɔ ka mian / nelɔ ɔmɔlɔb /
sɔluwɔ gelɔ miɛni /
I want it / you can give to me / I want that
very thing / I'll give you salt /

⁵Hɛh?!
What do you mean?!

Mobiya's response to Abi's attempt to take the salt from her (lines 1 and 3) is identical to what he has heard many times from his mother and other siblings. His response (line 4: "You can give to me. . . . I'll give you . . .") clearly expresses his understanding of what sharing and reciprocity are about. He wants something that she can give, and in the future he will respond in kind (*wɛl*). Her response (line 5: "What do you mean?!") to his offer of future return indicates her doubt and expresses her dissatisfaction with his behavior.

Individuals angered by someone's taking something of theirs can take one of a number of different stances ranging from indirect to very direct. Indirect comments include challenges of ownership ("Is it yours?!") and third-party threats ("Someone will say something!") if the item belongs to someone absent from the situation; more direct approaches are expressed through negative imperatives ("Don't take!"). In addition, speakers may use the phrase "Did I say . . . ?!" to directly challenge someone's taking, either to prevent the action or to add force to expressions of anger once it has been taken. The underlying force of the rhetorical question is "I didn't say . . . ," meant to confront and shame the one who takes. Unlike other expressions in which the speaker is not a referent, this challenge puts the speaker into the proposition conveyed and claims that the speaker did not give permission. This phrase is the most confrontational of the rhetorical questions speakers use. Because of its speaker stance and involvement, it is infrequently used and occurs only when speakers are angry. This expression is not used very often by younger children. Mɛli uses it collaboratively with her mother when teasing her father, but it is in a mock-angry frame. Even in the example below, Isa, who is angry, does not use the phrase "Did I say . . . ?!" (*Ɛlabeyɔ?!*) in the presence of her father.

Example 6.13. Isa (8:6) has just come home with some water. Wanu, Binalia, and her mother, Wadeo, are sitting around eating.

¹Mother → Isa: Bring a little water.
Hɔn desu diɛhamana.
[Isa looks around and can't find her ripe banana.]
²Isa → Mother: Mother, my ripe banana, who ate it?
Nɔ! ni magu genɔ abe nabeyɔ?
³Mother → Isa: Your father (did), you eat these, these two.
Golɛ, no we gɔnɔ maya, ɛlɛ we.
[She offers Isa two unripe bananas.]
⁴Isa → Mother: What's this! Did I say to him, "Eat!"?!
Ama! Emo "Nɛbi!" Ɛlabeyɔ?!
⁵Mother → Isa: Your father obviously finished it all.
Golɛ sandalɛloboga!
⁶Isa → Mother: I didn't finish any of mine!
Nɔnɔnɔ andomo tandalɛke!
[Whining]   ⁷feel sorry, Isa, I want water /
                                       wɔ, Isa, hɔnɔ nɛlɔwɛ /
⁸Isa → Wanu: What water?! Your own water (urine) is there!
Obɔ hɔnɔ?! Gɛ hɔn kowo!

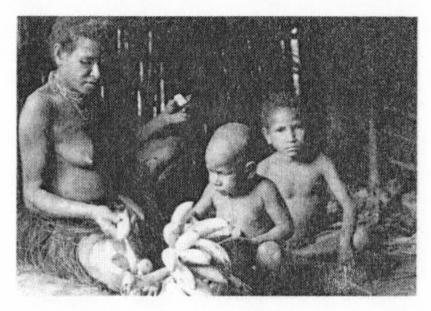

Figure 22. Ulahi sharing food with Abi and Yogodo.

This is a typical angry reaction to the discovery that someone has taken something without asking. Even after Wadeo's buy-off offer (*henulab*) of two unripe bananas (line 3), Isa is not calmed. Her anger continues, as is seen in her response to Wanu's request for water; she tells him in essence to drink his own urine (line 8).

Among older children, "Did I say . . . ?!" is used to do more than refuse a request; it is a put-down.

Example 6.14. Ea (8 yr) and Isa (8 yr) having collected *bigi*, prepare it with water. Binalia watches and begs for some.

Isa → Ea: Did I say, "Binalia will eat together with us two!?"
Binalia nain menɔwɔ?! ɛlalokɛ.

In this case, Binalia is not only being refused, but is cut off altogether, since Isa is talking to Ea and not addressing her rhetorical question to Binalia directly. "Did I say . . . ?!" is a rare but powerful refusal that does not get answered.

Refusing to share

Socializing refusals

Caregivers also directly instruct in strategies for refusing to share. These strategies provide ways for children to refuse without hurting others' feelings.

Figure 23. Abi refusing to share food with Yogodo.

Several teasing routines ranging from the playful to the serious are socialized to enable children to refuse to share. One set of teasing formulas is used only when responding to requests for food or objects when one intends to keep them for oneself. One responds to the request with words, not with the desired food or object. These formulaic expressions are used to taunt others by showing that you have something good and are unwilling to share. This particular construction is without a lexical or affixed negative, and is used only in the 2nd person for teasing. Within this pragmatically restricted context, only two verbs, "eat/drink" (*maya*) and "take" (*dima*), are used – in itself socially significant, indicating the special linguistic marking of teasing around sharing and eating. The construction is composed of a focused form of the 2nd person pronoun, *gi* 'you', with the 2nd/3rd person form of the verb minus the final consonant.[4] The present and future forms are as follows:

	Nonteasing form	Teasing form
Present tense	*gi nab* 'you eat'	*gi na* 'you don't eat'
	gi diab 'you take'	*gi dia* 'you don't take'
Future tense	*gi mɛib* 'you will eat'	*gi mɛi* 'you will not eat'
	gi diɛib 'you will take'	*gi diɛi* 'you will not take'

Adults socialize young children with ɛlɛma to use these playful taunts as refusals to share, directing the teasing phrases to other children and to adults. Children use them spontaneously with each other and to adults, but they are not used among adults, and only when annoyed do adults direct these phrases to children (see also Examples 6.4, line 2; 6.12, line 3; 6.23, line 1; 8.7, lines 14, 20, 25; 8.8, line 29).

Example 6.15. Mɛli (28.3) is with her mother and her mother's sister, Faili, sitting around the cooking fire. Mɛli's maternal grandfather, Kiliyɛ, has just brought a small marsupial (yɛsi) and given it to Mɛli. After talking about how he killed it and how he has given it to his granddaughter, Faili reaches for it.

¹G'fa → Mɛli →> Faili: A! Mɔmiɛnɔkɛ! – ɛlɛma.
No! I won't give it! – say it.
Ninɛli mɛnɛ, ninɛli mɛnɔ.
Only I will eat, only I will eat.
Faile, gi na! – ɛlɛma.
Faile, you don't eat! – say it.
[To mother]   ²nɔ Faili we sanama! /
                                         Mother, hit this Faili! /
³G'fa → Mɛli →> Faili: Gi na! – ɛlɛma.
Faile, you don't eat! – say it.
[To Faili]   ⁴gi nankɛ! /
                                         you usually eat! /
⁵Mother → Mɛli →> Faili: Gi nɛli! – ɛlɛma.
You will not eat! – say it.
[To Faili]   ⁶gi mɛibkɛ! /
                                         you will eat! /
⁷G'fa → Mɛli →> Faili: Gi mɛi! Gi nɛli! Gi na!
You won't eat! You won't keep eating! You don't eat!

In her three turns in this exchange, in spite of using the appropriate assertive force, Mɛli does not correctly repeat the utterances that her grandfather and then her mother have told her to say. In line 2 she tells her mother to hit Faili, which is an unacceptable response, and the adults encourage Mɛli to use rhetorical skills instead. In lines 4 and 6 Mɛli utters phonologically similar but semantically different regular verb forms following ɛlɛma instruction – first the habitual plus an emphatic particle (nan + kɛ 'one usually eats') and then the 3rd person future with an emphatic particle (mɛib + kɛ '3rd person will eat!') – both of which convey an affirmative meaning, which is opposite to what she is being told to say. Her grandfather then uses this teasing construction in three different tense forms (line 7), future (mɛi), future + continuative aspect (nɛli), and present (na). Mɛli, however, does not repeat, and Faili makes no further move on the yɛsi.

The adults turn to discuss the details of the yɛsi (size, sex), followed by instructions once again to Mɛli to direct these formulaic teasing expressions to Faili. Mɛli still does not repeat them, but instead produces forms with the regular inflectional endings (future and habitual) as before. Finally, her mother makes an important link for Mɛli in a discourse sequence that uses the teasing form *gi mɛi*. She says to Mɛli:

Naino yɛsiyɔ elɔ miɛsabo! Ni yɛsiyɔ gi mɛikɛ! – ɛlɛma.
Don't give our *yɛsi* to her! You [will not] eat my *yɛsi*! – say it.

Mɛli's mother makes the meaning of the teasing form explicit by following the regular negative imperative, which is transparent semantically (*miɛsabo* 'don't give'), with the teasing form (*gi mɛi*), which is not. The talk (all in a playful mode) then turns to all the reasons why Faili cannot have the *yɛsi*, followed by another set of *ɛlɛma* instructions to Mɛli using these formulaic expressions, which Mɛli still does not follow. Instead she tells her mother to hit Faili to prevent her from taking the *yɛsi*, but once again this is not acceptable to the adults. Later, when Faili appeals to Mɛli for the *yɛsi*, her grandfather once again instructs her to say, *Gi na!* 'You do not eat!', and Mɛli finally says it correctly with the appropriate force of delivery, several times in succession. Her grandfather then yells with delight, "She says, '*Gi na*'!" and the others laugh with expressions of approval.

Family members provide different cues to help children understand the meaning of this particular expression, which has a negative force without any surface negative marking. Without actually explaining the form to her, adults are persistent in encouraging her to use this expression in order to keep the *yɛsi*. The use of these expressions is contextualized within a recurring framework of teasing, in this case playful because Faili has not pressed her claim. Children are encouraged to think that the selection of the appropriate verbal form is critical to the desired outcome of the immediate situation. The appropriate use of these formulaic expressions is an important indicator of linguistic and social competence and is supported repeatedly throughout interactions.

Abi first uses these taunts in a playful manner, and by the age of 27.2 months was competently directing them to his siblings.

Example 6.16. Abi (27.2) is playing in the house with his siblings.

[Showing his banana to brother Daibo]	Daibo / maguwɔ **gi nayo**! / X / X /
	you don't eat banana! / X / X /
[Daibo shows Abi that he has several of his own.]	
[To mother]	ni maguwɔ! / nuɔ hɛh? /
	my banana / where's another? /

Yogodo → Mother: E magu se mɔganigaifɔ.
He hasn't even swallowed his banana yet [and he is asking for another].

Here what initially looks like an offer from Abi to Daibo is actually just a tease. Daibo's response provokes Abi to try and get more bananas, and his sister Yogodo intervenes to let his mother know that he hasn't even finished eating what he has. When children are older, they use these teasing routines to taunt or, when asked to share, to refuse. Use of these forms usually does not have the consequences of other types of refusals, which are angry and threatening.

The right amount

In responding to a request, one is often faced with the dilemma of how to keep what one has and still give something. When sharing, one does not want to insult others by giving too small an amount, nor does one want to part with any more than is necessary. When offering food, how does one insure that the other takes only a fair share and not much more? On the other hand, one always tries to get more – at least half, but one will settle for just a little.

Daily food-sharing situations contain many disagreements about the right amount to keep and give. Since food items can be repeatedly broken into increasingly smaller portions, they are prime candidates for continued negotiation. Caregivers, however, in interactions with small children do not encourage endless bickering over just how much is enough. Often they intervene, using ɛlɛma, as a way of amicably settling differences in desire. For example, Osolowa provided different solutions to this common dilemma, for if good feelings are to be maintained, no one wants to feel taken advantage of. One such verbal strategy used often, a counteroffer, appears below.

Example 6.17. Mɛli (26.3) and Mama (3;6) are eating Mɛli's salt, and Mama is taking a lot.

[To mother]   Mama just took that salt! /
Mother → Mɛli → > Mama: Can't you take something else? – say
it.
[Mama stops taking salt.]

Here Osolowa supplies a line for Mɛli to repeat (albeit a vague offer to take something else), to let Mama know that she is taking too much salt. Osolowa's line is effective without Mɛli's repetition of it.

The issue of what is yours, mine, and the others is often negotiated in each encounter, and what is enough is also part of the negotiation. Many prolonged discussions, especially among older siblings, focus on ownership or rights and amount to be divided. This becomes an issue only after someone has in principle agreed to give. For example, during a trip to their mother's gardens, Waye digs up five sweet potatoes, and her sister Yogodo digs up two. After Waye cooks them all, she gives only one to Yogodo. Yogodo becomes angry, arguing that she brought back two, and Ulahi (her mother) supports Yogodo's claim that she should be given one more, but Waye will not give the second one to her. Abi then complains that he has none and appeals to Waye, who gives him two. Yogodo angrily protests, but this time no one intervenes on her behalf. Ulahi then complains to Waye that she has been given a small one. Waye's response is that Yogodo got the big one. Ulahi, in an unusually confrontational move, says to Waye, "You secretly put it somewhere, I saw it." Waye admits to doing that, but even after her admission, there is nothing Ulahi can do or say to persuade Waye to give her more. If Waye does not give, she cannot be made to do so.

eating food out of sight of others

Ulahi's accusation reveals a common strategy used to avoid sharing: eating food out of the sight of others. Whereas mothers frequently tell their children, "We all always eat together!" (*Nigili uwa nankε!*), they also hide food in net bags or in the rafters for someone who is not there but is expected, or for a baby who is not hungry at the time, or for themselves to eat later in secret. Kaluli claim that sometimes this "out of sight, out of mind" practice is resorted to to avoid the bad feelings that result from refusal, or to spare persons who cannot eat the item (because of taboos) the feelings they would have on seeing others enjoy food forbidden them. That this type of behavior occurs is not a secret to 3-year-old children, who search for foods put away for infants or for their mothers' snacks and eat what they find. When mothers discover that the food is missing, there is little they can do except verbally vent their frustration through angry rhetorical questions like "Who gave it to you?! Is it yours?!" When mothers are found out, the ideal of always sharing is challenged verbally by older children, often sarcastically. But just as older children deny having eaten food, mothers also deny having hidden it. Eating stealthily and alone is not social and is negatively evaluated, but it happens. What really matters is not getting caught doing it.

When people do not think they have gotten the right amount – what they are entitled to get – they talk about it as not sharing or refusing to give (*kidiab*).

Example 6.18. Waye (7;6) and Yogodo (4;8) are arguing about sharing a wild almond (*uka*) that they have found. Waye has done the work of splitting the husk and has given her sister a small piece of the edible nut. Ulahi is within hearing distance.

Yogodo → Mother: Waye kidiab!
Waye is not sharing!
Waye → Yogodo: No gelɔ mɔmiyɔ?! Gi galilaliyele?
And didn't I give you?! I wonder, did *you* split it in half?!
Yogodo → Waye: Alan badiyɔ gi diaka!
You took the *big piece*, of course!

There is no simple way to resolve this dilemma verbally, because when challenged, individuals say they give what they deem appropriate in that situation. Such responses and reasons are used rhetorically and are not presented as facts to be weighed in deciding a just outcome. When children argue, even when there is adult intervention, there is little anyone can do to make them give up what they already have or to give more than they have already given. Situations such as these, which occur regularly, highlight a critical tension among Kaluli, the tension between being sociable through sharing and holding onto food or objects that one wants and feels one has a right to have.

In family arguments over sharing food, individuals often challenge each other's right to keep what they have. One asks, "Did you plant it?! Did you pick it?! Did you carry it?! Did you cook it?!" in addition to numerous questions about who gave it. These challenges about rights and access are used to assert rhetorical force and thus to persuade another to share, and to indicate the depth of the speaker's desire to have the object. The assertive equivalents ("I picked it! I cooked it!") are not used as warrants for behavior. These assertions are always negotiable; they do not guarantee outcomes.

Example 6.19. Ulahi has given Waye (7:6) cooked sweet potatoes and then realized she had kept none for herself. Yogodo (4:8) and Abi (30.2) are standing nearby.

¹Ulahi → Waye: Giyɔ hɛbdɛsuwɔ nɔnɔbɔ mina.
Give a little half of yours back to me.
²Waye → Ulahi: Ɛm!
No!
³Ulahi → Waye: Ɔ nɛlo mayab.
I'm hungry too.
⁴Waye → Ulahi: Gɛ mɛnɔ, gelɔ mɔolɔsodaluwɔ?!
Your sago, shouldn't you have tube-cooked [shared] it?!
⁵Ulahi → Waye: Ɔ mɛno hɛh?!
What sago?!
[Abi tries to take sweet potato from Yogodo,
but she won't give it.]
⁶Ulahi → Abi →> Yogodo: Gɔnɔ elɔ difeyɔ?! – ɛlɛma.
Did you plant it yourself?! – say it.

gɔnɔ elɔ difeyɔ?! /
did you plant it yourself?! /

⁷Gasa ge, ne sambɛnikɛ!
You dog, I am going to hit you!

gasa ge, ne sambɛnikɛ! /
you dog, I am going to hit you! /

⁸Ulahi → Waye [softly]: Waye, giyɔ adɛlo banɛmifoma.
Waye, break yours for *adɛ*.
⁹Yogodo → Ulahi: Dogɔf mɔsolilɔb.
I obviously really only have the skin (of the potato).
¹⁰Yogodo → Waye: Waye! Gi waliyɔ?!
Waye! Did you dig up yours?!
¹¹Waye → Ulahi: Kɔmɛ!
There is none!

In spite of several verbal attempts made in this multiparty exchange, no food changes hands. Ulahi, who has cooked and given sweet potato to her daughters, asks for some back from her older one, but all she gets is a rhetorical challenge (line 4) charging that she has not shared her sago, which she denies having. After Abi tries to take sweet potato from Yogodo and she refuses to give it, her mother challenges her refusal ("Did you plant it yourself?!") and insults her ("You dog!" – a serious insult, for dogs covet and steal food and occupy a very ambivalent position symbolically). Ulahi then shifts and turns to Waye to beg on Abi's behalf; she is interrupted by Yogodo, whose response (line 9) to her mother's lines 6–7 is that she has only the skin – a minimalizing strategy used to keep what she does have.[5] She then returns a challenge to Waye for more potato, but Waye is still unwilling to give up what she has and responds, "There is none."

Waye's assertion "There is none" is yet another rhetorical strategy Kaluli use when they do not wish to share. Kaluli will claim not to have something even when the object is in plain sight. This claim of having none may be followed by begging for sympathy from the one who has asked, who knows or strongly suspects that the statement is not true. But once the claim of "none" has been made, there is no argument. Again, this is a rhetorically powerful way to refuse, as it asserts a particular reality. Once this occurs, little can be done to change anyone's stance.

Mothers' threats and the consequences of refusals

When older children refuse their mothers' requests, there is little to do. Ulahi and Yaloame drop their requests in exasperation. Wadeo uses third-party threats when she is not able to persuade her daughters to share. Her threats are angry and direct but are still within the rhetorical attempt to create authority where there is very little. As in most threats, the agent of the action is unspecified or absent.

One of Wadeo's most frequent threats after a refusal (leveled only at her daughters) was "Urine will pour out" (*Beyɔ sumeib*). In other words, as a result of the anger of the speaker, the child addressee will become so frightened that she will lose control of her bladder. Other threats include "You will cry" (again, from fear) and *W.ɔsɔ*, an expressive meaning "You will be sorry next time," as in the following examples.

Example 6.20. Wadeo (Wanu's mother) has asked her daughter Isa to cook some bananas for her father. Isa has refused, saying she is hot, and has told Wadeo to cook them herself. A few minutes later Wadeo asks Isa again. Binalia, Isa's younger sister, is watching.

Isa → Mother: Do you hear?! I'm really hot!
Ofabolɔb! Dɛdaya?!
Mother → Isa: You are really going to cry!
Yɛlimɛnigabkɛ!
Binalia → Isa: You can go and cook them.
Ka sobalifoma.
[Isa refuses and Binalia does it.]

Example 6.21. Isa has cooked a small lizard in sago, and her sister Binalia, friend Ea, mother Wadeo, and brother Wanu are asking repeatedly for some of it. Isa finally gives Wanu a small piece but refuses the others, who then sit and watch the two of them eat.

¹Ea → Binalia / Mother: Eyɔ heyɛsen. Gelɔ mɔmiɛnigakeyɛ.
He's always asking. She's really not going to give to you.
[Showing his food to me]   ²Babi niyɔm! /
                                            Bambi my very own /

³Mother → Isa: Sɛsagɛnɔ ne.
Lizard to me.

⁴Isa → Mother: ɔ sɛsagɛn we obibɛsolɔbo?!
And how many lizards are obviously here?!
⁵Mother → Isa: **Wɔsɔ!**
You'll be sorry next time (for what you are doing now)!
[Soft voice] Wɔ! ne. **Wɔsɔ!** Giyɔ ka hɛynankɛ.
Feel sorry for me! You'll be sorry! You're always asking.
[Seeing cooked lizard] Imilisiga!
There's one right there!
⁶Isa → Mother: Ɛh, imilisiya!
Yes, only one right here!

There are very few examples of the speaker's threatening and taking responsibility by naming herself as the agent. Wadeo is the only adult recorded
in an interaction with a child to claim that she would do something. When
Binalia repeatedly refuses to comply with a request from her mother, her
mother says to her, "I'm going to break that girl's back!" Notice, however,
that some of the force is taken away from the threat as she refers to Binalia in
the 3rd person, talking loudly so others will hear. Wadeo rarely struck either
of the girls, and there was little she could do to compel them to act. Much of
the time, they eventually complied with her requests, but only after angry or
extended verbal exchanges. Third-party threats are characteristic of interac-   *Third-party threats vs. 1st party threats*
tions between adults. First-person threats are potentially too dangerous and
explosive. One might be pushed to act on his or her threat, which would
defeat the point of the exchange. To be called on one's threat could shut the
interaction down, when the point is to continue using verbal means of social
control to achieve a particular end. In any case, given the difficulty individuals in this society have compelling one another to do something, regardless
of their age, verbal manipulation with threats that speakers cannot act on
reduces the direct confrontational nature of social control while maintaining a
high level of drama.

Adults refuse children's requests

In addition to observing mothers and older siblings refusing to comply with
each others' requests, young children participate in interactions where their
mothers refuse their requests. Both observation and active participation contribute to children's learning how and when to refuse to share. A mother's
refusing to give the breast, however, is different from refusing to give food
or objects: The same arguments cannot be made. One cannot say when refusing the breast that there is none, nor can one question ownership. Refusals of
the breast are particularly marked because they constitute the clearest case
where the decision is based on the mother's desire to give.

Mothers' outright refusal without a reason is rare in first-try requests. They
are, however, found when children demand rather than ask. Another response

is to issue a series of reasons whereby the speaker does not take responsibility for refusal and then issues a rhetorical question back to the child, forcing the child either to ask again or drop the request. Another way in which Kaluli avoid direct refusal of a request they do not wish to fulfill is to redirect the child's interest from his or her own situation to someone else's. This is frequently done using *ɛlɛma* routines.

Ignoring a request is also dispreferred. Kaluli adults insist that their presence be acknowledged in all face-to-face interactions. It is extremely rude to appear in someone's social space suddenly and without warning. When entering a house, they announce their arrival with loud verbal greetings and expect a return in kind to insure that they are acknowledged. It is unimaginable that one person would ignore another or not respond in some way unless one were ill or extremely angry. Too, when making requests, speakers without exception follow the convention of making sure that those being addressed have already acknowledged that talk is under way.

Children are rarely ignored except when they repeatedly ask for something and the addressee is unable or unwilling to fulfill the request. Something minimal, if only an acknowledgment, is usually given. Not responding to a request usually indicates the caregiver's frustration or unwillingness, not lack of attention. When addressees do not respond, children continue repeating the request, using vocatives, expressives, and emphatic particles as well as increasing volume to get attention. Nonverbal means of getting the addressee's attention (such as pushing, hitting, scratching) are dispreferred and are last resorts. Children are persistent. At a very early age, they learn that they will be attended to, but not always at the instant they indicate need or desire. Sooner or later, some type of response from the caregiver will be forthcoming. It is very hard for Kaluli not to respond to anyone for very long.

Osolowa's responses to Mɛli's requests for the breast

While Wanu's and Abi's mothers rarely refuse their sons' requests, they frequently refuse those made by their older daughters. In contrast, Mɛli is refused the breast quite often, perhaps for reasons of gender and/or perhaps because she has a younger brother close to her in age and her mother wants to discourage her nursing.[6]

Of the three children, Mɛli's requests for the breast were ignored more than Abi's and Wanu's requests for food and objects combined. For example, Mɛli (24.3) and her mother visit the pastor's wife, and Mɛli issues over ten requests and receives no response (see Example 7.1). No one intervenes on Mɛli's behalf, but clearly her assertive and persistent requests are positively viewed by the other visitors, as indicated by the smiles of approval. Mɛli continues with twelve additional requests to her mother, this time for the breast, each intensified with emphatic and expressive particles. She then begins to push and hit her mother as well. When her mother finally gives her the breast, she comments to the group, "She is always drinking from this good-tasting breast, this little retard here," which draws laughter from everyone. In repeated situations such as this, the child learns to persist. She may try to draw others in, but only she can ultimately move the addressee to a positive response.

Counteroffers as a form of persuasion (hɛnulab)

The term *hɛnulab* is used to describe behaviors that include calming crying babies (making soft sounds, gently rocking them, or offering the breast, food, or some object) and telling children to look at something else in order to divert their attention. Initially I viewed this as a strategy of distraction, where adults tried to take a child's attention away from an object or emotional state in the hope that the child would lose interest in that original object or state. However, *hɛnulab* also describes the following situation. After Wadeo has attempted for some time to persuade her daughters to retrieve a net bag of food that was left by the forest edge, and angry words have been exchanged as they have refused, she says to them:

¹Wadeo → Isa / Binalia: Junɔ nɛsɛgɛ . . .
After you eat *jun* . . .
²Isa → Wadeo: Obo junɔ?!
What *jun*?!

Speakers named the speech act in line 1 *hɛnulab*, and line 2 was named *ɛlɛnyab*, the term used for the noncooperative response common after such a bid has been made. Thus, rather than gloss *hɛnulab* as "distraction," it makes more sense to place it in the context of other acts of exchange that take place within a focused interaction and to see it as a counteroffer: a type of persuasion or buy-off.[7] From the perspective of the speaker, the addressee is exhibiting unacceptable or inappropriate verbal or nonverbal behaviors, from refusing to cooperate to crying, and the counteroffer is intended to change the behavior of the addressee and make it compatible with the speaker's desires. The offer entails giving something, rather than taking something away.

Hɛnulab is an important interactional strategy between adults and children and is consistent with the general preference of adults for not ending interactions through such moves as ignoring, refusing, or immediately rejecting the children's verbal or nonverbal behaviors. *Hɛnulab* involves an offer of one thing for another, for example an object or a conversational topic. It also describes offers to exchange objects/food for feeling states, especially sadness or anger. Ulahi frequently offered Abi food when he was sad in exchange for his sadness, and when Mɛli was very angry about not having any salt and could not be cajoled out of her mood, her mother, as a symbolic gesture, offered Meli a piece of her shinbone in exchange for her anger (*Ge oba? Ko, ni asɔk nɔnɔbɔ gulumina* 'What's the matter with you? That, my shinbone, break some off and give it back to me'). Kaluli-speakers also named these speech acts *henulab* 'persuade or buy-off'.

Henulab 'one persuades with a counteroffer' is a common response to non-compliance, part of a pervasive Kaluli pattern of offering alternatives to the speaker's desires that not only takes what the speaker has indicated as a starting point but refocuses the request according to what the addressee wishes to accomplish.

Example 6.22. Meli (28.3) has been making many requests for the breast.

[Whining]	[superscript]1[/superscript]Mother / give me the breast / Mother, look here! // give me the breast I said! look here! /
	Nɔ / ne bo me / Nɔ wekɛ // ne bowɔ mologa / wekɛ! /
[superscript]2[/superscript]Mother → Meli: *Bigi* (fruit) over there, *bigi*, go and get the *bigi*!	
Bigi haloga, bigi, bigiyɔ diehamana!	
[Getting angry, talking louder]	[superscript]3[/superscript]Mother, do you hear what I said? / give me the breast / I said give me the breast! // Mother, look here! / oh my! / give the breast / Mother, do you hear what I said? / X / Mother, give the breast!! /
	Nɔ ge siyɔwɔ dedaya!? / ne bowɔ me / ne bowɔ mologa // Nɔ wekɛ / Yagidi! / bowɔ me / Nɔ ge siyɔwɔ dedaya? / X / Nɔ bowɔ mo!! /

[superscript]4[/superscript]Mother → Meli: Feel sorry for me! My mother, I'm really hungry.
Wɔ! Nɔ, ne mayabe.
[Meli continues to beg and cry. Osolowa finally gives her the breast, telling her to have only a little.]

In this sequence Meli makes her request for the breast clear. Her mother's response (line 2) is a counteroffer of another activity, to go get a tree fruit (*bigi*) outside. Meli, not accepting this alternative, challenges her mother (line 3), asking her if she has heard what she has said, a rhetorical question suggesting that her mother has not. Meli continues her request, escalating with expressives and emphatics. Her mother again (line 4) does not directly refuse her, but instead offers a change of focus from what Meli wants to what she wants. She asks Meli to feel sorry for her, addressing Meli as *nɔ* 'my mother', telling her that she is hungry. Mothers will call their children (of either sex) *nɔ* when they want them to feel sorry for them and share some food with them as mothers always do.

Henulab socializes children into viewing counteroffers of objects, food, conversational topics, or attention as possible ways of redirecting their desires or interests.[8] In the context of ongoing relationships, there are several ways to get what one wants or at least not to suffer a loss. Immediate agreement to one's proposed topic or focus of attention is only one option. Through counteroffers, participation and focus are maintained, but participants have the possibility of renegotiating *what it is* (the topic or focus) that they are paying attention to, rather than *that* they are paying attention to each other. What matters is maintaining face-to-face contact and being in the relationship.

Refusals through teasing and intense emotional cycles

Osolowa used other strategies to discourage Meli while not directly refusing her. These involve teasing and provoking the child to intensely emotional states. These sequences for Meli are similar to hide-and-seek games for young boys, discussed in Chapter 8, where mothers and sisters provoke boys to tears in encouraging them to search for objects, exuberantly support their success while they calm down, and then repeat the cycle. With mothers and daughters, there are the excitation and the tears; here, food or the breast is the calming element. Similar patterns were consistently documented between mothers and older daughters.

Example 6.23. Meli (28.3) is nursing while talking to her mother, who is cooking bananas and wants Meli to stop nursing.

¹Gi na magu we. Gi mɛi! Mɛli!
You don't eat this banana.
You won't eat! Mɛli!
[No response.]
²Mɛli, magu balima.
Meli, turn the banana (in the fire).

           obɛ? /
           what? /

⁴Maguwɔ.
The banana,

           ɛh /
           yes /

⁶balimɛ!
turn it!

           giba balimɛ! /
           you turn it! /

⁸Niba balimɛ?
I turn it?

           ɛh /
           yes /

¹⁰Ge mɛnɔ mɔbiaba? Wa?
Are you unwilling to eat it (banana)? Huh?

           mɔbiabɛ! /
           I'm unwilling! /

¹²Mɔbiabɛ?
You are unwilling?

> ɛh /
> yes /

¹⁴Nafa!
Good!
[Mɛli continues nursing.]
¹⁵Hobowɔ ko yabko badaya? Bo nɛlabeyɔ hobowe!
Do you see the blood coming there? The breast you were just
drinking, blood!
[Mɛli whines; mother tries gently to push her away.]

> ¹⁶nɔ! / bowɔ mɛ /
> Mother / give the breast /

¹⁷Bowɔ mɔmenɔwɔ?
You won't drink the breast?

> ¹⁸Nɔ! / ne bowɛ! / Nɔ ge siyɔwɔ dɛdaya? /
> X / Nɔ wekɛ / bowɔ mɛ /
> Mother! / my breast! / Mother, do you hear
> what I said? / X / Mother, look here! / give
> the breast /

[Mɛli takes the breast.]
¹⁹Seligiwɔ sɔwɔ.
Seligiwɔ is dead.
[Mɛli stops nursing.]

> ²⁰Nɔ Seligiwɔ abamiyɔ? /
> Mother, where is Seligiwɔ? /

²¹Seligiwɔ anelɔbo.
Seligiwɔ is obviously gone.
[Mɛli starts crying.]

> obɛ? /
> what? /

²³Wayu anelɔbɔwɛ!
He really went to Wayu (the mission)!

> ²⁴Nɔ Seligiwɔ abamiyɔ? / Nɔ wekɛ! Se-
> ligiwɔ! /
> Mother, where is Seligiwɔ? / Mother, look
> here! Seligiwɔ! /

²⁵Seligiwɔwɔ baya hando siyɛlɛkɔkɔ baya handokɛ.
Seligiwɔ is already going around outside in the yard, outside in
the yard.
[Crying very hard]

> ɛm? /
> huh? /

²⁷E Wayu henɛno ɛlɛta.
"I'm going to Wayu," he said.
²⁸Anelɔbɔkɛ!
He obviously went!
[Very distressed, screaming]

> ²⁹Nɔ Seligiwɔ abamiyɔ? / X /
> Mother, where is Seligiwɔ? / X /

[Seligiwɔ makes some noise while sleeping
in the corner.]
[Looks and stops crying]

> ³⁰wega! /
> right there I see! /

[31]Uhmm?
Huh?
[Pointing to him]

        [32]wekɛ! /
        look here! /

[Whining]

        [33]Nɔ nε bowɔ mε / Nɔ ge siyɔwɔ dε-
        daya? /
        Mother, give me the breast / Mother, do
        you hear what I said? /

[34]Dɔdɔl kɔsega –
I hear, but –
[Mɛli and her mother discuss for 15 more turns how much she will drink: only a little;
both are now laughing. After a short nurse, her mother takes the breast to put it back
in her dress.]

        nɔ /
        Mother /

Kɔmɛ!
That's enough!

        nɔ ɔisa *disalifowa /
        Mother, then *I put away /

[Mɛli takes the breast.]
Wa?
Huh?

        bo *disalifo / bo *disalifowɛ /
        breast *I put away / X /

*Bo disalifowɔ?
Breast *I put away?

        ɛh /
        yes /

Bo dise ɛlan.
I put the breast in, one says.

        bowɔ / bowɔ *disalifo /
        breast / breast *I put away /

In this complex sequence, several different strategies of refusing the breast
are used. First, Mɛli's mother tries to divert her interest and redirects her
attention to cooking bananas (lines 1–14), but she is unsuccessful. Her next
ploy (line 15) is to scare Mɛli, telling her that she is drinking blood, an idea
that is especially repugnant to Kaluli. But this only temporarily dissuades
Mɛli. Her mother then tries to get her to verbally agree to stop nursing (line
17), but Mɛli will not accept that either. Next she tells Mɛli that her brother
has died (line 19). This gets Mɛli's attention, and she stops nursing immediately. While crying, she carries on a conversation about her little brother.
Finally Seligiwɔ makes some noise, and Mɛli spots him in the corner in a net
bag. She immediately requests the breast, fully recovered from her intense
emotional display. After more discussion, Mɛli nurses briefly; then she and
her mother successfully end that nursing session.

This type of teasing seems cruel from a middle-class perspective, but as in
other types of noncompliant response and third-party threats, Osolowa uses a
variety of rhetorical ploys to keep the interaction going. There is a delicate

balance to be maintained. One would prefer not to refuse directly and not to take responsibility (as in third-party threats), but attempts are repeatedly made to establish authority and control. Teasing in these contexts is variable in key. It can be completely playful, but, as in the example above, it can also escalate into scenes where children become completely frustrated and angry and lose control. While one generally does not frustrate or anger small children, these responses are deliberately provoked in situations where the child wants something that caregivers are unwilling to give. When this occurs, caregivers bring their children back to a calm state relatively quickly, offering them food or the breast as a way of rebalancing the relationship.

These interactions make sense in the larger perspective of Kaluli emotional life, in which cycles of intense emotional arousal followed by calm and compensation are extremely important. They reach a peak of intensity in ceremonial contexts, but they also occur when people are mourning or when they think of someone and miss him or her.[9] In major rituals, such as Gisalo, hosts are moved to tears when they are reminded of those close to them who have died. They burn the shoulders of dancers who have provoked them, and receive compensation from the dancers because they have been moved to tears. While "balance" is restored after each ceremony, another ceremony is called for to continue.

These emotional patterns are socialized in particular interactional situations when children want something and are not given it. For girls, it is usually food; for boys, it may be the object of interest used in hide-and-seek games. Example 6.23 is not isolated or idiosyncratic but part of a socializing repertoire. Throughout Meli's interactions, there are many similar events, starting when she is only 26 months old. For instance, at 28.3 months Meli is with her mother playing in the house. Her mother takes an old piece of adhesive tape that Meli claims is hers, and they proceed to argue.

Example 6.24.

¹Mother, I – this is mine! / X / oh my! mine! Mother! / Mother, look here! mine! /

²Where did you put this that I took?! [Whining]
⁴You've already had the breast! [Sings softly]
[Meli continues to sing softly, picking up some vegetable remains. Then, laughing, re breast]
[With no response from mother, singing again]
⁸Why didn't she give you the breast?

³Mother, I want the breast! / X /

⁵Mother doesn't give me the breast / X /

⁶I am going to take it! / X / X /

⁷Mother doesn't give me the breast /

⁹Mother doesn't give me the breast /

[10]You, "Breast, the breast" like that all
the time are saying, but she is – I am unwilling.
                                        [11]Mother, I'm hungry /
[Mother takes puppy, Dabulobe, out of firepit,
holding it up to Meli.]
[12]Sit and drink Dabulobe's breast!

                    [13]Mother, I want to drink the breast! /

[14]Dabulobe's little breast, you drink that.

                    [15]Mother, do you hear what I said? /

[16][High voice] Why are you angry?
[Mother offers puppy's breast to Meli.]
[Hits mother]   [17]Mother, do you hear what I said? /
                                 Mother! /

[Mother pushes puppy's backside at Meli.]
[18]You eat Dabulobe's behind!
[To dog] Hɔ! Hɔ! Hɔ! Hɔ! [What you say to encourage dogs to go
after small animals]
[Mother pushes dog at Meli, who is half laughing, half crying.]
[19]It's going to kill a *mogei* [small animal that lives in holes], yes,
kill this *mogei*!
[To dog,] *Mogei! Mogei! Mogei!* Hɔ! Hɔ!
[To Meli] Lie down!
[Mother pushes dog under Meli's skirt.
Meli is screaming.]   [20]Mother! /
[21]It's just going inside (a hole). The *mogei* is going first
[Meli is crying. Mother gently pushes dog on Meli's behind while
she cries.]
so Dabulobe can kill it!
[Screaming]   [22]Mother, look here! I'm going over
                               there! /

[23]It has not yet killed the *mogei* there!
[Mother pushes dog as Meli screams.]   [24]Mother, look here! I want the breast,
                                        said! /

[25]The *mogei* is really there!

                    [26]Mother, look here! give me the breast, I
                    said / Mother, look here! /

[Meli is crying very hard. Mother gently pushes the dog back and
forth on Meli's behind.]
                    yikes! / Mother, give me the breast! /
[27](The dog) didn't kill it!!
[Osolowa's sister-in-law Waye walks in and laughs. Osolowa talks with her while
Meli yells. She playfully hits Meli and then gives her the breast. Meli stops crying
and calms immediately. Then Osolowa puts her brother on the other breast.]

Scenes such as the examples above balance the portrayal of reciprocity and
sharing. Contexts of sharing are complex, and different socializing messages
are simultaneously conveyed. Children do not always get what they want,
especially if they are girls, and getting angry in these situations with mothers
and then being calmed is part of learning the affective components of sharing
and refusing.[10] Caregivers and children both have their own desires and goals,

often different. But what is consistent throughout these exchanges is that, no matter what, the relationship is eventually rebalanced and so maintained. The next request may be complied with more easily than the previous one.

Continuity of strategies into adult life: husbands and wives

The ways in which caregivers and children talk about giving and taking, especially regarding food and cooperation, are similar to conversations between husbands and wives when expectations are not fulfilled or are challenged. These informal conversations touched off by breaches make explicit the assumptions people hold about how people actually behave. In the sequence that follows, Baseo and Wadeo draw on rhetorical ploys similar to those between parents and children. These are the routines of familiarity in ongoing relationships.

Example 6.25. Baseo comes into the house complaining to his wife, Wadeo, that he is hungry.

¹Baseo → Wadeo: Worms! I'm hungry!
Watio! Mayakε!
²Wadeo → Baseo: Then try to cook some food there!
Amiyɔ mεno ko se sodεiba!
³Baseo → Wadeo: No! I'm hungry.
Εm! Ne mayab.
⁴Wadeo → Baseo: When you are hungry, do you just sit like that?!
Mayabolɔ olien tanolɔkε?!
⁵You said you are hungry, it's okay to eat.
Mayologa, mεnowɔ ɔli.
[Baseo pays attention to Wanu for about 10 minutes, then searches to see if there is any pandanus, but the trough is empty.]
⁶Wadeo → Baseo: Yeah, sit and squeeze [pandanus]!
Ε helεmesea!
⁷Did you do any weeding today in the pandanus garden?!
Kolayɔ ge oga fεdεlino?!
⁸Baseo → Wadeo: Geez, I'm a little hungry!
Shhh! Ne hεlu mayab!
⁹Wadeo → Baseo: You always come around saying you're hungry, haven't eaten.
Mayab εnɔ mεnɔlɔ mɔnaki ka yano εlalekε.
¹⁰Baseo → Wadeo: And what weeding did you do?!
Ɔ kɔlɔ hundεlaya?!
¹¹[Softly, as he leaves] I wonder if I'll squeeze [pandanus] here?
Wena hamεnowele?
[About 45 minutes later, Wadeo prepares some pandanus. Baseo returns and eats. Just as he is finishing his food]
¹²Wadeo → Baseo: Baked bandicoot is really good!
Mahi duɔfε nafayɔ!
¹³Baseo → Wadeo: If you know how to go and kill bandicoot, you can eat it [but if you don't, don't think about it!].
Mahilɔ sandanεiyɔ mahi nalunɔ.

¹⁴Wadeo → Baseo: Don't talk like that!
Ɛledɔ sɛlɛsabokɛ!
¹⁵Baseo → Wadeo: Who said you don't eat it?
Ge mɔnan ɛlɛbɔ abe salaba?
¹⁶If you know how to go and kill bandicoot, you can eat it [but if you don't, don't think about it!].
Mahilɔ sandanɛiyɔ mahi nalunɔ.
¹⁷Wadeo → Baseo: And when you don't even see one, then you never eat it. When you see one, then you eat it.
Ɔ no mɔ bɛdabami ɔsa mɔnan. No badamiyɔ o ka nan.

In Kaluli families, women are supposed to cook food and give it to the rest of the family. Refusals to do so are usually met with angry verbal or, worse, physical responses. After Baseo tells Wadeo he is hungry, she does not directly refuse to cook or agree to it, but instead gives the turn back to Baseo with imperatives (lines 2, 6) and rhetorical questions and comments (lines 4, 5, 7). Baseo's response (line 8) is sarcastic; he says he is a little hungry when he means he is very hungry. This type of sarcastic response, saying the opposite, is very common when people are annoyed, but is not to be interpreted literally. Baseo continues making his feelings known (line 10) by challenging Wadeo's rhetorical question that implied he didn't do any work, and asking what work she has done. Then, as he is leaving, speaking out loud to no specific addressee, he wonders whether he is going to squeeze, meaning eat, pandanus (one squeezes the pandanus juice off the cooked seeds).

When Baseo returns, he finds the prepared pandanus and eats. At line 12, as Baseo is finishing, Wadeo makes the comment that bandicoot is really good – a request for meat food, as she has supplied the vegetable food. Baseo responds in kind with a sarcastic comment, suggesting that one has to know how to kill one to eat one, which is actually a comment on his own hunting skills as well. She tops him by suggesting (line 17) that he never even sees one, implying that his skills as a hunter are inadequate and that he is not fulfilling his role in the domestic economy.

Socializing the meaning of food and objects

Family talk is laced with messages about sharing and exchange. They may be short one-liners without explanation, elaboration, or paraphrase, or longer discussions about what is expected. There are redundancy, sarcasm, and directness, but no matter what particular linguistic form is selected, all make certain points (repeatedly) about the kinds of behavior expected from others. For example, while eating, Kaluli talk about who gave them food, but they do not talk about what they have eaten on previous occasions. Once they have finished what is available, they will usually claim not to have had enough and still be hungry, especially for meat. Kaluli seem to have the notion that if one has not shared food, one should not talk about eating it This dispreference is invoked in interactions with children, who will often violate the norm and talk about what they have eaten with those with whom they have not, but could have, shared. When at age 34.2 months Abi tells Yaloame, his father's co-wife, about the pandanus he had just eaten, her response is "*You* obviously didn't give *me* any pandanus!" (*Giyɔ ogayɔ nelɔ mɔmilɔbo!*). This line, used by others as well, expressed annoyance and indirectly poses two questions: "*Why* didn't you give me some?! [you should have]," and "*Why* are you telling me what you ate?! [you should not]." One does not share information about food one could have shared.

Except for items of clothing (skirts and pubic covers), and more recently the odd knife, Kaluli children usually own no durable objects. They are not instructed in the names of foods or objects just for the sake of knowing them or for use in naming routines. Using language just to name things does not fit with the essentially social view of language that Kaluli have. Children are socialized into the view that particular relationships obtain between people and objects, that objects play a role in the creation and maintenance of social life and in the coordination of relationships. Children are also socialized to see that personal relationships often depend on the exchange of objects, but that personal relationships come before one's attachment to objects. Objects are tools for social access, and interactions around them create social relationships. Food, unlike most objects, is ideally suited for sharing because it can be divided into almost endless pieces and shared, and thus at one point in time can belong to many people.

Young children frequently talk about objects in terms of whom they belong to and who gave them and ask, "Whose is it?" and "Who gave it?" rather than "What is it?" The source of an object and its current ownership are important social knowledge. When you want something, the first thing you must know is whom it belongs to so you know whom to ask for it and how to ask. Young children talk a great deal about who owns things and who will eat which piece of food when there is something, like a sago packet, to divide. These same interests in source and ownership are expressed by older children and adults talking about the flow of objects and the links they create in social relationships.

Wanu talks a lot about ownership, asking the question "Whose is it?" (*Abɛnowɔ?*) of family members about different things in the house. He does not solicit the names of the objects, most of which he already knows, just the names of the owners. Family members cooperate with his requests and say the names (though often they are not much interested and their answers are ad hoc responses). These exchanges have a playful quality, as Wanu repeats what someone else has said, naming a possible or alternative owner or adding his own commentary, such as "Is it yours?! It's mine! Who are you?!"

From 26 months of age, Meli frequently talks about food and objects in terms of who gave them to her. While playing with her cousin Mama, she shows her an empty tape dispenser and comments, "Mister Briggs [the Australian missionary] gave" (*Misita Biligɛ miyabe*). Most of her talk about this object centers on receiving it from Briggs while at the mission. This way of talking establishes both ownership of the object and source of the object; in other words, her relationship with Mr. Briggs is such that he gives her things. Children often talk about what others receive as well. They use the construction agent + ergative case marking + "give." For example, when showing an older cousin some fungus medication on her mother's arm, Mɛli says *Babiyɛ miyabe* 'Bambi gave'. This was appropriate and important information.[11] In conversations with visitors, Mɛli points out pieces of cooked pumpkin, for example, identifying each with the name of a family member plus the possessive suffix (e.g., *dowɛnɔ; Seligiwɔano* 'it's Father's; it's Seligiwɔ's') or with a possessive pronoun (*nɛnɔ; gɛnɔ; numɛ ɛnɔ* 'mine; yours; someone's') but often without naming the object itself. When she doesn't know whose it is, she asks her mother. These questions are answered patiently.

Children learn early on to talk about objects in these ways, linking them to the people who gave them or own them. Objects are also associated with their owners in third-party threats, such as "The ax will say something" (*Kabiyɛ samɛib*), where the named objects evoke or stand for their owners. This focus on ownership and source is consistent across all families and is not restricted to food. Children talk this way about dogs, pigs, and objects such as net bags, blankets, knives, and sago-processing tools. This information is part of object knowledge and is discussed repeatedly, in both playful and nonplayful exchanges, among adults as well as children. It was a little surprising to me to hear a 2-year-old often speak up and offer the name of the owner and source of an object when a visitor made an admiring comment. This is the most relevant information about the object: the relationship in which it is embedded.

Kelediab 'trade'

Kaluli have a history of trading locally available items, such as black-palm bows, strings of dog teeth, hornbill beaks, and net bags, with their neighbors for highly desired objects that are neither locally produced nor available locally: for example, vegetable salt, cowrie shells, glass beads, and steel ax heads (E. L. Schieffelin 1976:13–14). This type of immediate short-term exchange is called *kelediab* (*kelegɔ* 'things' + *diab* 'take') and means circulation of items according to values, or trade. *Kelediab* refers to situations in which people come together for the purpose of trading, with or without expectations about future transactions. *Kelediab* also describes the exchange between Kaluli and anthropologists of fresh food for salt, soap, or fishhooks, and has been extended to purchasing commodities from trade stores at a fixed price with money.

In family interactions, *kelediab* is occasionally used by Kaluli to describe a type of verbal offer following a refusal, where one kind of object or service is explicitly offered in exchange for another seemingly equivalent object or service. One difference between *kelediab* 'trade' and *hɛnulab* 'counteroffer' is that with *hɛnulab* speakers offer nonequivalent objects, services, and even topics of conversation in exchange for the addressee's current state of attention. *Kelediab* carries the sense of a business transaction and not what one expects among intimates. For example, when Wanu repeatedly refused to let Binalia look at a piece of soap that he was holding, she offered to give him a comb to look at if he would let her hold and look at the soap. Or when Isa's mother would not give her uncooked sago after she repeatedly asked for it, Isa offered her mother a piece of the fish that she wanted to cook in the sago, and her mother agreed to her offer. Adults named these offers of immediate exchange *kelediab*.

These offers of objects to achieve immediate ends are not common in families in spite of the fact that people are continually asking one another for food, objects, and services. This type of exchange is dispreferred among intimates for a number of stylistic, affective, and social reasons. First, although the act ratifies the relationship, an object-for-object (or object-for-service) exchange is not mediated by or embedded in the expected affective dimensions of familial relationships, but instead focuses on the individual's desire for the object (or service) itself. Such exchanges, when they do occur, reframe the transaction as one between nonintimates, putting distance between participants. *Kelediab* as an interactional strategy is of little consequence for building familial relationships, as further refusals in light of such directness leave participants no more options for continued negotiation.

Caregivers actively guide their children's feelings about the role of objects in mediating relationships with others outside the immediate family as well as within. These feelings are made explicit in relevant everyday situations, not in abstract or prescriptive contexts. Asking a child to give to a non–family member is most common in Mɛli's family because of their wider Christian contacts, which create more opportunities for Mɛli to interact with nonkin. In addition, because girls are expected to cook and give food, Mɛli is encouraged to interact with the visitors and offer them food. For example, when Mɛli is 27.3 months old, Osolowa draws on an ongoing situation to make explicit that reciprocity is expected in nonfamilial relationships. One afternoon while I was tape recording, Mɛli was cooking bananas, and Osolowa told her to give one to me. Mɛli ignored the request, and Osolowa then reminded her that I always brought her a small gift of salt. Mɛli responded directly to me, "What will you take for salt?" – a formulaic question that Kaluli ask when they trade (*kelediab*), meaning, What do you want me to give you in exchange for the salt you have? Mɛli's response is one that is used to initiate trading; she did not understand her mother's hint to give me the banana as part of our social relationship. Osolowa's response, laughing at Mɛli, was "What do you mean, 'What will you take for the salt?'?!," indicating that Mɛli's understanding of the situation did not match her expectations. To encourage Mɛli to give to me, she then repeated her request.

To make small children more comfortable around unfamiliar persons, adults tell them what objects a person will give them or remind children of what has already been given. When Osolowa wants to leave an unwilling Mɛli in the care of a village pastor for a few hours while she goes off to the bush, her comment to Mɛli is "I'm sorry for you; he always gives you soap" (*Hɛyɔ sopɔ gemɔ miɛsen*). In other words, he gives you things; you have a relationship with him. Mɛli, who is still unwilling to stay with the pastor, responds with "What soap?!" (*Oba sopɔwɔ?!*), a speech act called *ɛlenyab* 'one doesn't care' that children use when they are not interested.

Mɛli, who spends more time at the mission than any other child, sees Kaluli using money to buy salt, fish, and rice, among other things, at the small mission trade store. She also sees the Australian missionaries and Papuan teachers buying food from Kaluli people with money, something the anthropologists do not do. She hears talk about buying things, and by 28.3 months she is asking many questions about exchange, about using money, and about exchanging trade items such as salt and soap for food items. However, even though money is entering the local exchange system and is highly valued and desired, the importance of social relationships still figures critically in the organization and meaning of everyday exchange. This short discussion is one of many that show her mother's responses to Mɛli's probing questions about this new system of exchange.

Example 6.26. Visiting Mɛli (28.3) and her mother, I ask Mɛli, who is cooking bananas, to cook one for me. She agrees, but after a few minutes she still has not started to cook mine.

Mother → Mɛli: If you don't cook the banana, she won't give you salt.
Maguwɔ mɔsɔfiabe, sɔluwɔ eyɔ mɔmiɛbkɛ.
        when we trade for salt, then I will eat it /
        sɔluwɔ ka kelediaki ɛnɔ menɔkɛ /
If you cooked her banana, she would give you salt.
Ɔgiyɔ e maguwɔ sɔfɛ kibabeyɔ ɔ sɔluwɔ mibabe.
[Seligiwɔ urinates, and they both attend to him.]

Here Osolowa uses yet another rhetorical strategy to shape Mɛli's understanding and expectations of reciprocity. Osolowa first states her proposition in terms of the negative consequences (no banana, no salt), and then, after Mɛli has not gotten that message, Osolowa restates her message in terms of the positive outcome (cook banana, get salt). Osolowa lays out the traditional option to Meli, one that involves long-term exchange and relationship, not a short-term business arrangement available to anyone with money. Kaluli do not think of objects or food being used to buy the child's affection or trust. Objects are mediators of personal relationships; they are an important medium through which relationships grow and develop. Objects represent to the individuals involved and to others the fact that a particular type of relationship exists, one that involves sources and owners. In talk about object exchanges, the prevailing expectation is that relationships that are fostered and encouraged will continue.

7. The development of children's requests

Every language provides linguistic resources so that the finer shades of affect and key can be expressed across a range of situations and social relationships.[1] Kaluli carries affective information through a rich system of evidential, affect, and emphatic particles and affixes; affectively marked pronouns; word order; and prosody in addition to other paralinguistic features that convey the expression of varying degrees of assertion and appeal. Input contributes directly to children's acquisition of the particular forms of language used in assertive requests as children participate in extensive ɛlɛma routines containing sequences with syntactically variable request forms. In contrast, there is no direct instruction in socializing children's requests based on appeal. Appeal is seen as the natural mode of children, the way they get what they want, whereas verbal assertion is seen as necessitating direct instruction through specific routines. Thus, young children can appeal to others with a limited linguistic repertoire, whereas assertion, which involves persuasion and more complex rhetorical skills, is conveyed by a larger set of linguistic expressions.

Young children are sensitive to the fact that language encodes a range of affect, and they easily acquire competence in affect-loaded grammatical forms and contexts. Data from Samoan children indicate that affect constructions may be particularly salient as children acquire high-affect forms before more neutral forms that identify the same object or have similar referential content (Ochs 1986). Kaluli children also use affect-marked pronominal forms, expressives, emphatics, evidentials, and prosody in order to display their feelings from the time they start producing single-word utterances (B. B. Schieffelin 1986a).

Requests are one of several speech acts that reflect children's maximum interest in using language to achieve particular ends. As initiating speech acts, requests usually demonstrate the full range of sociolinguistic resources that children can draw on when they want a positive outcome, in contrast to other types of speech acts, like answering questions, where children have to take into account what the previous speaker has said and formulate their utterances accordingly (Bloom, Rocissano & Hood 1976), or in responding to ɛlɛma routines, where children may just be complying and repeating. While young children use many of the same forms to encode affective distinctions made by adults, at particular points in developmental time they make additional distinctions not made by adults, particularly in requests. They select particular forms of the language to further mark particular speech acts, specifically requests made of their mothers. They create variation in form/function relationships in specific contexts that co-occur with specific classes of objects where the formal language does not. Furthermore, they consistently select certain syntactic constructions when requesting food and objects according to whether they are asking in an assertive manner or appealing. In addition, young children switch between conventional and special verb forms to encode whether the self or another person is to be the recipient of the object they are requesting, thus linking the expression of a specific feeling state and linguistic marking of an intended egocentric or sociocentric outcome. An examination of variation in the use of request forms and in particular verb forms in requests demonstrates how language is sensitively manipulated by young Kaluli children to express conceptual categories important to them. From the time they are very small, children are sensitive to the fact that language can express affect, index specific activities, and specify particular relationships. Furthermore, as children begin to use language, they find ways to use it according to their own perception of what is important.

[margin handwritten: lang at a very early age affecting behavior]

Making requests: family orientations

There were striking similarities as well as variation across the three children in the request forms they used for the breast and food items (the major objects of desire) as well as for objects (beads, knives, sticks, net bags, cloths). From 24 to 30 months, there were similarities in children's differentiation of requests according to whether food/breast as opposed to an object was requested. Distinctions between food and nonfood are not formally encoded in Kaluli. Requests for the breast, for example, varied in terms of linguistic construction and the social routines they initiated. Several factors contributed to the differences in children's linguistic and social behaviors, including different family orientations to traditional versus Christian ideology, nursing and weaning patterns, the birth order and gender of the child, and such psychological factors as temperament of the caregiver and of the child. In order to understand the linguistic and social variation, I shall present selected differences for the three families.

Abi's mother was very indulgent with Abi and almost never refused her firstborn son anything he wanted. She dressed in traditional Kaluli style, and her breasts were never covered. Since Abi could take the breast whenever he desired, asking for or negotiating the amount of time on the breast was not part of his verbal repertoire. In spite of Ulahi's pregnancy throughout a major part of the study, Abi was not weaned until the age of 31 months, after his

Figures 24 *(top)* and 25. Wanu begging food from his mother and receiving it.

brother was born. This did not conform to the Kaluli expressed preference for weaning a child before the birth of the next baby. In fact, during the late stages of his mother's pregnancy Abi was frequently offered the breast, especially to soothe him when he was angry. With several older sisters in his household, Abi had an extensive range of individuals of whom he could make requests based on either assertion or appeal. His linguistic repertoire developed in the context of negotiating what he wanted with older sisters as well as with his mother.

Wanu's mother also wore traditional Kaluli dress, making her breasts accessible. At the start of the study, Wanu was still nursing, and he would usually ask for the breast when he wanted it. However, unlike Mɛli and Abi, Wanu was weaned when his mother was in the late stages of pregnancy. His sister was born when he was about 27 months old. This followed the preferred weaning pattern that people talk about.[2] Requests for the breast were recorded only in the first sample, because by Sample 2 Wanu was losing interest in the breast and no longer asked to nurse. Wanu also had two older sisters to whom requests could be addressed. Wanu's extensive interactions with his father also provided him with many opportunities to develop a range of request forms.

Mɛli's situation was different. As a firstborn child, she did not have older siblings with whom she could regularly interact. Her household did include her cross-cousin, who was fifteen months older than herself, but their talk included few requests. Mɛli's requests were mostly made of her mother's sisters and of her mother. Because her parents followed local Christian beliefs, they no longer practiced the traditional postpartum sex taboo, and Mɛli had a brother seventeen months younger than herself. Her brother always had first right to the breast. Mɛli was not old enough to be weaned, but because she was bigger, her mother worried that she would take all of the milk; her nursing time was often short. Mɛli's mother usually wore a dress, making it impossible for Mɛli just to take the breast herself. Consequently, Mɛli always

Table 3. *Mɛli's requests for the breast*

Sample	Age[a]	Length[b]	No. of utterances	No. of requests for breast	% of utterances
1[c]	—	—	—	—	—
2	24.3	1.5	603	42	7
3	26	3	936	29	3
4	27.3	4	1,513	34	2
5	28.3	4	1,546	136	9
6	30.2	3	1,517	6	0.3
7	31.2	3.25	1,260	15	1
8	32.2	4.25	1,514	0	—

[a] In months and weeks.
[b] In hours.
[c] This sample consists of speech between Mɛli and her grandfather. It may be that it was not an appropriate context in which to use either construction.

Table 4. *Distribution of Mɛli's use of syntactic forms when asking for the breast*

Sample	Syntactic form selected[a]
2	1
3	1
4	1 (2 used as single utterances with no elaboration)
5	1 and 2 (2 followed by 1 as a sequence)
6	2
7	1
8	0

Note: Except in Samples 4 and 5, only one syntactic form per sample was selected.

[a] 1 = *nelɔ*; 2 = *mɛ*.

asked for the breast. She developed verbal routines for getting the breast and complex negotiations for determining how long she could nurse. She was always willing to nurse at the same time as her brother and expressed concern that he get enough. While her mother was frequently reluctant to allow Mɛli to nurse for a prolonged period, she was willing to engage in extensive discussions about it. Requests for the breast formed an important part of the verbal routines between Mɛli and her mother, and within these routines a number of critical syntactic and discourse features developed. Mɛli's requests peaked at approximately 29 months of age. After that, she became increasingly independent and shifted from spending most of her time with her mother to spending more time with other girls in the village. She gave up interest in the breast and stopped talking about it.

The development of request forms

Requests for the breast

Mɛli's requests for the breast were usually initiated by the vocative (*nɔ* 'my mother') or the shared name (*wi ɛlɛdɔ*) *ne bo* 'my breast' and used an affect-marked pronoun *nelɔ* 'to me' and verb forms (*dimina*), frequently repeated, forming elaborate sequences marked with a variety of emphatic suffixes. Asking for the breast was almost always marked with descending intonation contours, increased nasality, and the softer voice quality (*geseab*) that is widely used in requests based on appeal. Two syntactic constructions accounted for all instances of Mɛli's requests for the breast from 24.3 to 32.2 months of age (see Tables 3 and 4).

Construction 1 used the affect-marked pronoun *nelɔ* 'to me/I want' as a single-word utterance or followed by an inflected verb. It indicates a desired action.[3] Optional elements that can be inserted in this construction, such as possessive pronouns, emphatic particles, and inflected verbs, are indicated in parentheses.

Construction 1

(nɔ)	(gi)	(bo (-wɔ)ɔ)	(1) **nelɔ**-(2)	(nɔl-(3))
	(ne	bo)		
mother	your	breast	I want / to me	DRINK / EAT I P pres
	my	breast		

"(Mother), I want (to drink) (your) breast."

(1) Nominal modifiers
  hɛlu 'a little'
  ba hɛlu 'only a little'
  nodowɔ 'the other one'
  deyɔwɔ 'the swollen one'
"(Mother), I want (to drink) (your) (a little) breast."

(2) Emphatic particles for nouns
  -wɛ emphasis
  -wo intensified emphasis / intimacy
"(Mother), I really want (to drink) (your) breast."

(3) Emphatic particles for verbs
  -ɛ~-wɛ emphasis
  -o~-wo intensified emphasis / intimacy
  -ologa~-wologa I said (self-repetition for emphasis)
" '(Mother), I really want to drink (your) breast!' I said!"

Construction 2 is an imperative that uses a special reduced form (*mɛ*) of the present imperative form of the verb "give" (*dimina*).

Construction 2

(nɔ)	(ne)	bowɔ	**mɛ**
mother	(to me)	breast	GIVE imp

"(Mother), give (me) the breast."

Mɛ and its two more emphatic variants (*mo* and *mologa*) from *dimina/mina* 'give' are the only stable "baby" forms consistently found in the speech of small children. These three alternative forms of the verb are marked for affect (appeal); in addition, the suffixes -ɛ, -ɔ, and -*ologa* add emphasis or intensify the affect. A nonemphatic form *ma* from *dimina* was never used by the children in this study. These appeal forms are further marked by voice quality (*geseab*). Children do not use these baby forms as single-word utterances. They are always preceded by a noun (direct object) with elision of *mɛ* or *mo* with that preceding noun (often *bowɔ* 'breast' or the name of a food item). This suggests that children may be treating these verb forms as emphatic affective suffixes attached to the noun rather than as separate lexical items. Young children further distinguish requests with Construction 2, the *mε* forms in the appeal mode, from requests with the verbs *dimina/mina* in an assertive mode, as the verbs *dimina/mina* 'give' are used as single-word utterances as well as in syntactic constructions and are clearly treated as separate lexical items that themselves take the emphatic suffixes: (*di*)*minε*, and (*di*)*mino*, (*di*)*minologa*.

Kaluli has several concatenated verbs that combine with the verb *mina*. Forms heard frequently in family interaction include *gulumina* 'break off a part and give', *diεmina* 'take and give', *dagumina* 'peel and give' (as in bananas), *silimina* 'take out (of a bag) and give', and *ɔmina* 'chew and give'. These are contractions of the concatenated forms "having done *x*, give." Of these forms, *ɔmina* is the most commonly used by small children; it is a Kaluli practice to premasticate such foodstuffs as meat, cooked bananas, taro, and sugar cane for infants and small children. After chewing a portion of food, caregivers either put it directly into an infant's mouth or, upon request, hand it to a small child. While most 2-year-olds can chew their own food, *ɔmina* 'chew and give' is a common request form in children's speech until about 30 months. Kaluli children always use the full forms of these compound verbs. Even when begging for prechewed food, they always use the full form *ɔmina*, never reducing it to **ɔmε*.

Thus, there are several differences between young children and older children and adults in the use of *dimina/mina*. *Dimina* is used by older children and adults with a wide range of addressees, both assertively and in appeal; young children use it only in assertion to a range of addressees. All use *dimina/mina* as single words and in syntactic constructions. *Dimina/mina* differs from Construction 2, *mε*, in that *mε* is used (i) only by young children; (ii) only in appeal with *geseab;* (iii) never as a single-word utterance; and (iv), with few exceptions, only in address to mothers. Furthermore, these baby forms are used only when children are begging for the breast or for food or things they want for themselves.

It is not surprising that the only baby forms used by Kaluli children are derived from the imperative form of the verb "give," a critical word in a society where reciprocity and exchange are crucial in social relationships and where a preferred way to get what one wants is to ask. The use of *mε* entails asking but retains childlike appeal. Kaluli, however, do not talk about these forms as special baby forms. None of the three baby forms of the verb "give" are ever used by adults or older children when speaking to babies. As I mentioned earlier, Kaluli do not instruct children to appeal for what they want, nor do they use any baby-talk lexicon. Consequently, they never instruct children to use *mε/mo/mologa*, but instead instruct them to use *dimina* or *mina*. In addition, these special forms are rarely found in the speech of adults or older children when they are speaking to children already using them, and then only when requesting clarification following a young child's use of the form, when repeating the child's utterance to someone else, or when making fun of the child. One young woman did the last when Mɛli was repeatedly begging her mother for some bananas while her mother was talking to a group of friends.

Example 7.1. [Sample 2]. Mɛli (24.3). (Emphatics and special verb forms are in bold type.)

[To mother]   ¹Nɔ, magu genɛ / X / X / Mother, ripe ba-
                                          nana! / X / X /
²Dauwa [in high voice, playfully mocking Mɛli]: Nɔ, magu genɔ
mɛ!
Mother, give ripe banana!
[The women continue talking, ignoring
Mɛli, who becomes increasingly upset,
crying and whining]   ³magu genɔ **nɛ** / magu genɔ **mologa** / nɔ
                                          magu genɔ **mɛ** / X / nɔ magu genɔ **mo** /
                                          magu genɔ **mologa** / nɔ magu genɔ **mɛ** /
                                          give ripe banana /

After getting no response, Mɛli asks her mother, "Do you hear what I said?" (*Ge siyɔwɔ dɛdaya?*). Still getting no response, she turns to the others and asks, "Doesn't she hear?" (*Mɔdɛdabɛ?*) This finally gets her mother's attention, and Mɛli then begins to beg for the breast, switching from asking for a banana using Construction 2 (*mɛ* 'give') to asking for the breast using Construction 1 only (*nelɔ* 'I want').

Without comment, these reduced forms eventually disappear from usage as children approach their third birthday and thereafter use only the full forms of the imperative *dimina/mina* in assertion and appeal, distinguishing the two modalities by using prosody, volume, and affect-marked vocatives.

Mɛli's use of request forms: developmental order

Both Construction 1, the pronominal request form *nelɔ* 'to me/I want', and Construction 2, *mɛ* (imperative) 'give', appear in Mɛli's spontaneous speech starting in Sample 2 (age 24.3). In that sample as well as in Samples 3 and 4, Mɛli uses Construction 2 *mɛ* in begging for food, but she does not continue to use it to appeal for the breast. During these first four samples (with two exceptions), when Mɛli appeals for the breast she uses only *nelɔ* 'I want' (Construction 1). Construction 2 (*mɛ*), as we shall see, does not appear in requests for the breast until Sample 5, four months later.

Example 7.2. [Sample 2]. Mɛli (24.3), her father, Degelɔ, and her mother, Osolowa, are sitting around the firepit. Osolowa is nursing Seligiwɔ (7 mo), who is sick and half asleep. She is wearing a dress, and one breast is still inside. (*Nelɔ* and *mina* are in bold type.)

[Mɛli is about to strike Seligiwɔ.]
¹Father → Mɛli: Ah! Sandɛsabɔ! Ko walafkɛ!
No! Don't hit! That one is really sick!
²Mother → Mɛli: Hɛh?!
What's that about?!
³Father: We ne ɛya.
This is my "father."
[Whining]

⁴Nɔ bo **nelɔ** / Nɔ bo **nelɔ** nɔlo / Nɔ bo no-
dowa **nelɔ** nɔlo /
Mother, I want the breast / Mother, I want
to drink the breast /Mother, I want to drink
on the other breast /

⁵Mother → Mɛli: Oba bo nodowɔ?!
What other breast?!

⁶egɛ we *disalifɔ / X /
uh this put-away one /

⁷Ɔdisalife!
It's already put away!

⁸ɛh we disalife / ɔdisalife /
yes this put-away one / it's already put
away /

⁹Ɔdisalife!
It's already put away!

¹⁰we disalifeyɔ? /
is this the put-away one? /

¹¹Ɛm.
Yes.

¹²we diseyɔ?! / /
is this put in?! / /
Nɔ bo **nelowɛ** / Nɔ bowɔ nodowɔ **nelɔ** /
X / Nɔ bowɔ nodowɔ nɔl / X /
Mother, I want the breast / Mother,
I want the other breast / X / mother,
I drink the other breast /

[Seligiwɔ cries, and mother initiates ɛlɛma routine with Mɛli.]
¹³Mother → Mɛli →> Seligiwɔ Odiɛni yɛlaya?! – ɛlɛma.
Why are you crying?! – say it.
[To baby]

¹⁴odiɛni yɛlaya?! /
why are you crying?! /

¹⁵Yɛlɛsabo! – ɛlɛma.
Don't cry! – say it.

¹⁶yɛlɛsabo! /
don't cry! /

[To mother]

¹⁷Nɔ bowɔ **mina** / Nɔwɔ / bowɔ /
Mother, give (him) the breast / Mother /
breast /

[Mother gives Seligiwɔ the breast. Mɛli then tries to take the other breast out of the dress for herself, asking if she can just hold it. They talk about it, and both children finally nurse. The mother distracts Mɛli with another object, and she stops nursing.]

This sequence displays many of the salient features of Kaluli interactions with small children that are centered on requests. For one thing, requests based on appeal are frequently made after the child feels that he or she has suffered some type of disappointment or has not gotten what is wanted. This event starts when Mɛli's father, Degelɔ, tells Mɛli not to hit her brother, who is sick. Her mother also yells at her, followed by her father's referring to the baby as *ne ɛya*, an affectionate term.[4] After this negative attention directed toward Mɛli and positive attention toward her brother, Mɛli immediately requests the breast, using the affect-marked pronoun *nelɔ* 'to me' with the voice quality of appeal (*geseab*). Each consecutive utterance in this sequence of three becomes more elaborate as Mɛli adds additional verbal elements to her request.[5] With the additional syntactic complexity, she also increases the intensity of her demand as she indicates which breast she wants (the one on the other side, the one her brother does not have).

Her mother responds (line 5) with the rhetorical question "What other breast?!," meaning that there is no other for her. Mɛli responds to this as if it were an information question, answering "The put-away one." Her mother's response to this is to repeat what Mɛli has said, using the correct form of the verb that Mɛli has used incorrectly, to which Mɛli responds, "Yes, this put-away one" (using the correct verb form). She then repeats her mother's utterance again, adding the adverbial prefix ɔ- 'already'. Her mother repeats her utterance as a way of affirming it, which is followeed by a clarification request from Mɛli (line 10), which her mother confirms. Mɛli, however, is not satisfied with this as a response to her request and comes back with a rhetorical question (line 12), "Is this put in?!," as a way of continuing the discussion. Getting no response from her mother, Mɛli reinitiates the request, adding emphatic markers to *nelɔ* (-wɛ) and repeating herself in a whining manner.

Mothers rarely refuse young children's requests directly, though it does happen. Instead, like Mɛli's mother in the example above, they use rhetorical questions to challenge children's claims, and engage them in conversation throughout. Here Mɛli's mother tries to distract her by involving her in an ɛlɛma routine with Seligiwɔ. When Mɛli tries to take the breast out of her mother's dress and then tells her that she is unable to, her mother responds, "You can't take the breast out? Why is anyone taking this breast out at all?!" Mɛli again attempts to strike her brother and is admonished. She asks just to hold the breast, another request that moves her closer to her goal, and finally ends up nursing for a brief period until she is again distracted by her mother. Interactions such as these provide opportunities for young children to develop strategies for modulating their requests and to acquire ways of responding to refusals without feeling that they are being rejected. At no point is a definitive no given, and Osolowa's rhetorical questions give Mɛli the option of either dropping her request or finding another way to negotiate. In these cases, the ball remains in Mɛli's court.

A similar sequence was recorded three months later. Mɛli was still using Construction 1 (*nelɔ*) as her only form for requesting the breast.

Example 7.3. [Sample 4]. Mɛli (27.3) and her mother have been doing an *ɛlɛma* routine directed to me. As Mɛli tires, she begins to whine and requests the breast. Her mother ignores her requests. Mɛli finally pulls down the zipper on her mother's dress. (Emphatic morphemes are in bold type.)

	¹Nɔ ne bowɔ nelowɛ! / Nɔ ne bowɔ / Mother, I want my breast! / Mother, my breast /
²Mother → Mɛli: Ginowɔ?! Is it yours?! [Starting to cry] [Re breast]	³nelɔwɛ! / ɔ gɛ oba! / we ginowele?! / I want! / who are you?! / is this yours?! /
⁴Yagidi! Oh my! [laughing] [Mɛli unzips mother's dress.] [Taking out breast]	⁵oba? / oba? / ɔ we dugufanigɔ**bale**! / ɔ we ne mɛnigɔ**bale**! / what? what? / I'm really going to take this out! / I'm really going to drink this! /
[Mɛli starts to nurse.] ⁶Ai! [Mother pushes her away.]	⁷Nɔ ba hɛlu nelɔ nɔlɛ / Mother, I only want to drink a little /
⁸Ɛm? Huh?	⁹ba hɛlu nelɔ nɔ**loga** / I only want to drink a little, I said /
¹⁰Wah? Huh?	¹¹ba deyɔwɔ hɛlu nelɔ nolɛ / I only want to drink a little of the swollen one /
¹²Ba hɛlu gelɔ naya? You want to drink only a little?	¹³ɔ deyɔ / X / ba deyɔ hɛlu nelɔ nɔlɛ / the swollen one / I only want to drink a little of the swollen one /
¹⁴Ba deyɔ hɛlu gelɔ naya? You only want to drink a little of the swollen one?	ɛm / yes /
Ɛm. Yes. [Mɛli nurses.]	

In this example we see that syntactically Mɛli is able to add additional elements with each repetition. Her mother supports her talk with clarification requests and repetition. She sequences and elaborates her request with Construction 1 (*nelɔ*). Construction 2, with *mɛ*, occurs only twice in this long sample, which has a total of sixty-four requests, thirty for objects and thirty-four for the breast. Both instances of *mɛ* are isolated requests with no elaboration, one for the breast, which is ignored and Mɛli is distracted, and the other for a vegetable, which is responded to positively. Thus, in Sample 4 Mɛli is still relying heavily on Construction 1 (*nelɔ*) in requesting the breast.

As early as Sample 2 (24.3), however, Mɛli demonstrates her ability to use the full imperative forms *dimina* and *mina* and to switch between them and the highly affect-marked *mɛ/mo/mologa* forms. Her use of these two sets of verb forms shows her sensitivity to marking modality (assertion/appeal), and type of object requested (food/other items). Thus, for example, Mɛli uses the full forms *dimina* and *mina* in an assertive modality when requesting food for herself, but never when requesting the breast for herself.

Example 7.4. [Sample 2]. Mɛli (24.3) is with her father, who is cutting up some meat.

Father → Mɛli: Banɔ gemɔlɔ mɔmian.
The leg isn't given to you.

> nemɔ **dimiyɛ** / Do / nemɔ ***dimiyɔkɛ***!! /
> give it to me / Father / give it to me !! /

Again, in Sample 3 (26 mo) there are many examples of Mɛli's asking for objects using the full form of the verb *dimina* with different final emphatic particles (-ɛ, -ɔ), but the breast is never requested this way.

Mɛli asks for an object. (Emphatic morphemes are in bold type.)

> Nɔ / ne dimina / Nɔ / ɛnɔ ne dimina / dim-
> inɛ! / Nɔ ɛnɔ ne dimino! / ge siyɔwɔ dɛda-
> ya? /
> Mother / give me / Mother / give it to me /
> give! / Mother, give it to me! / do you hear
> what I said? /

Another dimension of Mɛli's sensitivity to the social implications of variation in language use is her ability to switch verb forms according to the intended recipient (self/other), as can be seen in Example 7.2, line 17. Before this point in the interaction, Mɛli's mother adopts the strategy of *hɛnulab* 'persuade/distract', taking advantage of the baby's crying to initiate an *ɛlɛma* routine with Mɛli. Mɛli participates in this verbal routine, directing her attention to the baby. After repeating two utterances issued by her mother (lines 14, 16), Mɛli spontaneously suggests to her mother that her mother give the breast to the baby (*Nɔ bowɔ mina / Nɔwɔ / bowɔ /*). Note that Mɛli uses the *mina* form of the verb as she offers her mother a solution to ease the baby's discomfort. There are many instances where Mɛli suggests to her mother that the baby be given the breast when he is crying, and in all cases she used the *mina* or *dimina* form, never the *mɛ* form.

At this same time (Sample 3, 26 mo), Mɛli also asks for sugar cane for herself and uses the imperative verb forms *ɔmina* and *ɔminologa* 'chew and give'. Other requests use *mina*. All of these are in an assertive mode, and the verb is never reduced to *me*. Meli has assigned each of the two sets of verb forms for "give" to self-as-recipient versus other-as-recipient in terms of appeal versus assertive modality and as marking the type of object in question. Meli selects the *me* forms when she is to be the recipient of the breast and (occasionally) other food she is begging for. Thus, Meli marks a distinction between sociocentric and egocentric intended recipient by her choice between forms. This distinction is not made by adults or older children.

For Meli, self-as-recipient with *me* requests co-occurs only with appeal, while other-as-recipient using *dimina* co-occurs only with an assertive mode. This demonstrates the child's creation of co-occurrence rules involving the use of specific linguistic forms tied to specific keys or modality. Meli is selecting one form for one function, with affect and recipient indexed by her choice. While the use of *elema* with assertive modality is another example of co-occurrence, it is explicitly displayed in the input. Also modeled, but in a less direct way, are caregivers' appeals to older siblings on behalf of younger siblings, but young children do not use the *ade* term or appeal in a sociocentric way.

Finally, in Sample 5 (age 28.3), which has the largest number of requests for the breast of any sample (136 of 1,546 utterances, or 9%). Meli adds Construction 2 (*me*) and uses both Constructions 1 and 2 in the same speech event (see Table 4 above). Meli sequences the two constructions, but only in the following order (Construction 2, Construction 1; marked in bold type).

| [To mother] | nɔ bowɔ **me** / X / ba helu **nelɔ** nɔlɛ / |
| | Mother, give (me) the breast / X / I want to drink only a little / |

Meli uses only common nouns when using the *me* form, never any deictics or demonstratives (such as **kowɔ me*). When she speaks in an assertive mode, she inflects the verb "eat/drink" in three different tenses (present, inceptive, future). When she appeals, however, using Construction 1, she uses the verb "drink/eat" inflected in only one tense, the present. Especially when compared with requests for other food and objects made in a more assertive modality, requests for the breast are compressed, routinized, and highly marked for affect.

Compare, for example, a sequence from the same time (Sample 5, age 28.3) when Meli's mother is cooking a small marsupial and Meli asks for it in the following ways in the same situation:

wafɔ	ne	*miyebiyo*	'give me the tail later' (after it is cooked)
tail	to me	GIVE fut imp emph	
wafɔ	ne	*mina*	'give me the tail now' (it is cooked)
		GIVE pres imp	
wafɔ	ne	*menɔ* (**mɛnɛ*)	'I will eat the tail' (reaching for the tail)
		EAT fut 1 P	

Mɛli asked for food, referring to the items with a variety of nouns, deictics, and demonstratives, and appropriately using different syntactic constructions, some of which are listed below. None of the following constructions were used when she asked for the breast.

mɛnɔ	*heh?*	'what about sago / food?'
sago	what about	
mɛnɔ	*abamiyɔ?*	'where's the sago / food?'
sago	where	
we	*abenɔwɔ?*	'whose is this?' (where ownership indicates access)
this	whose	
kɔnɔ	*wi*	'sugar cane over here' (toward me)
sugar	toward me	
mɛnɔ	*ne*	'sago / food to me'
sago	to me	
Ne mɛnɔ	*mayab.*	'I'm hungry (for food / sago).'
I food	hungry	

Before discussing why children linguistically differentiate requests based on appeal and requests made assertively, and additionally why they associate particular linguistic forms with requests for the breast and use other linguistic constructions for requesting other objects, I present data from the two other children in the study.

Abi's and Wanu's use of request forms: a developmental overview

In Sample 1 Wanu used Construction 2 (*mɛ/mɔ/mologa*) for all requests for food, including the breast (twenty-four tokens). As with Mɛli, these forms were never used as single-word utterances. Instead, they specified the name of the food or used the word for breast and were consistently said in a whining tone (*geseab*). Wanu also used Construction 1 (*nelɔ*), but only to request nonfood items (batteries, sticks, blanket), never to request food or the breast. In addition to *nelɔ*, Wanu used a limited number of deictics and directionals, such as *ko wiyɛ* 'that in my direction' and *nuwɔ we* 'some here' to ask for nonfood objects that he wanted. These forms were used with both assertive and appeal demeanors.

One month later, in Sample 2, Wanu did not nurse or ask for the breast once during the entire three-hour sample (taken over three days). During this time he was very actively focused on getting and playing with objects. The *mɛ* construction was not used at all, but the full forms *mina* and *dimina* were frequent. Several concatenated forms (including *asumina* 'tie and give'; *hagomina* 'take off and give'; *gulumina* 'break and give') were also used to request objects, though they were not always appropriate semantically. In this sample, *nelɔ* was used in requests for food as well as for objects.

Wanu was no longer nursing by Sample 3 (age 26.3), but *mɛ* returned in requests for both food and objects based on appeal, while *mina/dimina* were used only assertively. Wanu's pattern of using the *mɛ* construction only with appeals and using the full verbal forms assertively remained constant throughout the study (ages 24 to 32 mo). Except for two tokens in the later samples when *mɛ* was used in appeals to his father, Wanu used the *mɛ* forms only when appealing to his mother. He never used *mɛ* in speech addressed to his sisters, though he did appeal to them using other linguistic forms.

As mentioned above, Abi rarely asked for the breast, and he was never told to stop nursing once he had started. The few times he did ask for the breast, he used the *mɛ* construction accompanied by either soft voice or whining, but he rarely had to ask more than once or twice. In Sample 1 (age 25.1), Abi asked only for food (not objects) and used Syntactic Constructions 1 and 2 in addition to *dimina* and *mina* 'give'. Abi continued to use these forms throughout the study. In Sample 2 (25.3; taken at the mission health center), there was no food around. In his requests for objects, Abi used only Construction 1 and other nominal forms, but no verb forms at all (i.e., Construction 2 using *mɛ*). Unlike the other two children, Abi did not use object names in requests, but had several alternative ways of requesting objects using pronouns, directionals, and deictics. All of these constructions are grammatically correct.

amiy.ɔ ne then to me		'then to me'
ɛn.ɔ ne it to me		'it to me'
nil.ɔw.ɔ the one that is mine	*wiy.ɔ* toward me	'the one that is mine toward me'
ko nil.ɔw.ɔ that one that is mine		'that one is mine'
nil.ɔw.ɔ the one that is mine	*hɛh?!* what about	'what about the one that is mine?!'
nuw.ɔ ne some to me		'some to me'

These different constructions were used in both assertive and appeal modalities. The other two children did not exhibit this range of constructions for requests using nominal and pronominal forms even by the last samples (32 mo). Given the amount of individual variation in early language, this is not surprising.

By the third sample (age 27.2), Abi was using *mina* 'give'. But like Mɛli and Wanu, he used the *mɛ/mo/mologa* forms only in appeal with a soft, plaintive voice (*gesɛab*). Abi used this request form to ask for objects as well as for food. During this early sample, objects were often named in noun + *nel.ɔ* constructions and noun + verb constructions. Like the other two children, Abi used the *mɛ* forms only when appealing for food from his mother, and

used other linguistic forms when begging from his sisters. Such shifts in linguistic form occurred within the same speech event: In requesting something
from a sister using *nelɔ*, for example, and getting a refusal, he would request
the same thing from his mother and shift to *mɛ*, thus affectively intensifying
the request and marking his mother as addressee. As in the other families, the
mɛ form and its variants were never used in *ɛlɛma* routines, nor did adults
and older children use this form.

Another form, *niɛnɛ* 'I want' (*ni* 'I' + *ɛnɛ* 'it' emph), was used frequently
by the members of Abi's and Suela's family. It was said only when asking in
a soft, plaintive, singsong contour, but never when whining (*gɛseab*); it was
instructed (with *ɛlɛma*) to be used in first appeals for food. It was used frequently by Ulahi, Yaloame, and their older children when they asked each
other for food. In contrast to frequent use in Abi's family, this form was used
only four times in the combined Wanu and Mɛli corpus. Wanu himself never
used it; when it was used by his sisters, its pragmatic force was identical to
its use in Abi's family: as a type of appeal. Ulahi and Yaloame were from the
eastern Bosavi dialect area (Ologo); this form may have been more commonly
used in that area. It was understood but not frequently used by other speakers
in Sululib, where a more central Bosavi dialect was spoken.

Children's requests: forms, functions, and origins

During the time young Kaluli children are acquiring requests, they show a
particular sensitivity to the fact that language systematically varies across social contexts, and that such variation is part of the meaning of linguistic structures. Variable linguistic structures index the situational and affective conditions of use with which they are associated. In developing request forms,
children select particular linguistic forms to systematically differentiate modality (assertion and appeal), indirect object (self/other as recipient), and type
of direct object (food/breast/objects). Mɛli showed the most consistent and
wide-ranging variation, but the other children also differentially marked requests as well. In the early stages of multiword utterances, Mɛli varied her
use of several alternative linguistic constructions. When requesting the breast
for herself, *nelɔ* was the preferred request form for the first four samples, and
mɛ (a baby form) was used to ask for the breast at the point where Mɛli's
mother was actively trying to discourage nursing and Mɛli was asking for the
breast more frequently (Sample 5). It was during this time (age 28.3) that the
most elaborate verbal negotiations took place. Perhaps Mɛli was using this
baby form as a rhetorical strategy to convey to her mother her status as one
who should still have the breast. It should be noted that, with one exception,
Mɛli used the *mɛ* form only when appealing to her mother.[6]

Mɛli's requests for the breast showed very little change over developmental time compared with the growth and development of other kinds of complexity in her requests for other food and objects. Requests for the breast were highly routinized and showed little syntactic variation. She used one syntactic construction (*nelɔ* 'I want'), and though she added emphatic particles to pronouns and verbs and noun modifiers, she relied heavily on self-repetition of this one syntactic construction rather than on varying syntactic expressions. Again, it is clear from her other requests for food, especially those that were assertive or stated more neutrally, that Mɛli was fully capable of much greater complexity and variation in syntactic expression, choice of tense, and sequencing of propositions. Requests for the breast, and appeals in general, relied on a more restricted use of language, highly marked for affect and very repetitious.[7] It is as if during this time Mɛli is creating a particular speech register for requests for the breast, marking these routines very differently from others that are assertive and from cases where she is asking that something be given to someone else. Mɛli shifts between the *mɛ* forms, used only in appeal and when she herself is the intended recipient, to the full forms *dimina* and *mina*, which she uses assertively when her brother is the intended recipient of her request to give him the breast. *Nelɔ* is used largely for appeals; *dimina* and other syntactic constructions are used assertively. Thus, the speech act (request) and the addressee (mother) remain constant, but the demeanor and the recipient are different.

Mɛli's requests for the breast have a restricted format, whereas requests for other food and objects are expressed through a wide range of expressions. Why might there be this particular kind of linguistic variation? First, the special relationship between child and mother mediated through sharing the first food, breast milk, is culturally salient and highly marked for affect, as evidenced, among other things, by the culturally recognized first words *bo* 'breast' and *nɔ* 'mother', and a special shared name (*ne bo* 'my breast') used in appeals between mothers and nursing children. No other sharing is like it; only mothers can be asked to give and can give the breast. These requests, unlike all others, index the addressee in the request form itself. They also frame a social activity that has clear boundaries, one that requires cooperation from a consistent single partner. Affect marking is particularly salient in terms of the expressive importance of these particular requests, and children use special forms of language to mark them. In Mɛli's case, the restricted use of *mɛ/mo/mologa* can be seen as a type of register marking, one that is based on non-instructed baby forms. For all children, *mɛ* and its variants are used almost exclusively in address to mothers, not to fathers or older siblings, and only in appeal with the self as (intended) recipient. Thus, this baby form may be closely tied affectively to the earliest interactions between mothers and children, indexing that relationship – though it is not used exclusively to appeal for food from mothers. In other words, these restricted forms carry a powerful social meaning.

Wanu also used both syntactic constructions simultaneously at age 24.1, but he used them complementarily in requests for breast/food and nonfood items. Construction 1 (*nelɔ*) was reserved for nonfood items, while Construction 2 (*mɛ*) was used only for the breast and food. This choice suggests that for Wanu *mɛ* may have been an earlier form, used to ask for the breast as the first request, and later extended to food. *Nelɔ*, which is not a baby form, is used for objects, which are usually requested at a somewhat later time developmentally, and is supported by *ɛlɛma* instruction. However, this relationship between syntactic construction and object class was not maintained after the first sample. Another clear distinction emerged and was stable for many months. This was the use of *mɛ* only with whining and appealing and the use of full forms (*dimina/mina*) only in assertive requests. Thus, Wanu also selected particular forms to co-occur with particular affective demeanors. Like Mɛli, he used *mɛ* only when begging for himself, and the full forms (*dimina/mina*) when directing someone to give something to a third person.

While Abi's patterns were somewhat different, in part because of his own communicative and behavioral preferences, he nonetheless exhibited several similarities to the language used by Wanu. Like Wanu in earlier samples, he preferred Construction 1 (*nelɔ*) when requesting objects, reserving the *mɛ* forms when he requested the breast. Like the other children, he used the *mɛ* forms when appealing, but extended that construction to food and objects, and used the full forms (*dimina/mina*) when demanding things. All children used the *mɛ* forms consistently for appeal, using a baby form for what children are thought to do naturally: appeal so as to move people to feel sorry for them and thus give them food and objects without reciprocal obligation. Only as they acquire the forms *dimina* and *mina*, which are used assertively, do they enter the system of everyday reciprocity, and it is the use of these assertive forms that is emphasized in instruction and corrected by adults.

When they are small, children can only cry for the breast, but as they get older they must ask for it. (Mothers never ask children if they want the breast, though they offer it when children cry.) One obvious question is how these three children all come to use the same forms of *mɛ/mo/mologa* without hearing these forms from others. Several contributing factors can be offered, but, given the data we have, there is no definitive answer. The following hypothesis is based on perceptual salience, child phonology, input, and semantics. The most perceptually salient part of the emphatic imperatives are the final syllables, either *mine* (*mina/minologa*) from *dimina* or the final syllable **ne* (**nol*nologa*) from *minɛ* – a form expressed very frequently in the child's verbal environment. It may be that young children initially produce *mɛ* as early attempts at these lexical items. In fact, Mɛli (24.3) produces a number of *nɛ* forms (eight tokens, seven of which are for food; *nɛ* is an emphatic 1st person pronoun commonly used in family interaction). However, one token is used when she begs banana from her mother and is immediately followed by the *mε* form (see Example 7.1, line 3). While these forms are never explicitly corrected, alternative expressions are supplied in adults' next utterances (see note 7). Mεli also produced *dimiyε* and *miyε* numerous times (age 24.3; see Example 7.4) before she consistently produced *minε*. Stability of *m*- and not *n*- may be due to phonological and semantic reasons. In Kaluli there are relatively few verbs that are *n*-initial (many are *m*-initial). Additionally, *n*- has strongly paradigmatic associations with all of the 1st person pronouns. So the *mε* form may emerge from a combination of perceptual salience, production difficulties, and input considerations (such as the lack of verbal correction when *mε* is used, but reliable response to requests using it). The fact that *mε* disappears from use may also be due to the fact that it is not in the adult verbal environment and that as the child's language develops, there is great interest in guiding the acquisition of conventionalized forms through not only *εlεma* routines but also exceptionally persistent correction. This is all part of the "hardening" process.[8]

8. The socialization of gender-appropriate behaviors

Ea was pregnant and very anxious to have her baby. She had experienced two miscarriages, and her husband, impatient to have a child, had taken a second wife. This did not please Ea, and she was glad she was nearing the end of her successful pregnancy. One afternoon several women came by to tell me that Ea was in labor. While most Kaluli women usually go into the bush to have their babies, Ea was staying in the small house up on a little bluff that she shared with her husband, which was in sight of the village but away from the main living area. Her husband was off visiting at another village. He would not have assisted her during the labor in any case; men do not participate in such activities. A number of women from the village were with her, giving her water and keeping her company. I went up to see her after several women called out for me to come and join them. When I arrived, they expressed their worries to me, talking about how Ea had been in labor for such a long time and about how concerned they were over how exhausted she was becoming. They said they did not have any means for facilitating the birth and asked if I did. I had no suggestions for them but stayed to observe what was happening.

Ea was underneath her small house, which was on stilts about five feet off the ground, sweating profusely. With her were several women from the village. They were telling stories about other difficult births, adding details to one another's accounts of people's experiences. This did not seem to increase their anxieties but certainly increased mine. Ea was restless and very uncomfortable, but allowed herself to be supported by several women, who were holding her in a sitting position. She was drinking a little water but not taking any food. Periodically, as the contractions came, she would assume a position on all fours and push her hips against one of the house posts to counter the pain of the contraction. After several more hours of labor, Ea was becoming visibly exhausted. Several women were steadying her as she crouched on her heels, leaning slightly backward, supported under the armpits by one of her friends. Others were busy putting large fresh banana leaves under her as she gave birth. While one of the women cut the umbilicus with a small knife, others wiped the baby with small soft leaves. The baby was wrapped in large soft leaves and handed to Ea. Upon seeing her healthy daughter delivered onto these leaves on the ground, she commented, "I wish it were a boy."

Such dramatic events are rare, and the comments that are made during them must be considered in context. Throughout this study, however, mothers made casual statements about boys and girls that indicated their feelings about them. For example, after watching her 5½-year-old son Daibo making a lot of noise, teasing and chasing his 2-year-old sister and threatening her with a stick, and then sticking a rusty safety pin into a dog to torment it, Yaloame said to me in an exasperated tone, "Boys do bad things; girls go along quite easily." Other mothers just aired their sense of frustration to no one in particular, their expressive words and angry expletives comments on their young sons' unruly behaviors. Women frequently said that sometimes boys (and even grown men) would act in ways that they saw as very demanding.

Such behaviors are socialized. Threatening demeanors and aggressive self-presentations are not tolerated in girls, even from an early age. These differences are socialized in subtle ways and are not explicitly noted except for rare comments. Gender-appropriate behaviors are constituted and maintained by caregivers and others in everyday situations through what they do and what they say to each other and to young children. Maternal attitudes and ideologies affect the ways in which boys and girls are socialized to be different – that is, to assume gender-based roles.

In spite of the many expressions of frustration and anger toward sons, Kaluli mothers treat them in a preferential manner. They give them more food, especially more meat, and more attention than they give their daughters. In spite of the fact that they want their daughters to cooperate with them and act like them, they treat them abruptly and with sharp words. These contradictory attitudes affect the shape of everyday interactions between mothers and their children.

Comparative perspective

Given the descriptions of antagonistic male–female relations (for example, Hays & Hays 1982; Herdt & Poole 1982; Langness 1974; Meggitt 1964; Meigs 1976; Strathern 1980) and of traumatic male initiatory practices linked to ideologies of male gender formation and identity (Godelier 1986; Herdt 1981, 1982; Poole 1981, 1982) in many Papua New Guinea Highlands societies, the Kaluli can be located at one end of a continuum. Though relationships between men and women are affected by men's fear of female pollution and though concerns about male growth are articulated through institutionalized male homosexuality, Kaluli attitudes about sexual antagonism, domination, and male gender formation are played out to a more limited extent than in many other Highlands societies in terms of public and private practices. Spheres of domestic and ritual activity are not as strongly gender-marked as they are in many Highlands cultures. Publicly, people tend to talk in terms of expressed ideals, and men express their fear of female pollution. Women claim to know nothing of male homosexual practices. In fact, however, there is considerable latitude, depending on the context, and both private and public behavior often departs considerably from the norms.[1] While the daily routines of men and women are quite separate, Kaluli do not have separate men's and women's houses, nor do they have the extensive male and female initiations reported in the Eastern Highlands and elsewhere in Papua New Guinea (Herdt 1982). Among the Kaluli, "complementarity" and "cooperation" best describe the majority of daily and ritual interactions between men and women.

How boys and girls acquire gender-appropriate behaviors has been of interest to a number of anthropologists studying Papua New Guinea societies (Mead 1930; Whiting 1941). Some researchers have studied (implictly or explicitly) gender behavior in American society as a framework for understanding the cultural and biological origins of preferences elsewhere (Chodorow 1974). Others have sought explanation in adult relationships in Papua New Guinea societies. For example, they have looked at male initiation practices and inferred what must have occurred or what must be believed about the nature of boys and girls and their psychosocial development to conclude that boys in particular need to be radically separated from their mothers and made into men (Godelier 1986; Herdt 1982).

Both Herdt, in his accounts of Sambia childhood (1981), and Godelier, in his writing about Baruya (1986), claim that in these societies women are the exclusive socializers of young children until the male children are about 9 years of age. Godelier says that young Baruya boys live in a world of women, play only with sisters, and must be remade into men – a job that can be accomplished only by men through fear and pain. Both Godelier and Herdt focus on what happens to young boys from the age of 9 onwards. Critically lacking in these studies is detailed information about the nature of everyday interactions in the first seven or so years for boys and girls. We do not know how mothers, sisters, and others in the life of young boys are in fact treating them. We also do not know what, in fact, young boys are able to observe concerning the social relationships of men and women around them. We do not know how interactions are organized, framed, talked about. We do not know what kinds of ideology, language, affect are being displayed by mothers to their sons and their daughters. Are we to assume that sons and daughters are treated identically by their caregivers and that they themselves only associate with same-sex siblings and cousins? In most societies where we do have detailed observation of young children's social interactions, we know that caregivers treat boys and girls differently (Gleason & Greif 1983; Goodenough 1957; Rheingold & Cook 1975; Sidorowicz & Lunney 1980). These interactional differences reflect important ideological differences linked to expectations about how males and females will behave throughout the life cycle.

My data illustrate a different perspective toward understanding the ways in which Kaluli socialize their male and female children into gender-appropriate behaviors. I distinguish two levels of gender-appropriate behaviors. The first concerns the social organization of domestic and expressive activities; for example, the division of labor and the complementary roles of men and women in everyday and ritual events. The second focuses on the conventions and preferences within particular social interactions – that is, the participant structures of events (Philips 1972); how individuals interact with each other within events and the expectations and assumptions that underlie those interactions.

Kaluli mothers socialize their sons into masculine roles from the very beginning of their development. My data show that for the first three to four years of a child's life, Kaluli mothers are the major caregivers. In their interactions with their sons, they teach them gender-appropriate behavior, just as they teach their daughters appropriate ways to act. Unlike the ideologies of psychosocial development reported in Papua New Guinea Highlands societies, Kaluli ideology does not consider boys to be initially feminized or female-identified or to require radical separation from their mothers in order to become masculinized or male. In Kaluli society, boys are guided in the development of gender-appropriate behaviors through interactions in which they are treated differently from sisters and differently by older brothers and sisters. They are treated differently both in terms of the types of social interaction they have – for example, the social roles they take toward their siblings, their mother, and other relatives – and in terms of the activities in which they are encouraged to participate. The opposition is realized in the ways in which mothers play with, tease, and excite their infant sons – behaviors obviously different from the more matter-of-fact ways in which they treat their young daughters. In the Kaluli view, men must be energetic and able to project vitality, whereas women are expected to be steady, even, and controlled. One must remember that young boys interact not only with their mothers but with their sisters and brothers as well. The world of Kaluli women is never isolated from that of Kaluli men for very long.

The data to be examined and analyzed are primarily family members' interactional verbal and nonverbal displays in the course of everyday exchanges. What individuals say to each other, how they act toward each other, and their modes of self-presentation constitute the frames and events for analysis. One major focus is the organization of contexts in which young children participate and observe others.

An analysis of gender-appropriate behaviors must be sensitive to the context of relationships in which they are displayed. The specific constellation of gender-appropriate behaviors displayed varies according to the other relationships in play between the speaker/actor and the interactional partner in the social situation. For example, at any particular point in the life cycle, gender-appropriate behavior for an individual in one kin relationship may not be appropriate in another kin relationship. Thus, a girl's appropriate behavior may be different with her sister and with her brother, and, depending on his age, a boy may behave differently with his mother and with his father. Gender-appropriate behaviors, then, must be considered as interactionally dependent and socially variable. Children are socialized to display not a set of invariant gender-specific behaviors but a range of gender behaviors appropriate to specific contexts.

From interactions and commentaries, implicit notions about how girls and boys are to be treated and how they are expected to behave can be made explicit. Kaluli mothers play an important role in organizing and participating in everyday interactions with children in culturally specific ways. They display particular demeanors and preferences for social outcomes both verbally and nonverbally. As mothers are the principal caregivers in a young child's life, much of what the young child learns is strongly influenced by what she does and says, not only to her children but in their presence. Analytically, it is important to distinguish how Kaluli mothers treat their children in dyadic interactions and how they organize interactions between siblings and others. Five issues are central.

① The first concerns the social construction of social identity, in particular how mothers relate to and treat their sons and daughters in dyadic interactions. Gender differences in adult life are rooted in everyday childhood activities. I regularly observed differences in the ways sons and daughters were treated that have lifelong implications. For example, mothers often give preferential treatment to their sons. The best pieces of grilled meat and crayfish are given more frequently to sons than to daughters. Fewer demands are placed on sons to assist with household chores. In contrast, daughters are consistently encouraged to take responsibility and are told to bring in firewood, draw water, and tend the cooking fires. When girls are around 5 years old, they are told to watch over their younger siblings. Girls are consistently encouraged to give up what they want, or at least share what they have, in light of the expressed desires of their younger siblings and older brothers or the wishes of their mothers.

sans favored over daughter

② The second issue concerns the constitution of sibling relationships through speech activities. I compare the ways in which mothers support and manage the activities of opposite- and same-sex siblings in multiparty interactions. Mothers encourage cooperative acts between same-sex siblings; in cross-sex interaction, mothers generally encourage sons to take physically assertive and demanding stances while encouraging their daughters to adopt compliant and nurturing postures in response.

③ The third issue concerns the socializing of complementary gender roles through play: the processes of creating expectations, interactive patterns, and social roles in later life. I take as one example hide-and-seek games, in which sisters hide desired objects from their brothers, who must search for them. In these situations, sisters tease their young brothers, provoking them to continue searching for the hidden objects. This pattern of women provoking and cheering men to continue engaging in culturally important activities is seen again in adult life, most dramatically in the roles played by men and women in the major ceremonial events, such as Gisalo and Kɔluba (E. L. Schieffelin 1976:125). A second example is role play and what it tells us about children's social knowledge. We see how in a variety of everyday situations from a very early age children display gender-appropriate behaviors. The fourth issue is ④ related to this concern with social knowledge and examines the use of *ɛlɛma* routines as an important linguistic and interactional resource for girls but not for boys. Girls use it extensively with younger children and as part of verbal play and role play. It indexes the association between particular activities (caregiving) and language use.

The fifth issue examines breaches in gender-appropriate activities. All young ⑤ children practice or experiment with different ways of talking and acting, trying out what seems interesting to them and resisting what they do not like. Some of their experiments may be evaluated as inappropriate behavior from an adult's perspective. These situations, where the adult and child views do not match, are important to examine in that they show what mothers do – the manner in which they respond when there is a breach in conventional behaviors. When possible, mothers make sure that boys and girls act in gender-appropriate ways through recontextualizing and socializing activities. Within a playful frame, the shaping of gender-appropriate behavior affects the organization of everyday activities. Since these activities provide the social contexts in which children are taught about becoming Kaluli, it is important to examine them in detail.

Treating sons and daughters differently: social construction of social identities

The Kaluli word for infant, *tualun*, is not gender-specific. An infant, however, is frequently talked about as a *kalu sawa* or *kalu lɛsu* (male child or little male) as opposed to *nɔ sawa* or *ga lɛsu* (mother child or little female). Terms for son and daughter are *nɔl* 'my son' and *nɛlɛ* 'my daughter', but they are used primarily in address and not in reference. Personal names, which are given about two or three weeks after the child is born, are gender-specific and are given with a particular namesake in mind. Before being named, a child is called Dɔsali or Kobake, names of male and female characters who appear in traditional stories. Everyday child-care practices in the first six months of life are not particularly gender-specific. For example, Kaluli feed their infant girls and boys the same foods and attend to their needs with no apparent difference. There are no ritual activities for infants. Kaluli have few explicit gender-specific theories of child development; those that exist apply to children who are close to or entering puberty.[2] The practices of Kaluli mothers, however, implicitly express their ideology about gender differences.

When an infant is 6–8 months old, mothers begin to respond differently to their infant daughters from the way they do to their infant sons. The differences are often subtle, and Kaluli do not talk about them. Differential patterns can be observed in the ways mothers interact with their babies while nursing them. All Kaluli infants bite the breast when they teethe. No objects are put in their mouths or are available to them to suck or bite. When infants begin teething, they lose the intense interest that they once had in nursing and use much of the time at the breast for playing, looking around, and socializing.

When boys first bite the breast, mothers say to their infant sons, *A!* 'No!' or *Kadefoma!* 'Stop!' and pull the breast gently out of the infant's mouth. Then, laughing or smiling, they put the breast back in the infant's mouth. This often has the effect of encouraging the infant to bite again while he keeps an eye on his mother to see her reaction. Her response is usually the same: to say no, remove the breast, smile, and then allow the infant to repeat what he was doing. In this way, during nursing mother and son establish one of their first teasing games, combining the feeding time with a time of intimate play.

As little boys become older, other types of playing and teasing evolve in this situation and take on a routine, gamelike aspect. Such activities involve sons and mothers in tickling, hitting, biting parts of the body, close face-to-face contact, and more ambiguous messages like *A! Mabulɛsabo!* 'Don't bite!' and *A! Ne Sandɛsabo!* 'Don't hit me!' with smiles of encouragement and the opportunity to act again. Osolowa continued such interaction with her son until he was 17 months old.[3] Ulahi consistently played in this way with Abi until he was weaned at 33 months. From the time he was 26 months old, she was halfheartedly trying to wean him and alternating between yes and no in a way that led him to treat her words as encouragement. When Abi's brother was born, he was suddenly weaned. This was a very difficult and traumatic event for him; he cried a lot, hit his mother angrily, and for several months did not talk as much as before. Ulahi, like other mothers, found other ways and situations in which to extend this type of play with her sons (see Example 8.4, lines 16–24). The play routines continued after Abi was weaned.

Mothers play a teasing role with their sons and become their partners in teasing games. Originating during nursing, the games start with an invitation from the mother to interact intensely but playfully around food. During the son's first two and a half to three years, these situations develop into more elaborate physical play, including biting, poking, and climbing on the mother. These games affect the meaning of sharing food in later cross-sex relations.[4]

In direct contrast, when infant girls pull away from the breast and look away, or bite the breast and watch the mother for a reaction, that reaction is matter-of-fact and consistently signals disapproval. Little girls are taken off the breast, faced outward toward others and reoriented toward other activities. When girls become distracted while nursing or bite the breast, mothers give them the message that feeding and playing are not to be mixed and that biting is not tolerated. Mothers and daughters are not involved in as much physical play as mothers and sons. When little girls are 2 or 3 years old, they occasionally play grabbing and holding games with their fathers, but these are greatly limited in comparison with the frequency and elaboration of physical contact boys enjoy with their mothers until they are over 3 years old, or until the next child is born.

Contrasting reaction of mother to daughter

Mothers tend to treat their daughters with what I view as abruptness. The following is taken from field notes:

27 February 1976
When I first observed Meli (Nov. 1975 – age 22 mo.) she was outstanding in her amount of outgoing activity, curiosity, and friendliness. However, it seemed that as her brother Seligiwɔ (then 4 mo.) emerged as a person in his own right (very sunny disposition and the receiver of a lot of attention) Meli retreated. She competes with him for the breast; getting the breast is a strong source of anxiety and tears for her. Meli's babyhood was prematurely interrupted by Seligiwɔ's early arrival. (This is direct outcome of the fact that baptized Christians do not practice the traditional post-partum sex taboo.) Meli often screams for the breast, will be distracted, then given the breast until Osolowa decides it is enough and pulls it away. Then Meli begs, whines, cries til it is given briefly, then withdrawn. Meli acts aggressively towards her mother, never towards her brother in these situations.

1 April 1976
Abruptness: Several times Meli will be settled on her mother's lap, and suddenly she is put down, and mother walks away, which reduces her to tears. This abruptness is very reminiscent of the nursing situation when Osolowa would suddenly say "kɔm!" 'that's enough!' and pull the breast away. Sometimes withdrawing the breast would be accompanied by a light smack. Osolowa never did this with Seligiwɔ. This same pattern of abruptness was consistently observed in both Ulahi's and Wadeo's treatment of their daughters (who were older than Meli).

It is important to emphasize that these mothers were not acting in a harsh or punitive way, but simply appeared to be less patient with their daughters. While they did tease them with food, they did not establish playful routines around sharing food with them. Thus, starting in feeding situations and extending to others, mothers present themselves to their sons and their daughters with different demeanors and establish different frames for interacting. With their sons, they are playful partners, creating games that are mutually amusing. They carefully modulate the key of an interaction to provide it with an uncertain interactional edge, a tension of contradictory messages of refusal and acceptance. Through these practices, they shape emotional responses, redefine boundaries with their infant sons, and create expectations that this is an appropriate interactional mode. Toward daughters, mothers are more direct and unambiguous. They urge infant daughters to de-center and to attend to what is happening outside of the dyad rather than to focus on the relationship between mother and daughter.

Another situation in which mothers differentially respond to sons and daughters is temper tantrums. When little boys feel they have not gotten their due (food, objects, or attention) and become enraged, their mothers offer them food, the breast, or other objects to persuade them to give up their anger. For example, once when Wanu wanted to nurse, his mother wanted him to come to where she was sitting, and he wanted her to move to him. They argued for some time, with Wanu screaming and crying his angry requests and his mother offering him additional food to persuade him to move to her. In the end, she moved, offered him some banana to calm him down, and let him nurse. Kaluli refer to this as *henulab*: buying off or exchanging one form of attention, mood, or object for another.

In contrast, when little girls are enraged, they are often told, *Hamana!* 'Go away!' or *Kɔm!* 'That is enough!' or are threatened with third-party reprisals like "Someone will say something!" Mothers are more likely to express annoyance toward their daughters or to laugh at them. Sometimes they shame their daughters in front of others. Such negative comments are not heard when sons are distressed and angry. Mothers tolerate tantrums in boys or try to distract, dissuade, or influence them with offers of food and attention. They will maintain prolonged conversational exchanges until their sons have calmed down. Daughters are often left to cool themselves down.

Mothers encourage daughters to be independent and less demanding of nurturance – seen in the extent of physical contact a mother will maintain with a 2- or 3-year-old daughter. Except when nursing or being groomed for head lice, a daughter does not hang on her mother's body. In contrast, small sons are carried for longer periods and are allowed to sit on and stay close to their mothers with little encouragement to separate, especially before the next child arrives.

Mothers do not verbally instruct young daughters how to carry out specific tasks, such as making fires or cooking foods. Daughters spend a lot of time observing their mothers and are asked to do specific jobs to facilitate a task. For example, while mothers are cooking, they ask daughters to bring fire tongs, turn bananas over, pour water onto a steaming packet. Mothers encourage this assistance in domestic tasks, gradually adding new jobs as the child gets older. Once a new baby arrives, daughters are asked to help with simple caregiving tasks like fetching things and holding the baby. These responsibilities, combined with the mother's attitude toward her daughter, help shift a young girl out of the predominantly receiving role into the giving role at an early age, usually by 3 years. As part of the process of learning how to act like a mother, little girls from the age of about 3 are given responsibilities (not just play tasks) for daily chores, such as sweeping the garbage away from the sleeping areas, picking up wood chips from the floor, and fetching things the mother needs, like glowing embers to start cooking fires. While participating in these cooperative activities, young girls are socialized into expectations about how they are to act.

That these socialization messages are effective is demonstrated by the fact that girls as young as 30 months ask to take care of their infant siblings and will persist in their requests even when they are not really able to handle the activity. Meli wanted to bathe her brother, carry him around, and give him food. She displayed her knowledge of many aspects of caregiving before she was 3 years old. She knew how to distract Seligiwɔ by pointing out sounds, and when he cried she would tell him that his mother was right there. She paid attention to his vocalizations, often imitating them. Meli would tell her mother to nurse him when he cried. While many of these activities were supported by her mother as part of her learning appropriate mothering behavior, they were also an important component of her learning how to pay attention to others and be an older sister. These gender-appropriate attitudes and interests were frequently exhibited by Binalia, Isa, Yogodo, Waye, Mobiya, and other older sisters throughout a range of social interactions with younger siblings. Young boys rarely asked to assist in taking care of infants, nor did they show interest in cooking or food preparation unless they were in the receiving role. What they were interested in doing was emulating male activities (playing with fish traps and knives, carrying things around), but lack of interest in and nonparticipation in female activities were also a critical part of their social knowledge.

Relative personal detachment toward daughters and the encouragement of their independence form a contrast to the intimacy, playfulness, teasing, and encouragement of dependence that characterize a mother's relationship with her son. Mothers cook for and feed sons, in contrast to the encouragement that daughters get to participate in the cooking process. Also demands made on daughters to assist with domestic tasks, while sons are left free, further differentiate roles and responsibilities for each.

Through the alternately intimate and teasing quality of mother–son interaction, a sense of the relationship is communicated. The mother plays a particular female role as a way of developing the maleness in her son. He is different from his mother and does not do what she does. And by expecting her daughter to be an accomplice, the mother encourages similarity, setting down one constellation of gender-appropriate behaviors for women.

Let us examine this from a slightly different perspective. Over and over again, I had the opportunity to observe mothers giving preferential treatment to their sons when it came to being carried around the village or being given choice bits of meat and fish at mealtimes. Boys were often given food before girls, and they were usually given more as well. Mothers monitored their daughters, making sure that when they had food they shared it with their brothers. Boys of 4 and 5 would demand that their (half) sisters of the same age cook for them, and the girls would usually comply. Mothers responded in the same way to requests and demands, providing the desired goods and services. It should be noted that when girls (age 4 and up) were together, one of their favorite activities was to cook and eat food; boys of the same age did not do that when playing together.

Near the end of the study, I asked several women why they repeatedly give more food treats and special consideration to their sons. Their answers (given independently) were simple and consistent: "The boys are ours. If our husbands die, our sons will take care of us, so we want to take good care of them now. Girls are not ours. They grow up and get married and move to other villages. We don't see them, and we don't get things from them." While one may hesitate to suggest that all of the behaviors, attitudes, and feelings Kaluli mothers direct toward their children are based on such a strongly deterministic, future-oriented sense of payback, or, in other words, that all of their acts are investments in their future, their statements help make sense out of a collection of related behaviors, in particular notions of compensation (*su*) and exchange (*wɛl*). In Kaluli society, one expects some type of compensation or return for what is given, on both the formal level[5] and the informal level, as in the usual expectations of sharing food and domestic responsibilities. Though Kaluli do not have a formal rule about sons taking care of their mothers if their husbands die (as compensation for the care they have given their sons), in practice this is what occurs.

Kaluli gender-appropriate behaviors are socialized through interactional enactments of kin relationships. The young child initially develops a mother–child relationship. As the child gets older, that relationship becomes differentiated into a mother–son or a mother–daughter relationship, each having its own constellation of appropriate behaviors and feelings. As other individuals enter into children's lives, additional relationships are constructed, sensitive to expectations of classificatory male and female kin relationships and age. For example, a boy learns how to treat sisters differently from brothers; a girl learns to treat younger siblings differently from older ones. How does gender socialization proceed? What behaviors and attitudes are encouraged as more than one set of contexts is being presented?

While focused interactions – those where two people attend to and interact with one another (Goffman 1961a) – are important sources of knowledge, one should not lose sight of the fact that Kaluli children, by virtue of the organization of their living space, acquire social knowledge through other interactional routes. They often take the role of active observer in interac-

Figure 26. Men carrying patrol boxes for the government patrol.

Figure 27. Boys play at carrying patrol boxes in the yard.

tional contexts. A dyadic exchange between mother and son is informative also to an older daughter who observes it.

Young children continually have the opportunity to observe how things get accomplished in families; that is, what is said, what gets done, who does it. Almost all of the mother's activities are carried out in multiparty settings involving children. Children see mothers cooking, assisted by daughters, and giving food to husbands and children. In the bush, children accompany mothers and see them weeding and gathering food from gardens, collecting small lizards and land crabs in the process. Children also see men cutting down trees, building houses, making fish traps, bringing home small game, and negotiating bridewealth. Small children are constantly in the company of at least one person, usually more, and they are socialized to attend to what is going on around them and take important social information from what they hear people saying to each other.

In the first three years, children have close contact with their mothers and other women who live in the women's section of the house. Fathers and other men spend a great deal of time away from the house, off in the bush, and small children do not have many opportunities to observe what they do. Young sons do not accompany their fathers to the bush; they are considered too young to keep up with their fathers' activities. On those occasions when several families join together on fishing trips, set themselves up in sago camps, and engage in other garden-related activities, young boys (and girls) do observe their fathers, uncles, and older brothers. For young boys, these are also opportunities to be directly involved in men's work.

The experience for sons and daughters is asymmetrical. Daughters usually have much less contact with fathers than boys have with mothers. Sisters do have contact with their brothers, and within that relationship they experience the details and examples of behaviors and expectations that are different, while in the relationship with their mothers they experience an emphasis on similarity. To discern the socialization of gender, it is not enough to examine the mother–child relationship exclusively. One must consider the variety of other relationships into which young children are socialized. Gender identities are constituted in the course of learning how to act in same-sex and cross-sex relationships in the context of the larger kinship and relationship structure of Kaluli society.

Constituting siblingship through speech activities

In addition to being actively involved in constituting relationships with their children, Kaluli mothers are critical in the socialization of relationships between their children. Between same-sex siblings, they consistently encourage cooperation in a variety of situations. They tell older siblings to comply with

Figure 28. Yaloame beating sago while Suɛla pretends to cook food nearby.

Figure 29. Suɛla pretending to beat sago at a sago camp.

the wishes of younger ones and ask younger siblings to seek the assistance and company of older ones. Between opposite-sex siblings, however, mothers encourage younger brothers to tease and provoke their older sisters in sometimes extended events. Mothers also tell younger brothers to ask older sisters to do things for them, such as cook food and carry them. Mothers initiate and support games in which brothers are physically assertive toward their sisters and sisters are compliant.

Most of these social orientations provide a basis for future relationships between siblings. As teenagers, brothers who live together in a village are expected to cooperate and to provide assistance to each other in a variety of tasks, for example hunting and fishing and making gardens. Once they marry, brothers continue to assist each other in activities like house building and help each other by sharing tools and other resources. This pattern of cooperation continues through life, as brothers tend to reside in their natal village and carry out a wide range of activities together.

The pattern between sisters is different. While growing up together in the village, they spend a lot of time together and cooperate in gardening and domestic chores, mostly under the direction of their mother. As part of the family unit, they contribute their labor and share in what is produced. Once they marry, however, they separate, move to their husbands' villages, and begin the process of establishing new relationships with women who live there. Thus, the frequent and familiar patterns of cooperation between sisters are not easily sustained once they marry, though sisters may visit each other when it is convenient.

The encouragement of cooperative acts between same-sex siblings

The following example shows how one mother, Ulahi, encouraged cooperation in play between her two sons.

Example 8.1. Ulahi is holding her infant son, Bage (3.). Abi (35.) is holding a stick on his shoulder in a manner similar to that in which one would carry a heavy metal patrol box. (Such a box would be hung from a pole carried on the shoulders of two men.)

[To baby]   ¹Bage! / do you see my box here? / do you
                                             see it? / X /
²Mother [high nasal voice, talking as if she is the baby, moving
the baby, who is facing Abi]: My brother, I'll take half, my brother!
[Holding stick out]   ³Mother, give him half / X / Mother, my
                                             brother – here, here, take half / X /
⁴My brother, what half do I take? What about it, my brother, put
it on the shoulder! [To Abi in her own voice, as if quoting the
baby] "Put it on the shoulder."
[Abi rests stick on baby's shoulder.]
⁵There, carefully put it on. [Stick accidentally
pokes baby.] Feel sorry, stop.

Figure 30. Baseo guides Wanu in scraping sago.

Young children will sometimes address questions to their infant siblings, initiating triadic sequences such as the one above. Mothers provide relevant responses "in the infant's voice" to keep the talk going. In this fantasy sequence that Abi directs to the baby, he is proposing an activity that he has observed: men carrying the heavy metal patrol boxes for the government patrols. Holding the infant as if he is responding, Ulahi speaks in a special register used when mothers talk for children. She draws on Abi's suggestion of carrying the patrol box to incorporate ideas about cooperation between brothers, one of the major organizational bases of work for Kaluli men. She is encouraging Abi to play a particular boys' game that reflects the ways in which men work. Additionally, Ulahi is socializing a set of gender-specific expectations surrounding the relationship between Abi and his infant brother. These interactions take the older child's interests into account but configure them according to gender-specific preferences of behavior.

Ulahi often encouraged Abi and his older brother Daibo to play together. As Abi got older, he would play this game of pretending to carry patrol boxes, marching around the yard carrying a stick on his shoulder while the other end was on Daibo's shoulder. When Ulahi saw other small boys who were classificatory brothers in the village, she frequently told Abi to call out and greet them as "my brother." This is one way men in the village often greet each other; Ulahi, like other mothers, took an active role in encouraging the development and awareness of that relationship by talking about it and providing verbal strategies through direct instruction (using *ɛlɛma*) to accomplish it.

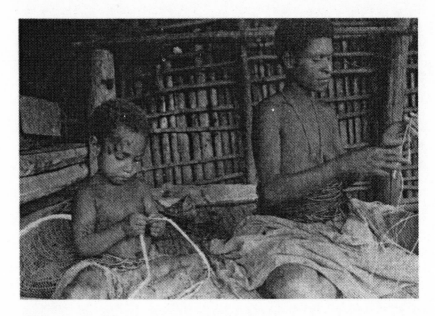

Figure 31. Ana and her mother making string out of bark.

Once Abi was on his own among children, he would have to manage his relationships himself, but as long as he was with his mother she was willing to verbally initiate and help sustain cooperative ventures among brothers.

Similarly, mothers encourage sisters to follow each other's examples of positively valued activities as models. Thus, when seeing a daughter engaging in a specific activity, mothers suggest to another daughter that she "do (some activity) like your sister is doing" (bring in firewood, carry water tubes, cook food). Kaluli do not talk about the importance of doing things in general or as abstract concerns, but rather point to specific individuals and particular actions that can be copied.

Once the younger daughter is at least 3 years old, mothers regularly direct their daughters to cooperate with each other in specific tasks. Both Ulahi and Wadeo frequently encouraged their daughters to help each other by doing together such chores as cooking, carrying heavy loads, and chopping firewood. Requests to carry out these activities took a variety of linguistic forms, from pleading and using address terms such as *nɔ* 'my mother' and *adɛ* to refer to siblings, to demanding, threatening, and reasoning. Like other requests, these were issued in situations where specific tasks had to be accomplished. Because authority was not given in any situation, these interactions were often complex because of the manipulative stance taken by the mother to accomplish her goals. Since negotiation is allowed, daughters have to be able to respond to the mother's verbal ploys when they do not wish to comply. Older daughters often resist their mothers' attempts to direct them, and deliver sharp responses in return for bribes and threats.

I observed no interactions in which mothers encouraged their same-sex children to fight or be aggressive with each other, engage in threatening or other assertive acts, or insult each other by name calling (e.g., "you dog" [*gasa ge*], "big breasts" [*bo badio*], "witch" [*sei*]). However, these same behaviors are characteristic of mother-supported interactions between children of different sexes, almost exclusively in the direction of boys toward girls.

Fostering aggressive acts between cross-sex siblings

One of the most striking socializing practices from the perspective of an outsider is one in which a mother or grandmother encourages a young boy to hit an older sister, who complies with this act. I observed such interactions many times in different families. Older children, however, are never encouraged to hit younger children.

Example 8.2. Mɛli (28.) is with her brother Seligiwɔ (11.), being cared for by her paternal grandmother, Wayabe sulɔ, who lives with them. Grandmother tells Mɛli to get a stick and give it to her brother, who is being held in the grandmother's lap facing forward. Mɛli gets the stick and gives it to her grandmother, who gives it to the boy.

¹G'mother → Seligiwɔ: Hit Mɛli with this! [She guides his hand.]
[Jumping around in front of her brother]   ²here! / X / X / X /
³Like this! [She guides baby's hand.] Like this!
[Mɛli tries to take the stick.]
⁴G'mother → Mɛli [pleading voice]: Don't take it, it's *adɛ*'s.
[Pointing to another stick] Go get him that short one.
[Mɛli does and gives it to him.]
                                 ⁵yes, hit me / X / wa! / X /

Two reciprocal roles are being socialized here: the one who hits (agent) and the one who gets hit (patient). Mɛli sees what her grandmother is doing and hears her instructions to her brother, evidenced by her response as she jumps around to get her brother's attention. Mɛli also observes how her grandmother guides her brother to act appropriately, both verbally and nonverbally. When Mɛli tries to take the stick, her grandmother shifts focus and addresses Mɛli, begging her first not to take the stick, which is in her brother's possession, and second, to get him another stick. In giving a reason why Mɛli should not take the stick, she uses the term *adɛ* (line 4), the relationship term used between younger brothers and older sisters that conveys the expectation that Mɛli will give in to her younger brother's wishes. Mɛli complies with the request and gets another stick, and the interaction continues with Mɛli verbally encouraging her small brother to hit her. Through repeated occurrences, these types of interaction become integrated into the usual course of events for both boys and girls.

Mothers sometimes comment about interactions in which sons hit daughters. On a number of occasions, Abi's mother called out after Abi had hit his sister Yogodo, bringing on tears from too hard a smack, "Abi hit his wife!" or after Abi repeatedly hit her, "Abi keeps hitting his wife." Ulahi's husband hit her when he thought she was not being cooperative. Like other Kaluli women who were hit, she cried but never fought back. Neither did Yogodo fight back when Abi hit her, and it may be that she had learned by the age of 5 that boys hit girls, husbands hit wives, and women do not hit back and say very little about it. While their loud crying informs the village, no one intervenes in domestic quarrels.

Compare the following with Example 8.2.

Example 8.3. Wanu (27.3) is at home with sister Isa (8 yr) and his mother (Wadeo).

[Chases Isa with my rubber thong,
threatening her]   ¹Ei! / X / X / X /
²Isa [as she runs] → Wanu: Wanuwa, Wanu!
³Mother → Wanu →> Isa: I'm going to hit you – ɛlɛma.
                                             ⁴I'm going to hit you! /
⁵Isa → Wanu: Oh, my brother! [Runs a bit out of his reach. Wanu throws the thong at her.]
[Wanu then takes Isa's skirt belts and throws them all around the floor. Isa grabs them, Wanu cries, she gives them back to him, and he throws them again.]

In this situation, Wadeo supports Wanu's actions by providing him with explicit verbal lines. Using the directive *ɛlɛma*, she tells him to tell his sister (line 3) what he plans to do: hit her. His sister not only encourages him, but when he throws her skirt belts around, she retrieves them and quickly returns them to him when he begins to cry, thus pacifying him and soothing his anger with the offer of an object. Sisters are often involved in teasing play that provokes strong emotional responses in their younger brothers. They learn to be in control of these situations, and can regulate the intensity of them by making new verbal and interactional moves. Unlike their mothers, they are free to leave the play situation when it no longer suits them, which puts an end to the immediate provocation.

The mother is an important social force in constituting these interactions between brothers and sisters.

Example 8.4. Abi (30.) and his sisters Waye (8;6) and Yogodo (5;6) are playing a hide-and-seek game. The two girls are hiding, and Abi is searching for them. Their mother, Ulahi, assists Abi. After he finds them, they run off and hide again.

[Abi is going to look for the girls.]
[Picking up a piece of firewood]   ¹I'm coming! /
²Yogodo → Abi: You come!
³Mother → Abi: One doesn't hit with a stick, just grab them with your hands, don't hit with a stick!

⁴Yogodo → Abi: Abi! Come!
⁵Mother → Girls: He's coming, bringing a stick!
⁶Mother → Abi: Don't take it [re stick]! Don't take it! One doesn't hit with a stick!
[Abi finds his sisters; they grab each other; girls hide again; Abi looks for another stick.]
⁷Mother → Abi: One doesn't hit with a stick! [Abi picks up a stick. Mother substitutes a piece of bamboo.]
⁸Yogodo → Abi [seeing stick]: I'm unwilling!
⁹I'm coming to hit! /
¹⁰I'm really unwilling!
¹¹I'm coming to hit! /
¹²Abi, brother, don't hit (me).
¹³I'm coming /
[Girls grab him, take stick, tickle him; he runs to mother; she tickles girls; they try to tickle Abi.]
¹⁴I'm unwilling! /
¹⁵Mother → Girls: Don't tease him; he said, "I'm unwilling!"
[Girls run out. Abi nurses, cuddles and then bites mother.]
¹⁶Mother → Abi: Amaye! Open your mouth! [She laughs.]
[Abi pinches her.]
¹⁷[Laughing] I'm going to hit you!
¹⁸[Abi pinches her.] I'm going to hit you when you are doing that! Open it! [re his hand, which is pinching her]
[Laughing and pulling on her bead necklace]
¹⁹I'm going to cut your neck! /
²⁰Mother, I'm going to cut your neck /
²¹[Mock concern] Oh my, my neck!
[Abi pretends to cut necklace with a stick.]
²²Are you cutting my neck!
²³Yes, I'm cutting (it) / X /
²⁴Oh dear! [Abi pulls away.] I'm afraid! [Abi laughs.]

Abi's mother encourages him in this hide-and-seek game, as do his sisters, but when there is a possibility that he might actually hurt them, his mother alerts the girls (line 5) and tells Abi repeatedly not to use the firewood. Yogodo expresses her unwillingness to be struck, and both girls assert themselves, grabbing him and taking the stick. They have, after all, some control over the outcome of the immediate situation – they can leave it. When the girls try to tease Abi, he seeks support from his mother, who takes his side, and the girls do in fact leave. But what continues while he is excited are the physical intimacy, teasing, and playing between a mother and her young son that I discussed earlier.

The messages that mothers send to their sons and daughters about the roles they can take differ. In this interaction as well as many others, Ulahi verbally encouraged Abi to chase, threaten, excite, and hit his older sisters but did not want him to hurt them. Since her words to Abi can also be heard by his sisters, they too get the message that their mother thinks it is acceptable for them to be threatened, hit, and chased by a male. They will be warned, but there will be no more direct intervention to protect them. Mothers do not encourage their daughters to act in these physically assertive ways with each other or to direct such acts against their brothers.[6]

These examples do not imply that older sisters never take an opportunity to provoke or tease their younger brothers. In fact, sisters, particularly those between the ages of 5 and 9, find ways to frighten or anger their young brothers, especially when they are out of their mother's view. These events can be emotionally intense and involve screaming and crying. Older sisters, those age 9 and up, are less inclined to push a younger child to tears and tantrums, but will not intervene when teasing is initiated by someone else. Yogodo, the younger of Abi's two older sisters, frequently taunted him about his mother's being away, causing him to cry and call out for her in a panic-stricken voice. Frequently, Ulahi was just out of sight, clearing weeds by the side of the house or the outhouse, but only her presence would calm him down. Yogodo did other things to provoke Abi. She mocked his speech when he spoke to her, which would confuse him; she offered him dirty food and tabooed food items, things she knew he was not supposed to eat. When given the opportunity, she encouraged him to do things that she knew were really not allowed. Waye more closely followed her mother's model of taking care of Abi, with one important difference. She rarely tormented Abi herself, but she never told Yogodo to stop tormenting him.

A similar pattern was observed in Wanu's family. Binalia, the younger of Wanu's two older sisters, had many fights with Wanu and teased him often. While Isa was generally more benevolent, she nonetheless took many opportunities to join Binalia in her efforts to agitate and tease her brother when she was away from her mother's view. The girls threatened to touch him with what he believed to be stinging nettles, offered him food and then pulled it back, and threatened to leave him alone by the stream, all of which caused protests and frightened tears. As young boys grow older, around the age of 4 or 5, they become less vulnerable to the taunts and threats of their older sisters and have increasingly less contact with them as caregivers; they are becoming more involved in their own peer groups and activities.

Socializing complementary gender roles through play

Hide-and-seek

Playful routines provide predictable interactions within which novices learn sequences of action and disposition and complementary roles, and experiment with what is acceptable and what is not within a particular frame. Kaluli have few special child games, and most of those have no name, but the games they do have are important in socializing roles, affect, and other cultural content.

One game of young Kaluli children is peek-a-boo with mothers and sometimes with older sisters. This involves covering the child's eyes with the child's hands and the mother's putting her face very close to the child's face. When the eyes are uncovered and the child sees the face of the mother unusually close, the child lets out a shriek of surprise and fear, and the mother pulls back and laughs. This game continues until the child begins to talk. It is one of the very few situations in which Kaluli put their faces into such proximity.

When children are between 18 and 24 months old, they are encouraged to play another game that is an elaboration of the hiding and disclosure routine. The child will cover himself with a cloth, wait until someone calls his name to ask where he is, and then pull it off and shriek. Another variation involves someone else covering the child and pulling off the cloth as the child sits still. When the cloth comes off, both child and partner yell out at the same time. These games of hiding and revealing are times of great excitement for young children: A lot of attention is focused on the child, and noise accompanies surprise. When the child learns to initiate the game, he or she is able to generate attention toward the self and enjoys the exclamations of surprise that sometimes create an intense, almost fearful, reaction that is encouraged by others. When this game is played with older siblings, the child's response may send him running to his mother and clinging to her, sometimes crying and talking about being scared (*Tagidab!* 'I'm afraid!'). After the child is calmed and reassured, he enthusiastically reinitiates the game again with whoever will play. The game usually ends when someone gets tired of it. Out of this basic routine, another more elaborate routine develops involving more people and different participant roles for boys and girls.

Once children are old enough to initiate the game (18–24 mo), mothers discourage girls from playing. When girls attempt to initiate the game, it invariably falls flat; no one is interested in playing, and girls soon learn not to try. For boys, things are different. These games become a reliable source of attention to self and provide a cycle of intense excitement followed by calming down. When boys cover themselves up, whoever is around (mother, father, sisters) asks questions like "Where is Wanu?" and call out his name as if searching for him. When boys pull off the cover, they are greeted with recognition and delight and become excited themselves, jumping around and making noise. Boys no longer show fear or say that they are afraid.

Wanu's mother and sisters were capable of sustaining this game for long periods. At the age of 22–26 months, Wanu himself began to hide small objects by sitting on them or putting them in his armpit or in the fold of his thigh while saying, *Andoma* 'All gone'. An audience of his mother and sisters would search him, tickle him, and focus attention on him, all the while asking where the object was hidden. When he finally pulled out the object, he would exclaim *Wego!* 'Right here!' and would then look for another hiding place.

In another frequent play-related game, his mother and sisters would take something that Wanu was interested in (a marble, a stick, a piece of food, my sandal) and hide it. Acting as if it were misplaced, they would ask him where it was. He would then search for the object, threatening to stop looking when he could not immediately find it. They would tease and provoke him, often until he cried out of frustration, but they would also encourage him to keep on looking until he found it. When Wanu located the hidden object, there was always a celebration on the part of his mother and sisters, and any tears or anger would be gone. He would be all smiles as they cheered his success. The game would usually be initiated again by Wanu once the cheering subsided.

Young boys participate in many hiding routines in which they experience emotional provocation, followed by support and the encouragement of a successful outcome. Kaluli repeatedly provide contexts in which small children undergo this type of emotional cycle. For Abi, the searching that took place was not for hidden objects but for hiding sisters, as in Example 8.4. Again, the mother is both audience and support system, expressing appreciation for her son's efforts and at the same time organizing her daughters as collaborators. For Meli, these provocations were set during negotiations for the breast and in other contexts of teasing.

Although I observed no interactions in which girls were the seekers in these games (they were always involved in hiding objects or themselves), I do not wish to suggest that girls (and women) never search for objects. Women and girls are often involved in searching activities in the bush. They look for crayfish in the rivers and collect numerous other foodstuffs in the bush: wild eggs, land crabs, small animals, edible insects. These activities are thought of quite differently from the activities of men. Collecting small protein foods is a casual activity, part of the routine domestic activities of women. They are not specially marked (linguistically or socially) like men's hunting or fishing, which are thought to require special training and knowledge. This was made clear when I asked Ulahi whether young girls ever play games in which they have to search for hidden objects or individuals. When she answered that they did not, I asked why. Ulahi told me, "Women plant the gardens; they always know where the banana trees or pandanus plants are. They don't have to look for them. Men, on the other hand, have to hunt and chase animals. They have to search for them and be persistent." Men are praised for bringing home meat and can tell stories about how difficult the hunt was or what the dogs did not do. No such excitement exists in providing garden foods; they are depended on and expected daily. These patterns and expectations for later life work are set down in play at an early age. One of the ways in which this is accomplished is in the basic routines of hide-and-seek.

Role play

Another perspective from which to examine what young children do is in terms of how their activities reflect what they know about gender-appropriate behavior. Children learn not only what to do but also what not to do in the course of observing what goes on, playing with each other, and practicing these activities by themselves.

Once young girls are about 2 years old, their mothers start asking them to help in preparing and cooking food. Around the age of 3, they begin to participate regularly in cooking activities with older girls, acting in ways that suggest they are becoming competent in gender-appropriate skills. For example, a group of 3- to 5-year-old girls will get together and collect firewood, make a small cooking fire, and cook a bit of food for themselves. But even before they do this, before they are using language and playing with others in a coordinated manner, little girls engage in solitary play activities that are gender-appropriate. These playtimes afford the child opportunities to practice, and at the same time demonstrate to the analyst the salience and importance of these activities and the child's ability to understand the details and sequences that constitute them.

Before she was putting two words together (at approximately 18 months), Suela performed an elaborate "play monologue," a routine she enacted by herself, silently, in which she evinced knowledge of all the steps involved in food preparation. She prepared a pretend cooking fire, wrapped up a small piece of firewood ("food") in a leaf packet, placed it in the fire with a pair of tongs she made from a twig, turned the packet over several times, pulled it out and inspected it for doneness with the appropriate look of concern, and returned it to her fire for further cooking. After some time had passed, she took out her leaf packet, blew on it to cool it off, and placed it on a safe and level spot. She carefully opened it and removed the "food." Then she offered it to an unnamed imaginary individual. Then, rewrapping the "food" in a leaf, she repeated the entire procedure several times. This was done while she was sitting by herself in a sago camp while her mother was processing sago (her back to Suela) about twenty-five feet away. Suela was not doing this for an audience, but simply for and by herself.

Such practices preface carrying out real cooking activities months later. For example, at $2\frac{1}{2}$ years and in the presence of her mother, Meli would cook bananas. She would blow on the fire so it would burn hotter, turn the bananas at the right time, retrieve them from the fire with tongs, and peel them, still hot, when they were done. I have no recorded observations of boys cooking food if a female (over the age of 3) was around, nor did boys ever pretend to cook food, either alone or with their sisters. Boys learned at an early age that such activities were not appropriate for them if their mothers or sisters were around.

Young girls are sensitive to other tasks expected of women as part of nurturing and caregiving, such as teaching children how to talk, cleaning up after infants' accidents, and attending to infants in net bags when they are distressed. Meli, along with other girls under 3, would tell even younger children what to say to others, something that their mothers did with them and their

Figure 32. Suela inspecting the contents of her net bag.

younger siblings. Meli would ask to help her mother clean up after her brother before he was toilet trained, a task only women do. This often came as a surprise to her mother, who had never asked her to assist in that specific task, and she refused to let Meli help, saying Meli was too young to do it right. To Meli, however, it seemed a perfectly appropriate task for her, something she had seen her mother do many times. Before Suela's baby brother was born, she often played with a net bag, stuffing it with an old piece of blanket and carrying it around on her head the way a woman carries a baby. Periodically she would stop, jiggle it, and then take it off her head, sit down, put the bag in her lap and look inside to check on the baby, as one does when the baby cries. These fantasy sequences, which modeled women's activities in great detail, were carried out as both solitary and social activities.

Similarly, Meli (27.3) often tried to get her baby brother into a net bag and carry him around. One time Meli was playing with my small net bag, putting things in it while she was also cooking some bananas with her mother. When she told her mother she wanted to put her 11-month-old brother in the bag, her mother distracted her by reminding her to attend to the bananas. When Meli asked again later, her mother raised two concerns: "Will he fit?" (the bag was very small) and "Won't Bambi mind?" (it was my bag). The issues of permission and size of the bag were discussed at length. Meli argued that he would fit and claimed that I had given her the bag to keep, neither of which

Figure 33. Abi playing with an ax while Suɛla looks on.

was true. Mɛli's proposal was not accepted that time, since there was pressure from her mother to cook and Mɛli became distracted.

However, three months later, Mɛli suggested a similar plan to her mother. She wanted to carry her brother around on her shoulders, another way young children are carried by mothers and older sisters. After unsuccessfully trying to dissuade her, her mother finally assisted her by putting the little boy, then more than 13 months old, on her shoulders, but he was too heavy for her to carry. Mɛli insisted that they keep on trying, and Osolowa kept laughing, as Mɛli could barely move under the weight of her brother. Finally, she told Mɛli to give it up, that her thigh bones would break because Seligiwɔ was too heavy, but Mɛli persisted. Osolowa attempted to persuade her to put him in a bag – an offer of an alternative solution. But as often happens with young children, Mɛli became distracted by hearing others playing outside and decided just to carry the empty bag. She ran out to join the other activities. Boys did not want to carry their younger siblings, nor did their mothers ever ask them to. Their fantasy play did not portray these domestic concerns.

While both men and women are expected to work with bush knives and axes in the gardens and to take care of pigs, these are the activities that boys focus on for play. By 28 months, both Abi and Wanu had small pocket knives given to them by their parents, who had obtained them by working for the anthropologists. These knives, and their frequent temporary and ultimately permanent loss, were an important topic of conversation for sons and members of their families. Both boys liked to carve off pieces of wood whenever possible from the house posts or the bed platforms, something men would do absentmindedly while talking whenever they were standing near a tree, a stump, or anything made of wood. Abi and Daibo pretended that they were killing pigs, and they generated many cooperative fantasies on that theme. Abi also liked to play with a large bamboo fish trap, carrying it to the top of a little rise in front of his house and back again. One day it accidentally rolled down the incline, and he chased after it yelling, "The pig is running away," as he ran and "captured" it. After that, he would drag it up the hill and, letting it go, would repeatedly run after it. Small boys also spend time marching around the yard with sticks as if carrying boxes, digging in gardens, shooting birds, accompanying older boys, or fishing in small nearby streams. These activities are usually carried out in groups of mixed age.

Socialization of gender identities through *ɛlɛma* routines

In Chapter 4 the analysis of *ɛlɛma* as a language-socializing practice was considered in terms of content, form, function, and the pervasiveness of this practice across social relationships. *Elɛma* sequences display to children culturally appropriate social and linguistic skills. Once the child is able to perform these skills alone, the work of the caregiver is over in this regard. *Elɛma* sequences are used not only by mothers but also by children to tell others what to say and how to say it. Children's use of *ɛlɛma* tells us what they know about gender-appropriate speech behavior.

In spite of the fact that all young children participate in *ɛlɛma* as addressees, only girls initiate these direct instruction sequences, telling others, particularly younger children, what to say. Although fathers occasionally use *ɛlɛma* with their children, I recorded no examples of boys – participants in the study or their young friends and relatives – using it. In striking contrast, Mɛli's older female cousins and Abi's and Wanu's older sisters initiated *ɛlɛma* routines frequently with younger children.[7]

Given the division of labor in Kaluli society, in particular the strong association between women and caregiving, these findings lend strength to the idea that girls from a very early age emulate their mothers' nurturing behaviors. Showing language through *ɛlɛma* is one of these caregiving behaviors. In spite of the fact that boys are around younger children, they are not encouraged to play a nurturing role, nor do they spontaneously take such a role. On the other hand, mothers tell girls what to say to their younger siblings, as we saw with Mɛli in Example 4.6. Thus, girls are increasingly put in a position to tell younger children what to say while protecting and supporting them.

Young girls' use of *ɛlɛma* demonstrates their social knowledge and communicative competence. Girls just over 2 years of age are able to produce ɛ*lɛma* sequences identical to those produced elsewhere by much older caregivers. One important caregiving routine involves calming a fussy baby; as early as 27.3 months, Mɛli was able to produce such lines spontaneously.

Example 8.5. Mɛli (27.3) is at home with her brother Seligiwɔ (11.) and grandmother, Weyabe. Her brother is restless and whining.

[To Seligiwɔ]	my mother! – ɛlɛma /
[The baby babbles.]	
	what? / Mother went away! /

Mɛli first tells her brother to call out for his mother, as hearing the mother's voice is one way to reassure an unhappy child. In response to the baby's babbling, she requests clarification and then tells him that his mother is not there. Later she says to him, "Mother is about to come." She already knows what to say to calm an anxious child waiting for his mother.

In another situation, which occurred several months later, Mɛli is playing with her classificatory daughter Ana. From around this developmental point, Mɛli more actively told younger children what to say as her own language improved and her mother's use of ɛ*lɛma* with her diminished greatly.

Example 8.6. Mɛli (32.2) is at home with her mother and Ana (23.), who is her classificatory daughter and whom Mɛli calls *nelε* 'my daughter'. Ana calls Mɛli *nɔ* 'my mother'. Mɛli's classificatory mother Auwe (one of two adult sisters of her mother's) is visiting. Mɛli has a packet of salt and is sharing it with Ana. Auwe has repeatedly requested some, and Mɛli has not answered her.

Auwe → Mɛli [annoyed]: What about the salt?!
Mɛli → Ana →> Auwe: what salt?! – elema /
[Before anyone can answer, there is a loud noise from the cooking area, and everyone is distracted.]

In this recurring rhetorical exchange regarding sharing, Mɛli, in directing Ana to speak to Auwe, is responding exactly like her own mother telling Mɛli what to say following a request that she has not responded to. Mɛli's rhetorical question was interpreted by Kaluli as a refusal, though in a somewhat playful key. Mɛli, however, should not have refused her classificatory mother in this way (through Ana), but everyone was distracted by an accident in the cooking area and the matter was dropped. In other similar interactions around this time when Mɛli refused Auwe, Auwe held her accountable, pressuring her to reciprocate and share by reminding Mɛli of what she had always been given. The introduction of accountability was a change from the way in which adults responded to Mɛli's refusals when she was younger. They would no longer just let the matter drop.

Older girls use ɛ*lɛma* throughout interactions to tell younger children what to say in much the same ways their mothers use it. Mama (3;6) frequently corrected Mɛli's speech, using ɛ*lɛma* both dyadically and triadically, when

Mɛli was 27.3 months old – a practice that sometimes infuriated Mɛli. In particular, the assertive use of language to claim or challenge ownership, or to tease and shame individuals into realigning themselves through sharing, dominates the ways in which older girls use *ɛlɛma*. Issues of giving and taking are always central in the negotiation of social relationships.

In the following example, *ɛlɛma* is used to regulate a range of social relationships. This sequence comes from an early sample from Suɛla. Her family used *ɛlɛma* the same way other families did. In this example, Suɛla's older sister Mage (10 yr) plays a major role in telling Suɛla what to say.

Example 8.7. Suɛla (23.), her mother, sister Mage (10 yr), and brother Daibo (5 yr) are at home. I have given Suɛla a small packet of salt as part of my routine visiting gift, and Mage and Daibo rush over to see what she has.

¹Mage: I wonder what kind (of thing) it is.
²Daibo → Suɛla [begging/whining]: Suɛla, we two will eat.
³Mother: Look at her salt!
⁴Daibo → Suɛla [begging/whining]: Salt we two will eat.
⁵Mother → Suɛla →> Daibo: Is it yours?! Is it yours?! – ɛlɛma.
                                          ⁶is it yours?! /
[As Daibo comes closer to her]   Mother! /
⁷Mage → Suɛla →> Daibo: Bambi gave! – ɛlɛma.
⁸Mother → Suɛla →> Daibo: Bambi, Bambi gave! – ɛlɛma.
                                          ⁹I--- /

¹⁰Mage → Suɛla: Speak.
¹¹Daibo → Suɛla: Suɛla, eat.
¹²Mage → Suɛla →> Daibo: What are *you* eating?! –ɛlɛma.
                                          ¹³salt /
¹⁴Mage → Suɛla →> Daibo: You don't eat! – ɛlɛma [*Gi na!*].
[5-sec pause]
¹⁵Daibo → Suɛla [whining]: Salt –!
¹⁶Mother → Daibo [angry]: What do you keep talking about?!
¹⁷Mother → Suɛla [re salt, persuasively]: Suɛla, *I* put it down.
                                          ¹⁸ɛm!(neg) /
¹⁹Mother → Suɛla: No.
²⁰Mage → Suɛla →> Mother: You don't take! – ɛlɛma. [*Gi dia!*]
                                          ²¹you don't take! / [*gi dia!*]
²²Mother → Suɛla [begging]: No, *nɛsu.* Salt to me.
[To mother]   ²³ɛm!(neg) /
²⁴Mother → Suɛla [begging]: No, I put it down.
²⁵Mage → Suɛla →> Mother: You don't take! – ɛlɛma. [*Gi dia!*]
²⁶Mage [looking at salt wistfully]: Oh, what a lot of salt here!
²⁷Mother → Suɛla [appealing]: No, my Suɛla.
                                          ²⁸ɛm! /
²⁹Mother → Suɛla [annoyed]: What's this "Ɛm"?! Yes!
³⁰Mage → Suɛla →> Mother: Really good! – ɛlɛma.
[Later Mage begs salt from Suɛla, and her mother uses a similar teasing routine directed at Mage.]

When Daibo sees the salt I have given to his sister Suɛla, he begs for it in a whining voice (*geseab*) to make her (and everyone else) feel sorry for him and give some to him (line 2). Both the pronoun he selected (*nani* 'only we two' dual emphatic) and verb form (intentive) are frequently used in begging to assert a special sharing relationship between the two parties ("Only we (and no one else) will eat"). After his repeated begging, his mother tells Suela to challenge him with a rhetorical question (line 5), "Is it yours?!" This is said to shame Daibo (*sasindiab*) for his somewhat inappropriate behavior and to curtail his begging. Both her mother and Mage urge Suela to say, "Bambi gave it," using ɛlɛma. Since this is a traditional way to acknowledge the source of a gift, this socializes some social graces. As Suela falters (line 9), her sister urges her to speak to Daibo and thus assert herself verbally.

In Daibo's next turn (line 11), he tells Suela to eat, which she is already doing. The purpose of such a comment is to make someone angry (*enteab*). Mage tells Suela what to say back to Daibo (line 12), pointing out sarcastically that Daibo has nothing to eat. Suela apparently does not understand and instead answers the rhetorical question as if it is an information-seeking question directed to her.

Mage (line 14) uses one of the formulaic expressions (*gi na* 'you don't eat') that children are encouraged to learn and use in teasing routines around sharing. Daibo persists in begging, but he is largely ignored until his mother shames him (line 16), using another formulaic expression meaning "You have nothing to keep talking about (so be quiet)." The mother then begins a series of requests directed to Suela to try to get the salt for herself (lines 17–19).

Mage initiates another teasing routine (similar to line 14) using ɛlɛma, which Suela repeats. The mother counters with an appeal, speaking in a soft, persuasive voice and addressing her daughter as *nɛsu* (see also Example 6.6) in an attempt to divert her attention from Mage, who uses ɛlɛma again (line 25) to elicit teasing from Suela toward her mother. The mother continues to appeal, addressing her daughter in increasingly intimate terms, while Mage tries to get Suela to refuse. Since the salt was given to Suela, the mother cannot forcibly take it. That would violate the child's rights. Appeal is the only strategy. However, after the third rejection, the mother becomes annoyed and challenges Suela (line 29) with "What's this 'No'?!" The interaction continues with Mage providing teasing lines for Suela to say to her mother. When Mage begs for the salt, Suela hands it to the mother, and the mother uses ɛlɛma to tell Suela what to say (another teasing routine) to her brother and sister, who now are both quite intent upon getting some of the salt themselves.

Mage takes her sister's situation quite seriously and puts pressure on her to assert herself and use specific linguistic routines to squelch the begging of her brother and mother. Like many older sisters, she tells her little sister what to say, just as they will both do with their children in the future.

In addition to using ɛlɛma to accomplish the serious work of social interaction, girls also take it as a linguistic resource for nonserious purposes. Such playful uses of language are especially revealing about what children know about social relationships and linguistic resources. There is no model for the ways in which girls play with *εlεma* in adult-initiated *εlεma* sequences. The interesting inversions of the practice reflect something only a child can do with *εlεma* – play with it.

Prior to the sequence below, Meli and her mother have been teasing each other and laughing a lot. A playful mood has been established, and Meli takes it from there.

Example 8.8. Meli (30.2) is standing on the opposite side of the room from her mother.

[Calling out]	¹Mother! / bedbug – εlεmo! /
²Huh?	
	³bedbug – εlεmε! /
⁴Bedbug.	
	⁵bedbug *lobus* – εlεma /
⁶Huh?	
	⁷bedbug *lobus* – εlεmε! /
⁸Do I say bedbug *lobusi?*	
	⁹yes /
¹⁰Bedbug *lobusi.*	
	¹¹this bedbug *lobusi* – εlεmε /
¹²Bedbug *lobusi*	
	¹³enough / X /
¹⁴Yea, enough?	
	¹⁵yes /
¹⁶Yea.	
	¹⁷bukobuk – εlεma /
¹⁸Huh?	
	¹⁹bedbug – .,
²⁰// Huh?	
	²¹*bukobuk* – εlεma /
²²Do I say *bukobuk?*	
	²³yes /
²⁴*Bukobuk!* [Both laugh.]	
	²⁵enough /
²⁶Enough?	
	²⁷yes /
²⁸Yes.	
	²⁹you don't eat! [*gi na!*] /

Meli takes the initiative in this dyadic *εlεma* sequence, calling to her mother and telling her to say "bedbug." As there is nothing in the prior discourse or situational context to indicate why she should start a conversation with the word "bedbug," her mother requests clarification, and Meli exuberantly repeats the command, using the emphatic form *εlεmε*, appropriate for a repeated request. After her mother complies, Meli continues, adding her version, *lobus*, of the Tok Pisin word *rabis* 'bad' that she has heard her father use. Here the juxtaposition of Kaluli and Tok Pisin (line 5) – *gayamu lobus* 'bedbug rubbish/bad' – strikes both of them as funny. After playing with this phrase, Mɛli adds another word from Tok Pisin, *bukbuk* 'crocodile', pronouncing it *bukobuk*. She succeeds in getting her mother to say these words, then shifts into a mock teasing routine as a continuation of their play frame (see Examples 4.14 and 4.15, which use *gi na*).

This ɛlɛma sequence is different in several important ways from others that took place between mothers and children. In terms of the structure and function of ɛlɛma sequences, this one is, first, initiated by the child, not the mother. Second, it is the longest dyadic ɛlɛma sequence in the entire corpus. Third, it consists of only explicit ɛlɛma. Fourth, there are no other situations in which Mɛli uses these Tok Pisin words. She is not referring to any specific bedbugs or crocodiles; there are none in sight. Thus, this ɛlɛma sequence becomes a speech event consisting of her mother's repeating Mɛli's funny words. These differences, plus the repetition of a limited number of words – "bedbug," *lobusi*, and *bukbuk* – mark this interaction as purely playful. And because the words are well formed and the ɛlɛma framework known to both participants, this type of word play works. Though ɛlɛma is used by mothers to initiate games with their children, there are no other recorded sequences in which one person tells another to say the names of things the way Mɛli asks her mother to do. In fact, saying the names of things is exactly the opposite of what ɛlɛma and the ideology of language instruction are about.

On the interactional level, the social roles are here reversed. Mɛli is taking the mother's role and telling her what to say, following the conventions down the line. Both partners make sure throughout the interaction that they have understood one another, with constant clarification checks (lines 6, 8, 14, 18, 20, 22, 27). The mother makes sure what she says is right, and Mɛli provides the requested confirmation (lines 9, 15, 23, 28) that the exact form has been repeated. The requests for clarification made by the mother are like the ones made by a child when the mother tells her what to say; thus, a balance is maintained (see also Examples 4.11 and 8.9 in which the child directs clarification requests to the mother). Both parties cooperate so that Mɛli can take the lead.

This give and take in verbal play is rooted in the increasingly egalitarian nature of mother–daughter relationships. That is, the child can ask the mother to do what the mother has been telling the child to do for the last ten months: use language for social and expressive ends. This is represented on a number of levels – in terms of role play, role reversals, and interactional rules. As in all play, if it is to be successful everyone playing must know the rules and act systematically when reversing them. For example, in nonplay situations, Kaluli mothers address their young children as *nɔ* 'my mother', but only when they appeal to them to give food or plead with them to act in a particular way. Feeling sorry for the mother (as mothers do for children) is always in the mode of appeal. Children do not address their mothers as "my child." In this role reversal during play, Mɛli adheres to that cultural convention, since she is not putting her mother explicitly in a child role, nor is she acting in the appeal modality. Mɛli calls to her mother as "my mother"; the mood is playful and assertive. Mɛli's use of the assertive key with ɛlɛma demonstrates her association between the two. In this and all other examples, when young girls use ɛlɛma the appropriate mood is maintained.

Finally, this is an example of role play. Little girls view ɛlɛma as something mothers do with their children. As an egalitarian society, Kaluli have no chiefs or bigmen or persons of special rank, nor are there any stores, hospitals, or other institutions that might provide role models for children. The major roles available for emulation are male and female, and they are kept well separated. This sequence is in fact a situation of role reversal and role play, with emphasis on the play with language itself providing a framework.

Breaches in gender-appropriate activities: recontextualizing and socializing

Sometimes children act in ways that do not conform to adults' or older children's notions of conventional gender-appropriate behavior. These violations demonstrate to children how problematic incidents are resolved and how they are to feel about them. We see here how one mother, Ulahi, handles such an incident with Abi. Her responses are typical of other Kaluli mothers in similar situations.

Example 8.9. Abi (28.3), Suɛla (21.), Mobiya (7 yr), Daibo (5 yr), and their mother are at home. Suɛla is walking around with a net bag containing an old cloth; she is bouncing it as if she were quieting a fussy baby.

¹Mobiya [re Suɛla]: She's going around with a tiny baby there!
[Requesting a net bag]   ²yagdiyo! / Suɛla one for me / Suɛla! //
[Teasing]   ³Suɛla's baby right here / newborn baby right
                                              here / what a huge one right here! / do you
                                              see the little baby! /
⁴Mother → Abi: Is she carrying around a little one there?
[Pointing to a net bag]   ⁵yes / Mother / me too / Mother, I too want
                                              to do like that / that's mine /
⁶Suɛla [as she leaves]: outside /
⁷Mother → Abi: You too put one on out there. [Mother enlists
Daibo to get the bag and a little cloth; he does.]
⁸[Giving Abi the bag] Go out like that.
[Re cloth]   ⁹Mother / give me mine /
[Mother puts cloth in: fixes bag.]
¹⁰Yes, take it outside like this.
[Abi takes it.]
¹¹Abi.
                                              ¹²yes? /

[13]Is that a newborn baby?

[14]Daibo → Abi [teasing]: Newborn baby!

[15]Mobiya → Abi [high-voice teasing]: Oh, newborn baby! Oh, my newborn baby!

[16]Mother → Abi: It's Daibo and Obali's baby! [Everyone laughs.]

[Abi takes bush knife; has bag on his head the way women carry it.]

[17]What do you have in there?

[18]huh? /

[19]Cloth!

[Pulling bag off, giving it to mother]   [20]this is your bag /

[21]Huh? Do I put it on myself?

[22]Was it born yesterday [re baby]?

[23]huh? /

[24]Was it born yesterday?

[Re bag]   [25]hold (it) /

[26]What? What? The cloth?

[27]Mother, you take the cloth /

[Abi runs outside with the knife.]

Initially, Abi begs Suɛla for a net bag (line 2), but then he teases her, using a routine sequence (line 3). Children often use the tease "It's a big one" in a variety of situations implying a vaguely sexual reference. Abi then requests a net bag for himself (line 5), and after assisting him with it, Ulahi teases him (line 13), and his siblings join her (lines 14–15). Recall that men have nothing to do with newborns and to transgress is both inappropriate and potentially dangerous, as it violates certain taboos. Ulahi confronts Abi about what is in the bag (lines 17–19), breaking the fantasy by telling him that it is a cloth and not a baby in the bag. Abi takes the bag off his head and discontinues his fantasy. Even though the children were teasing Suɛla early on about her "newborn baby" (lines 1, 3), they do not contradict or break her fantasy, which is appropriate for little girls. During this and similar situations where she is teased, she does not give up the bag or the fantasy, whereas Abi does.

In addition to which actions are appropriate, children have to learn gender-appropriate appearance. Hairstyles are the same for boys and girls: A shaved head with a small topknot is typical. During the first year, boys and girls are usually dressed similarly (and minimally); they wear a little string about their waists in which to tuck a cloth or leaf pubic cover. Mothers do make small bark-fiber skirts that they put on their little girls when they go visiting or when they show them off around the village, but before the introduction of Western clothing (shorts, trousers) there was no special clothing for small boys. Girls at the age of 2 or 3 can wear pubic covers (often under their skirts), but it is never appropriate for a boy to put on a skirt, except when he is trying to provoke a sister. This was brought out in many interactions involving Abi and his sister Yogodo. In the following situation with their mother at the swimming hole, both children are naked.

Example 8.10. Abi (33.2), Yogodo (6 yr), and their mother are at the Solɔ stream, washing and playing. Yogodo is in the water; Abi, on the bank.

[Picking up Yogodo's skirts]　　　　　¹oh Waye's skirt right here / and your skirt right here /

²Yogodo → Abi: Oh, mine! Mine!
[Holding skirt]　　　　　　　　　　　³no / this is mine! /
[Yogodo offers a tiny shrimp to Abi.]
⁴This shrimp, you take this. Give me back my skirt. Abi, the shrimp is right here. Shrimp, yes, take take this. You take this! [No response from Abi.]
⁵I'm going to put on your pubic cover. [There is none there.]
⁶Abi! Abi! Say something. Give me my skirt!
　　　　　　　　　　　　　　　　⁷It's mine! /
⁸You take another shrimp.
[Mother puts skirt on Abi.]
⁹Mother → Yogodo: Look at Abi in a skirt!
[To Yogodo]　　　　　　　　　　¹⁰do you see it? /
[To mother, looking for skirt]　　¹¹another? / X /
¹²Mother → Abi: There aren't others.

　　　　　　　　　　　　　　　　¹³no! / I'll put on another / give (me) another /
[Mother is laughing.]　　　　　　¹⁴Mother /
¹⁵Huh?

　　　　　　　　　　　　　　　　¹⁶give me your skirt / put it on · I want to put it on /
¹⁷Oh, do you wear skirts?!
　　　　　　　　　　　　　　　　¹⁸Mother / give (me) a skirt /
¹⁹You put on some leaves! Pubic cover.
²⁰Yogodo → Abi [teasing]: You put on some leaves! Pubic cover!
　　　　　　　　　　　　　　　　²¹Mother / Mother /
²²Mother → Abi: What?
　　　　　　　　　　　　　　　　²³give me a skirt /
²⁴I have none! [She is wearing one.]
[Abi pulls off her skirt, whining]　　²⁵give me your skirt / X / Mother! /
²⁶What! look at the one you have on!
[Mother pokes his penis through skirt.]
²⁷My little girl, your privates are showing! Look right there! What's that?
　　　　　　　　　　　　　　　　²⁸Mother / X / give your skirt /
²⁹[Poking him again] Wai! [She laughs and starts to wash him.]
³⁰Yogodo → Abi: I'm going to put on your pubic cover.
³¹Mother → Abi →> Yogodo: What do you mean?! – ɛlɛma.
　　　　　　　　　　　　　　　　³²what do you mean?! /
³³Yogodo → Abi: Is it yours?! Is it yours?!
[Abi takes his mother's breast and nurses. After a while Abi and Yogodo tease each other; the mother tells Abi to take off the skirt, and after several requests he does.]

In response to Yogodo's claim to her skirt (line 2), Abi counters with a tease that it is his. Yogodo offers to exchange the shrimps she has caught for her skirt. When Abi doesn't agree to her offer, Yogodo changes her strategy and threatens him, saying she will take his pubic cover (which isn't there). When he still does not answer, she demands that he return her skirt, and he teases her back, claiming, "It's mine!" (line 7). Yogodo escalates her earlier offer and adds another shrimp to facilitate the exchange. But to tease her further, Ulahi puts Yogodo's skirt on Abi, after which Abi (line 11) requests yet another skirt and argues with his mother. Abi (line 16) asks his mother for her skirt, and she teases him, "Oh, do you wear skirts?!" – a rhetorical question meaning "You don't wear skirts!" In response to his insistence, she is explicit (line 19) about what he should wear: leaves and a pubic cover. When he demands the skirt again, she denies she has one (line 24). When he continues, she gently mocks and teases him about the appropriateness of his request, reminding him that he is not a girl, making the evidence explicit (line 27). When he doesn't stop and requests her skirt again (line 28), she teases and distracts him by giving him a bath. Yogodo joins in the tease (line 30), only to have her mother turn on her, enjoining Abi to tease his sister. After Abi nurses, the skirt is taken off without fuss.

The issue of modesty is raised with Mɛli in the guise of trying to persuade her to wear a skirt. Osolowa's argument centers on the argument that pubic covers are for brothers; Mɛli's point is that she would rather wear a pubic cover than a skirt. In this situation, Mɛli does get what she wants.

Example 8.11. Mɛli (29.), who is wearing nothing, is with her mother in the house.
[1]Mother → Mɛli: Your privates are showing there, put on a skirt.
|Mɛli gets a pubic cover.| Give up with pubic cover, *nɛsu*.
[2]no! /
[3]No!
[4]no! pubic cover · pubic cover (I) will wear! /
[5]Huh?
[6]I will wear (the) pubic cover! /
[7]No! You wear skirts; Seligiwɔ wears a pubic cover.
[8]I will wear (the) pubic cover! /
[9]Are you a boy?!
[10]I will wear (the) pubic cover! /
[11]You wear skirts, you wear belts.
[12]Mother! I will wear (the) pubic cover! /

The topic of gender-appropriate behavior or gender identity is never discussed abstractly and becomes an issue only in instances of inappropriate behaviors. These concerns were talked about in the following ways. For example, in response to Mɛli's wanting to wear a pubic cover, her mother posed a rhetorical question: "Are you a boy?!" Mɛli did not answer and also did not put on the pubic cover. When Abi became too serious about wearing a skirt and was not just teasing his sister with it, his mother in a mocking and teasing way called him "my little girl" and then pointed out the contradictory aspect of her statement by poking playfully at his penis. In yet another situation, Abi asked whether he was a boy or a girl, and his mother made the point emphatically: "You're a boy," adding, "Yogodo is a girl, and it is okay for her to wear a skirt."

Example 8.12. Abi (35.2) is playing with himself and notices a wart on his testicles. His mother is making a woman's skirt.

[To mother]	[1]my wart here /
[2]Mother → Abi [teasing]: You aren't saying the truth!	
	[3]yes wart! /
[Watching his mother]	[4]Mother, will I wear (it) on here / I'm a
[Touching waist]	boy / I'm a girl / it goes on here!
[5]You're a boy!	
	[6]no /
[7]Yogodo is a girl.	
	[8]no, I'm a girl /
[9][Re skirt] It's okay for Yogodo to put it on.	
	[10]oh, I'm a girl /

[Abi then turns his attention to the baby. About an hour later, Abi reintroduces this topic with me, asking me if I am a girl.]

Mothers are gentle with their children but will tease them to get the point across. They help their children act in gender-appropriate ways through verbally guiding and manipulating them in a variety of interactions that focus on the ways in which they play, dress, and act. From the beginning, ideas concerning the proper socialization of boys and girls affect how mothers respond to children differentially. This behavior is consistent and pervasive, and like other socializing practices affects the direction and flow of everyday interactions. Expectations concerning mothers' relationships with their children (and other relationships as well) guide ways to act and feel as Kaluli males and females are socialized in and through social interaction.

9. Conclusion

The preceding chapters offer social, linguistic, and affective perspectives on the lives of several Kaluli children and their families. Their world is linked, of course, to a larger cultural and linguistic one that helps shape the ways in which children are socialized. Language socialization – the perspective that children are socialized to use language and socialized through the use of language – relies on the assumption that an explicit connection exists between the processes of learning language and learning from language. These are not invisible or natural processes but cultural ones.

The microethnographic methods used in this study enable one to specify and interpret the words, interactions, relationships, and contexts in which cultural meanings are displayed to young children and reproduced by them. We have seen, for example, that who participates in a conversation and what happens in a conversation affect how and what children learn. The conversational transcripts with annotation illustrate how cultural beliefs are displayed in and organize ordinary conversations. Fine-grained analyses of interactional strategies reveal assumptions that speakers hold about those with whom they interact. These in turn can be analyzed in conjunction with what individuals state about these assumptions. Language socialization allows the close investigation of major relationships between form and function in language, and of the processes by which these relationships are acquired and used. Further, if one is to understand how children come to acquire what they know, process and practice must be taken into account. As cultural ideology and everyday practice organize each other, what happens in interaction must be considered in detail and in relation to other types of cultural activities. Since cultural and social values are constructed continually through interactions, examining socializing interactions in relation to the larger social and linguistic world provides insights into not only what is being taught about language and culture but also the relationships that hold between the two.

"Methods link data – what we construe to be observations of some particular reality – with theory, our proposals for understanding reality in general" (Frake 1977:1). This study shows how language is a resource for social theory. How do we locate the practices and processes of social reproduction in

239

talk? What has been illuminated here is a particular view of language as a set of discourse practices that are the bridge between practical and discursive consciousness. Through talk, a form of action as well as a symbolic system, practical consciousness can become a type of discursive consciousness, if only for a few moments of an interaction, or repeatedly until understanding is achieved and nothing more needs to be said.

Kaluli believe that language use is not merely a verbal skill in and of itself, but a social skill central to relationships between people. This study also represents that viewpoint. In the concluding discussion that follows, I explore three structural themes in Kaluli society that have emerged from the study of Kaluli language socialization: (1) autonomy versus interdependence, (2) authority, and (3) gender and reciprocity. Each theme concerns relationships between people, and from each I draw a set of theoretical conclusions concerning how language practices are implicated in the articulation of social life. The first two of these themes – autonomy versus interdependence and authority – emerge out of analyses of interactional strategies and discourse practices. They articulate certain dilemmas or tensions that exist in Kaluli society. These two themes are expressed as stances in relatively direct ways through specific linguistic resources and interactional routines. In contrast, language is implicated in a less direct way in the third theme, gender and reciprocity. The fact that gender is indirectly expressed through discourse practices hides the critical connection between language and gender as well as between gender and reciprocity. However, through a close examination of discourse practices, one can discover an engendered cultural view, a view of reciprocity that considers the roles of all participants and how these roles are instantiated.

Autonomy versus interdependence

Two related themes continually recur in family conversations and other verbal genres in Kaluli society: the assertion of autonomy and the expression of interdependence. Not only are they continually negotiated in everyday conversations, but these same themes are repeatedly contemplated in such myths and poetic genres as *sa-yɛlab* 'sung–texted weeping' and Gisalo song texts. Kaluli recognize each theme as a value, and recognize their problematic nature as well. Rather than treat autonomy and interdependence as disembodied values, it is useful to delineate the dialogic forms in which they are embedded as stances in social life. Autonomy and interdependence are associated with particular sentiments, which in turn are keyed by participants' affective stances. Depending on how one is asserting autonomy or expressing interdependence in a given activity or with a particular set of interlocutors, varying discourse structures are used to articulate and negotiate social stance. While autonomy may be the stance taken initially by one party in an interaction, depending on the response of the other there may be a shift to a stance of interdependence, (i.e., cooperation, sharing) accompanied by a shift in affective display.

The relation between the assertion of autonomy and the recognition of interdependence creates cultural dilemmas for people everywhere. In a nonstratified and relatively small-scale society like Kaluli society, the lack of hierarchical structure results in responsibility continually being placed on individual members to negotiate interpersonal boundaries. Members make maximal use of the expression of sentiments – affection, obligation, compassion – appropriate to relationships and activities in mobilizing others' responses to their needs and desires. Rather than having a structural position from which to operate, they deploy personal sentiments such as compassion. Writing about the Pintupi (Western Desert of Australia), Myers points out that "underlying the concept of compassion is a recognition of 'relatedness' – a recognition of shared identity or empathy between the person who is compassionate and another. This identity is the source of the other's legitimate claim on one's compassion (1986:113)." Unless managed very carefully, not to be moved can be misread as "not in relation" among the Kaluli as well. We saw this articulated in the myth of the boy who became a *muni* bird and in other daily encounters. As among Pintupi, there is a "negotiated quality" (Myers 1986:286) to Kaluli daily life. Throughout Kaluli interactions, momentary and ever-shifting positions of autonomy and interdependence are continually articulated and negotiated. In every interaction involving a request for food, objects, cooperation, or attention, or where ownership or rights are contested, autonomy and interdependence may also be at issue.

Why sentiment plays such an important role among Kaluli in negotiating social life cannot easily be determined. Detailed accounts of the importance of sentiment in the lives of people in quite different nonstratified societies, such as Kaguru in Tanzania (Beidelman 1986) and Pintupi (Myers 1986), suggest both the unreliability of resources and the need people have for each other (labor, protection, support) in the long term. It is in this context that Myers talks about "compassion" and "pity" as highly adaptive qualities for Pintupi, stressing their valued status as social practices reproduced in both material and symbolic circumstances. Unreliability and scarcity of material resources and the implications for sharing (Lee 1982; Silberbauer 1981) do not account for the prevalence of these and other displayed sentiments in Kaluli life, where resources are reliably available. Among the Kaluli, uncertainty lies in relationships and the problematic nature of interdependence rather than in natural resources. The prominence of compassion and other displayed sentiments is a response to something problematic in this egalitarian society itself, not something external to it. In the absence of objectified authority, Kaluli draw on other resources, namely sentiments, to structure their relationships culturally. These sentiments are expressed through interactional strategies of assertion and appeal.

Kaluli are often caught in a dilemma: They want to do what is sociable or expected in relationships, and they want to have or do something for themselves. Sharing is one locus of the more central issue of how and when to display one's autonomy and to express one's relationship with others. These might appear to be absolute contradictions, but in fact they are not. Such dilemmas are the stuff of "moral imagination" (Beidelman 1986) throughout the world. This tension and the consequences of choosing are recognized and played out through the thematic cores of Kaluli myths as well as in everyday interactions, and are often expressed through differing expectations involving sharing and reciprocity.[1] Both choices are socialized – that is to say, given value – as children are encouraged both to share and to refuse. While sharing and reciprocity are expected, the *how* and *when* of these practices are negotiable and socialized.

[margin note: socialized → given value]

Caregivers socialize skills necessary for assessing how and when to assert one's autonomy or express one's relationship by guiding young children's participation in verbal activities. In socializing contexts, children are repeatedly encouraged to be sensitive both to the relationship between participants and to the affective key of interaction. What matters is how and when one responds to the displays of others. For example, in refusing someone, one must know whether a compassionate or a teasing manner is more what one might call "feelingful." Importantly, offering compassion itself and recognizing the relationship are seen by Kaluli as equivalent (*wɛl*) to giving something material. Similarly, a sharp, stinging tease can leave the other feeling pushed away in addition to having nothing.

Equally important is when to respond in a particular way. Children are not known for their patience, and they must learn that delays are part of the temporal configuration of human exchanges. This focus of Kaluli culture is particularly illuminated in language socialization. For Kaluli, much of what is learned through daily interaction is about the nature of interactional and social time. Children learn about sequencing and order in interaction, and also about how giving something now can mean getting something back later. They learn that relationships are enduring and that connections are created through shared activities, including talk. These are critical cultural constructions. Continuity over time builds trust, and the quick trade, which does not imply trust, is dispreferred among intimates. Returns are layered or staggered over time, which results in people's feeling owed and satisfied at different points in different relationships. Children are learning expectations about relationships in time and over time.

For Kaluli, the emphasis is not on showing or doing what one really feels, as would be the case in societies that value sincerity. In some sense, that is too much of a social risk and is seen as too similar to what children do before they acquire the social etiquette of personal relationships. Instead, what matters is the acknowledgment of socially valued relationships, the verbal and nonverbal display of appropriate feelings, which may or may not reflect one's internal state. Kaluli acknowledge that this is how it is when they say that one cannot know what another really thinks or feels. One can only go on what is displayed.

Complementary to the recognition of the problematic nature of interdependence as expressed in myths and everyday interaction, and on ceremonial occasions maintained in memory through *sa-yɛlab* 'sung–texted weeping' and Gisalo song texts, is a profound respect for personal autonomy. As Kaluli say, when a person does something for his or her own reasons, "having thought of it himself or herself" (*inɛli asulɛsɛgɛ*), this itself is a warrant for action. People can do their own thing, and others are careful not to violate their autonomy. Obviously, however, one must be sensitive to others' input and desires in considering doing what one wants. How to think about this, too, is not left to chance, but is actively socialized by caregivers and articulated by very young children, as Example 9.1 illustrates.

Example 9.1. Mɛli (32.2) is at home with me and her mother. Seligiwɔ (15.) puts on my rubber thong and is walking with it.

> Bambi, do you see that? / Bambi, do you see that one (who) has put (it) on and is going? /
> Babi honobadaya! / Babi hono sɛgɛlefɔhenayo badaya? /

BBS: Yikes!
Yagidi!
Osolowa → Mɛli: Number one! He does it by himself.
Namba wan! Inɛli dimɛdab.

> he does it by himself, his /
> inɛli dimɛdab · ene · /

Having thought of it himself,
Ene asulɛsɛgɛ,

> having thought of it himself /
> ene asulɛsɛgɛ /

he does it.
dimɛdab.

> dimɛdab /
> he does it /

One should not say anything; he will do his own thing.
Mɔsɛlaluwɛ; ene dimɛdɛmɛib.

Here we see one way in which Kaluli practice socializes an underlying ideology that encompasses both sensitivity to input and direction and to autonomy. Two modes of action are represented; "showing language" (*ɛlɛma* 'say it') is differentiated from guiding activity (*ɛlɛfoma* 'do it'). This is a proposed solution to another dilemma. Mɛli, in true Kaluli fashion, points out something to me, directing my attention toward something interesting in the environment. She is talking to me about the activity of her little brother rather than addressing him and commenting to him about his action. Her mother's response, *Namba wan* in Tok Pisin is followed by an oft-repeated comment regarding autonomy, "He does it by himself." Mɛli begins to supply the reason, which is formulaic, but as she pauses it is supplied by her mother as part of an implicit ɛlɛma routine – "having thought of it himself." Thinking of things yourself and doing them, especially those things that demonstrate competence, is evidence of independence, which is highly valued in young children. As Mɛli's mother points out, one should not tell a small child what to do in this area, though obviously Kaluli tell small children to avoid dangerous situations. In contrast, one "shows" a young child who does not know what to say how to speak.

Other Kaluli practices, such as asking for verbal clarification without offering paraphrase, could be viewed as placing a heavy burden on the child speaker, as providing no assistance. But from a Kaluli perspective, the speaker's autonomy of expression, no matter how inarticulate, should not be violated through offers of possible verbal alternatives. One "shows language," but one does not put words to the unarticulated thoughts of others. How does one know what another thinks? One only knows what another should be thinking. Autonomy and interdependence each play a role in socialization ideology and practice.

Authority

Authority, the right to tell others what to do, is another problematic theme in this nonstratified society. Authority is not "given," nor is it assumed without question. It can be, and frequently is, however, verbally asserted by anyone, adult or child. In spite of many assertions of authority over relatively minor as well as more serious issues, Kaluli are reluctant to take responsibility themselves for carrying out any threat or challenge, verbally or otherwise.[2] Authority is typically expressed with third-party threats ("Someone will say something or do something") rather than first-person threats ("I will say something or do something"), rhetorical questions that cannot be answered ("Who are you?!"), and words meant to shame ("Is it yours?!").[3] These linguistic resources, among others, are given as "reasons" why someone should or should not act in a particular manner. They do not however, necessarily focus on objective facts, but are "closely associated with the moral accountability of activity, . . . inevitably caught up in and expressive of, the demands and conflicts entailed within social encounters" (Giddens 1979:58). These rhetorical devices, combined with speakers' interactional endurance, create the semblance of authority in most everyday interactions, if only for the duration of the negotiation until a particular outcome is reached and there is the assurance that relationships remain intact. Everything may be up for grabs in the next interaction. This uncertainty, largely created through dramatic rhetorical displays, adds to the excitement of discussions and arguments. While there is no formal or static hierarchy, in the context of village life everyone is free to try to assert some authority verbally, if only for a moment.

All, including children, believe that they are able to negotiate some control in social relationships. Kaluli children learn that there are limits to control: One can never compel another to act. One can appeal and try to move others to act, or assert what one wants. Language is the major vehicle for attempting to express these stances.[4] Kaluli children must develop a sense of confidence in their face-to-face verbal skills, as such skills are what make the difference in influencing others and attempting to control them. These skills are socialized through verbal routines initially linked to particular persons and speech activities. In these contexts, children develop a security of being, come to depend upon a particular predictability of the world, and assume that they have a certain degree of control – what Giddens calls "ontological security" (1984:50). Expectations of predictability lead to the development of feelings of trust among those participating in these routine activities. It is within such contexts that children are enabled to learn how to learn according to the preferred ways of their social group.

However, as Giddens points out, "the flow of action continually produces consequences which are unintended by actors, and these unintended consequences also may form unacknowledged conditions of action in a feedback fashion" (1979:27). Thus, there are culturally preferred ways to insert order into chaos, to create feelings of authority and distribute control; yet there is also a tension between predictability and ambiguity. Children learn through participation in speech activities that particular outcomes are not guaranteed and that their personal control extends only so far. Whatever personal control one can achieve is largely accomplished through talk, which includes expression of sentiment, the major resource for moving others to more predictable and desirable states. Language provides the medium for articulating, even if for only a moment in a particular exchange, how two people relate. For example, in the everyday sharing of food, one must ask, and a reciprocal relationship or kinship term is selected for this purpose. Once one has asked for and been given food, that transaction becomes reportable. One can show the food to others and talk about who gave it. It becomes the visible link between persons, if only for a very short time. Once the food is eaten, there is no proof of the transaction such as one would have if a durable item were given. Address terms such as reciprocally used relationship names and talk about the giving remain and are what continue the memory of it for all who have participated. This is one way in which "subjective meanings become objective facticities" (Berger & Luckmann 1967:18). These are the created social facts that endure.

An individual's interactive history provides the frames by which he or she

[margin note:] predictability + ambiguity in control

organizes experience and through which reality is perceived. These frames are created by participation in a variety of verbal genres that are linked culturally, linguistically, and aesthetically. Each must be viewed in light of the other as they help define and give meaning to the complex set of cultural and linguistic resources that are at the center of any society. In poetic and more formal genres, language is the medium for remembering fragile relationships of interdependence in a more enduring manner.

An orientation to authority is also provided in the discourse structure of verbal genres themselves. For example, Kaluli myths (e.g., "The boy who became a *muni* bird") provide contemplative narrative discourses for imagining possible outcomes to events that mirror the problematic nature of relationships in everyday life, such as sharing and refusing to share. The teller can evoke the sentiments of the participants in a compressed discursive space using reported speech, and while there is provided an outcome to which a response is certain, that response is not given by any authoritative or judgmental stance of the teller. For Kaluli, it appears, it is up to listeners to construct appropriate sets of meanings; authority does not reside in the narrator. Nor does it reside in the text itself. Thus, for example, in the *muni* story there is no moral or explicit negative evaluation of the older sister's refusal to share with her younger brother, her *ade*. Each listener draws his or her own conclusions from the consequences of her refusal. Each listener may be reminded of his or her *ade*, of times shared that are no longer possible.

Since Lévi-Strauss (1958), much has been made of the significance of myth in articulating such cultural dilemmas. But a similar case can be made for the everyday interactions between young children and others. These too are explorations of what is and is not possible, or at least culturally preferable. These are contexts in which children learn the meaning of getting what they want and of not getting what they want. Everyday activities provide contexts in which boundaries can be defined and redefined, different courses can be taken, and intuitions can be developed and checked. As in Kaluli myths that have no explicit evaluation, no person is given an authoritative stance in routine events. Anyone may issue advisories, threats that some other person will say or do something, or challenges that may be returned, but no one person predetermines or dictates the way in which a given event will take shape. The design of everyday interactions is drawn from the participation of many, just as those who listen to a story make their own interpretive comments and draw their own conclusions.

Gender and reciprocity

The importance of gender ideology, in particular the role of women in the analysis of exchange systems, has emerged since the mid 1970s as central to understanding social and political relationships in many Papua New Guinea societies.[5] Women play a variety of roles in the organization and redistribution of wealth and everyday consumables, as well as being primarily responsible for socializing children into the practices and values of reciprocity. One suspects that from the perspective of women in these socializing contexts, reciprocity might have a different dynamic compared with that of men, who are more visible in formal arenas. Furthermore, while the symbolic logic of exchange in a particular society may be largely shared, men's and women's expectations about giving and receiving, the roles they play, and the affective stances they take in those transactions may be different because of the types of daily interaction that constitute their lives. It would be very surprising, therefore, if a study of language socialization in a Papua New Guinea society did not have anything to offer to current debates about gender and exchange.

The relationships between gender and language, however, are extremely subtle and remain relatively elusive next to recent contributions to the analysis of gender and other symbolic systems.[6] As Ochs has so eloquently stated, "The relation between language in interaction and gender ideology is not a simple straightforward mapping of the linguistic form to social meaning of gender. Rather the relationship of language to gender is constituted and mediated by the relation of language to other stances, social acts, social activities and other social constructs" (ms.: 2–3). A case in point is Lederman's (1984) study of access to formal contexts of discourse, in particular political meetings and decision making among the Mendi of Papua New Guinea. She observed that formal meetings are male and that women as a group are excluded. She argues that what difference this makes, and how it is valued, is a way to identify the "political" meaning of gender in formal settings, a way to read these behaviors as ratifying a particular reality with implications for gender ideology. Mendi women listen in silence, unable to challenge their subordination to an egalitarian male polity because it is formally acted out but never explicitly articulated. This asymmetry is culturally constitutive of political hierarchy in a society that, like Kaluli, is relatively egalitarian.

Informal settings and acts involving reciprocity and sharing are another resource for the investigation of gender ideology. In this study, reciprocity and sharing have been examined from different levels of social and linguistic detail and as well from a developmental perspective. The proposals that follow are generated from interactonal practices between adults and children rather than from formal prestations among adults. They are constructed through a set of associations of different activities and social constructs, all mediated by language. To start, cooperation is always encouraged in domestic tasks, which themselves are delineated through assigned gender-appropriate roles, in contrast to sharing, which is not always encouraged except between older sisters, who are asked to give to younger brothers or to younger sisters. Therefore, in cooperation, the tasks to some extent determine who will cooperate with whom; with regard to sharing and reciprocity, gendered relationships also guide the preferred outcome. Because these social acts are organized according to gender ideology, there are implications for how reciprocity is constructed and what it means in these settings.

Analyses of exchange start with a particular event or point in time. The Kaluli "opposition scenario" presented by E. L. Schieffelin (1976:110–11) to account for Kaluli reciprocity starts with someone's suffering a loss, either material or emotional, either voluntarily as in a formal prestation (e.g., giving a sister in marriage) or involuntarily in the form of injury or insult at the hands of another. This results in the need to rebalance, to put aside the feelings of being owed. To accomplish this, the recipient (in cases of marriage) or perpetrator (in cases of injury or insult) gives something, either an equivalent (*wel*) in the case of marriage, or compensation (*su*) in the case of injury, to balance a loss. In this account of reciprocity, the emphasis or starting point is the loss that must be redressed. E. L. Schieffelin suggests that "if Kaluli can interpret a set of events as involving a loss and opposition, there is a shared ideology about the appropriate course of action" (1980:506). While this framework articulates a cultural logic applicable to formal prestation, an analysis of language-socialization activities provides another perspective, one that has important gender distinctions.

That a different starting point exists is apparent when one examines expectations of reciprocity in everyday interactions between caregivers (who are predominantly women) and children. One is struck by the importance of mothers' giving to create and sustain relationships. Women initiate interactions with giving and respond to their children's (and husbands') requests by giving. They socialize their daughters to do the same as themselves, giving to brothers and to other male relatives. Giving is predominantly cast as being in relationship; that is what is socialized in most contexts. It is not primarily associated with rebalancing a loss, though obviously this too occurs when caregivers give to children who are angry or upset. And here is where an important gender difference arises.

As we saw earlier, boys and girls are treated differently in terms of what they are given and how they are responded to emotionally. Because of the preferential treatment they receive, sons come to expect more material things, especially food, and more emotional support and attention from mothers and sisters. Over time, they come to "feel owed" in terms of what can be given as well as done for them. Mothers encourage such expectations through their own treatment of sons as well as through socializing older daughters to treat their brothers the same way. Daughters, in contrast, are made fewer offers and given less attention, and learn quickly that "feeling owed" as a general orientation is neither valued nor appropriate for them. These are not strict categorical differences, however, and obviously there are times when little girls are angry or upset and given attention, but the generalization holds.

What I suspect, then, is that "feeling owed" is a stance more closely associated with males and more appropriate to males, regardless of age, while giving to redress their perceived loss constitutes a major role for females, regardless of age. How, we may ask, are discourse practices in socializing contexts implicated in articulating these engendered roles?

Gender is indirectly encoded in the discourse practices of family interactions in terms of reciprocity – who asks and gets, and who is refused:

1. Brothers can always ask their sisters for food or assistance, but sisters cannot make the same demands on their brothers. I argue that this affects the distribution and meaning of linguistic forms, including the ways in which affect is expressed.
2. Men display the exuberant self, they are "hard" and assertive, but they also appeal, especially to women. No matter how they ask, they expect to be given to and can easily "feel owed" if they are not. Women are most often in the giving position, responding to the appeals and demands of others, particularly men and children; less often, women.
3. Men display a greater range of emotionality and are generally more labile (given to tantrums, angry tirades, spontaneous weeping), while women are more steady in both everyday and formal contexts (Feld in press).

These discourse practices are connected through complex social and symbolic meanings across verbal genres. Through analysis of discourse practices, we can see how such gender positionings are socialized and sustained, even made invisible to participants. Further, by situating these discourse practices more broadly in terms of how they are mediated by their relationship to other social constructs, we can render the relation between gender and reciprocity visible and coherent.

The study of language socialization enables one to understand the nature of the culture and its cultural idioms. The verbal environment contains important cultural keys, tropes, metaphors, and rules. It also provides the material for learning one of the most important cultural systems and how to use it: language itself. To see culture, to make the invisible visible, we have to examine the role language plays in its workings.

Appendix: Transcription conventions used in examples

1. The utterances of the child under study appear on the right side of the page; those of all other speakers appear on the left side. Information about the situational and discourse context appears on the left and is enclosed in brackets.

2. In dyadic exchanges, the speaker–addressee relationship is identified by a single arrow (→), e.g., Speaker → Addressee. In triadic exchanges, where the speaker wants the addressee to repeat speech to a third person, a double arrow (→>) indicates the intended addressee, e.g., Speaker → Addressee →> Intended addressee. These same speaker–addressee relationships hold across turns unless otherwise indicated.

3. An action or event that occurs simultaneously with the child's utterance appears parallel to it; otherwise, it precedes or follows it, depending on its temporal relation to the utterance.

4. Adult utterances follow the usual conventions of capitalization and punctuation. Child speech is not capitalized except for proper names and place names. Punctuation is as follows:

- Child utterance boundaries are indicated by a single slash (/). When a longer-than-usual pause occurs between utterances, a double slash is used (//).
- Exclamation points follow child utterances when they are emphatic.
- Question marks follow utterances that have an interrogative particle.
- A question mark followed by an exclamation point (?!) indicates a rhetorical question.
- An asterisk (*) indicates that an utterance is ungrammatical or judged unacceptable by a native speaker.
- An unintelligible utterance is indicated by three dashes (---) before the utterance boundary slash.
- Complete and exact repetition of the speaker's own utterance is represented by X.
- An utterance-internal pause is indicated by a dot (·).
- A pause of over 5 seconds between utterances is indicated by three horizontal points (. . .) across the center line.

These conventions have been adapted from Bloom & Lahey 1978.

250

· A longer pause with intervening topics is indicated by three vertical points
(:) in the center line.
· When one speaker interrupts the speech of another, two sets of lowered
slashes (*// //*) indicate the point of overlap.
· A colon (:) indicates vowel lengthening.

5. Expressive or nontranslated Kaluli words are in italics. English words
are italicized to indicate stress or focus.

6. Words in parentheses that are part of the speaker's utterances are provided for purposes of translation, but are not overtly present as separate morphemes or words in Kaluli speech.

Glossary of Kaluli terms

Nouns in this list have no case markings.

adε	reciprocal relationship term for older sister and younger brother used in appeal
adɔ	'sister'
ao	'brother'
asugɔ	'understanding, thoughts'
εlεma	'say like this', a contraction of *εlε* 'like this' + *sama* 'say/speak'
εlεfoma	'do like this/that'
babo	'mother's brother'/'sister's son'
bale to	'turned-over words', a central metalinguistic complex that includes euphemism, metaphor, and, in everyday discourse, irony and sarcasm
ba madali to	'talk to no purpose', nonsense sounds
bo	'breast'
Bosavi to	'Bosavi language'; includes the four dialects Kaluli, Ologo, Wisesi, and Walulu
daiyo	'namesake'; also used as relationship term
dedab	'one repeats'
dikidiab	'one teases'
dimina/mina	'give'
do	'my father'
dogɔf wanalo kalu	'yellow-skinned people', Europeans
enteab	'one talks angrily'
geseab	'one speaks plaintively'
hala siyɔ	'mispronounced'
halaido	'hard', a central Kaluli metaphor for growth, strength, vitality
halaido domεki	'making hard', the process of hardening that applies to the development of linguistic and social competence
hεnima	'ask'
hεnulab	'one persuades, distracts, buys off'
heg	'underneath', a metalinguistic term referring to nonreferential or hidden meanings
heyo	expressive term that elicits or offers pity or empathy for another
holema	'call out' (with expectation of response)
kegab	'one talks angrily without threat'
kelediab	'one trades'

kelisɔ hen	Christian land
kidiab	'one refuses to share'
mɛmu	reciprocal kin term between grandparents and grandchildren; also between distant relatives
mahagale siyɔ	'said in a pragmatically inappropriate manner'
mayab	'I am/one is hungry'
memelab	'one begs with the eyes'
nɛ	'I/my' (emphatic)
nɛlɛ	'my daughter'
nɛsu	reciprocal relationship term between those who give/receive bridewealth
nelɔ	'I want', 'to me', 'for me'
ne bo	'my breast'; reciprocal term between mothers and nurslings
niɛnɛ	'I want'
nofɔlab	'one feels sorry'
nɔ	'my mother'
nɔl	'my son'
nosɔk	'my cross-cousin'
ɔbɛ to	'bird talk'
sa-yɛlab	'sung–texted weeping'
sama	'speak/say' (make speech)
sasindiab	'one teases'
sawalɛsu	'toddler'
sawa	'child'
sei	'witch'
su	'compensation'
tɛlɛnyab	'I am hungry for meat'
togode siyɔ	'said in a grammatically incorrect way'
tolema	'speak, say words, language' (speak language)
to nafa	'good talk, good words'
to halaido	'hard words, hard language'
to sɔmian	'one gives thoughts, understanding'
to widan	'one shows language'
tualun	'infant'
wanalo to	'yellow words', English
wesɛli salab	'one curses'
wi ɛlɛdɔ	lit. 'with two names'; reciprocal relationship term based on special food shared by two people
wɔ	expressive term used to elicit pity or empathy for oneself

Notes

1. Introduction

1 Additional major publications on the Kaluli include: Feld 1981, 1982b, 1983, 1984, 1985, 1986, 1987, 1988; E. L. Schieffelin 1977, 1980, 1981a, 1981b, 1982, 1983, 1985.

2 A. Weiner (1984) points out that in the Trobriands "hard words" means dangerous words.

3 Young children, whose early language resembles the call of the bird *nene* (the chanting scrubwren), are in complex symbolic relationships to birds (Feld 1982a:79).

4 For additional discussion of these concepts and their metalinguistic significance across genres and in acquisition, see Feld & Schieffelin 1982.

5 Like most of the other languages spoken in Papua New Guinea, Kaluli has no published grammar. The first work on the language was done by the Unevangelized Field Mission (now Asia Pacific Christian Mission) linguist Murray Rule in 1964. Rule, working through translators speaking related languages, spent six weeks in the Bosavi area and put together a short preliminary grammatical sketch designed to help Australian missionaries coming into Bosavi. Since that time, the only linguistic work in Bosavi has been carried out by Steve Feld and myself. E. L. Schieffelin has provided additional insights and assistance.

6 The fact that linguistic forms are sensitive to variation in social context has been discussed by Gumperz 1977; Hymes 1962, 1974; and Labov 1972. The point is especially well documented in two sociolinguistic studies carried out in Western Samoa. Ochs (1988, chap. 5) has pointed out the importance of sociolinguistic variation for language acquisition, in particular that one must investigate the extent to which individual features are actually in use in the speech environment of the language-acquiring child. Duranti (1981) has emphasized the importance of linguistic and ethnographic methods in relation to a more formal genre, the Samoan *fono*.

7 Kaluli orthography (Feld 1982:18–19):

Print	Phonetic symbol	Notes on pronunication
Vowels		
/i/	[i]	Like English "beet"
/e/	[e]	Like English "bait"
/ɛ/	[ɛ]	Like English "bet"

254

Print	Phonetic symbol	Notes on pronunciation
/a/	[a]	Like English "bother"; in initial position it is short, like English "bat"
/u/	[u]	Like English "boot"
/o/	[o]	Like English "boat"
/ɔ/	[ɔ]	Like English "bought"
Plosives		
/b/	[p]	Voiceless initially, finally, and
	[b]	usually medially; some speakers voice it medially for emphasis
/t/	[tʰ]	Highly variable with [s], but there are some words where all speakers use [tʰ]
/d/	[t]	Voiceless initially, voiced or
	[d]	voiceless medially, and unaspirated like English /d/
/k/	[kʰ]	
/g/	[k]	Voiced or voiceless medially
	[g]	
Fricatives		
/f/	[f]	
/s/	[s]	
/š/	[ʃ]	As in English "shoe" or "bush"
/h/	[h]	
Affricate		
/j/	[ǰ]	As in English "judge"
Nasals		
/m/	[m]	Voiced initially and medially; voiceless finally
/n/	[n]	Voiced initially and medially; voiceless finally; in final position alternates with /m/ for most speakers
Lateral/flap		
	[ɾ]	Alveolar flapped lateral; preced-
	[ʈ]	ing back vowels it is also retroflex
Nonsyllabic semi vowels		
/w/	[w]	Like English /w/
/y/	[y]	Like English /y/

8 See B. B. Schieffelin (1987) for more extensive comparison of conversation with stories and sung–texted weeping. See Feld (1982a) for details of song and sung–texted weeping.

2. Language as a resource for social theory

1 Like Feld's book on the Kaluli, this one is also "deliberately eclectic" (Feld 1982a:14). Many have contributed to the formulation of this work; the influence of the following is especially acknowledged: Bourdieu 1977; Cicourel 1973; Garfinkel 1967; C. Geertz 1973; Giddens 1979, 1984; Goffman 1959, 1974, 1979; Hymes 1974; Malinowski 1978, 1935; Myers 1986; Sapir 1921, 1927; Schegloff 1987; and Vygotsky 1962, 1978.

2 For work representative of developmental pragmatics, see Bates 1976; Garvey 1984; Ochs & Schieffelin 1983; and the edited collections Ervin-Tripp & Mitchell-Kernan 1977 and Ochs & Schieffelin 1979.

3 The collaborative work of several psychologists and sociolinguists resulted in *A Field Manual for Cross-Cultural Study of the Acquisition of Communicative Competence* (Slobin, Ervin-Tripp, Gumperz et al. 1967). This pioneering attempt to develop a method for collecting comparable cross-linguistic data resulted in several dissertations, most notably Blount 1969 (Luo), Kernan 1969 (Samoa), and Stross 1969 (Tenejapa Tzeltal). For a methodological critique of this project, see B. B. Schieffelin 1979.

4 Whiting, Child & Lambert (1966) and Whiting & Whiting (1975) represent a major tradition in socialization studies. The Jahoda & Lewis (1986) collection includes an annotated bibliography of recent anthropological work on socialization. Poole (1985) presents a very detailed account of infants in another Papua New Guinea society from the perspective of folk psychology, and Mayer's (1970) collection presents socialization largely in terms of formal events and from the perspective of social anthropology.

5 An extensive review of studies on language socialization appears in B. B. Schieffelin & Ochs 1986a. B. B. Schieffelin & Ochs 1986b contains a selection of articles on language socialization in different cultures, while Ochs & Schieffelin 1984 compares aspects of language socialization in three cultural contexts. Other work that exemplifies this perspective is found in Corsaro 1985; S. Heath 1983, 1984; Miller & Sperry 1987; Miller & Moore 1989; Ochs 1988; Watson-Gegeo & Gegeo 1986b; and Ward 1971.

6 For example, see Baugh & Sherzer 1984; Bauman & Sherzer 1974; Duranti 1984, 1988; Gumperz & Hymes 1972; Hymes 1967, 1974.

7 In particular, Berger & Luckmann 1967; Giddens 1979, 1984; Goffman 1959, 1961b, 1974; Schutz 1967; Wentworth 1980.

8 Wentworth 1980 provides a historical account of changes in theoretical formulations of socialization. The work of Cicourel (1973), Corsaro (1985), Ochs (1988), and Schieffelin & Ochs (1986b) exemplifies the interactive approach to the study of socialization.

9 Work in the sociohistorical school has been extremely influential in formulating the relationship between culture and cognition. As such work pertains to developmental processes, see Cole & Cole 1989; Wertsch 1985.

10 Bourdieu's notion of *habitus* – "laid down in each agent by his earliest upbringing, which is the precondition not only for the coordination of practices but also for the practices of coordination, since the corrections and adjustments the agents themselves consciously carry out presuppose their mastery of a common code . . . and since undertakings of collective mobilization cannot succeed without a minimum of concordance'' (1977:81) – shares many ideas with Giddens (i.e., practical consciousness, duality of structure) regarding the nature of agents and their actions in socializing contexts.

11 Related ideas have been articulated in Gumperz's formulation of contextualization cues (1977), Bateson's notion of metacommunicative frames (1972), Goffman's keyings (1974), and Hymes's concept of keys (1974). Bruner & Sherwood (1975) discuss frameworks and contingent responses in early play routines.

12 For a discussion of the acquisition of communicative competence through metacommunicative routines, see Briggs (1986:65–88). Cicourel (1970), Corsaro (1979), and Ochs (1979) address similar points from related theoretical perspectives.

13 Discussions about the heterogeneity of cultural knowledge can be found in Aberle 1960, Sankoff 1972, and Wallace 1961.

14 The main modification to Bloom's approach was that in my study it was caregivers, not the investigator, who interacted with children. In line with the anthropological goals of my study there was more variety of activities and contexts than in Bloom's research.

15 In the original research design, I planned monthly half-hour videotaped recordings, and took video equipment to the field. But videotaping in a Kaluli house proved not to be feasible in the smoky darkness of the household interior, especially the women's section. My attempts to change the context and record outside the house radically changed the behaviors, so I decided not to continue with the video portion of data collection.

16 See Bateson 1972, esp. p. xviii; Duranti 1987; Moerman 1988; and Ochs 1979.

17 For different approaches to transcription, see C. Goodwin 1981; M. Goodwin 1980; Ochs 1979; and Sachs, Schegloff & Jefferson 1974.

18 For work on children's language and caregiver speech that relies on transcripts of naturally occurring speech, see Corsaro 1979; Ervin-Tripp 1979; Ervin-Tripp & Mitchell-Kernan 1977; Garvey 1984; M. Goodwin 1980; Ochs 1988; Ochs & Schieffelin 1979; B. B. Schieffelin & Ochs 1986b.

19 See Feld in press for a discussion of this issue, especially as it pertains to his experience with Kaluli.

20 See Malinowski 1978/1935, pt. iv, p. 3.

3. Kaluli children: ideology and everyday life

1 Ages are presented in months and weeks for Abi, Suela, Wanu, and Meli in the form ''25.3.'' Infants' ages are in months, and children's ages over 3 years are presented in terms of years and months (''8;6''). Ages are given in terms of age of child at the beginning of tape-recorded samples. Taping itself began after three months of observation.

Since the Kaluli keep no written records of a child's birth, I determined the age of each child by approximation using several sources that I checked against each other: (1) birth dates on record at the mission (for younger children), (2) ethnographic field notes from Sululib from October 1966 through December 1968, (3) written records of significant events in the area recorded by government personnel and missionaries (e.g., the construction of certain buildings; visits by patrol officers). With this material, I was able to determine the relative birth order of all children in the village and then to link births to known dates, thus achieving a fairly reliable system for assigning birth dates. For purposes of this assignment, I assumed that all children were born on the first of the month unless otherwise documented.

2   Kaluli do not discuss children's comparative linguistic and social competence among themselves. When I asked several mothers to evaluate the children in terms of their development, Wanu was consistently said to be behind (*fɛsa* 'at the back') Abi and Mɛli. Asked why this might be the case, these women said that his mother "didn't show him language" (*to mɔwidɔ*).

This evaluation could not possibly be based on any objective measures. Perhaps it was based on a general sense that Wanu's mother went off without him more than other mothers did, leaving his father to take care of him, or it may have been an answer to a question that made little sense culturally. Nonetheless, I compared the frequency of *ɛlema* routines for the three children and found that Wanu received more direct instruction than the other two, in many cases by a factor of two. Wadeo, however, did not build extended discourse structures with Wanu, and in general her language to him was less syntactically complex than that of the other mothers. Wanu's developmental course was somewhat different from the other children's in that he had more errors in morphology and tended toward self-repetition (B. B. Schieffelin 1986a).

3   Osolowa's mother died when she was an infant, and her father moved to an Ologo-speaking area. Her first five or so years were spent with an Ologo-speaking relative. Her dialect was definitely Ologo, but people maintained that she was a Kaluli-speaker because of her clan association with the central Kaluli area.

4   This was acknowledged to be a difficult situation, since both children had to be nursed simultaneously. This is one of several reasons given to explain why infanticide was traditionally practiced when twins were born.

5   Kaluli literacy and Mɛli's book-reading events are analyzed in B. B. Schieffelin & Cochran Smith (1984). Below are listed some of Mɛli's Tok Pisin and *wanalo to* 'yellow words' vocabulary. *Wanalo to* is a metalinguistic term from *dogɔf wanalo kalu* 'yellow-skinned people', a current name for Europeans based on skin color. *Wanalo to* are English-based words that have been modified according to Kaluli phonology.

Tok Pisin
bukbuk (crocodile)
lobisi > rabis (rubbish, no good)

Wanalo to
sɛs (church)
fili (file)
masini (machine)
belɛdi (bread)
bisikis (cookies, biscuit)
andapani (underpants)
siti (shirt)
tɛlasis (trousers)
buti (boot)
sifuno (spoon)
pileti (plate)
disi (dish)
raisi (rice)
miti (meat)
bada (butter)
bukɔ (book)

Tok Pisin	*Wanalo to*
	penecilɔ (pencil)
	tapelekɔdɔ (tape recorder)
	pikisa (camera or picture
	batele (battery)
	sɔlu (salt)
	sob (soap)
	mabolo (marble)

6   In June 1984, I saw Meli, who was attending school at the mission station and was considered the brightest child in her class. In June 1989, I received a letter from her, written in English, telling me that she was now in the sixth grade and was seriously thinking of going on to high school.

7   For comparative material from Papua New Guinea on concepts of the child and ritual activities in childhood, see Poole 1982 and papers in the volumes edited by Marshall (1985) and White & Kirkpatrick (1985).

8   The only magic anyone mentioned concerning children was a spell to promote the whiteness of their permanent teeth. The child's shed baby teeth are put together with a white feather from a sulfur-crested cockatoo, and the mother asks that the teeth be like the feather.

9   Kaluli have always distinguished different skin tones among themselves, ranging from *gelaudɔ* 'light-skinned' to *heyɔn* 'dark-skinned'. When Kaluli first came in contact with Europeans, they called them *kalu gelaudɔ* 'light-skinned people'. In the early 1970s, the Australian missionary used the term *dogɔf wanalo kalu* 'yellow-skinned people' to refer to Europeans without knowing the negative connotation of yellow to the Kaluli, and this term was adopted. As far as I know, Kaluli make no negative symbolic associations between yellow-skinned people and death.

10   The types of prohibited bananas do not take longer to mature or cook than other types. Kaluli have several ways to cook sago. Some, like roasting directly on the fire, are very quick, and others, like baking in leaf pockets, take more time. Cooking sago in a tube does not take an especially long time, but perhaps the symbolism of containment marks this method as one to be avoided in pregnancy. Kaluli could not give a reason.

11   Lexical substitution is commonly used when adults talk with each other and do not want young children to understand. This is part of a larger complex of linguistic resources, *bale to* 'turned-over words', that figure importantly in many Kaluli speech genres. The specific example of lexical substitution is only effective until children learn about that kind of *bale to*. See note 7 in Chapter 4.

12   These developmental states are perhaps connected with indicators used to end the postpartum sex taboo. Parents resume sexual relations once the child is walking independently and has back teeth.

13   Mushrooms were the only frequently available food that Osolowa, who did not follow food taboos, would not let her young son eat. This was not surprising, since mushrooms not infrequently made people ill, and infants were especially vulnerable.

14   Kaluli did not in fact leave their babies unattended. They did, however, in order to explain the rare dwarfs in the population suggest that such behavior must have occurred.

15   When I explained baby talk as used by white middle-class Americans and the cultural notions that underlie it, Kaluli expressed dismay. It is not a good idea to teach children childish forms, they told me, since it is important for children to

hear "hard language" as spoken by adults if they are to learn to speak that way as well. They advised me to tell Americans to stop using baby talk. In addition to no baby-talk lexicon, other linguistic modifications characteristic of white middle-class baby talk are notably absent and this fact is reflected in Kaluli children's relatively error-free acquisition of certain linguistic forms, for example the shifters, the personal pronouns. Adults and older children never speak about themselves in the 3rd person, using proper names or kin terms, but always use 1st person pronouns. Except for vocatives, in addressing a child they use only 2nd person pronouns, never the child's name, kin term, or other 3rd person referent. (I never heard the equivalent of "Mommy wants Abi/baby to . . .") Instead, adults would say, "I want you to . . ." Kaluli children always use 1st person pronouns when talking about themselves, and 2nd person pronouns when speaking to others (B. B. Schieffelin 1986a).

16 The one exception to this is notable. When a toddler shrieks in protest at the assaults of an older child, mothers will way, " 'I'm unwilling,' he said" (*mɔido* = *mɔib* 'unwilling' plus *-do*, a quotative particle for immediate quoted speech).

17 See Ochs & Schieffelin 1984 for a comparison of these communicative contexts with white middle-class Anglo-American and Western Samoan behaviors.

4. *Elema* as a socializing practice

1 The importance of language-socialization routines in which caregivers instruct children on what to say and how to speak ("Say . . .") has been reported among diverse cultural groups including Mexican-Americans (Briggs 1986; Eisenberg, 1982), Wolof in Senegal (Wills 1977), Kwara'ae of the Solomon Islands (Watson-Gegeo & Gegeo 1986a), Basotho of Lesotho, southern Africa (Demuth 1986), Western Samoans (Ochs 1988), and English-speaking families in South Baltimore (Miller 1982), Hawaii (Iwamura 1980), and Boston (Greif & Gleason 1980). Although these "say it" routines are widely found, the ideological underpinnings are culturally specific. Groups differ in terms of the form, frequency, function, and relationship of these routines to other cultural and linguistic ideologies. See Demuth 1986 for a general comparison of these language-socialization practices.

The practice of speaking through others also occurs in seances in several Papua New Guinea societies. See E. L. Schieffelin (1977) for a study of Kaluli mediumship and performance and Wagner (1977) for similar practices of Daribi. However, both form and meaning of speaking through others in these contexts are different from *elema* routines.

2 In a sample of eighty-three hours of interaction in three families, when dyadic and triadic use of *elema* was compared, *elema* was used triadically over 80 percent of the time. In the two samples where percentages were less, the third participant was myself rather than one of the usual intended addressees, i.e., siblings and other Kaluli.

3 By the age of 20 months, children usually respond correctly and repeat what is said when they hear *elema*. They know to repeat when no explicit command to do so is forthcoming. See also Examples 4.3, 4.4.

4 In his discussion of the use of vocatives by children learning a number of languages, R. Brown (1973) claims that vocatives occurred in all samples, usually accompanying a greeting. "Stage 1 children control such forms, but they have little grammatical or semantic interest" (p. 180). This observation may be an artifact of the particular social or cultural situations studied by the researchers

Brown sampled, where information about social relationships is not extensively encoded through a variety of names.

5 Calling-out routines described by Watson-Gegeo & Gegeo (1986a) for the Kwara'ae share many social and linguistic features with Kaluli routines.

6 The majority of triadic *elema* exchanges are directed to older children. Kaluli children under 3 years of age rarely engage in same-age peer interaction; they usually interact with siblings and cousins who are older than themselves.

7 *Heg* is a metalinguistic term meaning 'underneath' and is part of the most significant complex of linguistic resources that make up a Kaluli way of speaking called *bale to* 'turned-over words' (Feld & Schieffelin 1982). *Bale to* covers a range of linguistic devices (like lexical substitution and manners of speaking: sarcasm, rhetorical questions, euphemisms) to achieve a variety of ends. It is used in joking, challenging, teasing, and shaming among other speech acts, and it is salient across modes of language use (conversation, stories, sung–texted weeping, and song), speech acts, and contexts. Words or phrases with a *heg* usually have veiled or nonobvious meanings that have to be searched for. There is a range of hiddenness of meanings that depends on the speech act and the participants. Rhetorical questions are one of the most pervasive, and in many ways the least complex, of a wide-ranging set of linguistic devices that are said to have a *heg*. Other forms require specific background cultural knowledge to get beneath the referential and surface meaning (B. B. Schieffelin 1986b).

   While some linguistic forms may be used only as information-seeking questions, others may be used either in that way or as confrontational rhetorical questions. Prosodic contour is crucial in the interpretation of questions: it differs in information-seeking questions from those that are asked rhetorically. The important difference is the final pitch contour and the length of the final vowel. Information-seeking questions have a perceptible rise and lengthened final vowel. Rhetorical questions have a perceptible fall and clipped final vowel. In addition, participants and context contribute to the appropriate interpretation of these speech acts.

8 Wanu has actually said *saya* 'sit' (2nd person present interrogative) instead of *salaya* 'say' (2nd person present interrogative). For a similar situation, where a word selected is not correct but is interpreted according to the rhetorical force of its presentation, see Example 4.8, lines 17, 19.

9 These teasing routines are about loss and having no family members with whom to share food and experiences.

10 For a musical discussion of *heyalo*, see Feld 1982a:35–6. For an ethnographic description of the ceremony, see E. L. Schieffelin 1976:225–9. Both Abi's mother and Steve Feld independently recognized Abi's vocalization as being like *heyalo*. I thank Steve for helping with the details of the musical material.

11 People do not talk to themselves, but women report singing alone in the bush. While most Kaluli singing is public and social, and some composing is done in company, mediums are unique in that they engage in monologue. They compose (*samolab*) and sing alone (*ineli molab*).

12 For work on sound play in children, see Garvey 1977; Jakobson 1968; Keenan & Klein 1975; and Weir 1962.

5. Socialization of appeal and the *ade* relationship

1 Kaluli do not talk about these different demeanors of assertion and appeal as being associated with developmental stages; that is, when adults appeal, they are not

seen as childlike. The only time I heard Kaluli talk about an adult acting like a child was when a man became angry at his elderly father and, while yelling, assumed a posture in which his knees were bent. The father claimed that his son's posture was like that of a child having a temper tantrum. This was taken as such an insult that the son struck the father, to the horror of everyone watching.

2   This analysis is based on ninety-seven tape-recorded occurrences (both reference and address) in family interactions. Others were observed and noted. Because of the family context in which the data were collected, there are only a few tape-recorded examples of adults using the *adɛ* term in address to each other. Four examples are between adult sisters who appealed to each other for food and assistance (many others were observed): one was from an older sister to her teenage brother asking him to bring firewood so she could cook for him; and one exchange was between a brother and sister, who used *adɛ* to tease each other in a request to clean up dog excrement.

3   An exception is in funerary sung–texted weeping (*sa-yɛlab*), where the *adɛ* term may be used with possessives and other limited constructions (Feld 1982:35, 157–8). The term *adɛ* is used more in song than in sung–texted weeping, specifically in formulas, e.g., calling out ("Come and see me"; "I'm alone orphaned") as well as in such vocatives as *Wadeyo!* 'Oh, *adɛ!*'

4   Examples are given to illustrate sibling terms, but this discussion applies to sociolinguistic rules for using kin terms in general.

6. Socializing reciprocity and creating relationships

1   In requests to children from older siblings and adults, the person asking for the food is not the person who has given it. This is in keeping with the Kaluli preference for not sharing or eating what one has given. For example, if Wanu's mother had given food to Wanu, then other family members could ask for some, but not his mother; or if Mɛli's grandfather gave her something, her parents could both ask, but she could not give back to her grandfather. Knowing this, I once refused some banana that Mɛli offered me, banana that I had given to her and had told her to eat. When she turned to her mother to tell her I was unwilling to eat it, her mother said to her, *Babiyɛ miyabe* 'Bambi gave' to explain my behavior.

2   Thinking about giving in this way was inspired by reading Myers's (1988) thoughtful essay on Pintupi ideas about ownership and identity. There are many important similarities between Pintupi and Kaluli with regard to sentiment and the social meaning of objects.

3   See B. B. Schieffelin 1986b for the developmental details.

4   Another form of refusal used especially by Wadeo and her daughters and less frequently in the other families was composed of the 1st person focused pronoun *ni* 'I' followed by a verb inflected for 3rd person. The meaning carried by these assertions was an angry negative, e.g., *Ni diɛhɛnab!* 'I certainly won't bring it!'

5   Cf. P. Brown & Levinson 1978 regarding the linguistic expression of politeness and other face-saving moves.

6   Since there was only one young girl in the study, I cannot be sure whether these patterns of refusal are gender-specific or whether refusals are more frequent in Mɛli's interactions because of the nursing situation.

7   The Tok Pisin translation of *hɛnulab* is *grisim*.

8   Young children are aware of and name this activity. For example, at 32.2 months

Meli, while watching her father calming her crying brother by making hushing sounds, says to me, *Henulab* 'He distracts/persuades'.

9   See Feld 1982a; E. L. Schieffelin 1976.

10 In general, girls are socialized to be more constant, to accept the idea that they can't always get what they want, in contrast to boys, who are socialized to feel that they are owed. Feld similarly observes: "For Kaluli, men are by far more typically and stereotypically culturally constructed as the emotional gender, the more unpredictable, potentially irrational, the more moody, prone to burst out in tears at any moment, or become flamboyantly seized with tantrums of rage or sadness. Kaluli men seem to have more trouble controlling anger and upset than do Kaluli women and this fact is clearly recognized. Men's crying . . . is less controlled, momentary, hysterical and often accompanied by physical trembling and angry gestures. Women's crying . . . is more melodic, texted, controlled, reflective and sustained. These qualities parallel general emotional display patterns: Kaluli women act more steady, reliable and even-tempered in everyday matters, and the obvious composure under intense stress that is indicated by their *sa-yelab* performances is an expressive extension of that constellation" (in press, p. 20).

11 This is one of the most frequent and earliest constructions with ergative marking on agents. The distribution of verbs and the particular forms in which they are used provide additional evidence for the importance of social acts guiding children's acquisition and use of particular linguistic forms. Young Kaluli children use *dimina* 'give' in the present imperative ("you give") and in the past tense ("Mother gave"), but not in the 1st person present ("I give") or the negative imperative ("don't give"). In contrast, the verb *dima* 'take' occurs in the 1st person present ("I take"), in the negative imperative ("don't take"), and with a 3rd person agent in the past ("he/she took") but rarely in the imperative ("you take") or any future tense. Thus, while inflected verb forms are produced early in the developmental process, they are restricted to a limited set of verbs in specific tenses that are socially salient (see B. B. Schieffelin 1986a:574 for further discussion of the acquisition of verbs).

Other linguistic forms show the important influences of social factors. For example, genitive constructions display the first case markers used with any regularity in obligatory contexts. All children from 24 months on used a variety of genitive constructions, lexical and morphological, in a range of speech acts, expressing the importance of possession in everyday talk (B. B. Schieffelin 1986a:537–8). Platt's (1986) detailed account of the acquisition of Samoan deictic verbs and Ochs's (1986) analysis of Samoan pronoun acquisition strongly support this position.

7. The development of children's requests

1   Research on the linguistic expression of affect has shown its importance to a wide range of ethnographic and sociolinguistic concerns (P. Brown & Levinson 1978; Heelas 1986; Irvine 1982, in press; Ochs & Schieffelin 1989; Watson-Gegeo & White 1990). Recent work on the acquisition and socialization of this critical aspect of communicative and social competence is reported in Miller & Moore 1989; Miller & Sperry 1987; Ochs 1988; Schieffelin & Ochs 1986a, b.

2   Kaluli mothers say that one should wean a nursling before the next child is born. There is no ritual marking of this transition. Mothers wean by increasing the

amount of solid food and distracting children who request the breast with offers of other food. They make excuses not to nurse, and if the child persists in his or her demands, go off to the bush for two or three days without the child, which effectively ends nursing.

3   While 2nd and 3rd person forms exist (*gelɔ* and *elɔ*), they do not have this affective meaning and simply express indirect object "to you" and "to him/her" respectively. *Nelɔ* co-occurs with verbs inflected for 1st person only in present, intentive, and future tenses. Children use it almost exclusively with two verbs, *maya* 'eat/drink' (52%) and *boba* 'see/look at' (30%), and only in requests for objects. This is because of pragmatic rather than syntactic or semantic constraints. Children made no errors in tense or speech-act use with *nelɔ* 'to me/I want'.

4   Use of the 1st person possessive pronoun *ne* 'my' with the word for father (3rd person) *ɛya* is a poetic form used in *sa-yɛlab* 'sung–texted weeping' when expressing sentiments about one's father (Feld personal communication). Fathers address young children as *dowɔ* 'my father' in requests based on appeal, but here Degelɔ is simply expressing his affection toward his son, using an affect-marked form rather than the neutral form *nɔl* 'my son'.

5   Note that when an inflected verb follows *nelɔ*, Mɛli is able to add different emphatic markers to the verb (usually *nɔl* 'eat/drink'), which is consistent with adult usage.

6   Mɛli (24.3) is playing with her father, reaching out her hand.

Mɛli → Father [softly]:   ɔ giyɔ dagiyɔ **mɛ** /
                                your hand give /
Mother → Father: Ɔ giyɔ dagi dimindɔ
Give your hand, she said [exact repetition particle].
Mɛli → Father [loudly]:   ɔ giyɔ dagiyɔ **diminɛ!** /
                                your hand give!

7   Bloom & Beckwith (1989) in their longitudinal study on the developmental relations between children's speech and affect (ages 9–30 mo) found that when children were in highly affective states their language production was reduced compared with children in less aroused states. While their subjects were much younger and less linguistically advanced than the Kaluli children, one wonders whether the affective state is a counter to the motivation of topic initiation in spite of the fact that initiating requests should show greater linguistic complexity, given the high affect involved in appeal. One possibility is that children come to associate particular affective states with particular linguistic constructions because of the cultural and social meaning they carry. Thus, what may initially be a psychological stage (begging and whining and using a limited linguistic repertoire) may evolve into a particular speech register that, because of the developmental process and the fact that it is not culturally conventionalized, is transitory.

8   Note that the *-o* / *-ologa* suffixing is highly productive in Kaluli.

8. The socialization of gender-appropriate behaviors

1   Two events provide a pragmatic counterexample to men's expressed fear of female pollution and both sexes' reports of their lack of knowledge of male homosexual activities. In 1976 I was interviewing women about the births of their children: who attended, where the birth occurred. Women are usually assisted by a few close female relatives near the village, but one woman told me the story of how she was

alone with her husband far from the village when she went into labor. Unable to get any female assistance and having difficulties, she got her husband to assist her; he got birth blood on his hands while doing so. When asked about how other people responded to this culturally problematic event, she emphasized that no one knew that her husband had helped and that I was the first person whom she had told, because I "would not be afraid."

The second event was a public one that I observed in 1967. After Baseo (Wanu's father) was accused of being a witch, his mother ran into the yard in front of the longhouse. In an obviously agitated state, she spoke out loudly about how her son had been inseminated by a "hard" man (whom she identified), leading to proper growth, and not by a witch (*sei*), who could transmit *sei inso* (witch-child or witch essence), a highly negative element (E. L. Schieffelin 1976:128). The response of those within hearing was dismay: "One should not say those things," and older men gently tried to persuade her to return to her house and stop talking about it.

2   As in several other Papua New Guinea groups described, girls are thought to be able to reach physical maturity by themselves, without ritual assistance or special practices, while boys need facilitation, usually through initiation rituals and the ingestion of special substances (Herdt 1982). Before European contact in 1964, Kaluli males periodically went into seclusion and built a bachelor men's ceremonial hunting lodge (*bau a*). While in this specially constructed lodge, boys aged 10–14 followed a rigorous round of activities with young men, learning various hunting techniques, cooking and eating game, and acquiring ritual knowledge that made them manly. They also engaged in homosexual intercourse with bachelor partners to facilitate their growth and physical development (E. L. Schieffelin 1982). After 1964, when an Australian-based Christian mission began the construction of an airstrip in Bosavi, the hunting lodge was discontinued, as Kaluli did not want outsiders to discover this secret institution. In all likelihood, however, homosexual activity continued until the early 1970s, evidencing the belief that young boys needed semen so that they would mature (E. L. Schieffelin 1976:124). In the mid 1970s, there was no evidence that these activities were still being practiced. In any case, there was no discussion about it in my family interaction data – not surprising, for women were not supposed even to know about these practices. They certainly did not pertain to small children.

Upon reaching puberty, girls acquire additional food taboos (E. L. Schieffelin 1976:66), but since my focus is on younger children, those practices did not affect the everyday interactions I observed. I observed no gender-specific practices relevant to young children's physical development.

3   When Seligiwɔ was 17 months old, his family left Bosavi and observation ended; the game may have continued beyond that time.

4   While parents and children, and brothers and sisters, may freely share food, once Kaluli are of marriageable age there are social constraints on who may give food to whom. Offers of food to persons of the opposite sex who may be potential marriage partners may be seen as a strong indicator of interest. Accepting food may be seen as reciprocating that interest. When couples are first married, they often wait to begin sexual relations until the wife is settled into her new community and becomes comfortable with her husband. When she is ready to initiate intimate relations, she does so by offering him food and touching his hand (E. L. Schieffelin 1976:61).

5   For example, in bridewealth exchanges one gives an object of wealth as a contribution to the marriage arrangements of a son, and much later, when a daughter from that relationship marries, one can claim an equivalent object.

6   In addition to gender-relevant messages, other general interactional preferences
    are displayed, namely, the preference that the autonomy of the agent is assured
    while the recipient of an action is protected. Kaluli do not like to prevent or inhibit
    any individual from carrying out an action directed toward another, but sometimes
    they perceive the need to intervene on the recipient's behalf. Rather than restrain
    the person about to strike someone, an individual can intervene to protect the
    recipient of the blow by providing a buffer between the striking object and the
    person. For example, on ceremonial occasions such as Gisalo, people who are
    deeply moved and respond by burning the dancer are not prevented from carrying
    out their actions, but sympathetic onlookers may (and do) hold leaves on the dancer's
    back to protect him if they think the dancer is being burned too much (E. L.
    Schieffelin 1976:191). Similarly, in interactions involving children, one who wants
    to strike someone older is not discouraged from doing so, but the instrument may
    be modified. (In this case, a piece of firewood is too dangerous, but a piece of
    bamboo is not.) Thus, one's autonomy is preserved while at the same time the
    other is protected.

7   Men and women use *ɛlɛma* in other contexts and genres – but what children see
    are the socializing contexts.

9. Conclusion

1   See B. B. Schieffelin 1987 ms.

2   For thoughtful discussions about language in egalitarian societies, see Atkinson
    1984 and Myers & Brenneis 1984.

3   The emphasis here is on rhetorical strategies, though there are extensive linguistic
    resources in the lexicon and grammar for asserting a variety of affective stances.
    For example, the constellation of features used in displaying interdependence when
    appealing to *adɛ* includes prosody, voice quality, expressives, and specific syntac-
    tic constructions. When asserting one's autonomy, the various semantically differ-
    entiated 1st and 2nd person pronouns (*niba/giba* 'I not you/you not me'; *ninɛli/
    ginɛli* 'I alone/you alone'; *nɔnɔ/gɔnɔ* 'my own/your own', among others) are re-
    peatedly used.

4   Kaluli use of magic for influencing others and attempting to control them is limited
    compared with other Papua New Guinea societies such as the Trobriand (Weiner
    1984).

5   See, for example, Feil 1978; Josephides 1985; Strathern 1972; Weiner 1976.

6   Important theoretical and ethnographic studies that discuss the complex relations
    between gender and language include Gal in press; Keenan 1974; Lederman 1984;
    McConnell-Ginet 1988; Ochs ms.; Philips, Steele & Tanz 1987; Silverstein 1985.
    Some work has already been done on Kaluli (Feld in press; B. B. Schieffelin
    1987). We plan an extensive treatment of the role of Kaluli gender ideology and
    the distribution and meaning of linguistic resources.

References

Aberle, D. 1960. The influence of linguistics on early culture and personality theory. In G. Dole & R. Carneiro, eds., *Essays in the science of culture*. New York: Crowell, pp. 1–29.

Atkinson, J. 1984. "Wrapped words": poetry and politics among the Wana of Central Sulawesi, Indonesia. In D. Brenneis & F. Myers, eds., *Dangerous words: language and politics in the Pacific*. New York: New York University Press, pp. 33–68.

Bates, E. 1976. *Language and context*. New York: Academic Press.

Bateson, G. 1972. Social planning and the concept of deutero-learning. In *Steps to an ecology of mind*. New York: Ballantine Books, pp. 159–76.

Baugh, J. & Sherzer, J., eds. 1984. *Language in use*. Englewood Cliffs. N.J.: Prentice-Hall.

Bauman, R. & Sherzer, J., eds. 1974. *Explorations in the ethnography of speaking*. New York: Cambridge University Press.

Beidelman, T. O. 1986. *Moral imagination in Kaguru modes of thought*. Bloomington: Indiana University Press.

Berger, P. L. & Luckmann, T. 1967. *The social construction of reality*. Garden City, N.Y.: Doubleday.

Bloom, L. 1970. *Language development: form and function in emerging grammars*. Cambridge, Mass.: MIT Press.

Bloom, L. & Beckwith, R. 1989. Talking with feeling: integrating affective and linguistic expression in early language development. *Cognition and Emotion* 3, 4:313–42.

Bloom, L. & Lahey, M. 1978. *Language development and language disorders*. New York: Wiley.

Bloom, L., Rocissano, L. & Hood, L. 1976. Adult–child discourse: developmental interaction between information processing and linguistic knowledge. *Cognitive Psychology* 8:521–52.

Blount, B. 1969. The acquisition of language by Luo children. Ph.D. diss., University of California, Berkeley. Circulated as Working Paper no. 19, Language Behavior Research Lab, University of California, Berkeley.

Boggs, S. 1985. *Speaking, relating and learning: a study of Hawaiian children at home and at school*. Norwood, N.J.: Ablex.

Bolinger, D. 1975. *Aspects of language*. New York: Harcourt Brace Jovanovich.

Bourdieu, P. 1977. *Outline of a theory of practice*. Cambridge: Cambridge University Press.

Briggs, C. 1986. *Learning how to ask*. New York: Cambridge University Press.

Brown, P. & Levinson, S. 1978. Universals in language usage: politeness phenomena.

In E. Goody, ed., *Questions and politeness*. Cambridge: Cambridge University Press, pp. 56–289.

Brown, R. 1973. *A first language*. Cambridge, Mass.: Harvard University Press.

Bruner, J. & Sherwood, V. 1975. Early rule structure: the case of peekaboo. In J. S. Bruner, A. Jolly & K. Sylva, eds., *Play: its role in evolution and development*. Harmondsworth: Penguin, pp. 277–85.

Chodorow, N. 1974. Family structure and feminine personality. In M. Z. Rosaldo & L. Lamphere, eds., *Woman, culture and society*. Stanford: Stanford University Press, pp. 43–66.

Cicourel, A. 1970. The acquisition of social structure: towards a developmental theory of language and meaning. In J. Douglas, ed., *Understanding everyday life*. Hawthorne, N.Y.: Aldine, pp. 136–68.

1973. *Cognitive sociology*. Harmondsworth: Penguin.

Clancy, P. 1986. The acquisition of communicative style in Japanese. In B. B. Schieffelin & E. Ochs, eds., *Language socialization across cultures*. New York: Cambridge University Press, pp. 213–50.

Cole, M. & Cole, S. 1989. *The development of children*. New York: Scientific American Books.

Cook-Gumperz, J. & Gumperz, J. 1978. Context in children's speech. In N. Waterson & C. Snow, eds., *The development of communication*. New York: Wiley, pp. 3–23.

Corsaro, W. 1979. Sociolinguistic patterns in adult–child interaction. In E. Ochs & B. B. Schieffelin, eds., *Developmental pragmatics*. New York: Academic Press, pp. 373–89.

1985. *Friendship and peer culture in the early years*. Norwood, N.J.: Ablex.

Demuth, K. 1986. Prompting routines among Basotho children. In B. B. Schieffelin & E. Ochs, eds., *Language socialization across cultures*. New York: Cambridge University Press, pp. 51–79.

Duranti, A. 1981. *The Samoan fono: a sociolinguistic study*. Pacific Linguistics, ser. B, vol. 80. Canberra: Dept. of Linguistics, Research School of Pacific Studies, Australian National University.

1984. *Intentions, self, and local theories of meaning: words and social action in a Samoan context*. Center for Information Processing Technical Report 122. La Jolla: University of California, San Diego.

1987. Four properties of speech-in-interaction and the notion of translocutionary act. Paper presented at International Pragmatics Association meeting, Antwerp.

1988. Ethnography of speaking: towards a linguistics of the praxis. In F. Newmeyer, ed., *Linguistics: the Cambridge survey*, vol. 4: *Language: the sociocultural context*. Cambridge: Cambridge University Press, pp. 210–28.

Eisenberg, A. 1982. Learning language in a cultural perspective: a study of three Mexicano families. Ph.D. diss., University of California, Berkeley.

Ernst, T. 1978. Aspects of meaning of exchanges and exchange items among the Onabasulu of the Great Papuan Plateau. *Mankind* 11, 3:187–97.

1984. Onabasulu local organization. Ph.D. diss., University of Michigan, Ann Arbor.

Ervin-Tripp, S. 1972. On sociolinguistic rules: alternation and co-occurrence. In J. Gumperz & D. Hymes, eds., *Directions in sociolinguistics: the ethnography of communication*. New York: Holt, Rinehart & Winston, pp. 213–50.

1979. Children's verbal turn-taking. In E. Ochs & B. B. Schieffelin, eds., *Developmental pragmatics*. New York: Academic Press, pp. 391–415.

Ervin-Tripp, S. & Mitchell-Kernan, C., eds. 1977. *Child discourse*. New York: Academic Press.

Feil, D. 1978. Enga women in the *tee* exchange. *Mankind* 11, 3:263–79.

Feld, S. 1981. "Flow like a waterfall": the metaphors of Kaluli musical theory. *Yearbook for Traditional Music* 13:22–47.

1982a. *Sound and sentiment: birds, weeping, poetics and song in Kaluli expression*. Philadelphia: University of Pennsylvania Press.

1982b. Music of the Kaluli. 12″ stereo disc or audio cassette with notes, photos, maps. IPNGS 001. Boroko: Institute of Papua New Guinea Studies.

1983. Sound as a symbolic system: the Kaluli drum. *Bikmaus* 4, 3:78–89. Reprinted in C. Frisbie, eds., *Explorations in ethnomusicology in honor of David P. McAllester*. Detroit Monographs in Musicology 9. Detroit: Information Coordinators, 1986, pp. 147–58.

1984. Sound structure as social structure. *Ethnomusicology* 28:383–409.

1985. Kaluli weeping and song. 12″ stereo disc with notes in English and German. Musicaphon/Music of Oceania series BM 30SL 2701. Kassel: Barenreiter.

1986. Orality and consciousness. In Yoshihiko Tokumaru & Osamu Yamaguti, eds., *The oral and literate in music*. Tokyo: Academia Music, pp. 18–28.

1987. Dialogic editing: interpreting how Kaluli read *Sound and sentiment. Cultural Anthropology* 2:190–210.

1988. Aesthetics as iconicity of style, or "lift-up-over-sounding": getting into the Kaluli groove. *Yearbook for Traditional Music* 20:74–113; cassette supplement.

In press. Postscript 1989. In *Sound and sentiment: birds, weeping, poetics and song in Kaluli expression*, 2nd ed. Philadelphia: University of Pennsylvania Press.

Feld, S. & Schieffelin, B. B. 1982. Hard words: a functional basis for Kaluli discourse. In D. Tannen, ed., *Text and talk*. Georgetown University Round Table on Languages and Linguistics 1981. Washington, D.C.: Georgetown University Press, pp. 351–71.

Foley, W. 1986. *The Papuan languages of New Guinea*. New York: Cambridge University Press.

Foley, W. & Van Valin, R. 1984. *Functional syntax and universal grammar*. Cambridge: Cambridge University Press.

Frake, C. 1977. Plying frames can be dangerous. *Quarterly Newsletter of the Institute for Comparative Human Development* (Rockefeller University) 1:1–9.

Gal, S. In press. Between speech and silence: the problematics of research on language and gender. In M. diLeonardo, ed., *Towards a new anthropology of gender*. Berkeley and Los Angeles: University of California Press.

Garfinkel, H. 1967. *Studies in ethnomethodology*. New York: Prentice-Hall.

Garvey, C. 1977. Play with language and speech. In S. Ervin-Tripp & C. Mitchell-Kernan, eds., *Child discourse*. New York: Academic Press, pp. 27–48.

1984. *Children's talk*. Cambridge, Mass.: Harvard University Press..

Geertz, C. 1973. *The interpretation of cultures*. New York: Basic.

Geertz, H. 1959. The vocabulary of emotion. *Psychiatry* 22, 3:225–37.

Giddens, A. 1979. *Central problems in social theory*. Berkeley and Los Angeles: University of California Press.

1984. *The constitution of society*. Berkeley and Los Angeles: University of California Press.

Gleason, J. B. & Greif, E. B. 1983. Men's speech to young children. In B. Thorne, C. Kramarae & N. Henley, eds., *Language, gender and society*. Rowley, Mass.: Newbury House, pp. 140–150.

Godelier, M. 1986. *The making of great men: male domination and power among the New Guinea Baruya.* Cambridge: Cambridge University Press.
Goffman, E. 1959. *Presentation of self in everyday life.* Garden City, N.Y.: Doubleday.
    1961a. *Encounters.* Harmondsworth: Penguin.
    1961b. *Asylums.* Harmondsworth: Penguin.
    1974. *Frame analysis.* New York: Harper & Row.
    1976. Replies and responses. *Language in Society* 5, 3:257–313.
    1979. Footing. *Semiotica* 25:1–29.
Goodenough, E. W. 1957. Interests in persons as an aspect of sex differences in the early years. *Genetic Psychology Monographs* 55:287–323.
Goodwin, C. 1981. *Conversational organization: interaction between speakers and hearers.* New York: Academic Press.
Goodwin, M. 1980. Directive–response speech sequences in girls' and boys' task activities. In S. McConnell, R. Borker & N. Furman, eds., *Women and language in literature and society.* New York: Praeger, pp. 157–73.
Greenberg, J. H. 1966. Some universals of grammar with particular reference to the order of meaningful elements. In J. H. Greenberg, ed., *Universals of language.* Cambridge, Mass.: MIT Press, pp. 73–113.
Greif, E. & Gleason, J. 1980. Hi, thanks and goodbye: more routine information. *Language in Society* 9, 2:159–66.
Gumperz, J. 1967. On the linguistic markers of bilingual communication. In J. Macnamara, ed., Problems of bilingualism. *Journal of Social Issues* 23:48–57.
    1977. Sociocultural knowledge in conversational inference. In M. Saville-Troike, ed., *Linguistics and anthropology.* Georgetown University Round Table on Languages and Linguistics. Washington, D.C.: Georgetown University Press, pp. 191–212.
Gumperz, J. & Hymes, D., eds. 1972. *Directions in sociolinguistics: the ethnography of communication.* New York: Holt, Rinehart & Winston.
Haiman, J. 1979. Hua: a Papuan language. In T. Shopen, ed., *Languages and their status.* Cambridge, Mass.: Winthrop, pp. 35–90.
Hays, T. E. & Hays, P. H. 1982. Opposition and complementarity of the sexes in Ndumba initiation. In G. Herdt, ed., *Rituals of manhood; male initiation in Papua New Guinea.* Berkeley and Los Angeles: University of California Press, pp. 201–38.
Heath, J. 1975. Some functional relationships in grammar. *Language* 51:89–104.
Heath, S. 1983. *Ways with words.* New York: Cambridge University Press.
    1984. Language and education. In B. Siegel, ed., *Annual review of anthropology.* Palo Alto, Calif.: Annual Reviews, pp. 251–74.
    1986. What no bedtime story means. In B. B. Schieffelin & E. Ochs, eds., *Language socialization across cultures.* New York: Cambridge University Press, pp. 97–126.
Heelas, P. 1986. Emotion talk across cultures. In R. Harré, ed., *The social construction of emotions.* New York: Blackwell Publisher, pp. 234–66.
Herdt, G. 1981. *Guardians of the flutes.* New York: McGraw-Hill.
Herdt, G., ed. 1982. *Rituals of manhood: male initiation in Papua New Guinea.* Berkeley and Los Angeles: University of California Press.
Herdt, G. & Poole, F. J. P. 1982. "Sexual antagonism": the intellectual history of a concept in New Guinea anthropology. In F. J. P. Poole & G. Herdt, eds., *Sexual antagonism, gender and social change in Papua New Guinea Social Analysis,* special issue no. 12, pp. 5–28.

Hymes, D. 1962. The ethnography of speaking. In T. Gladwin & W. C. Sturtevant, eds., *Anthropology and human behavior*. Washington, D.C.: Anthropological Society of Washington, pp. 15–33.

1967. Models of the interaction of language and social setting. *Journal of Social Issues* 23:8–20.

1974. *Foundations in sociolinguistics: an ethnographic approach*. Philadelphia: University of Pennsylvania Press.

1980. What is ethnography? In *Language and education: ethnolinguistic essays*. Washington, D.C.: Center for Applied Linguistics, pp. 88–103.

Irvine, J. 1982. Language and affect: some cross-cultural issues. In H. Byrnes, ed., *Contemporary perceptions of language: interdisciplinary dimensions*. Georgetown Round Table on Language and Linguistics. Washington, D.C.: Georgetown University Press, pp. 31–47.

In press. Registering affect: heteroglossia in the linguistic expression of emotion. In C. Lutz & L. Abu-Lugod, eds., *Affecting discourse: language and the politics of emotion*. New York: Cambridge University Press.

Iwamura, S. 1980. *The verbal games of pre-school children*. New York: St. Martin's.

Jahoda, G. & Lewis, I. M., eds. 1986. *Acquiring culture: cross cultural studies in child development*. London: Croom Helm.

Jakobson, R. 1968. *Child language, aphasia and phonological universals*. The Hague: Mouton.

Josephides, L. 1985. *Production of inequality: gender and exchange among the Kewa*. London: Tavistook.

Keenan, E. Ochs. 1974. Norm-makers and norm-breakers: uses of speech by men and women in a Malagasy community. In R. Bauman & J. Sherzer, eds., *Explorations in the ethnography of speaking*. New York: Cambridge University Press, pp. 125–43.

Keenan, E. Ochs & Klein, E. 1975. Coherency in children's discourse. *Journal of Psycholinguistic Research* 4:365–80.

Keenan, E. Ochs & Schieffelin, B. B. 1976. Topic as a discourse notion: a study of topic in the conversations of children and adults. In C. Li, ed., *Subject and topic*. New York: Academic Press, pp. 335–84.

Kelly, R. 1977. *Etoro social structure*. Ann Arbor: University of Michigan Press.

Kernan, K. 1969. The acquisition of language by Samoan children. Ph.D. diss., University of California, Berkeley. Circulated as Working Paper no. 21, Language Behavior Research Lab, University of California, Berkeley.

Labov, W. 1972. *Sociolinguistic patterns*. Philadelphia: University of Pennsylvania Press.

Langness, L. 1974. Ritual, power, and male dominance in the New Guinea Highlands. *Ethos* 2:189–212.

Lederman, R. 1984. Who speaks here? Formality and the politics of gender in Mendi, Highland Papua New Guinea. In D. Brenneis & F. Myers, eds., *Dangerous words: language and politics in the Pacific*. New York: New York University Press, pp. 85–107.

Lee, R. 1982. Politics, sexual and nonsexual, in egalitarian societies. In E. Leacock & R. Lee, eds., *Politics and history in band societies*. New York: Cambridge University Press., pp. 37–59.

Lévi-Strauss, C. 1958. The structural study of myth. In T. Sebeok, ed., *Myth*. Bloomington: Indiana University Press, pp. 50–66.

Longacre, R. 1972. *Hierarchy and universality of discourse constituents in New Guinea languages*. Washington, D.C.: Georgetown University Press.

McConnell-Ginet, S. 1988. Language and gender. In F. Newmeyer, ed, *Linguistics: the Cambridge survey*, vol. 4: *Language: the socio-cultural context*. Cambridge: Cambridge University Press, pp. 75–99.

McDermott, R. P., Gospodinoff, K. & Aron, J. 1978. Criteria for an ethnographically adequate description of activities and their contexts. *Semiotica* 24:245–75.

Malinowski, B. 1978 (1935). *Coral gardens and their magic*, vol. 2: *The language of magic and gardening*. New York: Dover.

Marshall, L., ed. 1985. *Infant care and feeding in Oceania*. New York: Gordon & Breach.

Mayer, P., ed. 1970. *Socialization: the approach from social anthropology*. London: Tavistock.

Mead, M. 1930. *Growing up in New Guinea*. Harmondworth: Penguin.

Meggitt, M. 1964. Male–female relationships in the Highlands of Australian New Guinea. In J. B. Watson, ed., New Guinea: the Central Highlands. *American Anthropologist* 66:204–24.

Meigs, A. 1976. Male pregnancy and the reduction of sexual opposition in a New Guinea Highlands society. *Ethnology* 15, 4:393–407.

Miller, P. 1982. *Amy, Wendy and Beth: language learning in South Baltimore*. Austin: University of Texas Press.

  1986. Teasing as language socialization and verbal play in a white working-class community. In B. B. Schieffelin & E. Ochs, eds., *Language socialization across cultures*. New York: Cambridge University Press, pp. 199–211.

Miller, P. & Moore, B. B. 1989. Narrative conjunctions of caregiver and child: a comparative perspective on socialization through stories. *Ethos* 17:43–64.

Miller, P. & Sperry, L. L. 1987. The socialization of anger and aggression. *Merrill Palmer Quarterly* 33:1–31.

Moerman, M. 1988. *Talking culture: ethnography and cultural analysis*. Philadelphia: University of Pennsylvania Press.

Myers, F. 1986. *Pintupi country, Pintupi self: sentiment, place and politics among Western Desert Aborigines*. Washington, D.C.: Smithsonian Institution Press.

  1988. Burning the truck and holding the country: forms of property, time and identity among Pintupi Aborigines. In T. Ingold, D. Riches & J. Woodburn, eds., *Property, power and ideology in hunting and gathering societies*. London: Berg, pp. 52–74.

Myers, F. & Brenneis, D. 1984. Introduction. In D. Brenneis & F. Myers, eds., *Dangerous words: language and politics in the Pacific*. New York: New York University Press, pp. 1–29.

Ochs, E. 1979. Transcription as theory. In E. Ochs & B. B. Schieffelin, eds., *Developmental pragmatics*. New York: Academic Press, pp. 43–72.

  1986. From feelings to grammar: a Samoan case study. In B. B. Schieffelin & E. Ochs, eds., *Language socialization across cultures*. New York: Cambridge University Press, pp. 251–72.

  1988. *Culture and language development: language acquisition and language socialization in a Samoan village*. New York: Cambridge University Press.

  Ms. Indexing gender. In S. Duranti & S. Goodwin, eds., *Rethinking context*. Submitted to Cambridge University Press.

Ochs, E. & Schieffelin, B. B. 1983. *Acquiring conversational competence*. London: Routledge & Kegan Paul.

  1984. Language acquisition and socialization: three developmental stories and their implications. In R. Shweder & R. Levine, eds., *Culture theory: essays in mind, self and emotion*. New York: Cambridge University Press, pp. 276–320.

  1989. Language has a heart. *Text* 9, 1:7–25.

Ochs, E. & Schieffelin, B. B., eds. 1979. *Developmental pragmatics*. New York: Academic Press.

Olson, M. L. 1978. Switch reference in Barai. *Proceedings of the Fourth Annual Meeting of the Berkeley Linguistics Society* 4:140–57.

Philips, S. U. 1972. Participant structures and communicative competence: Warm Springs children in community and classroom. In C. B. Cazden, V. P. John & D. Hymes, eds., *Functions of language in the classroom*. New York: Columbia University Teachers College Press, pp. 370–94.

Philips, S. U., Steele, S. & Tanz, C. eds. 1987. *Language, gender and sex in comparative perspective*. New York: Cambridge University Press.

Platt, M. 1986. Social norms and lexical acquisition: a study of deictic verbs in Samoan child language. In B. B. Schieffelin & E. Ochs, eds., *Language socialization across cultures*. New York: Cambridge University Press, pp. 127–52.

Poole, F. J. P. 1981. Transforming 'natural' woman: female ritual leaders and gender ideology among Bimin-Kuskusmin. In S. Ortner & H. Whitehead, eds., *Sexual meanings: cultural construction of gender and sexuality*. New York: Cambridge University Press, pp. 116–65.

1982. The ritual forging of identity: aspects of person and self in Bimin-Kuskusmin male initiation. In G. Herdt, ed., *Rituals of manhood: male initiation in Papua New Guinea*. Berkeley and Los Angeles: University of California Press, pp. 99–154.

1985. Coming into social being: cultural images of infants in Bimin-Kuskusmin folk psychology. In G. White & J. Kirkpatrick, eds., *Person, self, and experience: exploring Pacific ethnopsychologies*. Berkeley and Los Angeles: University of California Press, pp. 183–244.

Rheingold, H. L. & Cook, K. U. 1975. The contents of boys' and girls' rooms as an index of parents' behavior. *Child Development* 46:459–63.

Rule, M. 1964 ms. Customs, alphabets and grammar of the Kaluli people of Bosavi, Papua.

Sachs, H., Schegloff, E. & Jefferson, G. 1974. A simplest systematics for the organization of turn-taking in conversation. *Language* 50:696–735.

Sankoff, G. 1972. Cognitive variability and New Guinea social organization: the Buang Dgwa. *American Anthropologist* 74, 3:555–66.

Sapir, E. 1921. *Language*. New York: Harcourt Brace.

1927. The unconscious patterning of behavior in society. In E. S. Dummer, ed., *The unconscious*. New York: Knopf, pp. 114–42.

1949. Cultural anthropology and psychiatry. In D. G. Mandelbaum, ed., *Selected writings of Edward Sapir in language, culture and personality*. Berkeley and Los Angeles: University of California Press, pp. 509–21. Reprinted from *Journal of Abnormal and Social Psychology* 27 (1932):229–42.

Schegloff, E. 1968. Sequencing in conversational openings. *American Anthropologist* 70:1075–95.

1987. The routine as achievement. *Human Studies* 9:111–51.

Schieffelin, B. B. 1979. Getting it together: an ethnographic perspective on the study of the acquisition of communicative competence. In E. Ochs & B. B. Schieffelin, eds., *Developmental pragmatics*. New York: Academic Press, pp. 73–108.

1986a. The acquisition of Kaluli. In D. Slobin, eds., *The cross-linguistic study of language acquisition*. Hillsdale, N.J.: Erlbaum, pp. 525–93.

1986b. Teasing and shaming in Kaluli children's interactions. In B. B. Schieffelin & E. Ochs, eds., *Language socialization across cultures*. New York: Cambridge University Press, pp. 165–81.

1987. Do different worlds mean different words? An example from Papua New

Guinea. In S. U. Philips, S. Steele & C. Tanz, eds., *Language, gender and sex in comparative perspective*. New York: Cambridge University Press, pp. 249–60.

1987 ms. Context and interpretation. Paper presented at International Pragmatics Association meeting, Antwerp.

Schieffelin, B. B. & Cochran-Smith, M. 1984. Learning to read culturally. In H. Goelman, A. Oberg & F. Smith, eds., *Awakening to literacy*. Exeter, N.H.: Heinemann, pp. 3–23.

Schieffelin, B. B. & Ochs, E. 1986a. Language socialization. In B. Siegel, ed., *Annual review of anthropology*. Palo Alto, Calif.: Annual Reviews, pp. 163–91.

Schieffelin, B. B. & Ochs, E., eds. 1986b. *Language socialization across cultures*. New York: Cambridge University Press.

Schieffelin, E. L. 1976. *The sorrow of the lonely and the burning of the dancers*. New York: St. Martins.

1977. The unseen influence: tranced mediums as historical innovators. *Journal de la Société des Océanistes* 33, 56–7:169–78.

1980. Reciprocity and the construction of reality. *Man*, n.s., 15:502–17.

1981a. The end of traditional music, dance and body decoration in Bosavi, Papua New Guinea. In R. Gordon, ed., *The plight of peripheral people in Papua New Guinea*, vol. 1: *The inland situation*. Cambridge, Mass.: Cultural Survival, pp. 1–22.

1981b. Evangelical rhetoric and the transformation of traditional cultures in Papua New Guinea. *Comparative Studies in Society and History* 23:150–6.

1982. The *bau a* ceremonial hunting lodge: an alternative to initiation. In G. Herdt, ed., *Rituals of manhood: male initiation in Papua New Guinea*. Berkeley and Los Angeles: University of California Press, pp. 155–200.

1983. Anger and shame in the tropical forest: on affect as a cultural system in Papua New Guinea. *Ethos* 11:181–91.

1985. Performance and the cultural construction of reality. *American Ethnologist* 12:707–24.

Schutz, A. 1967. *The phenomenology of the social world*. Evanston, Ill.: Northwestern University Press.

Shatz, M. & Gelman, R. 1973. *Development of communication skills: modifications in speech to young children as a function of listener*. Monographs of the Society for Research in Child Development 38, no. 152. Chicago: University of Chicago Press.

Sidorowicz, L. S. & Lunney, G. S. 1980. Baby X revisited. *Sex Roles* 6:67–73.

Silberbauer, G. 1981. *Hunter and habitat in the Central Kalahari*. Cambridge: Cambridge University Press.

Silverstein, M. 1981. The limits of awareness. Sociolinguistic Working Paper 84. Austin, Tex.: Southwest Educational Development Laboratory.

1985. Language and the culture of gender: at the intersection of structure, usage and ideology. In E. Mertz & R. Parmentier, eds., *Semiotic mediation*. New York: Academic Press, pp. 220–60.

Slobin, D., Ervin-Tripp, S., Gumperz, J. et al. 1967. *A field manual for the cross-cultural study of the acquisition of communicative competence*. Language Behavior Research Lab, University of California, Berkeley.

Strathern, M. 1972. *Women in between*. London: Seminar Press.

1980. No nature, no culture: the Hagen case. In C. MacCormack & M. Strathern, eds., *Nature, culture and gender*. Cambridge: Cambridge University Press, pp. 174–223.

Stross, B. 1969. Language acquisition by Tenejapa Tzeltal children. Ph.D. diss., University of California, Berkeley. Circulated as working paper no. 20, Language Behavior Research Lab, University of California, Berkeley.

Tannen, D. 1979. What's in a frame? Surface evidence for underlying expectations. In R. Freedle, ed., *Discourse processes*, vol. 2: *New directions*. Norwood, N.J.: Ablex, pp. 137–81.

Voorhoeve, C. L. 1975. The central and western areas of the Trans–New Guinea Phylum. In S. A. Wurm, ed., *Papuan languages and the New Guinea linguistic scene*. Pacific Linguistics, ser. C, no. 38. Canberra: Department of Linguistics, Research School of Pacific Studies, Australian National University, pp. 345–59.

Vygotsky, L. S. 1962. *Thought and language*. Cambridge, Mass.: MIT Press.

1978. *Mind in society: the development of higher psychological processes*, ed. M. Cole, V. John-Steiner, S. Scribner & E. Souberman. Cambridge, Mass.: Harvard University Press.

Wagner, R. 1977. Speaking for others: power and identity as factors in Daribi mediumistic hysteria. *Journal de la Société des Océanistes* 33, 56–7:145–52.

Wallace, A. F. C. 1961. On being just complicated enough. *Proceedings of the National Academy of Science*. 47:458–64.

Ward, M. 1971. *Them children: a study in language learning*. New York: Holt, Rinehart & Winston.

Watson-Gegeo, K. & Gegeo, D. 1986a. Calling out and repeating routines in Kwara'ae children's routines. In B. B. Schieffelin & E. Ochs, eds., *Language socialization across cultures*. New York: Cambridge University Press, pp. 17–50.

1986b. The social world of Kwara'ae children: acquisition of language and values. In J. Cook-Gumperz, W. Corsaro & J. Streeck, eds., *Children's worlds and children's language*. Berlin: Mouton, pp. 109–28.

Watson-Gegeo, K. & White, G., eds. 1990. *Disentangling: Conflict discourse in Pacific societies*. Stanford, Calif.: Stanford University Press.

Weiner, A. 1976. *Women of value, men of renown*. Austin: University of Texas Press.

1984. From words to objects to magic; "Hard words" and the boundaries of social interaction. In D. Brenneis & F. Myers, eds., *Dangerous words: language and politics in the Pacific*. New York: New York University Press, pp. 161–91.

Weir, R. 1962. *Language in the crib*. The Hague: Mouton.

Wentworth, W. M. 1980. *Context and understanding: an inquiry into socialization theory*. New York: Elsevier.

Wertsch, J., ed. 1985. *Culture, communication and cognition: Vygotskian perspectives*. Cambridge: Cambridge University Press.

White, G. M. & Kirkpatrick, J., eds. 1985. *Person, self and experience: exploring Pacific ethnopsychologies*. Berkeley and Los Angeles: University of California Press.

Whiting, J. 1941. *Becoming a Kwoma*. New Haven: Yale University Press.

Whiting, J., Child, I. & Lambert, W. 1966. *Field guide for the study of socialization*. New York: Wiley.

Whiting, J. & Whiting, B. 1975. *Children of six cultures*. Cambridge, Mass.: Harvard University Press.

Wills, D. 1977. Culture's cradle: social structural and interactional aspects of Senegalese socialization. Ph.D. diss., University of Texas, Austin.

Index